BOTTLES

IDENTIFICATION and PRICE GUIDE

BOTTLES

IDENTIFICATION AND PRICE GUIDE

FIRST EDITION

MICHAEL POLAK

The CONFIDENT COLLECTOR™

AVON BOOKS  NEW YORK

Important Notice: All of the information, including valuations, in this book has been compiled from the most reliable sources, and every effort has been made to eliminate errors and questionable data. Nevertheless, the possibility of error always exists in a work of such scope. The publisher and the author will not be held responsible for losses which may occur in the purchase, sale, or other transaction of property because of information contained herein. Readers who feel they have discovered errors are invited to *write* the author in care of Avon Books so that the errors may be corrected in subsequent editions.

THE CONFIDENT COLLECTOR: BOTTLES IDENTIFICATION AND PRICE GUIDE (1st edition) is an original publication of Avon Books. This edition has never before appeared in book form.

AVON BOOKS
A division of
The Hearst Corporation
1350 Avenue of the Americas
New York, New York 10019

Copyright © 1994 by Michael Polak
The Confident Collector and its logo are trademarked properties of Avon Books
Interior design by Robin Arzt
Photographs by Jennifer M. Polak, Fred Holabird, Dale Mooney, The H.J. Heinz Company
Published by arrangement with the author
Library of Congress Catalog Card Number: 93-36606
ISBN: 0-380-77218-3

Library of Congress Cataloging in Publication Data:

Polak, Michael.
    Bottles : identification and price guide / Michael Polak.—1st ed.
        p. cm.
"The Confident Collector."
"The complete guide to old and new—from beer bottles to antique-figured flasks."
Includes bibliographical references.
1. Bottles—Collectors and collecting—Catalogs. I. Title.
NK5440.B6P58   1994   93-36606
748.8'2'075—dc20   CIP

First Avon Books Trade Printing: March 1994

This book is dedicated to my family for all the years of their support in my never-ending search of that elusive rare antique bottle in the deserts of Nevada. The search goes on.

And to the two newest bottle diggers in the family, my grandsons, Michael and Kevin.

Acknowledgments

When it comes to writing a book of this kind, there is a special group of individuals who provide a large amount of support in all areas. This writer had plenty of that sort of help from those with real expertise and I'd like to say thank you to those special people.

Jennifer M. Polak—To my daughter for putting in all those long hours of taking pictures, providing inputs on picture selection and format, and for putting up with Dad always getting in the way.

Fred Holabird—Thank you for all of your help over the years. Your understanding of bottles and of the art of bottle collecting have been invaluable. Thanks also for your fine contribution to this book, the special chapter on "Bottles of Nevada," and for your great friendship.

Jacque Pace—Thank you for all of your patience and long hours proofreading and providing editing assistance, for invaluable moral support.

Dale Mooney—Thank you for your help in providing not just photographic assortments and pricing inputs but also for information on digging techniques and special schooling on how the auction world operates.

Derek Abrams—Thank you for providing assistance in understanding the history of California bottles and for your offer of a future digging expedition.

Contents

New Bottles   289

Foreword

I would like to take a minute to introduce myself. I've been an antique bottle collector/junkie for approximately twenty years and have enjoyed writing this book with the help of other bottle collectors.

In order to write a book that would be informative, a good reference and pricing guide, as well as enjoyable reading, I decided to provide the beginner collector—as well as the veteran collector—with a cross section of material from across the United States. As a bottle collector, I've always known what I wanted in a good collectors' book. But in order to make this book the best reference available, I asked numerous bottle clubs across the United States for their ideas, their favorite digging spots, and their pricing input. Based on their input, as well as my own research, I feel that I have written a bottle collectors' resource that will be informative and fun for everyone.

After digging and collecting for so many years, I still find the thrill of bottle collecting is making that special find. I want others to experience that same excitement and I hope this book will help to guide you on your way in the great hobby of bottle collecting.

Good bottle collecting and digging,

Michael Polak
The Antique Junkie

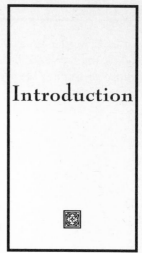

Introduction

Welcome to the world of antique bottle collecting. Over the years while selling at antique shows, flea markets, or just talking with friends, these are the most frequently asked questions: What makes a bottle old? What makes a bottle interesting? What makes a bottle valuable? Invariably someone asks how does one get started in antique bottle collecting. In writing this book, I have included essentials such as the history and origin of bottles, how the beginning collector gets started, a detailed section on basic bottle facts, bottle sources, handling suggestions, and a good guide for bottle digs. Also included are separate pricing and information sections for old bottles (pre–1900) and new bottles (post–1900). And, for reference and research purposes, there are sections on trademarks, bottle clubs and dealers, a bibliography, and a glossary of commonly used terms.

Over the past few years bottle collecting has risen rapidly in popularity. As a result, bottle clubs continue to form throughout the United States with more and more collectors spending their free time digging through dumps, foraging through ghost towns, digging out old "outhouses" (that's right), exploring abandoned mine shafts, and searching out favorite swap meets, flea markets, or garage sales. For many collectors and dealers, bottle collecting is big business, as evidenced by the prices in this book. It is worth noting that many bottles of recent make and origin have become greatly sought after due to limited availability.

Most collectors, however, look beyond the type and value of a bottle into its origin and history. In fact, I find that researching the history of bottles has at times proved to be more interesting than finding the bottle itself, largely because it is closely tied to the history of settling the United States and the early methods of merchandising.

How to Use This Book

This book is designed to assist collectors—from the complete novice to the seasoned veteran. The table of contents clearly indicates those sections, such as "The Beginning Collector," that veterans will want to skip over. However, other introductory sections, including those on history, facts, sources, handling, and Fred Holabird's chapter on Nevada bottles, I hope will contribute something to even the expert's store of knowledge about bottles and collecting.

The pricing information is divided into two main sections. The first begins on page 47 and covers older collectibles, almost exclusively manufactured before 1900, broken down into categories based on physical type and the bottle's original contents. Where applicable, trade names are listed alphabetically within these sections. In some categories, such as flasks, trade names were not embossed on the bottles, so pieces are listed by embossing or other identification that does appear on the bottles themselves. Descriptive terms used to identify these pieces are explained in the introductory sections and are also listed in the glossary at the end of the book. The second pricing section, which begins on page 289, is a guide to pieces produced after the turn of the century, and is broken down by manufacturer alone.

Since it's simply impossible to list prices for every available bottle, I've produced a cross section of collectibles in various price ranges. The dollar amount attached to any listing indicates the value of that particular piece. Similar but not identical bottles could be more or less valuable than those specifically mentioned, but this listing still provides a good starting point for pricing pieces in your collection or those you're considering as additions.

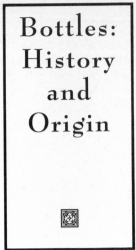

Bottles: History and Origin

Glass bottles are not as new as some people might think. In fact, the glass bottle has been around for about 3,000 years. In the late first century B.C., the Romans began to make glass bottles to use as small pharmacy vials that the local doctors and pharmacists used to dispense pills, healing powders, and potions. These were small cylindrical bottles, three to four inches in length and very narrow. As we will read later, the majority of early bottles produced after Roman times were sealed with a cork or a glass stopper, whereas the Romans used a small stone rolled in tar to seal vials. Also, the finished bottles contained many impurities such as sand particles and bubbles due to the crude glass-producing process. Because of the thickness of the glass and the crude finish, Roman glass was very resilient compared to the glass of later times, which accounts for the survival and good preservation of some Roman bottles that have been dated as 2,500 years old. The Romans also get credit for originating what we think of today as the basic store bottle and early merchandising techniques.

The first effort to manufacture glass in America is thought to have taken place at the Jamestown settlement in Virginia around 1608. It is interesting to note that the majority of glass produced at the Jamestown settlement was in fact earmarked for shipment back to England (due to its lack of resources) and not for the new settlements. As it turned out, the Jamestown glasshouse enterprise ended up being a failure almost before it got started. The poor quality glass produced simply couldn't support the needs of England.

The first successful American glasshouse was started in 1739 in New Jersey by Caspar Wistar, a button manufacturer who emigrated to the United States from Germany. The next major glasshouse operation was started by Henry Stiegel in the Manheim, Pennsylvania, area between 1763-1774. He later established several more. The Pitkin glassworks was started in East Hartford, Connecticut, around 1783 and was the first American glasshouse to provide figural flasks. It also became the most successful glasshouse of its time, until it closed around 1830 due to the high cost of wood for fuel. In order to understand early glasshouse history, both the successes and far more numerous failures, we need to understand the problems of availability of raw materials and the concerns of constructing the glasshouse itself.

The glass factory of the nineteenth century was usually built near abundant sources of sand and wood or coal, and in close proximity to numerous roads and waterways for transportation of the raw materials to the glasshouse and the finished products to major eastern markets such as Boston, New York, and Philadelphia. Finding a suitable location was usually not a problem, but once production was under way resources would quickly diminish.

The glasshouse building itself was usually a large wooden structure, which housed a primitive furnace that was shaped like a beehive about nine feet in diameter. A major financial drain on the glass companies, and the major reason so many of the businesses went broke, was the large pot that fit inside the furnace to hold the molten glass. The melting pot, which cost about $100 and took eight months to build, was made by hand from a long coil of clay and was the only substance known that would not melt when the glass was heated to 2,700° Fahrenheit. Although the material could withstand the temperatures, the life span of each pot was only about eight weeks; the high temperatures over a long period of time caused the clay itself to turn into glass. The cost of regularly replacing these melting pots proved the downfall of many an early glass factory.

Throughout the nineteenth century, glasshouses continued to come and go due to changes in demand and technological improvements. Between 1840 and 1890, there was an enormous demand for glass containers to satisfy the whiskey and beer businesses and the medicine and food-packing industries. Due largely to this steady demand, glass manufacturing in the United States finally expanded into a stable industry. This demand was due in large part to the settling of the western United States and the great gold and silver strikes between 1850 and 1900. Unlike other industries of the time that saw major changes in manufacturing processes, the process for producing glass bottles remained the same. It was a process that gave each bottle special character, producing unique shapes, imperfections, irregularities, and various colors until 1900.

At the turn of the century, Michael J. Owens invented the first fully automated bottle-making machine. Although many fine bottles were manufactured between 1900 and 1930, Owens's invention ended an era of unique bottle design that no machine process could ever duplicate. In order for a bottle collector, especially a new bottle collector, to better understand the history and origin of antique bottles, it is important to take a look at the chronological history of bottle manufacturing.

Free-Blown Bottles: First century B.C.-1860, see Figure 1

During the first century B.C., the blowpipe, which was nothing more than a long hollow metal rod, was invented. The tip was dipped into molten glass, and by blowing into the other end, a glassblower formed the desired bottle, bowl, or other container.

Pontil Marks: 1618-1866

Once the bottle was blown, it was removed from the rod through the use of a three-foot metal pontil rod, which was dipped into the tank of molten glass and applied to the bottom of the bottle. The neck of the bottle was then touched with a wet rod or stick, which separated it from the blowpipe.

The finishing process could include a variety of applied and tooled rings and collars. In the final step, an iron was inserted into the neck of the bottle, or held by tongs, while the pontil was separated from the bottle. If the bottle was to be molded for body form, the gather was inserted in a mold and further expanded to take on the shape of the interior of the mold, usually cylindrical, square, or polygonal.

Snap, Cases, Snap-Cases: 1860-1903, see Figure 2

Between 1850 and 1860, the first major invention for bottle making since the blowpipe itself appeared, an instrument known as the snap, which replaced the pontil. The basic snap-case was a five-foot metal rod that had claws to grasp the bottle. A snap locked the

Free-Blown Bottle Making Process
Figure 1

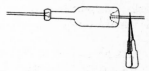

1. The blowpipe was inserted into the pot of red-hot metal and twisted to gather the requisite amount onto the end of the pipe.

2. The blowpipe was then rolled slowly on a metal table to allow the red-hot gather to cool slightly on the outside and to sag.

3. The blower then blew into the pipe to form an internal central bubble.

4. The gathered amount of metal was further expanded and sometimes turned in a wooden block that had been dipped in cold water to prevent charring by the hot metal, or possibly rolled again on the metal table.

5. The body and neck were then formed by the bottom of the bottle being flattened with a wooden paddle called a Battledore.

6. One of the irons (pontil) was attached to the center bottom of the bottle for easy handling during the finishing of the bottle neck and lip. At this time, a kick-up could be formed in the bottom of the bottle by pushing inward when attaching the iron.

7. The bottle was whetted, or cracked off the blowpipe by touching the hot glass at the end of the pipe with a tool dipped in cold water.

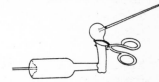

8. With the bottle held on a pontil, the blower reheated the neck to polish the lip and further smoothed it by tooling.

Snap, Cases, Snap-Cases: 1860–1903
Figure 2

Snap Case Open

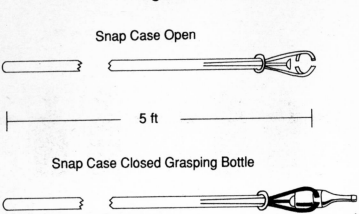

5 ft

Snap Case Closed Grasping Bottle

claw into place in order to hold the bottle more securely while the neck was being finished. It should be noted that each snap-case was tailor-made to fit bottles of a certain size and shape. These bottles have no pontil scars or marks, which left the bases of the bottles free from lettering or design. There may, however, be some minor grip marks on the side as a result of the claw device.

The snap-case instrument was used for small-mouth bottle production until the automatic bottle machine came into existence in 1903.

Molds: First century B.C.-1900
The use of molds in bottle making, which really took hold in the early 1800s, actually dates back to the first century with the Romans. As detailed earlier, in the free-blown process the glassblower shaped the bottle, or vessel, by blowing and turning it in the air. When using a mold, the glassblower would begin in the same way, then take a deep breath while lowering the red-hot shaped mass into the hollow mold. The blower would continue blowing air into the tube until the glass compressed itself against the sides of the mold to acquire the finished shape.

Molds: First Century B.C.–1900
Figure 3

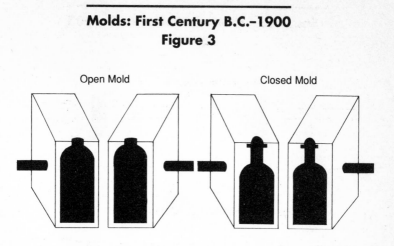

Open Mold   Closed Mold

Molds were usually made in two or more sections in order to enable the mold to come apart. The hardened bottle could then be easily removed. Since it was impossible to have the molds fit precisely, the seams show on the surface of the finished article, giving a clue as to the manufacturing methods used in the production of the bottle. The molds were categorized as "open," where only the body of the bottle was forced with the neck and lip being added afterward, and "closed," in which the neck and lip were part of the original mold (Figure 3). Later two specific types of molds came into use: the three-piece mold, in use from 1809-1880, which consisted of two main types; and the turn mold or paste mold, in use from 1880-1900. The three-piece mold helped the bottle industry become stronger in the nineteenth century.

Three-piece Molds, Figure 4

Three-piece dip mold—the bottom section of the bottle mold was one piece, and the top, from the shoulder up, was two separate pieces. The mold seams appeared circling the bottle at the shoulder and on each side of the neck.

Full-height molds—The entire bottle was formed in the mold and the two seams run vertically to below the lip on both sides of the bottle.

Three Piece Mold
Figure 4

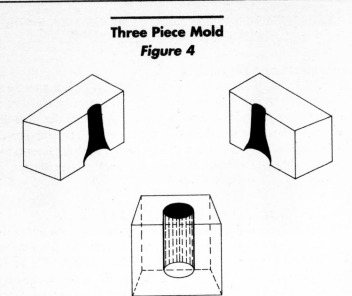

Turn Mold or Paste Mold
Wooden molds used in the manufacture of bottles were kept
wet to prevent them from igniting, but as the hot glass came
into contact with the mold, the walls of the mold became
charred. By turning the mold, however, manufacturers discovered that they could erase seams and mold marks, give a high
finish to the completed bottle, and prevent charring. After
metal molds replaced wooden ones, manufacturers used a paste
inside the mold that allowed the bottle to slide easily during the
turning process, which explains the origins of the terms "turn
mold" and "paste mold."

Mason Food Jars: 1858
In 1858, John Mason invented the wide-mouth jar that became
famous as a preserved food container. His new screw-top neck was
formed in the same mold as the body. The jar was then broken
away from the blowpipe and sent to the annealing oven to temper
the glass, making it more resistant to breakage. After this, the
jagged edges of the rims were ground down. In fact, earlier jars can

be distinguished from later ones by looking for rough and sharp edges produced by this grinding process.

Press-and-Blow Process: 1892
In 1892, a semiautomatic process called "press and blow" was invented. This process could only be used in the production of wide-mouth containers formed by pressing molten glass into the mold to form the mouth and lip first. Then a metal plunger was inserted through the mouth and applied air pressure formed the body of the bottle. This process was utilized for the production of early fruit jars and milk bottles.

The Automatic Bottle-Making Machine: 1903
Michael J. Owens is recognized as the inventor of the first automatic bottle-making machine. Owens first introduced his invention in 1899 but the machine was not perfected until 1903. In the beginning, the Owens machine made only heavy bottles since the demand for them was the heaviest. In 1909, improvements to the machine made it possible to produce small prescription bottles. Between 1909 and 1917, numerous other automatic bottle-making machines were invented and soon all bottles were formed automatically throughout the world.

In 1917, another invention of mechanized bottle manufacturing provided a way of forming a measured amount of molten glass from which a bottle could be blown. It was called a "gob feeder." In this process, a gob of glass is drawn from the tank and cut off by shears.

One last note about bottle making concerns the process of producing screw-top bottles. Early glassblowers produced bottles with inside and outside screw caps long before the bottle-making machines mechanized the process. Because early methods of production were so complex, screw-top bottles produced before the 1800s were considered specialty bottles and expensive to replace. Today they are considered to be rare and quite collectible. In fact, the conventional screw-top bottle did not become common until after 1924, when the glass industry standardized the threads.

The Beginning Collector

Now that you have learned something about the history and origin of bottle making, it's time to provide information about how to approach the hobby of bottle collecting, as well as suggestions on books and reference guides, start-up costs, old versus new bottles, and some information on bottle clubs.

So, what approach should you take toward getting started, and what might influence that approach? The first thing to understand about antique bottle collecting is that there aren't set rules of any kind. Everyone's finances, spare time, available storage space and preferences are different and will influence your individual approach. As a collector, you will need to think about whether to specialize and focus on a specific type of bottle or group of bottles, or whether you're more of a general or "Maverick" collector who acquires everything that becomes available. The majority of bottle collectors I have talked with over the years, myself included, took the "Maverick" approach as new collectors. We grabbed everything in sight, ending up with bottles of every type, shape, and color. Now, after twenty years of collecting, my recommendation to newcomers is to specialize. Of course, taking the more general approach in the early years has given me a wider spectrum of knowledge about bottles and glass in general. But specializing has distinct advantages over the "Maverick" approach:

- It reduces the field of collection, which helps to organize study and research.
- The specialist becomes an authority on bottles in a particular field.
- Trading becomes easier with other specialists who may have duplicate and unwanted bottles.

- By becoming more of an authority within a specialty, the collector can negotiate a better deal by spotting those bottles that are underpriced.

I need to mention, however, that specialized collectors will always be tempted by bottles that don't quite fit into their collections. So they cheat a little, and give in to that Maverick urge. This occasional cheating sometimes results in a smaller side collection, or, in extreme cases, turns the collector away from a specialty and back to being a Maverick. But that's alright. Remember, there are no set rules, with the exception of having a lot of fun.

Now, what does it cost to start a collection and how do you know the value of a bottle? Aside from digging excursions, which have travel and daily expenses, starting a collection can be accomplished by spending just a few dollars or maybe just a few cents per bottle. Digging, which we will discuss in detail later, is in this writer's opinion the ultimate way of adding to your collection.

Knowing what and where the best deals are obviously takes some time and experience. But the beginner can do well with just a few pointers.

Over the years, I've developed a quick-look method of buying bottles by grouping candidates into one of three categories:

- Low End or Common Bottles
  Bottles reflect noticeable wear and the label is usually missing or not very visible. In most cases the label is completely gone and there is never embossing. The bottle is dirty (which can usually be fixed), with some scrapes, and free of chips. These bottles are usually clear and colorless.
- Average Grade/Common Bottles
  Bottles reflect some wear and a label may be visible but is usually faded. They are generally clear in color and free of scrapes or chips. Some of these may have minimal embossing.
- High End and Unique Bottles
  These bottles can be empty or sometimes partially or completely full, with the original stopper and label or embossing. The color is clear and the bottle has no chips or scrapes and very little or no wear. If it has been stored in a box it is very likely in good condition. Also the box must be in good condition.

We will discuss price ranges just briefly here since values will be covered in detail in the two price sections. Usually, low end bottles can be found for 50 cents to $1, average grade bottles will range from $3 to $10, and basic high end bottles will range from $10 to $25. Anything over $25 should be looked at closely by someone who has been collecting for a while.

As a general rule, I try not to spend more than $1 per bottle for the low end and $3 for the average grade. It's easier to stick to this guideline when you've done your homework, but sometimes you just get lucky. During the 1992 Reno, Nevada, Bottle and Antique Show (one of the best, by the way), I stopped at a table where the seller had "Grab Bags," shopping bags full of bottles for $2 a bag. Well, I couldn't pass up this bargain. Later, when I had time to examine my treasures, I discovered a total of nine bottles, some purple, all earlier than 1900, in great shape, with embossing, for a total cost of 22 cents per bottle. Now what could be better than that! In the high end category, deals are usually made after some good old horse trading and bartering. But, hey, that's part of the fun. Always let the seller know that you are a new collector with a limited budget. It really helps. I have never run across a bottle seller who wouldn't work with a new collector to try to give the best deal for a limited budget.

A collector should also be aware of old bottles versus new bottles and what distinguishes an antique bottle from an old bottle, and either from a new bottle. Quite often, new collectors assume that any old bottle is an antique and that if a bottle isn't old it is not a collectible. By collectible, I mean a relatively rare and/or valuable bottle, or one that holds special interest for the collector (for its historical value, perhaps). This is not necessarily the case. In the antique world, an antique is defined as any article more than 100 years old. But you will see quite a number of bottles listed in this book that are less than 100 years old and are in fact just as valuable, perhaps more, than those that are antiques. I'm referring to bottles made between 1900 and 1950. As we discussed earlier, the history, origin, background, use, and rarity of the bottle can possibly gain more points with the bottle collector than how close the bottle comes to the 100-year mark.

The number and variety of old and antique bottles is greater than the new collectible items in today's market. On the other hand, the

Jim Beams, Ezra Brooks, Avons, and recent Coke bottles, and other types of figurals manufactured more recently, are very desirable and collectible and are in fact made for that purpose. If you decide you want to collect new bottles, the best time to buy is when the first issue comes out on the market. When the first issues are gone, the collectors' market is the only available source, and limited availability will drive prices up considerably. In mid-1992, the Coca-Cola Company reissued the eight-ounce junior-size Coke bottle in the Los Angeles area in an attempt to garner attention in a marketplace full of cans. This eight-ounce bottle has the same contour as the six-and-one-half-ounce bottle that was a Coke standard from the 1920s into the 1950s. (The six-and-one-half-ounce bottle is still available in a few parts of the United States, most noticeably in Atlanta, Georgia, where Coca-Cola has its headquarters.) When the eight-ounce bottles were issued in Los Angeles, the "heavy-duty collectors" literally paid in advance and picked up entire case lots from the bottling operations before they hit the retail market.

For the beginning collector, and even the old-timer, books, reference guides, magazines, and other similar literature are readily available at libraries and bookstores. I still make it a point to read as much as possible since someone is always discovering something new. As a help, there is a bibliography in this book of various types of literature to get you started. Also, joining a bottle club can be of great value since clubs pool numerous sources of information as well as offer occasional digging expeditions. Various bottle clubs and dealers are also listed at the end of this book, beginning on page 431.

Now, get out to the antique shops, flea markets, swap meets, and antique and bottle shows. Pick up those bottles and handle that glass. Ask questions and soon you will be surprised by how much you have learned, not to mention how much fun it is.

Bottle Facts

In order for a new bottle collector to better understand the hobby, there are certain specifics such as age identification, bottle grading, labeling, and glass imperfections and peculiarities that are very important to familiarize yourself with.

As mentioned in the introduction, usually the first question from a novice is "How do you know how old a bottle is?" or "How can you tell that it is really an antique bottle?" Two of the most common methods for determining the age are by the mold seams and the color variations. Also, details on the lip, or top of the bottle, will provide some further clues.

Mold Seams (Figure 5)

Prior to 1900, bottles were manufactured with a blowpipe using the free-blown method or with a mold (in use after 1860). In either process, the mouth or lip of the bottle was formed last and applied to the bottle after completion (applied lip). An applied lip can be discerned by examining the mold seam, which will run from the base up to the neck and near the bottom of the lip. In the machine-made bottle, the lip is formed first and the mold seam runs over the lip. Therefore, the closer to the top of the bottle the seam extends, the more recent the bottle.

For the earliest bottles, manufactured before 1860, the mold seams will end low on the neck or at the shoulder. On bottles made between 1860 and 1880, the mold seam stops right below the mouth, which makes it easy to detect that the lip was formed separately. Around 1880, the closed mold was utilized, wherein the neck and lip were

Age Identification Mold Seams of Bottles
Figure 5

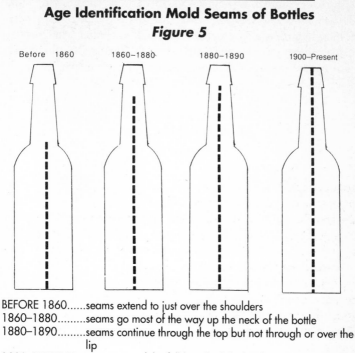

Before 1860   1860–1880   1880–1890   1900–Present

BEFORE 1860......seams extend to just over the shoulders
1860–1880.........seams go most of the way up the neck of the bottle
1880–1890.........seams continue through the top but not through or over the lip
1900–PRESENT ...seams extend the full length of the bottle and over the lip

mechanically shaped and the glass had to be severed from the blowpipe. The ridge that resulted was evened off by hand sanding or filing. This mold seam usually ends within one-quarter inch from the top of the bottle. After 1900, the seam extends clear to the top. Since the lips, or tops, were an integral part of the bottle-making process, it is important to understand some of that process.

Lips and Tops (Figures 6 and 7)

One of the best ways to identify bottles manufactured prior to 1840 is the presence of a "sheared lip." This type of lip was formed by cutting, or snipping, the glass free of the blowpipe with a pair of shears, a process that leaves it with a stovepipe look. Since hot glass can be stretched, some of these stovepipes have a very distinctive appearance. Around 1840, bottle manufacturers began to apply a glass ring around the sheared lip, forming a "laid-on-ring" lip. Between 1840 and 1880, numerous variations of lips or tops were produced by utilizing a variety of different tools. After 1880, manufacturers started to pool their processing information, resulting in a more evenly finished and uniform top. As a general rule, the more uneven and crude the lip or top, the older the bottle.

Neck Finishing Tools
Figure 6

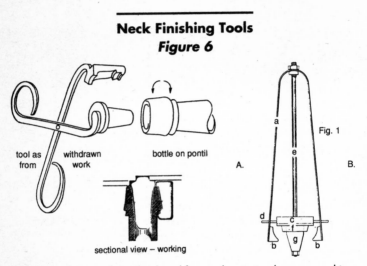

tool as
from

withdrawn
work

bottle on pontil

A.

sectional view – working

a

e

Fig. 1

d   c
g
b   b

B.

A. The line drawings were developed from a description that appeared in the 7th edition (1842) of the *Encyclopaedia Britannica*, Vol. X, p. 579: "The finisher then warms the bottle at the furnace, and taking out a small quantity of metal on what is termed a ring iron, he turns it once round the mouth forming the ring seen at the mouth of bottles. He then employs the shears to give shape to the neck. One of the blades of the shears has a piece of brass in the center, tapered like a common cork, which forms the inside of the mouth, to the other blade is attached a piece of brass, used to form the ring." This did not appear in the 6th edition (1823), though it is probable the method of forming collars was practiced in some glasshouses at that time.

B. The exact period in which neck-finishing tools evolved having metal springs with two jaws instead of one, to form collars, is undetermined. It doubtless was some time before Amosa Stone of Philadelphia patented his "improved tool," which was of simpler construction, as were many later ones. Like Stone's, "the interior of the jaws [was] made in such shape as to give the outside of the nozzle of the bottle or neck of the vessel formed the desired shape as it [was] rotated between the jaws in a plastic state . . ." U.S. Patent Office. From specifications for (A.Stone) patent No. 15, 738, Sept. 23, 1856.

Bottle Lips/Tops Identification
Figure 7

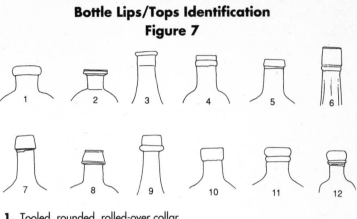

1. Tooled, rounded, rolled-over collar
2. Tooled, flanged, with flat top and squared edges
3. Tooled, rounded above 3/4" flat band
4. Tooled, flat ring below thickened plain lip
5. Tooled, narrow beveled fillet below thickened plain lip
6. Tooled, broad sloping collar above beveled ring
7. Tooled, plain broad sloping collar
8. Tooled, broad sloping collar with beveled edges at top and bottom
9. Tooled, broad flat collar sloping to heavy rounded ring
10. Tooled, broad flat vertical collar with uneven lower edge
11. Tooled, double rounded collar, upper deeper than lower, neck slightly pinched at base of collar
12. Tooled, broad round collar with lower bevel

English ink bottles reflecting the "sheared lip," 1830–1840.

Closures/Stoppers (Figure 8)

As discussed earlier, the Romans used small stones rolled in tar as stoppers. Later centuries saw little advancement in the methods of closure. For most of the fifteenth and sixteenth centuries, the closure consisted of a sized cloth tied down with heavy thread or string. Beneath the cover was a stopper made of wax or bombase (cotton wading). Cotton wool was also dipped in wax to be used as a stopper, along with coverings made of parchment, paper, or leather. Corks and glass stoppers were still used in great numbers. The cork was sometimes tied or wired down for use with effervescent liquids. When the "close mold" came into existence, however, the shape of the lip was more accurately controlled, which made it possible to invent and manufacture many different capping devices.

***

S. A. Whitney, Bottle Stopper
No. 31046 Patented Jan. 1, 1861
Figure 8

Fig. 1

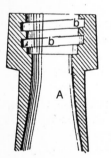 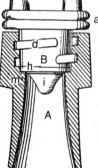

Fig. 2

From Samuel A. Whitney's specifications for his "Bottle Stopper," patent No. 31046, Jan. 1, 1861. Fig. 1 shows the grooves in neck of the bottle. Fig. 2, on which "h" is a cork washer, shows the stopper in place. "The stopper is formed by pressing or casting the molten . . . glass in molds of the desired shape . . . Although . . . applicable to a variety of bottles and jars, it is especially well adapted to and has been more especially designed for use in connection with mineral-water bottles, and such as contain effervescing wines, malt liquors, &c., the corks used in this class of bottles, if not lost, being generally so mutilated as to be unfit for second use when the bottles are refilled." (U.S. Patent Office.)

Glass stoppers,
1850–1900.

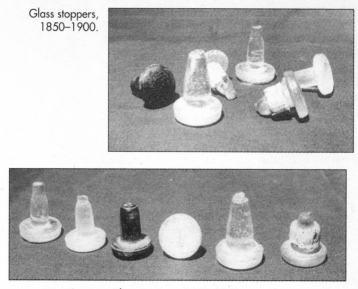

Glass stoppers, 1850–1900.

One of the most unique was developed in 1873 when a British inventor, Hiram Codd, invented a bottle with a glass marble confined inside its neck so that when it was used with an effervescing liquid, the pressure of the gas forced the marble to the top of the neck, sealing the bottle. From 1879 to the early 1900s, the Hutchinson stopper became a common bottle closure. It used a heavy wire loop to control a rubber gasket that stayed inside the neck of the bottle. The Lighting stopper, used from 1880 to the early 1900s, was a porcelain or rubber plug anchored to the outside of the bottle by means of a permanently attached wire. The wire formed a bar that controlled the opening and closing of the bottle.

In 1897, William Painter invented the crown cap, which revolutionized the soft drink and beer bottling industry. A crown cap was formed from a circular tin plate crimped on the outer edge to fit tightly over the rolled lip of the bottle. The inside of the cap was filled with a cork disk that created an airtight seal. A modified version of this cap is still used on beer and soft drink bottles today.

Finally, in 1902, threads were manufactured on the outside of the lip to enable a threaded cap to be screwed onto the mouth of the

Dumfries Ale (English) reflecting inside threads.

Dumfries Ale (English), full-bottle view reflecting inside threads.

bottle. This was not a new idea. Early glassblowers had produced bottles with inside and outside screw caps long before bottle-making machines came along. Early methods of production were so complex, however, that screw-top bottles produced before the 1800s were considered specialty bottles. They were expensive to replace and today are considered rare and quite collectible. In fact, the conventional screw-top bottle did not become common until after 1924, when the glass industry standardized the threads.

Glass Color

The next most common method for determining the age of a bottle is by examining the color of the glass. The basic ingredients for glass production (sand, soda, and lime) have remained the same for 3,000 years. These ingredients, when mixed together, are collectively called the "batch." When the batch is heated to a molten state, it is referred to as the "metal." In its soft or plastic stage, the metal can be molded into objects that when cooled become the solid material we know as glass.

Producing colored and perfectly clear glass were major challenges for glass manufacturers for centuries. In the thirteenth and fourteenth centuries the Venetians produced clear glass by using crushed quartz in place of sand. In 1668, the English tried to improve on this process by using ground flint to produce clear glass, and by 1675, an Englishman named George perfected lead glass. Today, this lead glass is referred to as "Flint glass." Prior to 1840, intentionally colored or colorless glass was reserved for fancy figured flasks and vessels. The coloration of bottles was considered unimportant until 1880, when food packers began to demand clear glass for preserved food products. Since most glass produced prior to this time was green, glass manufacturers began using manganese or delenium to bleach out the green tinge produced by the iron content of the sand. Only then did the clear bottle become common.

Iron slag was used up to 1860 and produced a dark olive-green or olive-amber glass that has become known as "black glass" and was used for wine and beverages that needed protection from light. Colors natural to bottle glass production are brown, amber, olive-green, and aqua.

The true blue, green, and purple colors were produced by metallic oxides added to the glass batch. Cobalt was added for blue glass, sulfur for yellow and green, manganese and nickel for purple, nickel for brown, copper or gold for red, and tin or zinc for milky colored glass (for apothecary vials, druggist bottles, and pocket bottles). Since these bright colors were expensive to produce, they are very rare and are sought after by most collectors.

"Purple glass" is the product of a number of imposed and natural forces and many collectors prize it above other colored glasses. As discussed earlier, the iron contained in sand caused glass to take on color between green and blue. Glass manufacturers used manganese, which counteracted iron's blue effect and produced clear glass. Glass with this manganese content, which was most common in bottle production between 1880 and 1914, takes on a rich purple color when exposed to ultraviolet rays. This "purple glass" has come to be known as "desert glass" or "sun-colored glass" since the color is actually a result of exposure to the sun. One last note, glass that was produced

Johnson and
Ramdohr Crown
Top Soda—
Amethyst,
Winnemucca
Bottle Works,
Winnemucca, NV.

between 1914 and 1930 is most likely to change to an amber or straw color.

Imperfections

Imperfections and blemishes are also clues to how old a bottle is and often add to the charm and value of an individual piece. Blemishes usually show up as bubbles or "seeds" in the glass. In the process of making glass, air bubbles form and rise to the surface, where they pop. As the "fining out" or elimination process became more advanced (around 1920), these bubbles or seeds were eliminated.

Another peculiarity of the antique bottle is uneven thickness of the glass. Often one side of the base has a one-inch-thick side that slants off to paper thinness on the opposite edge. This imperfection was eliminated with the introduction of the Owens bottle-making machine in 1903. In addition, the various marks of stress and strain, sunken sides, twisted necks, and whittle marks (usually at the neck, where the wood mold made impressions in the glass) also give clues to indicate that a bottle was produced before 1900.

Labeling and Embossing

While embossing and labeling were a common practice in the rest of the world before 1850, American bottle manufacturers did not adopt the inscription process until 1869. These inscriptions included information about the contents, manufacturer, distributor, and slogans, or other messages advertising the product. Raised lettering on various bottles was produced with a plate mold, sometimes called a "slug plate," which was fitted inside the casting mold. This plate created a sunken area, and these bottles are of special value to collectors. Irregularities such as a misspelled name add to the value of the bottle, as will any name embossed with hand etching or another method of crude grinding. These bottles are very old, very collectible, and very valuable.

Inscription and embossing customs came to an end with the production of machine-made bottles (1903) and the introduction of paper labels. In 1933, with the repeal of Prohibition, the only letter embossing on bottles, usually those containing alcohol, is "Federal Law Forbids Sale or Re-Use of this Bottle."

Bottle Sources

Antique or collectible bottles can be found in a variety of different locations and sometimes where you least expect them. Excluding digging for bottles, which we'll discuss later in detail, the following sources comprise what I think is a good list for potential hiding places of that much sought after bottle.

Flea Markets, Swap Meets, Thrift and Secondhand Stores, Garage Sales, Salvagers

For the beginner collector, these sources will likely be the most fun (next to digging) and yield the most bottles at the best prices. As we discussed earlier, a little bit of homework can result in opportunities to purchase bottles of endless variety for an extremely low cost. As a rule, the majority of bottles found at these sources will fall into the common or common but above average category.

When looking around at flea markets, swap meets, and thrift stores, be sure to target in on household goods. It's a good bet they will have some type of bottle. When looking through the paper for garage sales, try to concentrate your search in the older areas of town since the items being presented for sale will be noticeably older, more collectible, and more likely to fall into a rare category. Salvage stores or salvage yards are great places to search for bottles since these businesses deal with companies that have contracts to demolish old houses, apartments, and businesses, and on occasion, will come across treasures. One New York salvage company that contracted to clean out some old storage buildings came across an untouched illegal

Prohibition setup complete with bottles and unused labels. What a find!

Local Bottle Clubs and Collectors

By joining a local bottle club or working with other collectors, you will find yet another source for your growing collection. Members will usually have quantities of unwanted or duplicate bottles that they will sell very reasonably, trade, or sometimes simply give away, especially to an enthusiastic new collector. In addition, bottle clubs are always a good source for information about digging expeditions.

Bottle Shows

Bottle shows not only expose you to bottles of every type, shape, color, and variety but provide you with the opportunity to talk with many experts in specialized fields. In addition, there are usually publications for sale relating to all aspects of the bottle-collecting hobby. Bottle shows can be a rewarding and learning experience for the beginning collector in particular but also for the veteran collector.

One last note: Make sure to look under the tables at these weekend shows. The vendor may consider these duplicates as less attractive items, but a real bargain could be lurking there.

Auctions and Estate Sales

Auction houses have become a good source of bottles and glassware over the last ten years. Try to find one that specializes in antiques and estate buy-outs. To promote and provide buyers with a better idea of what will be for sale, the house usually publishes a catalog that provides bottle descriptions, conditions, and photographs. Auctions are fun and can be a very good source of bottles at economical prices. I do recommend, however, that you visit an auction first as a spectator to learn a little about how the whole process works before you decide to participate and buy at one. When buying, be sure of the color and condition of the bottle and terms of the sale.

Estate sales by themselves, apart from an auction, are a great source for bottles if the items for sale are from a home in a very old neighborhood or a section of the city that has historical significance. These sales are a lot of fun, especially when people running the sale let you browse, look over and handle the contents. Prices are usually good and always subject to downward negotiation.

Knife and Gun Shows

What, bottles at a knife and gun show? Quite a number of gun and knife enthusiasts are also great fans of the West and keep an eye open for related artifacts. Every knife and gun show I've attended, or sold at, has had at least ten dealers with bottles on their tables (or under the tables) for sale. And the prices were right since they were more interested in selling knives and guns than bottles. Plus, these dealers will often provide information on where they made their finds, which you can put to good use later.

Retail Antique Dealers

This grouping includes those dealers who sell bottles at or near full-market prices. Buying from a dealer has its up side as well as its down side. Dealers usually have a large selection and will provide helpful information and details about the bottles. It is a safe bet that bottles for sale are authentic and have been priced in accordance with the true condition of the bottle.

On the other hand, to try to build up a collection from these dealers can be very expensive. But, their shops are good places to browse, learn, and try to fill out a collection.

General Antique and Specialty Shops

The differences between a general shop and a retail dealer are usually the selection (more limited with a general shop) and the pricing, which is happily much lower. This is in part due to the fact that these dealers are not as knowledgeable about bottles and therefore may incorrectly identify a bottle, overlooking critical areas that determine the value. If a collector can become knowledgeable, these general dealers create the opportunity to acquire quality underpriced merchandise.

Digging for Bottles

T here are many sources for finding that collectible bottle but, as I have mentioned before, the most fun for the collector is finding that bottle by digging for it. Even though the goal is to find a bottle, the adventure of the hunt is as much fun as the actual find. Also, from a beginner's viewpoint, it is an excellent way to start your collection relatively cheaply with a whole bunch of fun. In addition, there have been a number of important historical findings made due to the efforts of bottle club digging expeditions as well as those of independent diggers. These finds have uncovered valuable data about the early growth of our country and the history of bottle and glass manufacturing in the United States. Any discussion of an expedition should begin with locating the digging site.

Locating the Digging Site

Prior to any dig, you need to learn as much as possible about the area you plan to explore. By the way, this does not exclude your own community. There are a number of resources that will provide this information, such as the town library or historical society. Old city maps and directories depict what the town used to look like and may contain clues to where stores, saloons, hotels, red-light districts, and the town dump were located. These spots are ripe for exploring. Don't forget to consider residential areas either. Also, be sure to check with the local chamber of commerce, law enforcement agencies, and locals who have lived in the community for a number of years and who can all be very informative. Another great resource for publications about the area's history are local antique and gift shops, which will carry literature on the town, county, and surrounding communities.

Dale Mooney, owner of Western Glass Auctions, in the process of digging for bottles. This was a four-by-twelve-foot hole and fourteen feet deep (notice the additional items found around the bottles).

Since most early settlers handled waste disposal themselves, buried bottles can be unearthed almost anywhere, but a little thinking can narrow the choice of digging sites effectively. Usually, the garbage was hauled to the end of town and dumped within one mile of the town center. Often settlers or store owners would dig a hole about twenty-five yards out from the back of their residence for garbage and refuse. Many hotels and saloons had a basement or underground storage area where empty bottles were kept. For those with the stomach for it, one of the best places to find an old bottle is in an old outhouse or privy. Like household dumps, most outhouses were located behind the residence about thirty yards away. Because of the rich fertilized ground, an unexpected grouping of vegetation, such as a clump of bushes or trees, is good evidence of an outhouse location. Outhouses have been known to yield not only bottles but guns, coins, knives, and even toys. As a note of caution, the dirt surrounding these outhouses is very soft and can be very dangerous. I always recommend that people work these sites in pairs, taking as many safety precautions as possible. Also, cisterns, which were a means of water storage, are great sources of bottles and other artifacts.

Ravines, ditches, and washes are also prime digging spots because heavy rains or snow meltoffs often washed debris down from other areas. Quite often, bottles can be found beside houses and under porches where residents either stored their bottles or threw them away. Walks down abandoned roads where houses or cabins were located, wagon trails and old railroad tracks, have proven fruitful. And, if it is legal, old battlegrounds and military encampments are wonderful places to dig.

The first love of this bottle hound, and high on the list of most collectors, is an expedition to a ghost town. It's fun—and a lesson in history. The best places to conduct a search in a ghost town are near saloons, trade stores, and the red-light district, as well as the town dump.

Digging Equipment and Tools

When I first started digging, I took only a shovel and my luck. It was the hard way and resulted in a few broken bottles. Since then, I've refined my list of tools and equipment. The following list includes those items that I've found to be useful and others recommended by other veteran diggers.

1. Thin steel probing rod (push it into the ground until you hear it hit glass)
2. Long-handled shovel
3. Short-handled shovel
4. Potato rake (long-handled)
5. Small hand rake
6. Hunting knife
7. Spoons
8. Hard- or soft-bristle brushes
9. Gloves/boots/eye protection/durable clothing
10. Insect repellent, snakebite kit, first aid kit
11. Extra water and a hat
12. Dirt sifter for coins or other items (a two-foot-by-two-foot wooden frame topped by small-gauge chicken wire)
13. Heavy-duty sack (burlap) for carrying bottles

General Rules and Helpful Hints

I know, I said there were no rules, but there is one important one to heed. Always ask for permission to dig, and when the digging is complete, always leave the site looking better than when you started. That means filling in all holes and raking over the area. Take out your

Bottles found while digging near an old mining camp.

trash and any trash left by previous prospectors. The community or owner will thank you and future bottle diggers will be welcomed.

Try not to go out on a dig alone, but if you do, be sure to tell someone where you're going and for how long you will be gone.

Now, when you start to dig, don't be discouraged if you find no bottles. If you unearth other objects such as coins, broken dishes, or bottle tops, continue to dig but in a wider area and deeper. If bottles still do not appear, move to another spot. Work from the perimeter of a designated area to the center. Do not get discouraged. Even the very best have come home with empty bags and boxes.

When you do find that bottle, stop your energetic digging and remove the surrounding dirt a little at a time with a small tool, brush, or spoon. Handle the bottle carefully since old bottles are very fragile.

Now that you know the details, what are you waiting for? Grab that shovel, get those maps, and get started on your way to making the discoveries of a lifetime.

Bottle Handling

While selling bottles, and listening to buyers at various shows, a question always arises about how to clean old bottles. Some collectors take the attitude that cleaning a bottle diminishes its collectibility and desirability. The choice rests with the owner, but if you do decide to clean a bottle I recommend using the following techniques.

Bottle Cleaning

First off, never attempt to clean your new find in the field. It's easy to break or otherwise damage the embossing. When you return from your expedition, the first step is to remove as much loose dirt, sand, or other particles as possible with a brush or a quick warm-water rinse. Then, soak the bottles for a number of days depending upon the amount of dirt using a solution of warm water and bleach. Be sure to stir the mixture first. This should remove most of the excess grime. Other cleaning mixtures favored by collectors include straight ammonia, kerosene, Lime-A-Way, and Borax bleach.

After soaking, bottles can be cleaned with a bottle brush, steel wool, or a semistiff brush. At this point you may want to soak the bottles again in lukewarm water to remove any traces of cleaning materials. Then, either let the bottles air-dry or dry them with a soft towel. If the bottle has a label, the work will become more painstaking since soaking is not a cleaning option.

Bottle Display

Now that you have clean, beautiful bottles, display them to their best advantage. My advice is to arrange your bottles in a cabinet rather than on wall shelving or randomly set around the house. While the last two options are more decorative, they are also more susceptible to casual disasters. When choosing a cabinet, try to find one with glass sides since this will provide additional visibility and light. As an added touch, a light fixture could set off your collection beautifully. If you have picked up any other goodies from your digging—such as coins or gambling chips—scatter them around the bottles for a little Western flavor.

Bottle Storage

For those bottles you've chosen not to display, the best method for storage I have found is empty liquor boxes with cardboard dividers, which provide good protection. As added protection, you might want to wrap individual bottles in paper.

Record Keeping

Last but not least, it's a good idea to keep good records of your collection. Use index cards detailing where the bottle was found or purchased (include the dealer's name and price you paid). Also, assign a catalog number to each bottle, record it on the card, and then make an index.

Many collectors keep records with a photocopy machine. If the bottle has embossing or a label, put the bottle on the machine and make a copy of it. Then, type all the pertinent information on the back of the image and put them in a binder. When it comes to trading and selling, you will find your record keeping invaluable.

Bottles of Nevada by Fred Holabird

I *first met Fred in 1983 during a Western gun and knife show where he was selling (what else) bottles. After talking with him a while, I bought a book he had written and of course ended up buying a few bottles. It was the start of a great friendship. Fred has been collecting bottles since 1973, when he found his first embossed Pumpkin Seed Whiskey bottle in an old prospector's pit.*

Fred has been in the mining industry for more than seventeen years as a geologist and mining company executive. In 1983, he founded a company specializing in Western Americana documents and glass. Since then, he has been involved with numerous auctions, including the 1987 sale of Mel Fisher's Atocha *treasure at Caesars Palace in Las Vegas. He is currently working with Butterfield and Butterfield of San Francisco on a major Western Americana manuscript sale.*

I feel honored that Fred has taken time to tell us about the history and value of the bottles of Nevada.

Collecting embossed bottles from Nevada became a passion of mine over twenty years ago. It began as a hobby, as an outreach of my new home in Nevada. It became something of an obsession after I watched the market value climb regularly in the mid-1970s. Just when I thought the market had peaked, it would steady and take off again. So, I jumped in. . .

Two books and numerous magazine articles later, I became a recognized "expert" on the subject. Not by design, but because of the enthusiasm I had developed after researching many of the merchants

Hunter Creek Dairy, Reno, NV, 1925 (rare).

The N.E. Wilson Company Inc., Reno, NV, 1916–1937 (machine made, last of the Nevada embossed drugstore bottles).

who bottled their products in glass containers. It was like a giant mystery novel. I was continually digging up "new" information on merchants that I couldn't seem to find through the normal channels of researching in directories, newspapers, and tax records.

One of my favorite stories comes from an autograph session at a local bookstore. In walked a well-dressed elderly gentleman who introduced himself as John Shier's grandson (Shier had a drugstore in the little mining camp of Delamar, now a ghost town). I had been particularly stymied in my research on Shier's drugstore because of a lack of records. It seemed that very little had survived. Then in walked his grandson with the best stories you could imagine, complete with photographs.

Collecting soon became fun because of the people. I enjoyed not only the folks involved in research, but the families I met, the people at research institutions, the folks who let us dig in their back yards, and the wild-goose chases after elusive rare bottles. The hobby was fresh and there were a lot of collections to find.

While I began logging collections, the discovery of quite a few very beautiful bottles from Nevada came as a small surprise. In the mid-1970s, the common perception was that embossed bottles from Nevada were quite plain. Since Nevada was undeveloped until modern historical times, 1860s to 1870s, most people thought bottles from Nevada were "plain." Most of the Nevada bottles known to the collecting world of the 1970s were drugstores and a few plain whiskeys and sodas without any fancy colors. But the idea that Nevada bottles were nothing but plain was soon dismissed. As I looked at more and more collections, I noticed there were quite a few striking color variations of otherwise plain bottles. Some of the most strikingly beautiful bottles are, of course, quite rare (one or two known). Among these are the amber Higgins Ink and the Morrill Apothecary, both from Virginia City.

One of the great Nevada bottles today is the W.S. Wright soda from Virginia City. While the bottle carries only the proprietor's name, it is the only true example of a merchant's bottle from the Nevada territorial period (pre-October 1864). Manufactured by the San Francisco Glass Works, this soda exhibits all the traits of early

A.B. Stewart and Company, Goldhill, NV, 1877–1881.

A.B. Stewart and Company, Virginia City, NV, 1877–1881 (rare).

Smith Drug and Jewelry, Yerington, NV, 1908–1920 (rare due to misspelling "Drug and Jewerly").

crude Western glassmaking. Colors range from emerald and grass-green to aqua to shades of blue. As I collected color variations and displayed them at shows, I found people were as excited about the colors as they were about this newly discovered collectible.

One day I received an excited call from one of my digging friends in Virginia City. "We hit Wright's outhouse!" he exclaimed. In a hole about fifteen feet deep, they found several feet of broken glass . . . probably several thousand broken bottles. Only two or three mint Wright bottles made it through, one of which is the crudest dark green-aqua glass peppered with charcoal bits and pieces. About twenty-five whole bottles were found with cracks. Most of these were seriously flawed, with large pieces of charcoal or "pot stones," resulting in cracks. I kept a good cross section to show the variation in flawed bottles.

Other popular "ghost town" bottles include the crown-top soda from the Eagle Bottling Company, of Goldfield (exceptionally rare), and drugstore bottles from Ruby Hill, Tuscarora, and Seven Troughs. The Seven Troughs bottle has a large owl on the front, a symbol of the Owl Drug store but unrelated to the Owl Drug Company. Seven Troughs was a small mining camp in the high desert located up a

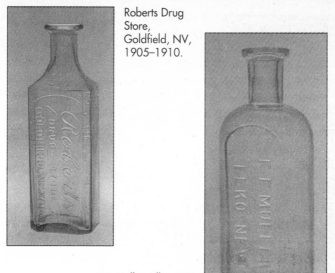

Roberts Drug
Store,
Goldfield, NV,
1905–1910.

F.F. Muller, Elko, NV,
1876–1888 (scarce).

canyon. Unfortunately for the folks of Seven Troughs, the canyon drained after it became a populated community. As providence would have it, a horrendous flood washed away part of the town about the same time the mines began to "peter out." Today nothing is left except a few rusty cans.

Sometimes collecting bottles in small towns that are all but vanished isn't all that easy since it's illegal in many areas. So the only hope of acquiring one of these rare bottles is buying from a collection or traveling to a neighboring town in the hope that digging there will uncover one of these rarities. The Seven Troughs bottle in my collection was dug from a deep hole in Lovelock, a town about ten miles from Seven Troughs. With its sixteen-ounce capacity, it remains the largest known example.

Digging in Nevada has been quite an experience. While nowhere near as experienced as some of my friends, I have dug my share of holes, probably a thousand or so. But this amounts to about 10 percent of what my fanatic and very successful friends have dug. My "Rule of Thumb" is that one hole in ten will have bottles and only one in ten of those will have a "good" bottle.

Once, while working in a small mining town, a nice lady let us dig in her back yard after she came home from work. We located the privy and began digging. As bottles began to fly out of the hole, she came out, dangled her feet over the edge of the hole and said she hoped we would find her father's broken plate, which she was told had been thrown out long before she was born. It was apparently the only missing piece in a set of china generations old. Fifteen minutes later, out came both pieces unstained. We made her day and she made ours.

The goal that I've had over the past fifteen years has been to assemble a complete collection of Nevada merchant bottles. Considering widespread bottle production, this would be an insurmountable task with most states. But in Nevada, a state lightly populated compared to others, the task is much easier. I am now only one bottle short of my original goal. The Nevada collection offers a spectacular array of colors, sizes, and shapes. But one prominent nationally collected color is missing from the rank of the Nevada embossed

G.P. Morrill, Virginia City, NV, 1863-1874 (apothecary bottle, extremely rare).

Frank Abadie, Eureka, NV, 1884–1886 (pumpkin seed flask).

Kane's Cafe, Reno, NV, 1914–1919 (amber pocket flask, only three specimens known).

A.M. Cole, Virginia City, NV, 1861–1908 (amber, rare).

bottles—cobalt. The only cobalt bottles from Nevada known are two seltzers, both from Reno. For years I had heard stories about a cobalt Delamar bottle. After some research I tracked down an exceptionally kind lady in Panaca who showed me her collection. And there they were. Two cobalt Delamar drugstore bottles. She had made them both herself using glazed pottery. We laughed over the stories based on those recreations that had circulated and grown. She had made a number of unique ceramic bottles that the Las Vegas Bottle Club gave away as prizes for displays, of which I have a few.

And there's always a story behind these ghost town bottles. The merchant history is every bit as fascinating. Sometimes the merchants would only last a few years in one town, moving on to another when the gold "dried up." Such was the case with Henry Schuldt of Tuscarora, who moved to Grass Valley, California. More of his Tuscarora drug bottles have been dug there than in Tuscarora. George Thaxter moved from Carson City to Redlands and W. H. Stowell moved from Eureka to Spokane. Bottles bearing these merchants'

The Cann Drug Company, Reno, NV, 1898–1931 (script embossing, extremely rare).

A. Livingston, Carson City, NV, 1885–1905 (coffin flasks).

Tonopah Soda Works, Tonopah, NV, 1902–1905 (aqua Hutchinson).

Johnson and Beckerk, Winnemucca Bottling Works, Winnemucca, NV, 1885–1922 (crown top soda).

names have been discovered in both towns. Other merchants such as A. B. Stewart started "franchising." A.B. Stewart stores operated nearly simultaneously in Virginia City, Gold Hill, Silver City, Bodie, Seattle, and later Exeter.

Collecting anything today is both an investment and a hobby and I've enjoyed all aspects of the hobby. Because of my passion, the investment has been worthwhile as well. Because antique bottles are aesthetically pleasing and their shapes and colors are an art form, we've seen their entrance into art auction markets. Once this move was made, collecting bottles as an investment became legitimized and has proven to be both fun and profitable.

When considering a bottle purchase as an investment, the following factors, listed in descending order of importance, will influence the decision:

1. Demand—Is there sufficient demand for the bottle to support the price indefinitely? A number of factors such as bottle color, clarity, crudeness, age, and collecting category all affect this demand. Major collecting categories are figurals, historical flasks, bitters, sodas, whiskeys, and medicines.

2. Market—Is the market for the bottle national, regional, or local? And does this market support the perceived demand? A national market means a broad support base with more collectors, therefore greater investment stability. Regional or local markets may be substantial enough to support a market long-term. The bottom line, though, is the number of collectors. The more collectors, the more competition, the more stable the price.

3. Condition—Is the condition of the bottle good enough to insure an easy sale? Broken, chipped, or cracked bottles are often hard to sell unless they have an exceptional demand. Initially, when bottles first became valuable collectibles, the only acceptable investment condition was "mint." True "mint" used to be defined as a bottle with no scratches, discoloration, potstones, stains, chips, cracks, or blemishes. Now the term "mint" applies to any bottle that has no chips or scratches. A minor stain is okay. Recently, rarity has become a significant factor. If a bottle is sufficiently rare the condition will affect the price, but the bottle still remains marketable and in high demand.

G.P. Morrill, Virginia City, NV, 1863-1870 (blob-top soda, rare, second oldest Nevada soda).

4. Guarantee—Will the dealer or collector selling the bottle guarantee its origin and condition? Will they give you your money back if you are not satisfied? Investment guarantee may be the stickiest negotiating point in a sale. When a bottle sold to a collector is warranted in a specific condition, it should be in just that condition. One popular West Coast dealer has often overlooked small chips on some of the bottles he has sold through the mail, but he has never hesitated to refund money if the customer is not satisfied.

In summary, use good judgment when buying bottles as investments. Display them as art at home or at the office. Know the market, how to buy and sell, and understand the key factors affecting bottles as investments. The thing to remember about collecting and investing is that it should be fun. I've had more than my share of fun doing this and if you share my passion for bottles, I'm sure you'll do the same.

Old Bottles

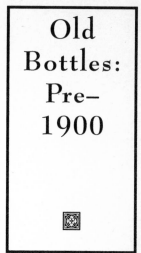

Old Bottles: Pre–1900

The bottles listed in this section have been broken down into individual categories by physical type and/or by the original contents of the bottle. For most categories, the trade names can be found in alphabetical order if they exist. Note that in the case of certain early bottles, such as flasks, a trade name does not appear on the bottle. These bottles have been listed according to the embossing or other identification on the bottle itself.

Since it is impossible to list every bottle available, I've tried to provide a good cross section of bottles in various price ranges and categories rather than listing only the rarest or most collectible pieces.

The pricing shown reflects the value of the particular bottle listed. Similar bottles could have higher or lower values than the items specifically listed in this book. This listing will still provide a good starting point for determining a price range.

Bottle Grading

Pricing, or putting a value on an old bottle, is dependent upon a number of variables, as well as on reliable sources. The guidelines below detail variables that are most often used by dealers and collectors to determine a value and are consistent with the methods that I have used over the years. These variables break down into the following three groups:

1. Rarity and demand for the specific bottle
2. Bottle type based on the original function
3. Unique features
   • Embossing
   • Labeling

- Pontil scars
- Whittle marks
- Imperfections in the glass
- Colors
    Purple (amethyst)
    Cobalt blue
    Milk glass
    Black glass

Bottles are then categorized into one of the following conditions.

Mint—An empty or full bottle (preferably full) with a label or embossing. Clear in color, clean, with no chips, scrapes, or wear. If there is a box, it must be in good condition.

Extra Fine—An empty bottle with the label (slight wear) or embossing. Clear in color, clean, no chips, no scrapes, some wear. Usually there is no box or the box is not in very good condition.

Very Good—Bottle reflects some wear and label is usually missing or not very visible. Most likely there is no embossing and no box.

Good—Bottle reflects additional wear and label is completely absent. Color is usually faded and bottle is dirty. It's common to see some scrapes and minor chips. Most likely there will be no box.

Fair or Average—Bottle shows much wear, the label is missing, and there is no embossing. The color is very faded and the piece has numerous scrapes and some chips or even cracks. Definitely no box.

Even with the above guidelines, it is important to have some additional resources for grading those rare or unique bottles that give the collector a real challenge and fun. The bibliography in this book will provide some additional references. And remember to ask other collectors or dealers for help. They're a valuable resource.

Ale and Gin

Since ale and gin bottles are almost identical in style and similar in other ways, it becomes difficult to determine what the bottle originally contained unless information is provided on the bottle itself. Ale bottles should not be confused with beer bottles, a common mistake due to the similarities in shape.

Ale was a popular beverage at a time when available wines were not as palatable. Even the very best ale was not expensive to make or buy so it's easy to understand the demand for it. The bottles used by colonial ale makers were made of pottery and imported from England. When searching out these bottles, keep in mind that the oldest ones had a matte or unglazed surface.

In the seventeenth century, a Dutch physician named Francesco De La Bor prepared gin as a medical compound for the treatment of kidney disease. While its effectiveness in purifying the blood was questionable, gin drinking became very popular. It became so popular that many chemists decided to go into the gin-brewing business full-time to meet the growing demand. During the nineteenth century, gin consumption in America increased at a steady rate.

The design of the gin bottle, which has a squat body, facilitated packing in cases by preventing shifting and possible damage in shipping. The first case bottles had very short necks and were octagonal. Designs that came later featured longer necks. Bottles with tapered collars are dated to the nineteenth century. Case bottles vary in size from a half pint to multiple gallons. The early bottles were crudely made and have distinct pontil scars.

Gordon's London Dry Gin,
clear, 1880–1900.

Amsterdam Croixd' Honneur 1895
Clear, 8¾ inches, clear top, pour spout ground for stopper ..$50–100
European 1895

Blankenheum and Nolets
Clear, 11⅞ inches, tooled top, smooth base $75–100
Dutch 1890–1910

Charles—London—Cordial Gin
Dark blue-green, 10 inches, applied top, smooth base $100–200
American 1860–1870

Clermont Brand Holland Gin
Dark olive-green, 10½ inches, applied top, smooth base $70–120
American 1880–1890

Dip Mold Case Gin
Dark olive-amber, 10⅞ inches x 3⅛ inches at base..............$150–250
Dutch 1780–1810

Dutch Gin
Olive-green, 10¼ inches, applied top, open pontil $75–150
Dutch 1780–1800

E.P. Shaw and Company LD. Ale, Wakefield, England, 1880.

Ale pottery bottles from England, 1880.

Dutch Gin
Olive-green, 9¼ inches, applied top, open pontil $75–150
Dutch 1780–1800

E. Kiderlen
Dark olive-green, 9¼ inches, applied top, smooth base $50–100
European 1860–1870

J.T. Daly, Club House
Dark emerald-green, 8¾ inches, applied top, smooth base ...$100–150
American 1860–1865

J.J.W. Peters, Hamburg, Trademark (dog with bird motif)
Orange-amber, 8⅛ inches, applied top, smooth base............$75–150
European 1870–1880

Lebens Trophen, John Carl Mitau
Clear, 9 inches, tooled top, smooth base $75–125
American 1880–1890

London/Jockey—Club House/Gin (man riding horse motif)
Amber, 9¼ inches, applied top, smooth base......................$150–225
American 1865–1875

Manyaofu/Dimaloila, Trademark (lion motif)
Light olive-green, 8½ inches, applied top, smooth base.....$150– 250
European 1870–1880

Palm Boom G. Meyer and C. Schiedam (palm tree motif)
Dark olive-green, 11 inches, applied top, smooth base.........$75–125
European 1870–1880

Rose Gin, F.P. Dilley and Company, Philadelphia
Clear with white enamel, tooled top, tied pontil $85–125
American 1890–1910

S.B. Rothenberg, Sole Agent, U.S. Pat. Applied For (applied seal)
Milk glass, 9 inches, applied top, smooth base.....................$75–125
American 1890–1900

Club House/Gin,
London/Jockey,
1865–1875
(amber).

Royal, I.A.I.N. Bataui (sealed gin)
Amethyst, 12 inches, tooled top, smooth base $100–150
American 1890–1910

Van Den Bergh and Company (bell motif)
Olive-green, 10½ inches x 2½ inches at base, applied top $75–125
Dutch 1840–1860

Wister's Club House
Dark blue-green, 9½ inches, iron pontil, applied top..........$100–200
American 1840–1850

Barber Bottles

Starting in the mid-1860s and continuing to 1920, barbers in America used colorful decorated bottles filled with various tonics and colognes. The finish of these unique and colorful pieces originated when the Pure Food and Drug Act of 1907 restricted the use of alcohol-based ingredients in unlabeled or refillable containers.

Very early examples will have rough pontil scars with various types of ornamentation such as fancy pressed designs, paintings, and labels under glass. The bottles were usually fit with a cork, metal, or porcelain-type closure.

Barber Bottle
Sapphire-blue, 6⅝ inches, melon sided, coin-spotted pattern....$80–120
American 1890–1910

Barber Bottle
Yellow, 7 inches, tooled top, smooth base, melon sided, coin-spotted pattern $80–120
American 1880–1910

Barber Bottle
Deep amethyst, 7 inches, tooled top, open pontil, ribbed with orange, white, and gold flower enamel..............................$100–150
American 1880–1910

Barber Bottle
Emerald-green, 7 inches, tooled top, smooth base, melon sided, coin-spotted pattern...$80–120
American 1890–1910

American barber bottles, 1880–1910.

Barber Bottle
Deep amethyst, 7½ inches, sheared top, open pontil, white, pink, and yellow enamel flower pattern......................................$100–150
American 1880–1910

Barber Bottle
Milk glass, 7½ inches, sheared top, open pontil, multicolored scene of three cherubs...$200–300
American 1880–1910

Wildroot Hair Tonic,
Wildroot Chemical
Company, Buffalo, NY,
1900–1920.

Barber Bottle
Deep amethyst, 7¾ inches, tooled top, open pontil, blue, red,
and yellow enamel...$80–120
American 1880–1910

Barber Bottle
Turquoise-blue/yellow and silver enamel sheared top, ribbed
Persian pattern...$100–150
American 1880–1910

Barber Bottle
Medium emerald-green, 7⅛ inches, tooled top, open pontil,
blue, red, and yellow enamel..$80–120
American 1880–1910

Barber Bottle
Purple, 8 inches, tooled top, pontil, white and blue enamel...$50–100
American 1890–1920

Barber Bottle
Colbalt-blue, 8⅛ inches, tooled top, smooth base, melon-sided
pattern $80–120
American 1900–1920

Kokens Tonique De Luxe,
The Liquid Head Rest,
hair tonic, 1890–1920.

Assortment of hair tonic bottles: Colgate and Company, New York; Wildroot Company Inc., Buffalo, NY; Ed Pinaude, Paris; 1880–1920.

Barber Bottle
Emerald-green, 8⅛ inches, tooled top, smooth base, melon-sided pattern $80–120
American 1900–1920

Barber Bottle
Milk glass, 8½ inches, tooled top, open pontil, multicolored scene $100–200
American 1880–1910

Barber Bottle
Blue milk glass, 9½ inches, tooled top, open pontil $75–125
American 1880–1910

Barber Bottle
Blue milk glass, 9⅝ inches, tooled top, open pontil $75–125
American 1880–1910

Beer Bottles

Attempting to find an American beer bottle made prior to the mid-nineteenth century is a difficult task, since up until that time, most of the bottles used for beer and spirits were imported. The majority of these imported bottles were black glass pontiled bottles made in a three-piece mold and rarely embossed. It's interesting to note that in spite of the large amounts of beer consumed in America up to 1850, beer bottles did not exist. Most of the beer manufactured during this time was made in the home or was drunk at the local tavern, where beer was dispensed from wooden barrels. Embossed bottles marked "Ale" or "Porter" started to appear about 1850. In the mid-1860s, the bottles were embossed with brewery names. This practice continued into the twentieth century. By 1870, beer was readily available in bottles in most of the country.

The first bottles used for beer in America were made of pottery, not glass. Glass did not become widely used until after the Civil War (1865). A wholesaler for Adolphus Busch named C. Conrad sold the original Budweiser beer from 1877 to 1890. The Budweiser name was a trademark of C. Conrad, but in 1891 it was sold to the Anheuser-Busch Brewing Association. Up until the 1870s, beer bottles used cork stoppers. Late in the nineteenth century the Lighting stopper was invented, a convenient way of sealing and resealing "blob top" bottles. In 1891, corks were replaced with the "Crown Cork Closure," invented by William Painter. This made use of a thin slice of cork within a tight-fitting metal cap. Once these caps were removed, they couldn't be used again.

P.B. Milwaukee, Ticoulet
and Beshorman,
1895–1906.

Up until the mid-1930s, beer came in green glass bottles. After Prohibition, brown glass came into use since it was thought to keep out the sun and preserve the freshness of the contents.

A. Cappeli and Company, Trademark (deer motif)
Amber, 11¾ inches, applied top (fewer than 5 known)...$600–1,000
American 1882 only, San Francisco, CA

Ahrens Bottling Company, Trademark (monogram motif)
Amber, quart, tooled top..$50–75
American 1893–1906, Oakland, CA

Alabama Brewing Company, Trademark (monogram motif)
Amber, half pint, tooled top...$30–60
American 1895–1900, San Francisco, CA

Alabama Brewing Company, Trademark (monogram motif)
Amber, half pint, tooled top...$50–100
American 1900–1906, San Francisco, CA

Common beer bottle, dark amber with porcelain stopper, 1900–1930.

Amreir Brown
Clear, pint, tooled top, smooth base.....................................$40–80
American 1890–1910, Philadelphia, PA

Angel's Brewery and Bottling Works, Ernest F. Hubler, Proprietor
Dark amber, quart, tooled top...$100–150
American 1890–1900

Antonio Ventresca
Aqua, pint, tooled top, smooth base....................................$40–60
American 1890–1910

A. Palmtag and Company
Aqua, pint, tooled top, smooth base....................................$30–60
American 1895–1906, Eureka, CA

A.W. Kenison
Aqua, quart, tooled top...$30–50
American 1895–1906, Auburn, CA

Barnold's B
Amber, half pint, tooled top..$30–60
American 1895–1906, Seattle, WA

B and J
Amber, half pint, tooled top...$40–60
American 1902–1906, Oakland, CA

Beer Steam Bottling Company, Wm. Goeppert and Son, Trademark ("W G & SON" in diamond motif)
Light amber, quart, applied top (fewer than 6 known).......$400–600
American 1882–1884, San Francisco, CA

Buffalo Brewing Company, S.F. Agency, This Bottle Is Never Sold (monogram motif)
Amber, half pint, tooled top...$100–150
American 1890–1900, San Francisco, CA

Buffalo Brewing Company, S.F. Agency (monogram motif)
Dark amber, pint, tooled top..$40–80
American 1895–1900, San Francisco, CA

Buffalo Brewing Company (Buffalo horseshoe motif)
Amber, pint, tooled top...$30–60
American 1902–1906, Sacramento, CA

Buffalo Brewing Company, This Bottle Not To Be Sold
Clear, quart, applied top, smooth base..............................$100–150
American 1880–1885, Sacramento, CA

Buffalo Brewing Company, This Bottle Not To Be Sold
Clear, pint, applied top, smooth base................................$100–150
American 1800–1885, Sacramento, CA

California Bottling Company, John Wieland's Export Beer
Dark olive-green, pint, applied top (fewer than 5 known)...$300–600
American 1885–1895, San Francisco, CA

California Bottling Works, John Wieland's Extra Pale-Sac
Amber, pint, tooled top...$100–200
American 1890–1902, San Francisco, CA

Capitol Bottling Works (monogram motif)
Dark amber, pint, tooled top...$50–100
American 1895–1902, Petaluma, CA

Capitol Bottling Works (monogram motif)
Amber, pint, tooled top...$40–60
American 1902–1906, Petaluma, CA

Castle Rock N.M. Spring Company
Black amber, half pint, tooled top (extremely rare)...............$50–100
American 1900–1910, Castella, CA

C.D. Postel, Trademark (sheath of wheat motif)
Amber, quart, applied top, smooth base.............................$250–350
American 1884 only, San Francisco, CA

Charles G. Frank
Aqua, pint, tooled top, smooth base.......................................$40–60
American 1890–1910

Charles Knorr
Clear, pint, tooled top, smooth base.......................................$40–80
American 1890–1910, Philadelphia, PA

Chicago Bottling Works, D. Meinke, Proprietor
Light amber, quart, tooled top $60–100
American 1895–1905, San Francisco, CA

Chicago Lager Beer, Chicago Brewing Company (label only)
Amber, quart, applied top..$300–500
American 1880–1885

Chicago Lager Beer, Chicago Brewing Company (monogram motif)
Amber, quart, applied top..$350–550
American 1887–1890

Consumers' Bottling Company (monogram motif)
Amber, quart, tooled top (fewer than 4 known)..............$500–1,000
American 1893–1906, Redwood, CA

Contra Costa Bottling Company
Amber, half pint, tooled top...$75–125
American 1895–1906

Daniel Minahan
Black-amber, pint, tooled top (rare in this color) $40–60
American 1895–1905, Vallejo, CA

Deininger/Vallejo Crown Distilleries Company (crown motif)
Amber, 6 inches, tooled top, smooth base $30–60
American 1900–1915, Vallejo, CA

Deininger/Vallejo Crown Distilleries Company (crown motif)
Amber, 7⅛ inches, tooled top, smooth base $30–60
American 1900–1915, Vallejo, CA

Deininger/Vallejo Crown Distilleries Company (crown motif)
Amber, 8 inches, tooled top, smooth base $30–60
American 1900–1915, Vallejo, CA

Eldorado Brewing Company (monogram motif)
Dark amber, half pint, tooled top $40–80
American 1893–1906, Stockton, CA

Enterprise Brewing Company (monogram motif)
Amber, half pint, tooled top $30–60
American 1895–1900, San Francisco, CA

Enterprise Brewing Company (monogram motif)
Yellow-amber, half pint, tooled top (rare in this color) $20–40
American 1895–1906, San Francisco, CA

Enterprise Brewing Company (monogram motif)
Amethyst, half pint, tooled top (rare in this color) $30–60
American 1895–1906, San Francisco, CA

Enterprise Brewing Company (monogram motif)
Yellow-amber, pint, tooled top (rare in this color) $40–60
American 1900–1906, San Francisco, CA

Enterprise Brewing Company (monogram motif)
Black-amber, pint, tooled top (rare in this color) $40–60
American 1900–1906, San Francisco, CA

Etna Brewery/Etna Mills
Dark amber, half pint, tooled top $30–60
American 1895–1906

Fancy S in Circle
Olive-green, quart, applied top, smooth base $50–100
American 1885–1895

F.O. Brandt
Amber, pint, tooled top..$50–100
American 1895–1906, Healdsburg, CA

Fredericksburg Bottling Company (monogram motif)
Amber, pint, tooled top, smooth base $30–60
American 1895–1906, San Francisco, CA

Fredericksburg Bottling Company (monogram motif)
Amber, half pint, tooled top..$100–150
American 1890–1900, San Francisco, CA

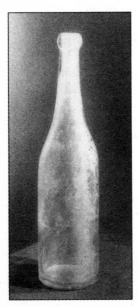

Blob-top beer bottle, aqua, 1880–1900.

Fredericksburg Brewery
Red-amber, quart, applied top, smooth base $40–80
American 1890–1895, San Jose, CA

G.B. Selmer's Celebrated California Pop Beer
Aqua, quart, applied top, smooth base $50–100
American 1885–1895

G. Gnauck
Honey-amber, quart, tooled top (rare beer in a nice color)...$75–150
American 1890–1900, Benicia, CA

Geo. Braun Bottler (shield monogram motif)
Amber, half pint, tooled top..$40–80
American 1902–1906, San Francisco, CA

Geo. Braun Bottler (shield monogram motif)
Clear, half pint, tooled top...$75–100
American 1900–1906, San Francisco, CA

Geo. Middleton
Clear, pint, tooled top, smooth base.....................................$40–80
American 1890–1910, Philadelphia, PA

Geo. A. Ticoulet, Sac
Amber, half pint, tooled top...$20–40
American 1900–1906

Golden Gate Bottling Works, Trademark (standing bear with glass of beer motif)
Amber, half pint, tooled top...$125–175
American 1902–1906, San Francisco, CA

Gold Medal Agency, C. Maurer, Proprietor
Amber, half pint, applied top...$75–150
American 1890–1895, San Jose, CA

Gustave Gnauck, Benicia Brewery
Amber, half pint, tooled top...$200–300
American 1895–1906, Benicia, CA

G.W. Angels
Amber, half pint, tooled top...$40–80
American 1890–1900

Independent
Aqua, pint, tooled top, smooth base......................................$40–60
American 1890–1910

Jackson's Napa Soda
Amber, pint, tooled top..$50–100
American 1895–1906, San Francisco, CA

J.J. Maenner
Clear, pint, tooled top, smooth base......................................$40–80
American 1890–1910, Philadelphia, PA

John J. Buck, This Bottle Not To Be Sold
Dark amber, 11⅛ inches, applied top (only 1 known)........$500–700
American 1880–1885, San Francisco, CA

John Rapp and Son
Yellow-amber, half pint, tooled top.......................................$40–60
American 1895–1906, San Francisco, CA

John Rapp and Son
Amethyst, half pint, tooled top (rare in this color) $30–60
American 1895–1906, San Francisco, CA

John Simon
Clear, pint, tooled top, smooth base......................................$40–80
American 1890–1910, Philadelphia, PA

John Wieland's Export Beer
Yellow-olive, 5½ inches, tooled top $200–400
American 1890–1900, San Francisco, CA

John Wieland's Export Beer
Red-amber, half pint, tooled top $60–100
American 1890–1895, San Francisco, CA

K.M.
Amber, half pint, tooled top...$20–40
American 1895–1906, Oakland, CA

Lynch's
Aqua, pint, tooled top, smooth base.....................................$40–60
American 1890–1910

Mirrasoul Brothers
Amber, half pint, tooled top...$20–40
American 1893–1906, San Francisco, CA

Mokelumne Hill Brewery
Amber, quart, tooled top, small base.....................................$50–75
American 1893–1900

N. Cervelli (monogram motif)
Amber, quart, tooled top...$100–175
American 1902–1906, San Francisco, CA

N. Cervelli (monogram motif)
Amber, half pint, tooled top...$60–100
American 1902–1906, San Francisco, CA

National Bottling Company, Trademark (eagle motif)
Amber, pint, tooled top...$60–100
American 1890–1900, San Francisco, CA

National Bottling Company, Trademark (eagle motif)
Amber, quart, applied top (fewer than 10 known).............$300–400
American 1888 only, San Francisco, CA

National Lager Beer, H. Rohrbacher, Agent (monogram motif)
Dark amber, pint, tooled top...$30–60
American 1895–1906, Stockton, CA

**North Star Bottling Works, Trademark (star motif), Bottle Not
To Be Sold**
Honey-amber, half pint, tooled top.......................................$40–80
American 1895–1906, San Francisco, CA

Blob-top beer bottle,
aqua, 1880–1900.

P.B. Milwaukee
Honey-amber, pint, tooled top..$30–60
American 1895–1906

Peter Eidenberg
Clear, pint, tooled top, smooth base......................................$40–80
American 1890–1910, Philadelphia, PA

**Philadelphia Bottling Company, Trademark (eagle motif), Lager
Beer, Lang Brothers Proprietors**
Amber, quart, applied top, smooth base fewer than 6
known)...$200–400
American 1886–1889, San Francisco, CA

The Prospect Brewing Company, This Bottle Not To Be Sold
Amber, 7⅛ inches, tooled top..$50–100
American 1890–1900, Philadelphia, PA

Raspiller Brewing Company, Trademark (eagle motif)
Amber, quart, tooled top...$75–125
American 1893–1906, Berkeley, CA

Richmond Bottling Works
Amethyst, half pint, tooled top..$50–100
American 1893–1906

S and L Trademark
Aqua, pint, applied top (rare this size) $100–150
American 1880–1885

S and L Trademark
Aqua, quart, applied top $75–125
American 1880–1885

San Jose Bottling Company
Amber, half pint, applied top...$75–125
American 1890–1895, San Jose, CA

San Jose Bottling Company
Reddish-amber, pint, applied top...$50–100
American 1890–1895, San Jose, CA

San Jose Bottling Company, C. Maurer
Dark amber, pint, tooled top..$30–60
American 1895–1906, San Jose, CA

Santa Fe Bottling Company
Amber, quart, tooled top...$50–100
American 1890–1900, San Francisco, CA

Seal Rock Bottling Company, John Kroger
Amber, half pint, tooled top (fewer than 4 known)................$40–80
American 1890–1900, San Francisco, CA

Sierra Bottling Company, Wieland's Best
Amber, pint, tooled top (extremely rare with label)............$200–300
American 1895–1900, Jamestown, CA

Stockton Wholesale Liquor Company, Trademark (monogram motif)
Amber, half gallon, tooled top (extremely rare)..................$250–350
American 1893–1906, Stockton, CA

T.D. Tweedie, Red Hand, Trademark (hand motif),
This Bottle Never Sold
Olive-green, half pint, applied top, smooth base $150–250
American 1885–1895, San Francisco, CA

T. Kagawa Company, Trademark (Japanese figures motif)
Amber, quart, tooled top..$50–75
American 1895–1906, San Francisco, CA

Ticoulet and Beshorman
Amber, pint, tooled top..$30–60
American 1895–1906, Sacramento, CA

Union Brewing and Malting Company
Honey-amber, pint, tooled top..$30–60
American 1895–1906, San Francisco, CA

Common beer bottle,
crown top, amber,
1900–1920.

Wielands Little Pop California Bottling Company, Trademark (crown motif)
Olive-green, half pint, applied top (extremely rare)............$100–150
American 1890–1895, San Francisco, CA

Wielands Little Pop California Bottling Company, Trademark (crown motif)
Amethyst, half pint, tooled top...$75–125
American 1890–1900, San Francisco, CA

Wiener Bottling Company
Amber, quart, applied top (fewer than 3 known)...............$200–400
American 1880–1885, San Francisco, CA

Wunder Bottling Works
Amber, half pint, tooled top..$20–40
American 1895–1906, Oakland, CA

Wm. Kayser
Clear, pint, tooled top, smooth base.......................................$40–80
American 1890–1910, Philadelphia, PA

Bitters

When looking at antique bottles as collectibles, bitters bottles have long been favorites. Because of their unique form, bitters bottles were saved in great numbers, giving the collector of today some great opportunities to build very special collections.

Bitters, which originated in England, is a type of medicine made from roots or herbs named for their bitter taste. During the eighteenth century, bitters were added to water, ale, or spirits with the intent to cure all types of ailments. Because of the pretense that these mixtures had some medicinal value, bitters became very popular in America, since colonists could import them from England without paying the liquor tax. While most bitters had a low alcohol content, some brands were labeled as high as 120 proof, higher than most hard liquor available at the time. As physicians became convinced bitters did have some type of healing value, the drink became socially acceptable. This thought process promoted sales to people who normally weren't liquor drinkers and also provided upstanding citizens a good excuse for having liquor in the home (for medicinal purposes, of course).

The best known among the physicians who made their own bitters for patients was Dr. Jacob Hostetter. After his retirement in 1853, he gave permission to his son David to manufacture it commercially. Hostetters Bitters was known for its colorful and dramatic advertisements. While Hostetters said it wouldn't cure everything, the list of ailments it claimed to alleviate with regular use covered most everything: indigestion, diarrhea, dysentery, chills, fever, liver ailments, and pains and weakness that came with old age (at that time, a euphemism for impotence). Despite these claims, David Hostetter died in 1888 from kidney failure, which could supposedly be cured by his bitters.

Most of the bitters bottles, over 1,000 types, were manufactured between 1860 and 1905. The more unique shapes, called "figurals," were in the likeness of cannons, drums, pigs, fish, and ears of corn. In addition, a variety of other forms produced bottles that were round, square, rectangular, barreled-shaped, gin-bottle-shaped, twelve-sided, and flask-shaped. The embossed varieties are the most collectible, older, and more valuable.

These bottles were most commonly amber (pale golden yellow to dark amber-brown), frequently aqua (light blue), and sometimes green or clear glass was used in their manufacture. The rarest and most collectible colors are dark blue, amethyst, milk glass, and puce (a purplish brown).

African Stomach Bitters, Spruance Stanley and Company
Reddish-amber, 9½ inches, applied top..............................$100–150
American 1875–1880

Alpine Bitters Decanter
Bright emerald-green, 6½ inches, applied handle.................$200–300
American 1885–1890

Celery Compound
Bitters, 1885–1895.

Angostura Bark Bitters, Engle Liqueur Distilleries
Amber, 6½ inches, tooled top, smooth base $40–60
American 1890–1900

Atwood's Jaundice Bitters, M. Carter and Sons
Aqua, 5⅞ inches, tooled top...$20–40
American 1860–1865, Georgetown, MA

Bakers Orange Grove Bitters
Light golden amber, 9½ inches, applied top, smooth base ...$250–350
American 1860–1870

Bennet's Wild Cherry Stomach Bitters, Chenery, Souther and Company, Sole Agents
Amber, 9⅞ inches, applied top, smooth base $300–500
American 1871–1879, San Francisco, CA

Bitter Witch, Trademark (horseshoe motif)
Amber with an olive hue, 8⅛ inches, applied top, smooth
base $300–400
American 1876–1880

Bourbon Whiskey Bitters
Medium strawberry-puce, 9⅜ inches, applied top, smooth
base $250–350
American 1860–1865

Botanical Society, Hierapicra Bitters, Extract of Figs, California Fig
Dark blue-aqua, 9½ inches, applied top, smooth base $250–350
American 1880–1890

California Fig Bitters (label only)
Clear, 9¼ inches, tooled top $40–60
American 1892–1897

Clarke's Compound Mandrake Bitters
Aqua, 7½ inches, applied top, smooth base $100–125
American 1865–1875

Lash's Bitters
Company,
1880–1890.

Clarke's Sherry Wine Bitters
Aqua, 9¾ inches, applied top, smooth base $75–125
American 1865–1875, Rockland, ME (one of the rarer Clarke's)

Cobalt-Blue Unembossed Barrel
Medium cobalt-blue, 9¾ inches, applied top, smooth base ...$600–800
American 1860–1863

Darkes Plantation Bitters, Patented 1862
Amber, 9⅝ inches, applied top, smooth base (one of the nicer
looking Darkes)..$150–225
American 1926

Darkes 1860 Plantation X Bitters, Patented 1862
Yellow with a hue of amber, 10 inches, applied top, smooth
base...$100–150
American 1862–1870

Dr. Geo. Pierce's Indian Restorative Bitters
Aqua, 7⅞ inches, applied top, open pontil $100–150
American 1857–1860, Lowell, MA

Dr. Harter's Wild Cherry Bitters
Amber, 8¼ inches, tooled top (rare) $75–150
American 1885–1895, Dayton, OH

Dr. Henley's Wild Grape Root IXL Bitters
Bright emerald-green, 12 inches, applied top, smooth base
(first of the IXLs)..$2,000–3,000
Extremely rare and unique in this color
American 1868

Dr. Henley's Wild Grape Root IXL Bitters
Very dark aqua, 12 inches, applied top.................................$75–125
American 1868–1872

Dr. Henley's Wild Grape Root IXL Bitters
Dark fire aqua, 12 inches, applied top, smooth base $50–100
American 1868–1872

Dr. Henley's Wild Grape Root IXL Bitters
Aqua, 12¼ inches, applied top, smooth base $60–100
American 1873–1878

Dr. Henley's Wild Grape Root IXL Bitters
Aqua, 12½ inches, applied top, smooth base $75–125
American 1879–1884

Dr. Henley's Wild
Grape Root IXL
Bitters,
1868–1872.

Dr. J. Hostetter's
Stomach Bitters,
1869–1872.

Dr. J. Hostetter's Stomach Bitters
Amber, 20 ounces, applied top, smooth base $30–50
American 1865–1870

Dr. J. Hostetter's Stomach Bitters L and W
Light olive-citron, 8⅞ inches, applied top, smooth base $250–350
American 1869

Dr. J. Hostetter's Stomach Bitters
Black-amber, 8⅞ inches, applied top, smooth base...............$75–100
American 1865–1869

Dr. J. Hostetter's Stomach Bitters L and W
Yellow-green-citron, 8⅞ inches, applied top.......................$300–400
American 1869

Dr. J. Hostetter's Stomach Bitters
Dark emerald with a hue of olive, 9¼ inches, applied top.....$60–100
American 1860–1865

Patd. 1884, Dr. Petzold's Genuine German Bitters Incpt 1862
Amber, 10¼ inches, applied top, smooth base...................$140–180
American 1884–1890

Dr. Renz's Herb Bitters
Amber, 9¾ inches, applied top, smooth base.....................$100–150
American 1868–1873

Dr. Renz's Herb Bitters
Olive with amber tones, 9⅞ inches, applied top, smooth
base $250–350
American 1862–1874

Dr. Renz's Herb Bitters
Dark amber, 10 inches, applied top, smooth base................$75–100
American 1874–1878

Dr. Soule Hop Bitters, 1872, Trademark (hop and leaf motif)
Black-red, 9⅛ inches, applied top, smooth base $125–175
American 1872–1882

Dr. Von Hopfs, Chamberlain and Company, Curacoa Bitters
Amber, 8 inches, tooled top, smooth base...........................$50–75
American 1890–1900, Des Moines, IA

Drakes Plantation Bitters, Patented 1869
Medium amber, 7⅞ inches, applied top, smooth base........$200–300
American 1862–1873

Drakes 1860 Plantation X Bitters, Patented 1862
Amber with olive hue, 9¾ inches, applied top, smooth base...$100–200
American 1862–1873

**E.J. Rose's Magador Bitters for Stomach, Kidney and Liver,
Superior Tonic, Cathartic and Blood Purifier**
Amber, 8¾ inches, tooled top, smooth base (rare)..............$100–150
American 1895–1905

E. Wideman and J. Chappaz, Lady's Leg Alpine Bitters
Copper-puce, 11½ inches, applied top, smooth base.......$700–1,000
Three-piece mold, extremely rare Western bitters (fewer than 10
known)
American 1861–1863, Marysville, CA

Electric Bitters, H.E. Bucklen and Company
Amber, 10 inches, tooled top...$20–40
American 1890–1900, Chicago, IL

Ferro Quina Stomach Bitters, Blood Maker
Amber, 9 inches, tooled top, smooth base...........................$75–125
American 1895–1909

Foster Milburn Company, Burdock Blood Bitters
Clear, 7½ inches, tooled top..$30–60
American 1915–1925, Buffalo, NY

Greeley's Bourbon Bitters
Medium copper-puce, 9¼ inches, applied top, smooth
base...$250–325
American 1860–1865

Greeley's Bourbon Whiskey Bitters
Medium puce, 9¼ inches, applied top, smooth base...........$175–250
American 1860–1862

Hall's Bitters, E.E. Hall New Haven, Established 1842
Amber, applied top, smooth base.......................................$150–250
American 1875–1885

Hellman's Congress Bitters
Amber, 8⅞ inches, applied top, smooth base......................$150–250
American 1860–1870, Saint Louis, MO

Holtzermanns Patent Stomach Bitters
Amber, 9⅞ inches, tooled top, smooth base........................$125–175
American 1889–1905

J. Walker's V.B
Grass-green, 8½ inches, applied top..................................$100–150
American 1863–1870

J. Walker's V.B.
Aqua, 8½ inches, applied top $100–150
American 1863–1870

Lediard's Celebrated Stomach Bitters
Dark blue-green, 10 inches, applied top, iron pontil...$2,500– 3,500
American 1850–1860

Marshall's Bitters, The Best Laxative and Blood Purifier
Amber, 8¾ inches, tooled top...$40–80
American 1902–1908

**O.K. Jacob Pinkerton, Y!!, Wahoo and Calisaya Bitters, Y!!,
Jacob Pinkerton, I.M.**
Amber, 10¼ inches, applied top, smooth base....................$225–275
American 1864–1870

Old Sachem Bitters and Wigwam Tonic
Honey-amber, 9½ inches, applied top, smooth base...........$150–225
American 1860–1865

Old Dr. Townsend's Magic Stomach Bitters, New York
Blue-green, 9¾ inches, applied top, smooth base.........$2,000–3,000
American 1858–1863

Oxygenated for Dyspepsia, Asthma and General Debility Bitters
Clear, 7¼ inches, applied top, open pontil $40–80
American 1850–1860

Peruvian Bitters, Trademark (shield monogram motif)
Amber, 9 inches, applied top, smooth base...........................$30–60
American 1871–1877

Pipifax
Amber, 9½ inches, tooled top...$30–60
American 1877–1885

Prickly Ash Bitters Company
Honey-amber, 9¾ inches, tooled top $50–100
American 1885–1895

Marshall's Bitters, The Best Laxative and Blood Purifier, 1902–1908.

Bitter bottles: Old Sachem Bitters and Wigwam Tonic, 1860–1865; Greeley's Bourbon Bitters, 1860–1865; Bourbon Whiskey Bitters, 1860–1865; unembossed Barrel Bitters, 1860–1863.

Prune Stomach and Liver Bitters, The Best Cathartic and Blood Purifier
Amber, 9¼ inches, tooled top, smooth base $50–100
American 1900–1910

Royal Pepsin Stomach Bitters, L. and A. Scharff Sole Agents
Amber, 8⅞ inches, tooled top...$100–200
American 1890–1900

S.B.C. Wild Cherry Tonic, Star Bitter Company
Amber, 8½ inches, tooled top..$40–60
American 1900–1910

The John W. Cope Company, Best in the World
Amber, 9 inches, tooled top, smooth base..........................$200–400
American 1890–1900

Toneco Stomach Bitters, Appetizer and Tonic
Dark amethyst, 9⅛ inches, tooled top....................................$50–100
American 1908–1917

Turner Brothers
Olive-green with an amber hue, applied top, smooth base....$350–450
American 1858–1861

Willard's Golden Seal Bitters
Aqua, 7¼ inches, tooled top, smooth base $50–100
American 1880–1892

Yerba Buena Bitters
Amber, 8 inches, applied top, smooth base..........................$75–125
American 1869–1875, San Francisco, CA

Yerba Buena Bitters
Olive with a yellow hue, 8¼ inches, applied top, smooth base $150–250
American 1869–1875, San Francisco, CA

Yerba Buena Bitters
Amber, 9⅝ inches, tooled top...$100–200
American 1898–1900, San Francisco, CA

Blown Bottles

As mentioned earlier, free-blown bottles, also called simply blown bottles, are made without the use of molds and were shaped by the glassblower. It is difficult to attach ages and origins to them, since many were produced in Europe and the United States for a long period of time before records.

Another type of blown bottle, the blown three-mold, was formed in a three-piece mold. These bottles were manufactured between 1820 to 1840 in Europe and the United States and it is quite difficult to distinguish bottles from different sides of the Atlantic. Since blown three-mold and pressed three-mold are similar, it is important to know how to differentiate between them. With blown glass, the mold impression can be felt on the inside, while pressed glass impressions can only be felt on the outside. Most blown three-mold bottles came in amethyst (purple), sapphire blue, and a variety of greens.

A. Dervieux, Gray (sealed champagne)
Olive-green, 11¾ inches, applied top, smooth base $50–100
French 1890–1900

Blown Rum or Beer
Black glass, 10½ inches, tooled top, open pontil...................$50–100
European 1830–1840

Blown Wine or Ale
Dark olive-amber, 8½ inches, applied string lip, open
pontil...$150–250
European 1800–1820

Black whiskey/ale
bottles, Johann Hoff,
1870–1890.

Blown Wine or Ale
Olive-green, 10⅛ inches, applied string lip, open pontil.....$100–200
European 1820–1830

Chestnut Grove, Whiskey, G.W.
Light amber with an olive hue, 8½ inches, applied top.......$200–300
Applied handle, open pontil (rare in this light color)
American 1850–1860

Chestnut Grove, Whiskey, G.W.
Amber with an olive hue, 8½ inches, applied handle, open
pontil...$175–250
American 1850–1860

Chestnut Grove Whiskey, G.W., Trademark (crown motif)
Reddish-amber, 9 inches, tooled top, applied handle, open
pontil...$150–250
American 1845–1855

Early Demijon
Medium apricot-puce, 11½ inches, sheared top, pontiled..$150– 250
European 1740–1780

Dutch Champagne'
Emerald-green, 9⅝ inches, applied top, open pontil...............$40–80
Dutch 1780–1820

Dutch Long Neck
Dark olive-amber, 11⅜ inches, applied string top, open
pontil...$75–125
Dutch 1760–1780

Dutch Onion
Olive-green, 7⅝ inches, applied string top, open pontil........$50–100
Dutch 1720–1740

Dutch Onion
Light olive with a yellow hue, 7¾ inches, applied string top...$50–75
Dutch 1720–1740

Dutch Onion
Emerald-green, 7¾ inches, applied string top, open pontil....$200–300
Dutch 1720–1740

Free-blown globular bottle,
1800–1820 (rare).

Black whiskey bottle, three-piece
mold, 1820–1850.

Free-Blown Globular Bottle
Blue-aqua, 10¾ inches, applied top, open pontil................$125–175
American 1800–1820 (rare in large size)

Free-Blown Globular Bottle
Blue-aqua, 7¾ inches, applied top, open pontil..................$100–150
American 1800–1820

Free-Blown Wine Sampler
Aqua, 5½ inches, rolled-in lip, open pontil.........................$100–200
European 1750–1800

Handled Chestnut
Light Amber, 8 inches, applied top and handle, open
pontil..$50–100
American 1830–1850

Huile D'Olive Surfine, Clarifiee, Bordeaux
Aqua, 10 inches, sheared top, open pontil $75–125
French 1850–1860

J.F.T. and Company
Orange-amber, 7¼ inches, applied top and handle, open
pontil..$50–100
American 1840–1850, Philadelphia, PA

Old Virginia Peach Brandy
Olive-amber, 11⅞ inches, applied top, iron pontil........$2,000–3,000
American 1845–1855 (extremely rare)

Pennsylvania Dutch Hat (Zanesville swirl pattern)
Deep amethyst, 1⅜ inch x 5⅛ inches diameter, open
pontil..$400–600
American 1815–1838

Snuff Jar
Medium olive-green, 10⅝ inches, flared lip $200–300
European 1780–1820

Black whiskey bottle assortment, 1820–1860.

Tokay (applied seal)
Aqua, 7¾ inches, applied top, smooth base $40–60
European 1860–1870

Vonthofen's Aromatic Scheidam Schnapps
Dark blue-green, 9¾ inches, applied top, iron pontil..........$100–150
American 1850–1860

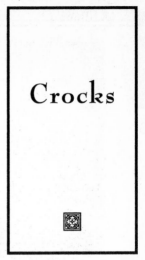

Crocks

While crocks are made of pottery and not glass, many bottle collectors also have crock collections since they have often been found wherever bottles are buried. Crock containers were manufactured in America as early as 1641, and were used extensively in the sale of store products during the nineteenth and early twentieth centuries. Store owners favored crocks since they kept beverages cooler and extended the shelf life of certain products. Crocks are appealing to collectors because of their interesting shapes, painted and stenciled decorations, lustrous finishes, and folk art value.

Upon the discovery of microbes in disease-causing bacteria in the late 1800s, many medicine makers seized the opportunity to push a fraudulent cure on unsuspecting consumers. The most infamous of these so-called cures were produced and sold in pottery containers by William Radam. He was given a patent for his "Microbe Killer" in 1886, and stayed in business until 1907, when the Pure Food and Drug Act ended his scheme. It seemed that his "cure" was nothing but watered down wine (the wine was only 1 percent of the total contents).

With the invention of the automatic bottle machine in 1903, glass bottles became more common and cheaper to produce. The production and use of pottery crocks and containers began a steady decline.

25th Annual Excampment, Gar, Department of Ohio 1891, Stevenville (bust of a man motif), Filson Helms
White, gold, and brown, 3⅜ inches (extremely rare) $150–250
American 1891

Common early crock
for beverage (possibly
whiskey), 1890–1910.

Armour and Company
Tan, white, and black, 8 inches...$50–100
American 1900–1910, Chicago, IL

Cal. Pottery Company
Salt glaze with a green hue, 10 inches x 8½ inches $250–350
Clamshell handles (extremely rare)
American 1890–1900, San Francisco and Oakland, CA

Compliments of W.B. Tobey (sample)
White and black, 3¼ inches (extremely rare).....................$300–400
American 1900–1910, Ethan, SD

Cruiskeen Lawn, Mitchell's Old Irish Whiskey (jug)
Tan, white, and black, 7¼ inches..$75–125
European 1890–1910

Deodorizer, The Pullman Company (jug)
Brown, blue, and white, half gallon....................................$100–150
American 1900–1910

Grannie Taylor's Liqueur Whiskey (lady holding jug motif)
Tan, white, and black, 7¾ inches..$75–125
European 1890–1910

Henry Bosquest, Old McKenna Whiskey, 245 4th Avenue, Souvenir (flower braid motif)
Brown, white, and blue, 2⅝ inches.................................:................$75–150
American 1910–1920, Louisville, KY

Henry-Brown Company, Trademark Brand, Sierra Club Ginger Beer, Contents Eight Ounces
Brown, black, and white, 6¼ inches $40–60
American 1910–1920, Glendale, CA

Herrington's Fluid Beer, Purest on Earth (handled crock)
Brown, white, and black, 6⅝ inches $40–80
American 1890–1900

Holy Water or Rosewater Bottle
White porcelain, 5 inches $50–100
American 1880–1900

J. Simonds
Blue and gray, 8¼ inches...$100–150
American 1850–1860

Crock—Herrington's
Fluid Beer—Purest on
Earth, 1890–1910.

J.W. Orr, Michigan Bar
Brown and tan, half gallon, 9⅜ inches $700–1,000
American 1859–1870, one of the first California potters

**L.C. Brown Company, Riverside Avenue, Phone 2291,
It's Groceries and Delicatessen, Eastern and Local Butter**
Gray and black, 3 pounds...$50–100
American 1895–1905, Southern California

**Moo Cow Beverages, Capitola, Cal., Brown's Little Brown Jug,
Contents 10 oz., Ginger Beer**
Brown, white, and black, 6¾ inches (extremely rare)............$50–100
American 1915–1925

O'Donnel's Old Irish Whiskey Cork (jug)
White and green, 8 inches..$100–150
European 1890–1910

Pattison's Morning Dew (jug)
Brown, white, and black, 7⅝ inches $50–100
European 1890–1910, lettering is on both sides

Pennsylvania Club Pure Rye Whiskey, K.T. and K. China
White and purple, 7½ inches...$150–250
American 1903–1907

**Radium Ore Reuigator Patd 7-16-12, Trademark, The Radium
Ore Reuigator Company, 280 California St., San Francisco, Cal.**
Cream colored with blue lettering, 12 inches.....................$125–175
American 1912–1915, (extremely rare in original condition),
(instruction on how to use on each side)

**Return to Sharpe Brothers, Health Beverages, Australia and New
Zealand—Persons Detaining Misappropriating or Trading with
This Jar Liable to be Prosecuted**
Tan, white, and black, 13 inches..$75–150
European 1900–1920

Stone Ginger Beer
Tan, white, and black, 7 inches...$30–60
European 1890–1910

Stone Ginger Beer
Tan, white, and black, 8 inches...$60–100
Australian 1890–1910

Strong, Cobb and Company, Wholesale Druggists, Cleveland
Gray, 9¼ inches, embossed and rare.....................................$75–125
American 1890–1910

Taddy & Company, Manufacturers of "Tobacco Snuff & Segars," Minories, London
Brown and tan, 9 inches x 6⅜ inches.................................$100–150
European 1870–1890

The Banner Liquor Store, Jos. Hoffarth, Prop'r., Winona, MINN (jug)
Blue and white, half gallon, Red Wing Stoneware Company....$250–350
American 1895–1905

Crock—Strong, Cobb
and Company,
Wholesale Druggists
(rare), 1890–1910.

Crock—Vihno Verde, Do Lavradoe; Pullnaer
Bitters Wasser, Genende Pullna (European),
1860–1880.

The Tappithen Hawthorn Dew
White and black, 7 inches..$50–100
European 1890–1910

**Victoria (motif of lady reverse side of bottle, motif of man),
Pottery-handled Whiskey**
Tan and brown glaze, ¾ inch x ½ inch................................$75–125
English 1810–1840

**Vulcanizing Solution, Manufactured by the Goodyear Tire and
Rubber Company, Akron, Ohio**
Black and white, 4¾ inches $40–80
American 1890–1900

Wm. Radam's Microbe Killer, Red Wing Stoneware Company
Gray, gallon (extremely rare)..$300–400
American 1890–1900

Cosmetic Bottles

This category includes those bottles that originally contained products to improve personal appearances, including treatments for skin, teeth, scalp (hair grooming and restoring agents), and perfumes. The most popular of these are the hair and perfume bottles.

Hair bottles are popular as collectible items due to distinctive colors such as amethyst and various shades of blue. The main producer of American-made perfume bottles in the eighteenth century was Casper Wistar, whose clients included Martha Washington. Another major manufacturer of that time was Henry William Stiegel. While most of Wistar's bottles were plain, Stiegel's were decorative and are more appealing to collectors.

In the 1840s, Solon Palmer started to manufacture and sell perfumes. By 1879, his products were being sold in drugstores around the country. Today, Palmer bottles are sought after for their brilliant emerald-green color.

Baldwin's Queen Bess Perfume
Labeled, ring top, 5½ inches..$10–15

California Perfume Company
Amethyst, rectangular, 5½ inches...$20–25

Christiani de Paris
Aqua, 3⅜ inches, open pontil, flared lip................................$35–40

Colgate and Company
Amethyst, 6¼ inches...$10–12

Colgate and Company, New York
Amethyst, 3⅛ inches, center of circle: "Perfumers" $5–7

Colgate and Company, Perfumers, New York
Amethyst, 3⅛ inches, long neck, rectangular $6–8

Countie of Boston, Magna Toilet Cream, C.J. Countie and Company, Chemists, Boston, U.S.A.
Blue transfer, ⅞ inches x 3¼ inches, label on base...............$200–300
American 1890–1900 (rare and unique with label)

The Crown Perfumery Company
Amber, 2½ inches..$7–10

Dagget and Ramsdell
Clear, 2¾ inches, screw-top, "Perfect Cold Cream"....................$3–5

Daybrooks Detroit Perfumers
Clear or amethyst, 6 inches..$6–10

Empress Josephine Toilet Company
Milk glass, 6¼ inches...$12–15

Florida Water
Clear, 7¼ inches, label with "568" on bottom..........................$6–10

Florida Water
Aqua, 8 inches, label, pontil..$10–15

Franco American Hygienic Company, Chicago
Amethyst, 6 inches, rectangular $10–12

Frostilla
Clear, 4½ inches, "Elmira, NY, U.S.A." on side $8–10

Gold Leaf with White Enamel (perfume), A and Q Warranted (base label)
Teal-blue, 3½ inches, smooth base $40–60
European 1895–1905

Gouraud's Oriental Cream
Clear, 4¼ inches..$6–8

Harrison's Columbian Perfumery
Clear, 2¾ inches..$10–12

Hilbert's Deluxe Perfumery
Clear, 3¼ inches, fattened heart shape with long neck...........$10–12

F. Hoyt and Company Perfumers, Philadelphia
Amethyst, 3 inches...$8–10

Richard Hudnut Perfumer, NY
Amethyst, 3½ inches, square $6–10

Imperial Crown Perfumery and Company
Clear, 5 inches $10–12

Dr. Koch's Toilet Articles, Winona, MINN
Amethyst, 5¼ inches, ring top $8–10

Lightner's Maid of the Mist
Milk glass, 6½ inches, Detroit, MI $20–25

Lightner's White Rose Perfumes
Milk glass, 6½ inches, Detroit, MI $20–25

Mack's Florida Water
Aqua, 8½ inches, tapered top $10–12

Murray and Lanman Druggists, Florida Water, NY
Aqua, 5½ inch body, 3¾ inch neck.......................................$8–10

Palmers, Larkin Soap Company
Emerald-green, 4¾ inches, tooled top $30–60
American 1900–1910

Ed Pinaud
Amethyst, 7 inches...$8–10

Ed Pinaud
Clear, 7 inches $8–10

Ed Pinaud
Aqua, 6 inches $6–8

Pompeian Massage Cream
Amethyst, 2¾ inches $7–10

Pond's Extract
Clear, 5½ inches, machine made, "1846" on bottom $7–10

Rieger's California Perfumes
Clear, 3¼ inch, crooked neck $6–10

Sun Burst Scent
Clear, 2⅞ inches, sheared and polished lip $75–150
American 1840–1860

Violet Dulce Vanishing Cream
Clear, 2½ inches..$6–8

Alfred Wright, Perfumer, Rochester, NY
Colbalt, 7½ inches...$20–25

Alfred Wright, Perfumer, Rochester, NY
Amber, 7½ inches..$20–25

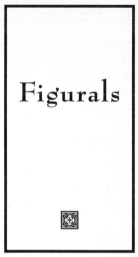

Figurals

Figural bottles were produced in large numbers in the late nineteenth and early twentieth centuries. These whimsical bottles took on the shapes of animals, people, boots, and books, among other things. They came in a wide variety of colors and sizes and were quite popular among the very rich and the aristocrats of the time.

Austria (nipper), "PT APPD FR"
White and brown pottery, 6¾ inches....................................$40–80
American 1910–1920

Boy Reading Book
Milk glass, 4¼ inches...$100–150
American 1895–1905

Figural Barrel
Lavender or purple, 9¼ inches, tooled lip, smooth base $75–125
European 1880–1900

Figural Bunch of Cigars
Amber, 5 inches, ground lip, smooth base $50–90
American 1890–1900

Candy Container
Milk glass figural suitcase, 2½ inches....................................$75–150
American 1920–1930

Figural Cluster of Grapes
Purple amethyst, 6⅝ inches, ground lip...............................$75–125
American or German 1880–1910

Figural Fish
Clear, 9 inches $75–125
American 1900–1910

Figural Gun
Amber, 10 inches long, "PATENT APPLIED FOR" above
trigger $75–125
American 1880–1900

Figural Man in the Moon Decanter
Yellow glass moon on black-amethyst base, 13 inches $600–900
American 1890–1910 (rare and highly desirable)

Figural pistol
Honey-amber, 4½ inches..$50–100
American 1900–1910

Figural Shoe (crown abc monogram motif)
Light aqua, 3½ inches, tooled top (rare) $40–80
American 1900–1910

Figural Spanish Senorita
Milk glass, 11⅞ inches, smooth base $50–80
European 1920–1930

L.M. (figural of a shoe)
Clear, 5 inches, sheared top with applied ring, pontiled.......$75–125
European 1850–1860

Match Holders with Silver Tops
Clear, 2 inches $30–60
European 1880–1900

Uncle Sam on a Battleship Mustard Dish
Milk glass, 4⅝ inches...$50–100
American 1890–1910

Van Dunck's Genever, Trademark, Ware and Schmitz
Red-amber, 8¾ inches, applied top $75–150
American 1880–1888

Violin
Bright lime-green, 7½ inches, tooled top $20–40
American 1900–1920

Figural Whimsy Cucumber or Zucchini
Medium cobalt-blue, 8¾ inches long, (rare) $125–175
American 1880–1890

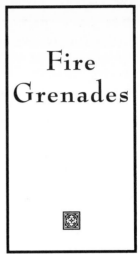

Fire Grenades

Fire grenades are a highly prized item among bottle collectors and represent one of the first modern improvements in fire fighting.

A fire grenade is a globular bottle about the size of a baseball that was filled with water. Its use was simple. When thrown into a fire, it would break and spread its contents, hopefully extinguishing the flames.

The first American patent on a fire grenade was issued in 1863 to Alanson Crane of Fortress Monroe, Virginia. The best known manufacturer of these highly specialized bottles was the Halden Fire Extinguisher Company in Chicago, Illinois, which was awarded a patent in August of 1871.

These grenades were manufactured in large numbers by companies with names as unique as the bottle itself: Dash-Out, Diamond, Harkness Fire Destroyer, Hazelton's High Pressure Chemical Firekeg, Magic Fire, and Y-Burn. The fire grenade became obsolete with the invention of the fire extinguisher in 1905. Many of these grenades can still be found with the original closures, contents, and labels.

American Fire Extinguisher Company, Hand Grenade
Clear glass, pint, 6⅛ inches, tooled top, smooth base $350–450
American 1860–1890 (rare)

Babcock Hand Grenade, Non-freezing, 325–331 South Des Plaines St., Chicago—"Manf'd by Fire Extinguisher Mfg. Co."
Deep cobalt-blue, 7½ inches, ground lip, smooth base ...$1,000–1,500
American 1880–1890

Babcock Hand Grenade, Non-freezing, 325–331 South Des Plaines St., Chicago—"Manf'd by Fire Extinguisher Mfg. Co."
Yellowish-amber, 7½ inches, ground lip, smooth base.....$700–1,000
American 1880–1890

Barnum's Hand Held Fire Extinguisher, Diamond, "Pat'd June 26th 1869"
Medium yellow with olive tone, 5⅞ inches, tooled top.......$500–700
American 1870–1880 (very rare in this color)

Descours and Company Fire Watcher, Hand Fire Grenade
Clear glass, 5¼ inches, (very rare).....................................$200–275
English 1890–1910

Firex Fire Grenade (unembossed)
Cobalt-blue, 4 inches $50–100
English 1890–1910

Grenade—Prevoyante—Extincteur
Medium yellowish-amber, 5⅞ inches, ground lip $400–600
French 1890–1910

Harden Star Hand Grenade—Fire Extinguisher—Patented "No 1 Aug 8 1871, Aug 14 1888"
Turquoise-blue, 6¼ inches, ground lip, smooth base..............$35–45
American 1885–1895

Harden Star Hand Grenade—Fire Extinguisher-"This Bottle Pat May 27 84"
Turquoise-blue, 6⅜ inches, sheared lip, smooth base $50–90
American 1885–1895

Harden Star Hand Grenade—Fire Extinguisher
Turquoise-blue, 6⅜ inches, sheared lip, smooth base.............$50–90
American 1885–1895

Harden Star Hand Grenade—Fire Extinguisher
Pale clear green, 6¼ inches, ground lip, smooth base $200–400
English 1885–1895 (very rare)

Harden Star Hand Grenade—Fire Extinguisher
Deep cobalt-blue, 6¾ inches, ground lip, smooth base $200–400
English 1885–1895

Harkness Fire Destroyer
Deep cobalt-blue, 6 inches, ground lip, smooth base $350–500
American 1880–1885

Hayward Hand Grenade Fire Extinguisher, No. 407 Broadway, NY (base: "Design H Patent")
Amber, 5⅞ inches, tooled lip, smooth base.........................$400–600
American 1875–1890 (rare in this color)

Hayward's Hand Fire Grenade—"Patented Aug 8 1871, S.F.," Hayward, 407 Broadway, NY
Cobalt-blue, 6 inches, ground lip, smooth base $200–250
American 1875–1885

Hayward's Hand Fire Grenade—"Patented Aug 8 1871, S.F.," Hayward, 407 Broadway, NY
Yellow-olive, 6⅛ inches, rolled lip, smooth base.................$175–250

Hayward's Hand Fire Grenade—NY
Aqua, 6⅜ inches, tooled lip, smooth base...........................$125–175
American 1880–1885

Hayward's Hand Fire Grenade—"Patented Aug 8 1871, S.F.," Hayward, 407 Broadway, NY
Clear glass, 6¼ inches, smooth base $175–250
American 1875–1885 (Hayward grenades are not often seen in clear glass)

Sulfuric Acid, 4 Ounce Line, Childs Fire Extinguisher, Utica, NY
Aqua, 6⅛ inches, tooled lip $35–45
American 1890–1900

W.D. Allen Manufacturing Company, Chicago, IL (motif of cresent moon)
Clear glass, 8¼ inches, sheared lip, smooth base $500–700
American 1870–1890 (very rare)

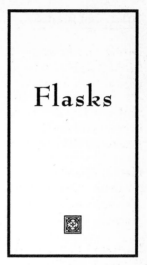

Flasks

Flasks have become a most popular and prized item among collectors due to the variety of decorative, historical, and pictoral detail featured on many pieces. The outstanding colors have had a major effect on the value of these pieces, more so than with most other collectible bottles.

Early history documents that American flasks were first manufactured by the Pitkin Glasshouse in Connecticut around 1815, and quickly spread to other glasshouses around the country. Early flasks were free-blown and represent some of the better craftsmanship with more intricate designs. By 1850, approximately 400 designs had been used that produced black graphite pontil marks. The pontils were coated with powdered iron, which allowed the flask's bottom to break away without damaging the glass. The flasks made between 1850 and 1870 had no such markings due to the widespread use of the newly invented snap-case.

Since flasks were designed to be refilled with whiskey or other spirits, more time and effort was expended in the manufacturing process than for most other types of bottles. Flasks soon became a popular item for use with all types of causes and promotions. Mottos were frequently embossed on flasks and included a number of patriotic sayings and slogans. One of the more controversial flasks was the masonic flask, which bore the order's emblem on one side and the American eagle on the other. Public feelings were high against this representation but the controversy soon passed. Masonic flasks are now a specialty item for collectors.

Also highly collectible are the Pitkin-type flasks, named for the Pitkin Glassworks where they were manufactured exclusively. While

Pitkin-type flasks and ink bottles are common, the bottles, jugs, and jars are very rare. German Pitkin flasks are heavier and straight-ribbed, while the American pattern is swirled or broken-ribbed with unusual colors such as dark blue.

The George Washington depiction was a popular face on flasks, as were the candidates of the presidential elections of 1824 and 1828. These promoted the likenesses of Andrew Jackson and John Quincy Adams. Events of the time also were reflected on these flasks.

Because of the use of flasks for the promotion of various political and special interest agendas, they represented a major historical record of the people and events of those times.

A.H. Powers and Company, Importers, Sacramento, CA
Clear, half pint, tooled top $30–60
American 1885–1887

Anchor Flask
Aqua, pint, applied top, smooth base $40–80
American 1865–1875

Andy Balich, 170 Pacific Ave., Santa Cruz, CA
Clear, half pint, tooled top $50–75
American 1908–1918

Flask—A.H. Powers and Company, Importers, 1885–1887.

Flask—Andy Balich, 170 Pacific Ave., Santa Cruz, California, 1908–1918.

Barney Schow, Wholesale Wines and Liquors, Willits, CAL.
Amber, half pint, tooled top..$100–150
American 1902–1905, (extremely rare, fewer than 10 known)

Berges and Garrissere, Wholesale Wines and Liquor Merchants, Salinas City
Clear, pint, tooled top..$50–100
American 1890–1900 (rare in this size, older embossing)

Berges and Garrissere, Wholesale Wine and Liquor Merchants, Salinas City
Clear, half pint, tooled top..$100–150
American 1890–1910

Berges and Garrissere, Wholesale Wine and Liquor Merchants, Salinas City
Amethyst, half pint, tooled top...$45–75
American 1900–1906

B.F. Jellison, Washoe Exchange, 544 California St.
Clear, half pint, tooled top...$100–175
American 1889–1900

Borgfeldt-Propfe Company (monogram motif), San Francisco
Dark amethyst, pint, tooled top $50–100
American 1907–1909

Flask—B.F. Jellison,
Washoe Exchange,
544 California St.
1889–1900.

Carroll Rye, Crown Distilleries Company (crown monogram motif)
Amber, 5½ inches, tooled top, smooth base $44–80
American 1900–1910

C.C. Goodale, Full ½ Pint, Rochester, NY
Amber, 6½ inches, applied top, smooth base.......................$75–125
American 1865–1875

C.C. Goodale, NY
Aqua, half pint, tooled top, smooth base................................$40–60
American 1875–1885

Chestnut Flask (30 Broken Ribs Swirled to the Left)
Clear, 5 inches, pontiled $125–175
American 1820–1840 (rare in this color)

C. Newman's, "Pat Oct 17th 1876"
Amber, pint $75–125
American 1876–1879 (C. Newman established the San Francisco Glass Works)

Cornucopia Urn
Deep olive-green, pint, open pontil.......................................$50–75
American 1830–1847

Cornucopia Urn
Medium olive-green, pint, open pontil................................$75–125
American 1845–1855

Crystal Palace (monogram motif), 5 Kearny Street
Clear, half pint, tooled top...$100–150
American 1890–1898 (extremely rare and desirable)

C. Tynan, J.H. Cutter Whiskey, Salinas, CA
Clear, half pint, tooled top, smooth base...........................$100–200
American 1905–1918 (extremely rare, fewer than 6 known)

D. Allen, 58 Water Street, Middletown, CT
Amber, pint, applied top, smooth base $40–80
American 1870–1880

Eagle—Eagle
Olive-amber, half pint, open pontil......................................$75–125
American 1840–1860

Eagle—Eagle
Aqua, half pint, applied top, smooth base..........................$40–70
American 1860–1870

Eagle—Eagle
Aquamarine, quart, open pontil......................................$100–200
American 1849–1855

Eagle—Eagle
Aqua, pint, applied top, smooth base...................................$30–60
American 1860–1865

Eagle—Eagle
Aquamarine, pint, applied top, smooth base.........................$20–40
American 1860–1865

Eagle (with banner in beak)
Medium emerald-green, quart, applied top, iron pontil $100–150
American 1850–1860

Eagle—Eagle, Pittsburgh, PA
Aqua, pint, applied top, smooth base...................................$20–30
American 1860–1870

**Edward Oullanhan, Pioneer Liquor House, Trademark
(E.O. diamond motif) Stockton, CA**
Clear, half pint, tooled top...$100–150
American 1886–1895

Fleckenstien and Mayer (monogram motif), Portland OREGON
Light amber, half pint, tooled top......................................$350–450
American 1880–1885 (fewer than 5 known)

For Pike's Peak, Old Rye—Eagle, Pittsburgh, PA
Aqua, half pint, applied top, smooth base............................$50–75
American 1860–1865

Flask—G.W. Chesley, Importer, 51 Front Street, Sacramento, CAL., 1890–1894.

Flask—H. McLoughlin, The Magnolia, San Mateo, 1907–1918.

For Pike's Peak, Prospector—Eagle
Aqua, half pint, applied top, smooth base $60–100
American 1860–1870

For Pike's Peak, Prospector—Eagle
Aqua, pint, applied top, smooth base $50–100
American 1860–1870

Goldberg, Bowen and Company, San Francisco, Oakland, Wine Merchants
Clear, pint, tooled top $75–150
American 1900–1918

G.W. Chesley, Importer, 51 Front Street, Sacramento, CAL.
Clear, half point, tooled top $75–125
American 1890–1894

H. Cohn and Company, Wine and Liquor Merchant, Eureka, CA
Clear, half pint, tooled top, smooth base $50–80
American 1890–1895

H. McLoughlin, The Magnolia, San Mateo
Light amethyst, half pint, tooled top $80–120
American 1907–1918

Herman's Corner, H. Windmuller, "N.W. COR. 12TH & WEBSTER STS," Oakland, CA
Clear, half pint, tooled top $40–60
American 1910–1912

Hunter—Fisherman
Medium copper-puce, quart, applied top, iron pontil $200–300
American 1850–1860

I.W. Harper Whiskey, Bottled by L. & V. Demartini, Petaluma, CA
Clear, pint (label only) $150–200
American 1904

J. Hayes & Company, Wholesale Dealers, Manchester, NH
Light amber, pint, applied top, smooth base $40–80
American 1875–1885

J.H. O'Brien, Wholesale Liquors, Stockton
Clear, half pint, tooled top $75–125
American 1885–1888

J.M. Roney, Wholesale Liquors, Santa Rosa
Clear, half pint, tooled top $100–150
American 1886–1895

Flask—Hunter–Fisherman,
1850–1880.

J. Schaufele, The Opera, Monterey, CAL. Net Contents, 5 Ounces
Amethyst, half pint, tooled top, smooth base $30–60
American 1900–1910

Jenny Lind (Calabash)
Aqua, quart, applied top, open pontil $50–100
American 1840–1850

John B. Drake, Tremont House, Chicago, IL
Orange-amber, half pint, applied top, smooth base............$100–150
American 1860–1865 (top has inside threads for glass stopper)

John W. Vogel, Newark, NJ
Dark amber, half pint, tooled top, smooth base.....................$30–60
American 1880–1890

Jones and Mathews, Santa Rosa
Clear, half pint, tooled top $150–250
American 1910–1916

Kohlberg and Cavagnaro, Wholesale Liquors, Stockton, CAL.
Light amethyst, pint, tooled top (extremely rare) $100–200
American 1893–1894

Label Under Glass Pocket Glass
Multicolored, 5⅝ inches, ground top...................................$500–700
American 1890–1910

Flask—Jones and Mathews,
Santa Rosa, 1910–1916.

Label Under Glass Pocket Glass
Multicolored, 6 inches, ground top $500–700
American 1890–1910

Lauenthal Brothers, San Francisco
Amber, pint, tooled top $40–60
American 1895–1906

Lilienthal and Company Distillers (crown shield monogram motif)
Yellow with a hue of amber, half pint, applied top $250–350
American 1883–1889 (extremely rare in this color and applied top)

Lilienthal and Company Distillers (crown monogram motif)
Light amber, half pint, tooled top, smooth top (rare) $200–300
American 1885–1889

Log Cabin—Spring Garden, Anchor Glass Works
Aqua, pint, applied top, open pontil $50–75
American 1850–1855

**M. Rothenberg and Company, Mendle's Game Cock Whiskey
(rooster motif), 423 Kearny Street**
Clear, half pint, tooled top, smooth base............................$125–175
American 1895–1906 (highly sought after Western coffin flasks)

Malcom Fraser and Company, Ancient Liqueur, "Contents 1‰ Oz"
Clear, pint, tooled top, smooth base......................................$30–60
American 1900–1920

Malcom Fraser and Company, Ancient Liqueur, "Contents 1‰ Oz"
Olive-green, 4⅛ inches, tooled top, smooth base....................$30–60
American 1900–1920

**Millers Extra, E. Martin and Company, Old Bourbon, Trademark
(shield motif)**
Olive with an amber hue, pint, tooled top..........................$500–700
American 1871–1879 (seldom seen in green)

Mountain Brook Whiskey, John L. Steward, Marysville, CAL.
Clear, pint, tooled top...$150–250
American 1885–1895

Flask—multicolored
lady (label under glass),
1900–1910.

Oberon, Louis Gnesa, Santa Rosa, CAL., "Net Contents 6 Oz"
Clear, half pint, tooled top, smooth base.............................$50–100
American 1913–1918 (fewer than 4 known)

Old Crow Bonded, "7th & BO'WY, OAKLAND," A.A. Dahlke
Aqua, half pint, tooled top...$150–200
American 1911–1918 (Shoo-Fly flasks, very few in aqua)

Old Gilt Edge Whiskey (crown motif)
Clear, pint, ground top..$40–60
American 1895–1906

Paul Friedman, San Francisco
Clear, pint, ground top, smooth base....................................$40–60
American 1895–1906

**Phoenix Bourbon (eagle motif), Naber Alfs and Brune,
San Francisco**
Clear, pint, tooled top..$150–250
American 1891–1906 (seldom seen)

**Phoenix Old Bourbon (eagle motif trademark), Naber, Alfs and
Brune, San Francisco, Sole Proprietors**
Amber, half pint, tooled top...$150–250
American 1879–1888

Pheonix Old Bourbon (eagle motif trademark), Naber, Alfs and Brune, San Francisco, Sole Agents
Light amber, pint, tooled top, smooth base $175–250
American 1879–1888

Pottery Flasks (bust on both sides)
Brown, 6½ inches...$75–150
American 1860–1880

Ravenna Glass Company—Eagle and Stars (anchor motif)
Aqua, pint, sheared top, iron pontil $150–250
American 1857–1860

Roth and Company, 214 and 216 Pint Street, San Francisco
Amber, pint, applied top (fewer than 10 known)...............$250–450
American 1880–1885

Roth and Company, San Francisco
Amber, half pint, tooled top, smooth base $30–60
American 1900–1910

Royal Hotel, Colne Road, Burnley
Aqua, 7½ inches, tooled top $20–40
European 1890–1900

S.B. Rottenberg, Importer, Oakland
Clear, half pint, tooled top (rare) $75–125
American 1887–1897

Scroll—Scroll
Blue-aqua, half pint, sheared top, open pontil.....................$60–100
American 1850–1860

Scroll—Scroll
Aqua, pint, sheared lip, open pontil.....................................$40–60
American 1850–1860

Sheaf of Grain—Westford Glass Company, Westford CT
Reddish-amber, pint, applied top, smooth base $75–125
American 1860–1870

Flask—Summer
Tree/Winter Tree,
1860–1865.

Shield and Clasped Hands—Eagle
Aqua, quart, applied top, smooth base $50–75
American 1860–1870

Shield and Clasped Hands—Eagle
Aqua, half pint, applied top, smooth base $40–70
American 1860–1870

Summer Tree—Winter Tree
Aqua, quart, applied top, smooth base $50–80
American 1860–1865

Strap Side Flask (Base), S
Light amber, quart, applied top, smooth base $20–40
American 1870–1876 (possibly from the San Francisco Glass Works)

Theodor Gier (monogram motif), Oakland CA
Clear, half pint, tooled top, smooth base..............................$60–100
American 1892–1910

The Arlington, M. A. Lindberg Proprietor, Bakersfield, CAL., PCGW
Golden orange-amber, pint, tooled top, smooth base.........$400–600
American 1907–1917 (extremely rare seed flasks, fewer than 6 known)

The F. Chevalier Company
Amber, pint, tooled top, smooth base $30–60
American 1900–1910

The Father of His Country, Washington—A Little More Grape, Captain Bragg Taylor
Aqua, quart, applied top, smooth base................................$50–100
American 1860–1870

The Father of His Country, Washington—General Taylor Never Surrenders, Taylor
Aqua, pint, applied top, smooth base....................................$35–65
American 1860–1870

The Father of His Country, Washington—General Taylor Never Surrenders, Taylor
Aqua, pint, applied top, smooth base................................$50–100
American 1858–1865

The New Louvre, 53 North First Street, San Jose, W.J. Fercoson
Clear, pint, tooled top..$100–150
American 1904–1912

Flask—The New Louvre, 53 North First Street, San Jose, W.J. Fercoson, 1904–1912.

Flask—The Noble Buffet, Belt Ink and Ritter, Oakland, CA, 1906–1915.

The New Louvre, 53 North First Street, San Jose, W.J. Fercoson
Clear, half pint, tooled top $80–120
American 1904–1912

The Noble Buffet, Belt Ink and Ritter, Oakland
Clear, half pint, tooled top $50–100
American 1906–1915

The Relay Company, Sutter and Fillmore Sts., San Francisco, Dealers in Wines and Liquors
Clear, half pint, tooled top (fewer than 3 known).................$75–150
American 1910–1915

Tholcke and Lapierre, 165–167 Main Street, Salinas
Clear, half pint, tooled top, smooth base............................$100–150
American 1895–1900

Union Clasped Hands, A.R.S. Eagle
Aqua, quart, applied top, open pontil $20–50
American 1850–1861

Union Clasped Hands Shield—Eagle, A and Company
Aqua, pint, applied top, smooth base....................................$20–40
American 1860–1865

Vanderhurst, Sanborn and Company, General Merchants, Salinas City, CA
Clear, quart, tooled top..$200–300
American 1886–1895 (there are only 2 different quart California flasks and both are extremely rare)

Washington Bust—Sheaf of Rye
Aqua, quart, applied top, smooth base $40–80
American 1858–1865

Washington—Jackson
Medium olive-amber, half pint, sheared top, open pontil...$150–250
American 1830–1850

Flask—Vanderhurst, Sanborn and Company, General Merchants, Salinas City, CA, 1886–1895.

Flask—Western Hotel, Santa Rosa, 1904–1918.

Washington—Sheaf of Rye
Aqua, pint, applied top, open pontil $60–100
American 1850–1860

Western Hotel, Santa Rosa, "Net Contents 5 Oz"
Amethyst, half pint, tooled top..$150–200
American 1904–1918

Westford Glass Co., Westford, CONN—Sheaf of Grain
Dark red in base and orange in shoulders, applied top.......$100–150
American 1860–1865

W.H. Cohen and Company, 229 Washington St., NY
Aqua, 8½ inches, applied top, iron pontil............................$75–125
American 1850–1860

Whiskey Merchants, San Francisco
Amber, half pint, tooled top, smooth base $30–60
American 1900–1910

Flask—Wichman and Lutgen, Old Gilt Edge—OK Bourbon, Sold Agents SF, 1889–1893.

Wm. Hoelscher and Company, Turk and Taylor SS, 1888–1906.

Wichman and Lutgen Old Gilt Edge, OK Bourbon, Sole Agents, San Francisco
Clear, half pint, tooled top $100–150
American 1889–1893

Willington Glass Company, West Willington, CT, Eagle Liberty
Emerald-green, pint, applied top, smooth base $250–350
American 1860–1870

Wm. Hoelscher and Company, Turk and Taylor Streets (mongram motif), San Francisco
Clear, half pint, tooled top $60–100
American 1888–1906

World's Fair (flag motif), Saint Louis, U.S.A., 1904
Clear, 6⅜ inches, half pint, screw ground top, smooth base...$75–125
American 1904

Flask—W.W. Ward, Grotto, Marysville, 1882–1907.

Variety of whiskey "warranted flasks," 1870–1890.

World's Fair (flag motif), Saint Louis, U.S.A., 1904
Clear, pint, screw ground top, smooth base $75–125
American 1904

Wormser Brothers, San Francisco
Dark amber, 8½ inches, union oval, applied top, smooth
base $150–250
American 1867–1872

Wormser Brothers, San Francisco
Golden orange-amber, pint, applied top, smooth base $200–300
American 1867–1872

Food Bottles

Food bottles are one of the largest and most diversified groups in the field of collectible bottles. They were made for the commercial sale of food products excluding beverages except milk. Because of the diversification of this category, food bottles are ideal for the beginning collector. Many collectors are attracted to food bottles for their historical value. Ninteenth- and early twentieth-century magazines and newspapers contained many illustrated advertisements for food products, and many collectors keep scrapbooks of ads as an aid to dating and pricing the bottles.

Prior to the introduction of bottling, food could not be transported long distances or kept for long periods of time due to spoilage. The bottling of foodstuffs revolutionized the food industry. With the glass bottle, grocers were able to use portion packaging, save labor, and sell to customers at some distance from their store. The glass bottle started a new chapter in American business merchandising and distribution.

Due to this newfound competition, many interesting bottles were created specifically to distinguish them from others. These included the Peppersauce bottles made in the shape of Gothic cathedrals with arches and windows (green and clear), mustard jars and chili sauce bottles with unique embossing, cooking oil bottles that are tall and slim, and pickle bottles that are large and square.

Two of the more common are the Worcestershire sauce bottles distributed by Lea and Perrins and the Heinz sauce bottles. The green Worcestershire sauce bottle was in high demand during the nineteenth century and is still quite common. Henry J. Heinz introduced his

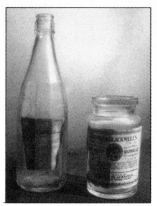

Apple Cider Vinegar, Safeway Stores; Crosse and Blackwell's Pure Orange Marmalade; 1910–1930.

Variety of food bottles: Heinz Pickled Onions, 1869–1873; Del Monte Brand Onions, 1900–1910; Lea and Perrins Worcester Shire Sauce, 1890–1910.

Common sauce bottle (possibly pickle), 1900.

sauces in 1869 with the bottling of horseradish, and didn't begin bottling ketchup until 1889.

The Abner Royce Company, Pure Fruit Flavor, Cleveland, OH
Clear, 5¼ inches $7–10

Armour and Company, Chicago
Milk glass, 5¼ inches, cathedral panels..................................$15–20

Armour and Company Packers, Chicago
Milk glass, 2¼ inches..$4–6

Baker's Flavoring Extracts, Baker Extracts Co.
Clear, one side "Strength & Purity," other side "Full Measure"...$5–7

Common food, sauce,
and pickle bottles,
1870–1890.

Becker's Pure Horse radish, Buffalo
Aqua, 4¼ inches $10–12

Borden's Condensed Milk Company
Milk glass, 4¼ inches..$8–10

Borden's Condensed Milk Company
Clear, 4¼ inches $8–10

Borden's Condensed Milk Company
Amethyst, 4¼ inches $8–10

Burnett's Standard Flavoring Extracts
Aqua, 5¼ inches $5–7

Food bottle assortment:
Curtice Brothers
Preservers, Rochester,
NY; Monogram Salad
Oil, Swift and
Company, U.S.A.; H.J.
Heinz Company;
1900–1920.

Heinz's Trieste Mustard—hand blown in Heinz glass factory in Sharpsburg, PA, 1885–1910.

Heinz's pre-served Sweet Pickles—hand blown in Heinz glass factory in Sharpsburg, PA, 1893–1905.

Candy Bros. Mfg. Co. Confectioners
Aqua, 12 inches, label..$8–10

Cathedral Pepper Sauce
Green-aqua, 8⅜ inches, applied top, smooth base $50–75
American 1860–1865

6–Sided Cathedral Pickle
Aqua, one gallon, 13 inches, applied top, smooth base $50–100
American 1860–1870

R.C. Chances's Sons, Table Talk Ketchup, Phila.
Clear, 9¼ inches, label..$8–10

R.C. Chances's Sons, Table Talk Ketchup, Phila.
Amethyst, 9¼ inches, label $8–10

Curtice Brothers Company
Clear, 8 inches $8–12

Curtice Brothers Company
Amethyst, 8 inches..$8–12

Curtice Brothers Company
Amethyst, 7¼ inches, preserves on the shoulders $5–7

Curtice Brothers Company Preserves, Rochester, NY
Clear, 8 inches, 10½ inches, and 12¼ inches $8–12

George M. Curtis, Pure Olive Oil
Clear, 17 inches $6–9

Dayton Prentiss and Borden, NY
Aqua, 7 inches, tooled top, open pontil (extremely rare)....$200–300
American 1851–1854

Heinz's Tabasco Pepper Sauce—hand blown in Heinz glass factory in Sharpsburg, PA, 1889–1899.

Heinz's Table Sauce—hand blown in Heinz glass factory in Sharpsburg, PA, 1895–1909.

Heinz's Keystone Ketchup—produced in Heinz glass factory in Sharpsburg, PA, 1889–1913.

Heinz Mince Meat—hand blown in Heinz glass factory in Sharpsburg, PA, 1893–1905 (has threaded metal-and-glass cap with wood and bail handle, very rare).

E.R. Durkee and Company, NY
Aqua, 4½ inches, pontil...$20–25

E.R. Durkee and Company Challenge Sauce
Amethyst, 4 inches, (sample) $8–10

E.R. Durkee and Company Salad Dressing, NY
Amethyst, 6½ inches, bottle "Patened April 17" on bottom.........$4–6

E.E. Dyer and Company Extract of Coffee, Boston, MA
Green, 6 inches, graphite pontil..$40–60

Ellwood Cooper Pure Olive Oil, Santa Barbara, CA
Aqua, 10⅞ inches, tooled top, smooth base (applied seal)......$30–50
American 1900–1905 (Most CA sealed bottles are rare)

Eno's Fruit Salt
Clear, 7 inches, "W" on bottom...$7–10

Evangeline Peppersauce
Clear, 5¼ inches, 12 panels $5–7

Extract Tabasco
Clear, 4¾ inches...$5–7

Folger's Golden Gate Flavoring
Amethyst, 5¼ inches, rectangular $4–6

G. Venarre—San Francisco
Aqua, 6⅝ inches, applied top, smooth base $30–60
American 1876–1887

Grapette Products Company, Camden, AR
Clear, 7¼ inches..$10–12

Charles Gulden
Clear, 4¾ inches...$5–7

Charles Gulden, NY
Clear, 5½ inches, flared collar..$5–7

H.J. Heinz Company, No. 37 Gothic Horseradish
Aqua, 6 inches $7–10

H.J. Heinz Company
Clear, 8¾ inches, 18 panels $5–7

H.J. Heinz Company
Amethyst, 9¼ inches, 8 panels...$5–7

H.J. Heinz Company, "69 Patd."
Clear, 6 inches $7–10

H.J. Heinz Company
Amethyst or clear, 4¾ inches, "122 Patd" on bottom $5–7

Assortment of Heinz products, 1885–1915.

Assortment of Heinz products, 1869–1873.

Keyhole Sauce (emerald-green, extremely rare), 1845–1855.

Lea and Perrins Worcester Shire Sauce, 1870–1900 (with glass stoppers).

Munger Brothers Company (food), Phoenix, AZ, 1900–1906.

H.J. Heinz Company
Amethyst or clear, 8¼ inches, "7 Patented" and "X" on bottom...$6–8

Heinz
Aqua, 7¼ inches, "No. 28" on bottom $5–7

Hires Improved Root Beer
Aqua, 4¾ inches, "Panel Mfg. by the Charles Hires Co" $7–10

Hodges and Cross—Yankee Sauce
Aqua, 7¼ inches, applied top, open pontil $60–80
American 1850–1860

Horlick's Trademark, Racine, WI, Malted Milk M.M. U.S.A., "1 Gal"
Clear, 10¾ inches $4–6

Keyhole Sauce
Emerald-green, 9⅝ inches, applied top, iron pontil $2,000–3,000
American 1845–1855 (extremely rare in this color, fewer than 4 known)

Lea and Perrins
Aqua, 11½ inches $5–7

Long Syrup Refining Company
Wine color, 4¾ inches...$10–12

McCormick and Company Spice Grinders, Baltimore
Amethyst or clear, 3¾ inches, sheared top, 8 panels.................$7–10

Moxie Nerve Food, Lowell MA, Patented
Lime-green, 9⅞ inches, applied top....................................$125–175
American 1885–1890

Munger Brothers Company (monogram motif), Phoenix, AZ
Amethyst, 9 inches, tooled top, smooth base (rare)...............$40–80
American 1900–1906

Old Duffy's 1842 5-Year-Old Apple Juice Vinegar
Amber, 6¾ inches, "Duffy's" in diamond shape and "1842" in circle
on neck, 8 panels...$15–20

Mellin's Food Company, Boston, U.S.A., 1900–1920.

Food bottle assortment: first three bottles common, fourth bottle is A-1 Sauce, 1900–1920.

Paskola's, The Predigested Food Company, Trademark
Amber, 6 inches, embossed pineapple $7–10

Pompeian Brand Virgin Lucca Olive Oil
Aqua, 7½ inches...$5–7

Primrose Salad Oil, Western Meat Company
Aqua, 9½ inches...$5–7

Red Snapper Sauce Company, Memphis, TN
Clear, 9½ inches, 6 sides $10–12

Robert Gibson, Manchester, England, E.C. Rich, NY, U.S. Agent
Aqua, 13 inches, tooled top, smooth base $50–100
American 1888–1895

Trapey's Tabasco Peppers
Clear, 6¾ inches...$4–6

Waters Brothers Olive Oil and Extracts, Oakland, CA
Light Aqua, 11½ inches..$7–10

Wood Cooper Pure Olive Oil, Santa Barbara, CA
Aqua, 11 inches $7–10

Fruit Jars

Unlike food bottles, fruit jars were sold empty for use in home preservation of many different types of food. The use of fruit jars was predominant in the 1800s, when foodstuffs were not available prepackaged and home canning was the only option. Though fruit jars carry no product or advertising, they aren't necessarily common or plain since the bottle manufacturer's name is usually embossed in large lettering along with the patent date. The manufacturer whose advertising campaign gave fruit jars their name was Thomas W. Dyott, who was in the market early, selling fruit jars by 1829.

With respect to closures, the most common of those used in the first fifty years was a cork sealed with wax. In 1855, an inverted saucerlike lid was invented that could be inserted into the jar to provide an airtight seal. The Hero Glassworks invented the glass lid in 1856 and improved upon it in 1858 with a zinc lid invented by John Landis Mason, who also produced fruit jars. Because the medical profession warned that zinc could be harmful, Hero Glassworks developed a glass lid for the Mason jar in 1868. Mason eventually transferred his patent rights to the Consolidated Fruit Jar Company, which let the patent expire. In 1880, the Ball Brothers began distributing Mason jars, and in 1898 the use of a semiautomatic bottle machine increased the output of the Mason jar until the automatic machine was invented in 1903.

Fruit jars come in a wide variety of sizes and colors, commonly aqua and clear. It's more difficult to find blues, ambers, blacks, milk glass, greens, and purples.

Abga Mason Perfect
Aqua, quart...$18–25
American 1890–1920

Agee Special
Amber, quart...$12–17
Australian 1920–1930

Agee Utility Jar
Clear, quart..$12–17
Australian 1920–1930

American (eagle and flag) Fruit Jar
Greenish-aqua, half gallon, ground lip..............................$150–200
Australian 1900

American (eagle holding flag) Fruit Jar
Pale apple-green, half gallon, ground lip, smooth base.........$75–100
Australian 1900

Atherhold, Fisher and Company, Philadelphia
Agua, quart, applied mouth, smooth base.........................$100–150
American 1865–1875

Atlas E-Z Seal
Cornflower blue, pint...$50–75
American 1870–1920

Assortment of Atlas fruit jars,
1865–1920.

Atlas E-Z Seal fruit jars,
1870–1920.

Atlas E-Z Seal
Amber, quart..$15–20
American 1915–1930

Atlas E-Z Seal
Deep aqua, quart...$15–20
American 1915–1930

Atlas E-Z Seal
Apple green, quart $15–20
American 1915–1930

Atlas E-Z Seal
Medium yellow-green, quart $15–20
American 1915–1930

Atlas E-Z Seal
Light blue, quart $15–20
American 1915–1930

Atlas Good Luck
Clear glass, half pint...$12–15
American 1930–1940

Atlas Strong Shoulder Mason
Cornflower blue, quart..$15–20
American 1915–1925

Atlas Strong Shoulder Mason
Teal-blue, quart $15–20
American 1915–1925

Atlas Strong Shoulder Mason
Light cobalt-blue, quart...$15–20
American 1915–1925

Atlas Strong Shoulder Mason
Light yellow-green, quart $15–20
American 1915–1925

Atlas Strong Shoulder Mason
Medium yellow-green, quart $15–20
American 1915–1925

Ball
Yellow-amber with deeper amber striations throughout jar, quart,
smooth base $350–500
American 1990

BBGMCO
Aqua, quart, smooth base, ground lip $40–50
American 1885 (aqua jar is one of the oldest Ball jars)

BBGMCO
Yellow-amber, quart, smooth base, ground lip.......................$40–50
American 1975 (reproduced to commemorate the early
Buffalo-made jar and the American Bicentennial)

Ball Root Mason
Aqua, quart..$15–20
American 1905

Ball Root Mason
Medium yellow-olive, half gallon $20–30
American 1905

Ball Mason
Light lime-green, quart, smooth base $15–30
American 1905

Ball Mason
Light lime-green, half gallon $15–30
American 1905

Ball Improved
Blue, pint, smooth base...$25–35
American 1910–1920 ("improved" has been slug-plated in)

Ball Perfection
Blue, pint, smooth base...$25–35
American 1910–1920

Ball Mason
Clear glass, pint, smooth base $90–125
American 1900 (jar has upside down embossing—very rare)

Ball Mason
Clear glass, pint, smooth base $40–50
American 1900

Ball Mason—"Mason's Patent Nov. 30th 1858"
Deep aqua, half gallon...$25–30
American 1900

The Ball Mason's Patent 1858
Aqua, quart, smooth base, ground lip $25–35
American 1900–1910

Ball Perfect Mason
Clear glass, quart, smooth base $35–45
American 1930–1940

Ball Perfect Mason
Clear, quart, smooth base...$7–10
American 1925–1950

Ball Perfect Mason
Aqua, 40 ounce, smooth base $7–10
American 1925–1950

**Ball Ideal and Ball
Perfect Mason,
1915–1930.**

Ball Perfect Mason
Amber, half gallon, smooth base $7–10
American 1925–1950

Ball Square Mason
Clear, quart...$6–9
American 1915–1925

Ball Perfect Mason
Light green, quart $6–9
American 1915–1925

Ball Mason's Patent
Clear, half gallon..$7–10
American 1915–1925

Ball Sure Seal
Clear, quart...$18–25
American 1910–1920

Ball Sure Seal
Clear, pint..$18–25
American 1915–1920 (rare in clear color)

Ball Sanitary Sure Seal
Blue, half gallon, smooth base...$20–30
American 1915–1920

L. Bamberger, Sure Seal Made for
Blue-aqua, pint, smooth base $15–25
American 1915

Bamberger's Mason Jar
Blue-aqua, quart, smooth base $15–25
American 1915

Bamberger's, The Always Busy Store, Newark
Aqua, quart, smooth base, ground lip $100–125
American 1900–1910

Ball Perfect Mason
Olive-amber, quart, A.B.M., smooth base............................$125–175
American 1910–1920 (extremely rare in this color)

Ball Standard
Medium olive-green, quart, A.B.M., smooth base................$250–350
American 1910–1920 (extremely rare in this color)

Bloeser Jar
Aqua, quart, ground lip, smooth base $200–250
American 1887–1895 ("Pat. Sept 27 1887" on glass lid)

Blue Ribbon
Clear, pint..$17–20
American 1920–1935

Buck Glass Company, Garden Queen, Baltimore, MD
Clear, quart..$17–20
American 1920–1935

Buck Glass Company, Farm Family, Baltimore, MD
Clear, pint..$17–20
American 1920–1935

Cohansey
Aqua, pint, ground lip $13–16
American 1872–1880

Cohansey
Aqua, quart, ground lip...$13–16
American 1872–1880

Cohansey
Aqua, half gallon, ground lip $13–16
American 1872–1880

Commodore
Aqua, quart, applied mouth, smooth base..........................$750–900
American 1865–1870 (very rare and desirable jar)

"Crown" (motif of crown)—T. Eaton Company Limited, Toronto and Winnipeg
Clear with slight tint of amethyst, smooth base $35–50
Canadian 1900

Cutting's Jams and Jellies, Trademark (griffin motif)
Clear, 4½ inches, tooled top, smooth base...........................$75–125
American 1885–1895 (rare)

Cutting Packing Company, Trademark (griffin motif), San Francisco
Clear, 3⅛ inches x 2½ inches..$20–40
American 1885–1895 (rare)

Drey Square Mason
Light green, half gallon $7–10
American 1915–1925

Electric (globe) Fruit Jar
Aqua, quart, ground lip, smooth base $50–60
American 1880–1890

Federal (flag) Fruit Jar
Light yellowish-green, quart, ground lip, smooth base.......$150–200
Australian 1900

Flaccus Brothers
steerhead fruit jar,
1890–1900.

Flaccus Brothers (grapes and leaves motif)
Clear, pint..$50–80
American 1890–1900

Fruit Jar (floral motif)
Clear, pint..$50–80
American 1890–1900

Gimbel Brothers Pure Food Store, Philadelphia
Aqua, quart..$18–25
American 1890–1920

H and C
Clear, quart, ground lip $18–25
American 1890–1920

J.J. Squire Jar
Aqua, 2⅞ inches (extremely rare) $60–100
American 1864–1865

The Leader
Amber, pint, ground top, smooth base.............................$300–400
American 1892–1895

Lighting, Trademark (base: "H W P, 269")
Yellow-olive with an amber hue, half gallon, smooth base...$250–350
American 1880–1885

Mason's CFJCO Improved Butter Jar
Aqua, quart, ground lip..$50–75
American 1870–1880

Mason's "Patent, Nov 30th, 1858"
Citron, 7⅛ inches, ground top, smooth base (rare color)....$200–300
American 1885–1895

Mason's "Patent, Nov 30th, 1858" (base: heart motif)
Dark blue-aqua, ground top..$75–100
American 1870–1880

Mason's "Patent, Nov 30th, 1858"
Dark blue-aqua, quart, ground top, smooth base $20–40
American 1870–1880

Mason's "Patent, Nov 30th, 1858" (moon and stars motif)
Aqua, half gallon, ground lip, smooth base $75–125
American 1895 (a rare Mason jar)

Mason's "Patent, Nov 30th, 1858"
Deep blue-aqua, pint, ground lip, smooth base......................$50–60
American 1890 (known as "the Christmas Mason")

Mason's "Patent, Nov 30th, 1858"
Golden amber, quart, ground lip, smooth base $100–125
American 1880

Mason's (keystone) "Patent, Nov 30th, 1858"
Clear, pint, ground lip, smooth base $50–75
American 1875

Mason's (keystone) "Patent, Nov 30th, 1858"
Medium yellow-olive, ground lip, smooth base......................$50–75
American 1875

Mason Brothers
common, trade-
mark, Mason's
improved,
1875–1880.

Mason Porcelain Lined
Aqua, half gallon, ground lip, smooth base $50–75
American 1870

Mason Porcelain Lined
Aqua, quart, ground lip, smooth base $50–75
American 1870

Mason's Fruit Jar
Lime-green, quart, ground top, smooth base.........................$50–75
American 1890–1940

Mason Fruit Jar, Texas
Lime-green, quart, ground top, smooth base.........................$50–75
American 1890–1940

Mason (base: "Made in Texas by Texans 13")
Clear, pint, ground top, smooth base $50–75
American 1890–1940

The Mason Jar of 1858
Aqua, half gallon, ground lip $37–50
American 1875

Mason's "Patent, Nov 30th, 1858," amber, 1880.

The Mason Jar of 1872
Aqua, half gallon, ground lip $37–50
American 1875

The Mason Jar of 1872, Whitney Glassworks, Glassboro, NJ
Aqua, quart, ground lip, smooth base $50–75
American 1872–1875

Millville Atmospheric, Fruit Jar—Whitall's "Patent, June 18th 1861"
Aqua, quart, applied top, smooth base $50–100
American 1861–1865

Mother's Jar
Aqua, quart..$12–15
American 1910

Mountain Mason
Clear, quart, smooth base..$15–20
American 1920–1940

Pacific Mason
Clear, quart, smooth base..$15–20
American 1920–1940

Pacific San Francisco Glass Works, "Patd Feby 9th 1864, Victory, Reisd June 22d 1867"
Dark blue-aqua, half gallon, ground top, smooth base $200–300
American 1867 only (rare Western jar)

Safety (base: "2")
Orange-amber, pint, ground top, smooth base...................$200–300
American 1890–1900 (extremely rare in this size)

Safety (base: "76")
Golden orange-amber, half gallon, ground top, smooth
base..$125–175
American 1890–1900

Ball Ideal and Ball
Perfect Mason
(different view),
1915–1930.

Safety Wide Mouth Mason—Salem Glass Works, Salem, NJ
Aqua, quart..$12–15
American 1910

**San Jose Fruit Packing Company, "Patented July 11 1893,"
Contents Sold Only**
Aqua, quart, ground top (rare)...............................$40–60
American 1893–1895

Safety Wide Mouth Mason
Aqua, quart..$12–15
American 1910

Sealfast, Sold by C.S. and B. Cummings, New Bedford, MA
Clear glass, quart..$50–75
American 1910–1915

Steers Head (steer head motif)
Clear, pint..$50–80
American 1890–1900

Suffragette Canister Jar and Postcard
Clear, quart, smooth base $100–150
American 1900–1920 (the woman has a pot turned backward on
her head, large knife in one hand, rolling pin in the other)

Yeoman's fruit bottle,
1860–1870.

Texas (map of Texas) Mason
Clear, aqua, smooth base $15–20
American 1920–1940

Tropical Canners—Florida
Clear, quart, smooth base..$15–20
American 1920–1940

Yeoman's Fruit Bottle
Aqua, 7¾ inches, applied top, smooth base..........................$75–150
American 1860–1870

Hutchinson Bottles

The Hutchinson bottle was developed in the late 1870s by Charles A. Hutchinson. What is most interesting about his development is that the stopper, and not the bottle itself, differentiated the design from others. The stopper, which Hutchinson patented in 1879, was intended as an improvement to cork stoppers since they eventually shrank and allowed air to seep into the bottle.

The new stopper consisted of a rubber disk that was held between two metal plates attached to a spring stem. The stem was in the form of a figure eight, with the upper loop larger than the lower to prevent the stem from falling into the bottle. The lower loop could pass through the bottle's neck and push down the disk to permit the filling or pouring of the bottle's contents. A refilled bottle was sealed by pulling the disk up to the bottle's shoulder, where it made a tight fit. When opened, the spring was hit, which made a popping sound. Thus, the Hutchinson bottle was the source of the phrase "pop bottle" and the story behind how carbonated drinks came to be known as "pop."

Hutchinson stopped producing bottles in 1912, when warnings about metal poisoning were issued. As collectibles, Hutchinson bottles rank high on the curiosity and price scales, but pricing varies quite sharply by geographical location, compared to the relatively stable prices of most other bottles.

Hutchinson bottles carry abbreviations of which the following three are the most common:

tbntbs—"This bottle not to be sold"
TBMBR—"This bottle must be returned"
TBINS—"This bottle is not sold"

Alameda Soda Water (shaking hands motif)
Lime-green, 6¼ inches, tooled top (rare in this color)........$100– 200
American 1890–1895

American Soda Works (flag motif), S.F.
Aqua, 6⅝ inches, tooled top $50–100
American 1890–1895

Ashland Bottling Works, Ashland, WI
Aqua, 7¾ inches, tooled top $15–30
American 1885–1900

B
Aqua, 7 inches, tooled top (rare Stockton, CA, hutch) $50–100
American 1890–1895

Bacon's Soda Works, Sonora, CAL.
Aqua, 6⅞ inches, tooled top $100–200
American 1893–1906 (extremely rare, fewer than 5 known)

Belfast Trademark (b triangle motif) Ginger Ale Company, S.F.
Aqua, 7 inches, tooled top $60–100
American 1885–1900

The Belfast Soda Water and Ginger Ale Company—San Francisco, CA
Aqua, 6⅞ inches, tooled top $60–100
American 1885–1900

Black Diamond Soda Works
Aqua, 6¾ inches, tooled top $40–60
American 1902–1906 (Pittsburg, CA)

J.I. Bliven and Company, Oakland, CA
Aqua, 7¼ inches, tooled top $30–60
American 1865–1875

Bay City Soda Water Co., San Francisco, CAL.
Aqua, 7¼ inches, tooled top $30–60
American 1865–1875

Bradley Spring Water Company (eagle motif), San Diego, CA
Aqua, 6½ inches, tooled top (fewer than 5 known) $250–450
American 1895–1906

California Bottling Works, T. Blauth, 407 K Street, Sacramento
Aqua, 6⅝ inches, tooled top $40–60
American 1895–1906

California Bottling Works, T. Blauth, 407 K Street, Sacramento
Aqua, 6¼ inches, tooled top, smooth base..............................$40–80
American 1890–1906

California Soda Works (eagle motif)
Aqua, 7 inches, tooled top $30–60
American 1890–1900

Cape Argo Soda Works, Marshfield, OR
Aqua, 6⅝ inches, tooled top $45–75
American 1902–1906

Capital Soda Works
Aqua, 6¼ inches, tooled top $60–100
American 1885–1900

Chico Soda Works (base: "C.S.W.")
Aqua, 6¼ inches, tooled top $40–60
American 1885–1895

Cider and Vinegar Company, Eureka, CA
Aqua, 6¼ inches, tooled top $75–125
American 1900–1906

City Soda Eureka Works, Postel and Schnerr, Sacramento, CA
Aqua, 6¼ inches, tooled top $60–100
American 1885–1900

City Soda Eureka Works
Aqua, 6¼ inches, tooled top, smooth base..............................$40–80
American 1890–1906

C.F. Riley
Medium cobalt-blue, 6⅜ inches, applied top $500–700
American 1875–1880 (fewer than 5 known)

Crystal Soda Works, Honolulu, HI (base: "Trademark J.A.P")
Aqua, 7 inches, tooled top, smooth base $30–60
American 1890–1900

Diamond, Trademark ("d" in a diamond motif)
Aqua, 6¾ inches, tooled top $30–50
American 1880–1906

Dixon Soda Works (base: "K")
Aqua, 6¼ inches, tooled top, smooth base $30–60
American 1890–1900

**Eagle Soda Water and Bottling Company, (eagle motif),
Santa Cruz, CA, This Bottle Never Sold**
Aqua, 6¾ inches, tooled top, smooth base $100–150
American 1900–1906

Eel River Valley Soda Works, Springville, CA
Aqua, 6¾ inches, tooled top, (fewer than 3 known) $200–300
American 1895–1900

**E.L. Billings, Sacramento, CA, Gravitating Stopper, Eureka, CA
(eagle motif)**
Aqua, 7¼ inches, applied top, smooth base $60–100
American 1870–1900

E. and J. Lodtmann, Santa Cruz Company, CA
Light aqua, 7¼ inches, applied top, smooth base $30–50
American 1870–1880

Empire Soda Works, Alameda
Dark aqua, 6½ inches, tooled top $50–100
American 1885–1890 (seldom seen: "Alameda, Calif.")

Enterprise Soda Works, S.F., A. and W.G.
Aqua, 7 inches, tooled top (rare)..$40–60
American 1890–1895

**Eureka California Soda Water Company, San Francisco
(eagle motif), (base: "E-C")**
Aqua, 6¾ inches, tooled top $50–75
American 1890–1895

Excelsior Soda Works Company Limited, Hilo
Aqua, 7¾ inches, tooled top, smooth base............................$80–120
American 1908–1910

F. Baumah Soda Works, Santa Maria, CA (base: "F.B.")
Aqua, 6¾ inches, tooled top (extremely rare) $100–150
American 1895–1906

F.B. Healdsburg, CA
Aqua, 6½ inches, tooled top (hard to find with the state name) ..$60–100
American 1900–1906

G.A.K.
Aqua, 6⅛ inches, tooled top $175–250
American 1887–1895, Winnemucca, NV (rare Nevada Hutch)

**Golden West Soda Works, San Francisco, CA (base),
(horseshoe motif)**
Aqua, 7⅛ inches, tooled top $75–100
American 1885–1895

**G. Norris and Company City Bottling Works, Detroit, MI
(base: "G.N. & CO.")**
Dark cobalt-blue, 6¾ inches, applied top, smooth base $200–300
American 1885–1890

G.W. Epler
Aqua, 7 inches, tooled top $50–100
American 1885–1890 (rare Walla Wall, WA, Hutch)

H Sac—P (base: "C.S.W. SAC")
Aqua, 7 inches, tooled top $45–75
American 1885–1895

Hayward's S.J. Simons Soda Works
Aqua, 6⅛ inches, tooled top $40–60
American 1885–1895, Hayward, CA

F.A. Heim's Bottling Works
Light lime, 7 inches, applied top, smooth base....................$50–100
American 1895–1900, Los Angeles, CA

Hugh Casey Eagle Soda Works
Dark aqua, 7 inches, tooled top $50–100
American 1885–1895

IXL Soda Works, Stollar Brothers, Santa Rosa
Aqua, 7 inches, tooled top, smooth base $200–300
American 1890–1900 (fewer than 6 known)

J.D. Stellmann, Palmyra, NJ (large "J" motif)
Aqua, 7¾ inches, tooled top $15–30
American 1885–1900

John Howell, Buffalo, NY
Aqua, 6⅜ inches, tooled top $15–30
American 1885–1900

Jackson Napa Soda—A Natural Mineral Water, Jackson's
Aqua, 6⅞ inches, applied top, smooth base $50–100
American 1895–1900 (extremely rare with applied top)

Klammer and Malz, San Rafael, CA (base: "M.B.W.")
Aqua, tooled top $75–100
American 1885–1890

Lahaina Ice Company Limited, Lahaina, Maui
Aqua, 7¾ inches, tooled top, smooth base............................$80–120
American 1908–1910

Martin Petersen, San Rafael, CA (base: "M.B.W.")
Aqua, 6⅝ inches, tooled top $75–125
American 1885–1890 (rare California Hutch)

Monroe's Distilled Soda Water, Eureka, CA
Light lime-green, 6⅞ inches, tooled top, smooth base $75–125
American 1900–1910 (very few California Hutches come in any
color other than aqua)

Moxie (base: "Moxie")
Aqua, 6⅜ inches, tooled top, smooth base $50–100
American 1895–1906

National Soda Works (horseshoe motif), Stockton, CA
Aqua, 7¼ inches, tooled top $40–60
American 1885–1895

Nevada City Soda Works (star motif), E.T.R. Powell
Aqua, 6⅝ inches, tooled top $50–75
American 1902–1906

Nevada City Soda Works, E.T.R., Powell, Monroe
Aqua, 6¾ inches, tooled top $75–125
American 1900–1906

New York Bottling Works, Los Angeles (base: "N.Y.B.W.")
Aqua, 6¼ inches, tooled top (seldom seen)...........................$60–100
American 1890–1900

Oceanview Bottling Works, N and B Proprietors, Mendocino, CA
Aqua, 6¾ inches, tooled top $50–80
American 1895–1906

**O.P.S.W. Company, Trademark (bottle motif), Oakland, CA,
Registered, Bottle Is Never Sold**
Aqua, 6⅝ inches, tooled top $40–80
American 1890–1895

P. Somps Soda Water Works, San Francisco, CA
Aqua, 6⅝ inches, tooled top (rare)...$40–80
American 1890–1895

Pacific and Puget Sound Bottling Company, Seattle, WA
Aqua, 7⅛ inches, tooled top $75–125
American 1890–1906

Pearson Brothers, Placerville—P
Aqua, 6⅜ inches, tooled top (extremely rare) $100–200
American 1885–1895

Pioneer Soda Works (shield motif), San Francisco
Aqua, 6½ inches, applied top $30–60
American 1880–1885

Patrick H. Quirk, Trademark (monogram motif), 413 West 16th Street, NY, Registered
Aqua, 7½ inches, tooled top, smooth base............................$40–80
American 1890–1906

R.H. Williams, Grass Valley (base: "330,H")
Aqua, 6⅞ inches, tooled top $50–100
American 1900–1906

Richmond Soda Works, R.S.W., Point, Richmond
Aqua, 6⅝ inches, tooled top (rare)......................................$75–125
American 1900–1906

Sammons Brothers, Jamestown
Aqua, 6⅞ inches, tooled top (fewer than 5 known) $200–400
American 1890–1900

San Francisco Soda Works
Aqua, 6¾ inches, tooled top $30–50
American 1880–1906

Santa Rosa Bottling Company (monogram motif), Santa Rosa, CA, Registered
Aqua, 6¾ inches, tooled top $40–60
American 1900–1906

S.C.O.N.M. Ass'n. (trademark registered), Sacramento, CAL.
Aqua, 6⅞ inches, tooled top $40–60
American 1895–1906

Soda Works Company, San Francisco
Aqua, 7 inches, applied top...$30–50
American 1880–1906

Soda Water Company, S.F.
Aqua, 6¾ inches, tooled top, smooth base...........................$60–100
American 1870–1900

Solano Soda Works, Vacaville, CA
Aqua, 6¾ inches, tooled top, smooth base...........................$50–100
American 1900–1910 (the only California Hutch that spells out
"California")

South Bend Soda and Bottling Company, South Bend, WA
Aqua, 6⅞ inches, tooled top $75–125
American 1890–1906

Spokane Soda Bottling Works, Spokane, WA
Aqua, 6¾ inches, tooled top, smooth base.............................$40–80
American 1892–1906

T and H, Sonoma, CA (base: "gravitating stopper")
Aqua, 7⅛ inches, applied top, smooth base $200–300
American 1864–1865 only (extremely rare, fewer than 5 known)

T. Hilderbrand, Gilroy, CA (base: "H")
Aqua, 7 inches, applied top...$50–100
American 1880–1890 (fewer than 8 known)

Temmett and Sons, Ogden, UT (base: "C.C.G.CO")
Aqua, 6⅝ inches, tooled top $20–40
American 1890–1900

Thomas Leonard, Sonora Soda Works, Sonora, CA
Green-aqua, 7 inches, tooled top $100–150
American 1895–1905 (one of the rare California Hutches)

Ukiah Soda Works, Ukiah, CA
Aqua, 6¾ inches, tooled top $40–60
American 1895–1906

W.E. Deamer—Nevada Soda Water Company, Grass Valley, NV (base: "gravitating stopper")
Dark aqua, 7 inches, applied top, smooth base (rare).........$100–150
American 1870–1880

Adam Wieser, Spokane, WA
Aqua, 6½ inches, tooled top, smooth base..............................$40–80
American 1892–1906

Willows Bottling Works, Willows CA
Aqua, 7 inches, tooled top (seldom seen)..............................$60–90
American 1890–1900

W.P. White, Danielson, CT, Registered
Dark amethyst, 7 inches, tooled top......................................$40–60
American 1890–1900

W. Tormey, Vallejo
Aqua, 7⅛ inches, applied top, smooth base, (rare) $40–80
American 1880–1890

Yonkers Mineral Water (monogram motif), Yonkers, NY, Registered
Aqua, 7½ inches, tooled top, smooth base..............................$40–80
American 1890–1906

Ink Bottles

Ink bottles are unique due to their centuries-old history, which provides collectors today with a wider variety of designs and shapes than any other group of bottles. People often ask why a product as cheap to produce as ink was sold in such decorative bottles. While other bottles were disposed of or returned after use, the ink bottle was usually displayed openly on desks in dens, libraries, and studies. It's safe to assume that even into the late 1880s people who bought bottles considered the design of the bottle as well as the quality of its contents.

Prior to the eighteenth century, most ink was sold in brass or copper containers. The very rich would refill their gold and silver inkwells from these storage containers. Ink that was sold in glass and pottery bottles in England in the 1700s had no brand-name identification and, at best, would have a label identifying the ink and/or its manufacturer.

In 1792, the first patent for the commercial production of ink was issued in England, twenty-four years before the first American patent was issued. Molded ink bottles appeared in America around 1815–1816. The blown three-mold variety was in use through the late 1840s. The most common shaped ink bottle, the umbrella, is a multisided conical that can be found with both pontiled and smooth bases. One of the more collectible ink bottles is the teakettle, identified by the neck, which extends upward at an angle from the base.

As the fountain pen grew in popularity between 1885 and 1890, ink bottles gradually became less decorative.

Miscellaneous inks, 1890–1910.

Miscellaneous inks, 1850–1910.

Bertinguiot Ink
Medium olive-green, 2 inches, sheared top, open pontil $300–400
European 1840–1850 (extremely rare in this color)

Writing Black, Felt Stationers Hall, Fluid Ink, NY
Brown, 4½ inches..$100–200
American 1830–1850 (rare American pottery)

Carter's 1897, Made in U.S.A. (base: "Cone Ink")
Medium olive-green, 2½ inches, tooled top $30–60
American 1897–1905

Carlton—Ink
Aqua with a green swirl, 2⅝ inches, tooled top, smooth
base $75–125
American 1870–1880

Carter's Cone Inks
Light amber, 2⅜ inches, tooled top..$20–40
American 1885–1900

Carter's 1897, Made in U.S.A. (base: "Cone Ink")
Light olive-green, 2½ inches, tooled top $30–60
American 1897–1905

Carter's (base: "Pat. Feb 14—99")
Lime-green, 7¾ inches, tooled top...$30–60
American 1900–1910

Carter's
Blue-green, 8½ inches, applied top with pour spout.............$75–100
American 1880–1900

Caw's Ink
Clear, 1¾ inches x 1½ inches, smooth base.............................$20–40
American 1880–1890 (small house shape)

Cone Ink
Dark blue-green, 2¼ inches, tooled top $50–70
American 1885–1895

Umbrella ink, Carlton,
1870–1880.

Carter's Ink, 8½ inches; Carter
8–sided ink 2½ inches;
1880–1900.

Cone Ink
Amethyst, 2½ inches, tooled top, smooth base $15–30
American 1890–1910

Cone Ink
Emerald-green, 2½ inches, tooled top, smooth base $15–30
American 1890–1910

Cone Ink
Dark olive-green, 2½ inches, tooled top, smooth base $15–30
American 1890–1910

Cone Ink
Very dark blue-green, 2½ inches, tooled top $60–100
American 1880–1890

Cone Ink (base: "Carter's")
Emerald-green, 2½ inches, tooled top $30–50
American 1890–1900

Cone Ink
Light olive-green, 2½ inches, tooled top $100–150
American 1885–1895

Cone Ink
Light amber, 2½ inches, tooled top...$20–40
American 1895–1905

Cone Ink, unembossed,
1870–1890.

Cone Ink, unembossed, 1890–1910.

Cone Ink
Turquoise-blue, 2½ inches, tooled top, smooth base $50–100
American 1880–1890

Cone Ink
Medium cobalt-blue, 2⅜ inches, tooled top, smooth base.....$50–100
American 1880–1890

Cone Ink
Cobalt-blue, 2⅜ inches...$60–100
American 1905–1915

Cone Ink
Yellow, 2⅜ inches, tooled top, smooth base...........................$50–75
American 1890–1900

Crockery Master Ink
Brown, 9¾ inches..$25–50
European 1860–1880

Crockery Master Ink
White, 5¾ inches..$25–50
European 1860–1880

Dessauer's Ink (Cone Ink)
Aqua, 2½ inches, tooled top (rare embossed ink) $50–80
American 1880–1890

Cone Ink, Dessauer's, 1880–1890.

Four Quill Pottery Inkwell
Brown, 2⅝ inches $100–200
American 1800–1830

G.E. Hatch, "Pat'd Dec. 27, 1875" (inkwell)
Milk glass, 2½ inches x 3⅞ inches, pontiled $300–400
American 1875–1880 (looks like a pear branch with a pear, extremely rare)

Geometric Ink
Black, 1½ inches x 2¼ inches, rolled lip, open pontil.........$100–150
American 1820–1840

Harrison's Columbian Ink
Blue-green, 1⅞ inches, rolled lip, open pontil $200–300
American 1850–1860

H.G. Hotchkiss Lyons, NY (base: "Master Ink")
Dark cobalt-blue, 9¾ inches, tooled top, smooth base..........$60–120
American 1885–1895 (with pour spout)

House Ink
Dark sapphire-blue, 2⅛ inches x 2⅜ inches x 1⅛ inches, ground top, smooth base...$150–250
American 1862–1867 (early San Francisco blown ink)

House Ink
Clear, 2¼ inches, tooled top..$200–300
American 1880–1890

House Ink—2 Windows and Door
Dark blue-aqua, 2⅜ inches x 2⅛ inches, burst top $200–300
American 1862–1865 (Western blown ink)

Inverted Funnel Ink
Cobalt-blue, 2 inches, open pontil $150–250
European 1860–1870

Inverted Funnel Ink
Dark cobalt-blue, 2½ inches, open pontil $75–125
European 1860–1870

Master Ink
Forest green, 7¾ inches, applied top, smooth base $40–80
American 1865–1875

Master Ink (with pour spout)
Cobalt-blue, 8 inches, applied top, smooth base $50–80
American 1865–1875

Master Ink
Olive-amber, 8¾ inches, applied top, smooth base $30–60
American 1860–1865

Master Ink (with pour spout)
Amber with a hue of olive, 9¼ inches, applied top $40–60
American 1865–1875

Miscellaneous inks, 1850–1870 (Note: middle back and front two inks have sheared lips).

NE (2 window and door) Fluid, House Ink
Dark aqua, 2⅝ inches, ground top, smooth base $350–450
American 1860–1870 (extremely rare Western house ink)

Pottery Ink
Tan, 3¾ inches $10–20
European 1860–1880

Pottery Ink
Brown, 3¾ inches $10–20
European 1860–1880

Pottery Ink
White, 2 inches...$10–20
European 1860–1880

Pottery Inkwell
Green-gray, 1¾ inches..$75–150
American 1800–1840

S.S. Stafford's Inks, Made in U.S.A., This Bottle Contains One Full Quart, colbalt-blue, 1890–1909.

Umbrella ink, Gibb, 1860–1870.

Russia Cement Company, "Sole Mf'rs of Signet Ink and Lepage's Glue")
Cobalt-blue, 7¾ inches..$40–80
American 1905–1915

S.S. Stafford's Inks, Made in U.S.A., This Bottle Contains One Full Quart
Cobalt-blue, 9⅜ inches, tooled top with pour spout.............$60–100
American 1890–1909

T & M—T & M
Light sapphire-blue, 2½ inches, rolled lip, open pontil...........$50–75
American 1850–1860

T & M—T & M
Dark blue-green, 2½ inches, rolled lip, open pontil............$100–150
American 1850–1860

T & M—T & M
Aqua with a dark green swirl, 2⅜ inches, rolled lip,
open pontil $75–125
American 1850–1860

Umbrella Ink
Puce, 2½ inches, rolled-in lip, smooth base $200–300
American 1860–1865

Umbrella Ink
Dark olive-green, 2½ inches, sheared top, open pontil $75–125
American 1850–1860

Umbrella Ink
Emerald-green with olive hue, 2½ inches, rolled-in lip.......$300–400
American 1850–1860

Umbrella Ink
Emerald-green, 2½ inches, rolled-in lip, open pontil..........$300–400
American 1840–1850

Umbrella Ink
Root beer brown, 2½ inches, sheared top, open pontil $200–300
American 1850–1860

Umbrella Ink
Yellow with orange hue, 2½ inches, rolled-in lip $400–600
American 1850–1860

Umbrella Ink
Dark blue-green, 2½ inches, rolled-in lip, open pontil........$100–150
American 1850–1860

Umbrella Ink
Blue-green, 2½ inches, rolled-in lip, open pontil $60–100
American 1850–1860

Umbrella Ink
Yellow, 2½ inches, rolled-in lip, open pontil $400–600
American 1850–1860

Umbrella Ink
Blue-green, 2½ inches, rolled-in lip, open pontil....................$50–75
American 1850–1860

Umbrella Ink
Medium olive-yellow, 2½ inches, sheared top, open pontil ...$150–250
American 1850–1860

Umbrella ink, unembossed,
1850–1860.

Miscellaneous inks, 1850–1870 (Note: middle ink has a sheared lip).

Umbrella Ink
Red-amber, 2⅜ inches, sheared top, open pontil $400–600
American 1840–1850

Umbrella Ink
Puce, 2⅜ inches, rolled-in lip, open pontil $300–400
American 1850–1860

Gibb (Umbrella Ink)
Dark blue-aqua, 2⅜ inches, burst top, smooth base............$200–300
American 1860–1870, Oakland, CA (fewer than 5 known)

Umbrella Ink
Olive-amber, 2⅜ inches, sheared top, open pontil..............$200–300
American 1840–1850

Umbrella Ink
Dark aqua, 2⅞ inches, applied top, open pontil $50–100
European 1840–1850

Medicine Bottles

The medicine bottle group includes all pieces specifically made to hold patent medicines. Bitters bottles and cure bottles, however, are excluded from this category due to the very questionable healing powers of these mixtures.

A patent medicine was one whose formula was registered with the U.S. Patent Office, which opened in 1790. Not all medicines were patented, since the procedure required the manufacturer to reveal the medicine's contents. After the passage of the Pure Food and Drug Act of 1907, most of these patent medicine companies went out of business when it became required to list the ingredients of the contents on the bottle. The public demand quickly diminished as consumers learned that most medicines consisted of liquor diluted with water and an occasional pinch of opiates, strychnine, and arsenic. I have spent many enjoyable hours reading the labels on these bottles and wondering how anyone would survive after taking the recommended doses.

One of the oldest and most collectible medicine bottles was manufactured in England from 1723 to 1900, the embossed Turlington "Balsam of Life" bottle. The first embossed U.S. medicine bottle dates from around 1810. When searching out these bottles, always be on the lookout for embossing and original boxes. Embossed "Shaker" or "Indian" medicine bottles are very collectible and valuable. Most embossed medicines made before 1840 are clear and aqua, the embossed greens, ambers, and blues are much more collectible and valuable.

A.H. Bull, Extract of Sarsaparilla, Hartford, CONN
Aqua, 6¾ inches, applied top, open pontil $25–50
American 1845–1855

A.H. Smith and COL , Amaryllis for the Complexion, San Francisco
Cobalt-blue, 5½ inches, tooled top, smooth base................$100–150
American 1880–1885 (extremely rare)

Amaryllis Van Schmidt and Company Chemist, San Francisco
Dark cobalt-blue, 5¾ inches, tooled top $100–200
American 1880–1890

A.M. Cole, Virginia City, NEVADA
Clear, 3¼ inches, tooled top $20–30
American 1861–1867

A.M. Cole Druggist, Virginia City, NEVADA
Clear, 5 inches, tooled top, smooth base............................$75–125
American 1861–1883

A.M. Cole Druggist, Virginia and Virginia, NEVADA
Clear, 6⅛ inches, tooled top, smooth base..........................$20–40
American 1861–1870

Assortment of medium-size medicine bottles, 1870–1900.

A.M. Cole Druggist, Virginia and Virginia, NEVADA
Clear, 5¾ inches, tooled top, smooth base $20–40
American 1861–1870

A.M. Cole Druggist, Virginia and Virginia, NEVADA
Clear, 5 inches, tooled top, smooth base $20–40
American 1861–1870

A. Lernhart Druggist, Virginia City, NEVADA
Clear, 5 inches, tooled top, smooth base $20–40
American 1865–1875

Aneola Root
Clear, 6 inches $10–15
American 1910–1940

**A Natural Medicinal Water—Santa Barbara—A Natural
Medicinal Water**
Light golden amber, 10 inches, tooled top, smooth base $40–80
American 1895–1905 (extremely rare)

Citrate of Magnesia, Goldfield Drug
and Jewelers, NV, 1890–1900.

Selection of common medicine bottles,
1870–1900.

The Cuticura System of
Curing Constitutional
Humors—Potter Drug
and Chemical Company,
Boston, MA, U.S.A.,
1880–1885.

Ayers Hair Vigor
Peacock-blue, 6⅜ inches, tooled top, smooth base $50–100
American 1900–1910

B.F. Foster, Carson City, NEV
Clear, 4¼ inches, tooled top, smooth base...........................$40–80
American 1874–1885

B.F. Foster, Carson City, NEV
Clear, 4⅞ inches, tooled top, smooth base...........................$20–30
American 1874–1891

**B.F. Roberts and Company—Golden Gate Medical Syrup,
CALIFORNIA**
Aqua, 10 inches, tooled top, smooth base $30–50
American 1890–1895 (extremely rare)

B and P, NY—Lyons Powder
Puce, 4¼ inches, rolled-in lip, open pontil $85–125
American 1857–1860

B and P, NY—Lyons Powder
Medium emerald-green, 4¼ inches, rolled-in lip, smooth base $30–50
American 1860–1862

B and P, NY—Lyons Powder
Medium olive-green, 4¼ inches, rolled-in lip, open pontil ...$150–250
American 1857–1860 (rare color)

Boericke and Runyon, Homeopathic Pharmacy, San Francisco, CAL., Branch Portland, OR
Amber, 9 inches, tooled top, smooth base..............................$50–80
American 1885–1895 (extremely rare in this large size)

Boericke and Runyon Pharmacists, San Francisco, CAL., and Portland, OR
Clear, 8¼ inches, tooled top, smooth base $30–60
American 1880–1890 (extremely rare)

Bowman's Oakland and Berkeley, CAL
Amber, 3½ inches, tooled top, smooth base $30–60
American 1900–1910 (rare)

Brown Chemical Co.
Amber, 8½ inches, applied top, smooth base.........................$15–25
American 1880–1910

Selection of Tonopah and Goldfield, NV, medicine bottles, 1890–1920.

Burton Family Medicines, Sacramento, CA
Aqua, 9¼ inches, tooled top $40–80
American 1890–1900

C. and B., San Francisco
Dark aqua, 6¼ inches, applied top, smooth base $100–150
American 1865–1875 (rare in this small size)

Carob—Blood and Nerve Tonic
Light golden amber, 7¾ inches, tooled top $75–150
American 1880–1890

Cary Gum Tree Cough Syrup (tree motif), San Francisco, U.S.A.
Dark aqua, 7¼ inches, tooled top (extremely rare) $100–175
American 1885–1890

Caswell Mark and Company, Omnia Vincitt Labor Chemists, New York and Newport
Dark cobalt-blue, 7½ inches, tooled top, smooth base........$100–150
American 1861–1868

Cattle Liniment—Breinig, Fronefield and Company
Aqua, 6¼ inches, applied top, iron pontil...........................$350–450
American 1850–1860

Celery Compound (celery compound motif)
Amber, 9¾ inches, tooled top...$100–150
American 1885–1895

Chief Tonic—Chief Tonic, San Francisco
Clear, 9¾ inches, tooled top, smooth base..........................$200–300
American 1893–1905

Citrate of Magnesia, The Sun Drug Company (winged mortar motif), Los Angeles, CAL.
Emerald-green, 8 inches, tooled top, smooth base $40–60
American 1895–1905

Crane and Brigham, San Francisco
Dark aqua, 8⅞ inches, applied top, smooth base $50–75
American 1865–1875

John Wyeth and Sons, cobalt-blue, 1870–1880.

Wakelee's Camelline, 1890–1900.

**Damascus, Trademark (bust of Arab, buildings and camel motif),
Stoddart Bros. Cor., Geary and Mason Streets, San Francisco**
Amber, 4½ inches, tooled top $100–200
American 1880–1885

Davis and Miller Druggist, Baltimore
Aqua, 5½ inches, applied top, open pontil $75–125
American 1850–1860 (has a backward S in "Davis")

Wholesale—Davis and Miller, Baltimore Druggists
Aqua, 6½ inches, applied top, open pontil.........................$100–150
American 1850–1860 ("Davis" and "Miller" are in slug-plate)

D.D.D.
Medium cobalt-blue, 7⅛ inches, tooled top.........................$50–100
American 1870–1876 (Western blown medicine)

**Dickey Pioneer 1850 Chemist, S.F.
(mortar and pestle motif)**
Dark cobalt-blue, 5¼ inches, tooled top, smooth base........$100–150
American 1867–1870 (rare in this dark color)

Dickey Pioneer 1850 Chemist, S.F. (mortar and pestle motif)
Medium cobalt-blue, 5¾ inches, tooled top, smooth base.....$75–100
American 1865–1870

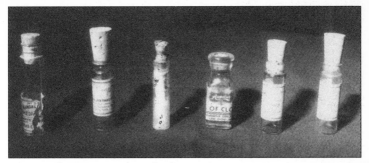

Selection of miniature medicine bottles, 1860–1890.

Dickey Pioneer 1850 Chemist, San Francisco (mortar and pestle motif)
Dark cobalt-blue, 5¾ inches, tooled top, smooth base $100–150
American 1865–1870 (rare in this dark color)

Dickey Pioneer 1850 Chemist, San Francisco (mortar and pestle motif)
Sapphire-blue, 5½ inches, applied top $40–80
American 1865–1870

Dr. A.M. Loryea and Company—Unk Weed Remedy Rheumatic Cure—OREGON
Dark aquamarine, 8¼ inches, applied top, smooth base...$750–1,250
American 1865–1870 (fewer than 5 known)

Dr. Bells
Clear, 6 inches $10–15
American 1910–1940

Dr. Bells Peptonized—Port
Amber, 9¾ inches, tooled top, smooth base $50–100
American 1890–1900

Dr. C.W. Roback's Scandinavian Blood Purifier, Purley Vegetable—Dyspersia—Liver Complaint
Dark aqua, 8¾ inches, applied top, smooth base $50–100
American 1860–1866

Florida Water coffin—Redington Company, San Francisco, 1890–1900.

Florida Water, Davis Bro's, San Francisco, 1875–1885.

Dr. D. Jayne's Expectorant, "Philad. A"
Aqua, 6½ inches, applied top, open pontil $40–60
American 1850–1860

Dr. E. Champlain Lignenous Extract Patented, Cloverdale, CA
Dark aqua, 5½ inches, applied top, smooth base $100–150
American 1864–1870 (fewer than 10 known)

Dr. Henley's Celery, Beef and Iron—C.B. and I. Extract Company, S.F., CAL.
Amber, 9½ inches, tooled top, smooth base $100–150
American 1884–1894

Dr. Hoofland's Balsamic Cordial—C.M. Jackson, Philadelphia
Aqua, 6¾ inches, applied top, open pontil $100–150
American 1852–1860 (rare)

Dr. James M'Clintock Family Medicines
Clear, 8½ inches, applied top, open pontil $100–150
American 1850–1860

Dr. J.B.B. Lefevre Druggist, Virginia City, NEV
Clear, 4 inches, tooled top $40–80
American 1868–1878

Dr. J.J. Hogan, Next to Post Office, Vallejo, CA
Cobalt-blue, 7¼ inches, tooled top, smooth base................$100–150
American 1890–1895 (extremely rare, fewer than 3 known)

Dr. J.J. McBride—King of Pain
Dark blue-aqua, 6⅛ inches, applied top, smooth base $80–120
American 1869–1875

Dr. Leppep's Electric Life
Aqua, 5⅞ inches, tooled top, smooth base..........................$100–150
American 1880–1885 (extremely rare with misspelling of "Lepper's")

Dr. Liebig's German Invigorator, 400 Geary St., San Francisco
Medium amber, 6¾ inches, tooled top, smooth base $50–100
American 1883–1897

Lydia E.
Pinkham's
Vegetable
Compound,
1905–1910.

Dr. Mary Putzman's Compound for Women
Amethyst, 9¾ inches, tooled top..$50–100
American 1890–1900

Dr. Mintie's Nephretiucm, San Francisco
Aqua, 6⅛ inches, applied top, smooth base $150–250
American 1877–1880

Dr. Rowell's—G.G. Burnett Apothecary No. 327 Montgomery St., San Francisco—Fire of Life
Aqua, 5⅞ inches, tooled top $40–80
American 1875–1886 (rare)

Dr. S.F. Stowe's Ambrosial Nectar (glass and grapevines motif), "Patented May 22, 1866"
Amber, 7⅞ inches, applied top $50–100
American 1868–1872

Dr. Wistar's Balsam of Wild Cherry, Philad—"I.B."
Aqua, 6⅜ inches, applied top, open pontil............................$25–50
American 1845–1855

Sheep Dip Poison, Goldfield Drug and Jewelers (NV), 1880–1890.

Atlas Baby Syrup, 1890–1900.

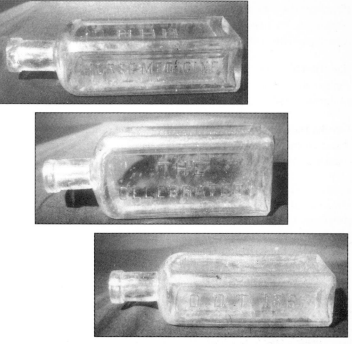

The Celebrated, Horse Medicine, DDT 1868 (three views), 1868–1890.

Druggist—Davis and Miller—Baltimore
Aqua, 4⅜ inches, applied top, open pontil $75–125
American 1850–1860

E.G. Lyons and Company, Ess, Jamaica Ginger, S.F.
Dark lime-green, 6 inches, applied top, smooth base $125–175
American 1886–1875 (rare in this dark color)

E. Anthony, New York
Cobalt-blue, 6 inches, tooled top, smooth base....................$50–100
American 1870–1880 (Anthony was a photographic supplier)

E. Frese, S.F.
Aqua, 5⅝ inches, applied top, smooth base $75–125
American 1860–1865 (extremely rare)

Ebener. Ellis—Boston, MASS
Dark aqua, 7¾ inches, applied top, open pontil $100–200
American 1840–1850

Electric Laxative
Amber, 8½ inches...$10–15
American 1910–1940

Eureka Hair Restoritive—P.J. Reilly—San Francisco
Aqua, 7¼ inches, applied top, smooth base $150–250
American 1868–1873 (extremely rare)

Farmer's Horse Medicine, S.F., CAL—XXX
Lime green, 6½ inches, tooled top, smooth base....................$50–80
American 1880–1890 (rare in this color)

F.L. Saylor Prescription Druggist, Swight Way and Shattuck Ave., Berkeley, CAL
Aqua, 7¾ inches, tooled top, smooth base.............................$30–60
American 1900–1910 (rare)

Forge's ASFT—Manna, Trademark Reg., Asthma, Bronchitis, Colds, Etc., S.B. Force M'F' Chemist, San Francisco, CA (base: "P C G W")
Amber, 8⅝ inches, tooled top, smooth base $100–150
American 1902–1906 (extremely rare)

Lamlough's Effervescing Pyretic Saline, 1880.

Assortment of miniature medicine bottles, 1870–1890.

Fort Bragg Hospital and Drug Company
Aqua, 7¾ inches, tooled top $50–75
American 1890–1900

Florida Water, Davis Bro's, San Francisco
Very dark aqua, 9¼ inches, applied top...............................$75–100
American 1875–1885

Florida Water Coffin—Redington Co., San Francisco
Aqua, 6½ inches, tooled top, smooth base $15–25
American 1880–1910

From Carson and Riley Pharmacists, Corner 2nd and Santa Clara Sts, San Jose, CAL
Aqua, 7½ inches, tooled top, smooth base............................$30–60
American 1885–1895 (rare)

G.C.N. Crittenton—Hale's Honey of Horehound Tar, NEW YORK
Aqua, 8½ inches, applied top, smooth base $50–100
American 1883–1888

Germ Bacteria or Fungus Destroyer, Wm. Radam's Mibrobe Killer (man clubbing a skeleton motif), "Registered Trade Mark Dec. 13, 1881, Cures All Diseases"
Amber, 10¼ inches, tooled top, smooth base $75–125
American 1887–1906

Glocken Gasse No. 4711 Kolna R
Clear, 9½ inches, tooled top, smooth base $20–40
American 1880–1900

Gogings Iron Tonic (monogram motif), 904 J. St., Sacramento
Aqua, 8⅛ inches, tooled top $50–100
American 1880–1885

The Golden One Minute Sterilizer (base: John O. Golden Portland, ORE)
Honey-amber, 3½ inches, tooled top $75–100
American 1880–1890

Golden Treasure
Aqua, 3½ inches, applied top, open pontil $250–350
American 1850–1860

G.P.O.B.—C.C.W
Aqua, 5⅛ inches, rolled-over lip, open pontil $30–60
American 1850–1860

Green's Lung Restorer, Santa Abie—Abietine Medical Co.—Oroville, CAL., U.S.A.
Aqua, 7¾ inches, tooled top, smooth base $75–125
American 1890–1900 (one of the rarer Santa Abie bottles)

H. Farmer's—Horse Medicine, S.F. CAL—XXX
Aqua, 8½ inches, tooled top, smooth base $20–40
American 1880–1900

Hall's Balsam for the Lungs—J.F. Henry Curran and Company—8 and 9 Collage Place, NY
Sapphire-blue, 7⅝ inches, tooled top, smooth base $50–75
American 1873–1880

Hall's—Hair Renewer
Peacock-blue, 7¼ inches, tooled top $150–200
American 1900–1910

Herbing
Amber, 8½ inches $10–15
American 1910–1940

**Hills, Trademark, (large H motif) Dys. Pep. Cu, Cures,
Chronic Syspepsia, Indian Drug Specialty Co,
St. Louis and Indianapolis**
Amber, 8¼ inches, tooled top, smooth base $75–100
American 1900–1905

Holdens Dysentery and Diarrhoea Cordial, Stockton, CA
Aqua, 5⅛ inches, applied top, open pontil $600–1,000
American 1850–1860(fewer than 5 known)

**Hop—Cel Company, San Francisco—Nerve, Blood and
Brain Tonic**
Amber, 9 inches, tooled top, smooth base............................$50–100
American 1870–1875

H.P. Wakelee, San Francisco
Aqua, 7⅛ inches, applied top, smooth base $40–80
American 1870–1875

H.P. Wakelee, San Francisco
Aqua, 7⅜ inches, applied top, smooth base $60–100
American 1870–1875 (rare)

**J.A. Folger and Company, Essence of Jamaica Ginger,
San Francisco**
Aqua, 5⅞ inches, tooled top, smooth base..............................$20–40
American 1880–1890

J and C Maguire Chemist and Druggist, Saint Louis, MO
Dark cobalt-blue, 7 inches, tooled top, smooth base $100–150
American 1860–1865 (rare)

J.J. Spieker Druggist—N.W. Corner 6th and K Sts, Sacramento
Aqua, 5⅞ inches, applied top, smooth base $40–70
American 1865–1875

J. Lipman—San Francisco
Dark aqua, 6½ inches, applied top, smooth base $75–100
American 1870–1880

James Dingles and Company, 99 Washington St., Boston, MASS
Amber, 9½ inches, applied top, smooth base......................$100–200
American 1874–1877

J.R. Nichols and Company—Chemist—Boston
Super dark cobalt-blue, 9⅛ inches, applied top,
smooth base...$200–300
American 1865–1872 (extremely rare in this color and size)

Kodol
Clear, 6 inches $10–15
American 1910–1940

Label Only Flasks
Clear, 6 inches, tooled top $10–20
American 1890–1900

Langley and Michaels, San Francisco
Aqua, 8¾ inches, tooled top, smooth base.............................$20–30
American 1895–1905

Langley and Michael Ess Jamaica Ginger
Aqua, 6 inches, tooled top, smooth base $20–40
American 1880–1890

Levarn's Hair Tonic and Dandruff Cure, Granville, NY
Clear, 7½ inches, label under glass, tooled top $100–150
American 1890–1906

Liebig Dispensary, 400 Geary St., S.F.
Aqua, 7¾ inches, tooled top, smooth base............................$50–100
American 1883–1888

LLewellyn, 1410 Chestnut Street, Phila
Cobalt-blue, 2½ inches, tooled top, smooth base...................$30–50
American 1890–1910

L.Q.C. Wishart's Pine Tree Tar Cordial, Phila—Patent (tree motif) 1859
Grass-green, 7¾ inches, applied top, smooth base.............$100–150
American 1860–1870

L.Q.C. Wishart's Pine Tree Tar Cordial, Phila—Patent (tree motif) 1859
Medium emerald-green, 7¾ inches, tooled top, smooth base ..$75–125
American 1860–1870

Lull's Antispasmodic for Coughs, San Francisco, CAL
Aqua, 4¾ inches, tooled top, smooth base.........................$250–350
American 1870–1875 (fewer than 10 known)

Lydia E. Pinkham's Vegetable Compound, 14 Oz
Dark lime-green, 8⅛ inches..$30–60
American 1905–1910

Lydia E. Pinkham's Vegetable Compound
Amber, 8½ inches, applied top, smooth base.........................$15–25
American 1880–1910

Mack's Florida Water
Aqua, 8⅞ inches, tooled top $20–40
American 1890–1900

Spirit of Nitrate,
Goldfield, NV, 1900.

Assortment of miniatures and medium-size common medicine bottles, 1870–1900.

Magivetic Liniment, Made by A.C. Grant, Albany, NEW YORK
Aqua, 5 inches, sheared top, open pontil $50–100
American 1850–1860

Mayhew and Wenzell, San Francisco
Dark cobalt-blue, 6 inches, applied top, smooth base $300–400
American 1869–1874 (possibly the only one known)

McElree's Wine of Cardum—Chattanooga Medicine Company
Clear, 8½ inches, tooled top $75–100
American 1896–1900

McClellan's Diphtheria Remedy
Aqua, 8¼ inches, tooled top, smooth base..........................$100–200
American 1875–1885

McCombie's Compound Restorative
Aqua, 6⅞ inches, applied top, open pontil $50–100
American 1850–1860

McMillan and Kester, Ess, of Jamaica Ginger
Aqua, 5⅞ inches, applied top $30–60
American 1865–1875

Moe Hospital, Sioux Falls, SOUTH DAK
Amethyst, 8¼ inches, tooled top, smooth base $30–50
American 1890–1910

Newell's Pulmonary Syrup, Redington and Company
Aqua, 7¼ inches, tooled top, smooth base.............................$30–60
American 1874–1880

Newell's Pulmonary Syrup, Redington and Company
Light lime-green, 7⅜ inches, tooled top..............................$100–175
American 1874–1880 (rare in this color)

Newell's Pulmonary Syrup, Redington and Company
Aqua, 7⅜ inches, applied top, smooth base $75–100
American 1874–1880

New York Pharmacal AS
Dark cobalt-blue, 12 inches, applied top, smooth base $150–250
American 1875–1880 (extremely rare)

Nichol's Injection
Dark aqua, 7½ inches, applied top, smooth base $150–200
American 1880–1885 (has an unusual sunken panel that is thought
to have been used for a syringe; very rare)

Nichol's Infallible Injection (dose glass), Nichol's Injection
Aqua, word "Dose" in lime-green, 7½ inches, applied top....$200–300
American 1880–1885 (very rare)

NY Medical University (graduating measurement motif)
Dark purple, cobalt-blue, 7¼ inches, tooled top, smooth base ...$75–100
American 1870–1875

NY Medical University (graduating measurement motif)
Aqua, 9½ inches, applied top, smooth base $75–100
American 1870–1875

NY Medical University (graduating measurement motif)
Clear, 7⅛ inches, tooled top, smooth base............................$75–100
American 1870–1875

NY Pharmacal Association
Cobalt-blue, 8 inches, tooled top, smooth base....................$60–100
American 1874–1880

O.P. Willis Apothecary, Carson City, NEV
Clear, 6¾ inches, tooled top, smooth base $75–100
American 1868–1878 (one of the more difficult Carson City
medicines to find)

O.P. Willis Apothecary, Carson City, NEV
Clear, 5⅛ inches, tooled top, smooth base $75–100
American 1868–1878 (one of the more difficult Carson City
medicines to find)

O.P. Willis Apothecary, Carson City, NEV
Clear, 4 inches, tooled top, smooth base $40–80
American 1874–1885

Owbridge's Lung Tonic—Hull
Sapphire-blue, 5⅛ inches, tooled top, smooth base $30–60
English 1890–1900

One Wing (owl motif)
Light amber, 2½ inches, tooled top $50–100
American 1895–1908 (one of the rarer amber medicines)

The Owl Drug Company (owl motif)
Clear, 3¼ inches, tooled top $25–50
American 1905–1910 (extremely rare, two-wing owl)

The Owl Drug Company (owl motif)
Milk glass, 3¼ inches, tooled top, smooth base $150–200
American 1900–1910 (extremely rare in this size)

Dr. Miles Restorative Nervine, 1880–1890.

One Wing (owl motif), The Owl Drug Company
Milk glass, 3⅜ inches, tooled top.......................................$100–200
American 1895–1905

Owl Motif in a Slug Plate
Light amethyst, 3¾ inches, tooled top $30–40
American 1892–1895 (one of the first Owl Drug Company bottles;
base: "Pat. Jan 5th, 1892")

The Owl Drug Company
Clear, 4 inches, one wing, tooled top $20–30
American 1900–1935

The Owl Drug Company
Clear, 3⅛ inches, two wings, tooled top $20–30
American 1900–1935

The Owl Drug Company
Clear, 2½ inches, two wings, tooled top $20–30
American 1900–1935

Dr. Miles Restorative
Nervine,
1880–1890.

One Wing (owl motif), The Owl Drug Company
Milk glass, 4⅛ inches, tooled top...$40–70
American 1900–1935

The Owl Drug Company (owl motif)
Light amber, 4⅜ inches, tooled top..$40–80
American 1895–1906

One Wing (owl motif), The Owl Drug Company
Amber, 4⅜ inches, tooled top...$60–90
American 1895–1908

One Wing (owl motif), White Pottery Store Display
White, 4⅝ inches..$300–400
American 1895–1908 (pottery displays are extremely rare)

One Wing (owl motif), The Owl Drug Company
Milk glass, 4⅞ inches, tooled top..$40–70
American 1895–1908

The Owl Drug Company
Clear, 3¼ inches, screw cap...$5–10
American 1910–1941

The Owl Drug Company
Clear, 4 inches, screw cap...$5–10
American 1910–1941

The Owl Drug Company
Clear, 4½ inches, screw cap...$5–10
American 1910–1941

The Owl Drug Company
Clear, 4¾ inches, screw cap...$5–10
American 1910–1941

The Owl Drug Company
Clear, 5½ inches, screw cap...$5–10
American 1910–1941

The Owl Drug Company (owl motif), Lewiston, IDA
Clear, 4¾ inches, tooled top $100–200
American 1900–1908 (extremely rare)

The Owl Drug Company
Clear, 1½ inches, screw cap..$7–10
American 1900–1945 (key chain with view of the Owl Rexall Drug)

The Owl Drug Company
Clear, 3½ inches, screw cap..$7–10
American 1900–1945

The Owl Drug Company
Clear, 4½ inches, one wing, screw cap.....................................$7–10
American 1900–1945

The Owl Drug Company
Clear, 5½ inches, one wing, screw cap.....................................$7–10
American 1900–1945

Owl Drug Company,
milk glass (extremely
rare), 1900–1910.

One Wing (owl motif), The Owl Drug Company
Milk glass, 5½ inches, tooled top..$60–90
American 1895–1908

Owl Motif in a Slug Plate
Clear, 5¾ inches, tooled top $40–60
American 1892–1895 (one of the first Owl Drug Company bottles, no patent date on the base)

One Wing (owl motif), The Owl Drug Company
Amethyst, 5⅜ inches, tooled top...$15–25
American 1895–1908

One Wing (owl motif), The Owl Drug Company
Amethyst, 5⅞ inches, tooled top...$15–25
American 1895–1908

The Owl Drug Company (owl motif)
Milk glass, 6 inches, tooled top $100–200
American 1895–1908 (rare in this size)

The Owl Drug Company, San Francisco
Clear, 6 inches, tooled top $15–25
American 1900–1908

Owl Drug Company,
cobalt-blue,
1895–1900.

Owl on Mortar Motif
Cobalt-blue, 6¼ inches, tooled top $60–100
American 1892–1895

The Owl Drug Company (owl drug motif)
Cobalt-blue, 6¼ inches, tooled top, smooth base.................$75–125
American 1895–1905

The Owl Drug Company, Bay Rum
Clear, 6½ inches, tooled top $25–45
American 1900–1910

The Owl Drug Company, Bay Rum
Clear, 6½ inches, tooled top $10–15
American 1895–1908

The Owl Drug Company, Medicine
Clear, 4 inches, tooled top $10–15
American 1895–1908

Owl Motif in a Slug Plate
Clear, 7 inches, tooled top $50–75
American 1892–1895 (one of the first Owl Drug Company bottles;
"Pat. Jan 5th, 1892" on base)

The Owl Drug Company
Clear, 7½ inches, barrel shape $20–30
American 1925–1933 (rare)

The Owl Drug Company, Two Wings (owl motif)
Clear, 4½ inches, ...$20–30
American 1925–1933 (rare)

The Owl Drug Company, One Wing (owl motif)
Clear, 3¼ inches, tooled top $25–50
American 1895–1908

The Owl Drug Company, One Wing (owl motif)
Clear, 7⅛ inches, tooled top $25–50
American 1895–1908

One Wing (owl motif) Standard Pharmaceuticals
Amethyst, 8 inches, tooled top...$35–50
American 1892–1908 (base embossed with "S.F." and "L.A. 16 oz")

One Wing (owl motif), Standard Pharmaceuticals
Amethyst, 6 inches, tooled top...$35–50
American 1892–1908 (base: "The Owl Drug Co., San Francisco")

The Owl Drug Company (owl on mortar and pestle motif)
Amethyst, 8¾ inches, tooled top, smooth base $100–150
American 1895–1900 (rare in this large size)

The Owl Drug Company, San Francisco, CAL
Amber, 8⅜ inches, rounded back $75–150
American 1895–1900 (extremely rare owl bottle)

The Owl Drug Company (owl motif), Bay Rum
Amethyst, 8⅞ inches, tooled top, smooth base $100–150
American 1900–1910 (rare in this large size)

The Owl Drug Company, Huile D' Olive
Clear, 9 inches, tooled top $100–150
American 1895–1905 (extremely rare)

Owl on Mortar Motif
Dark cobalt-blue, 9¼ inches, tooled top $400–600
American 1892–1895

The Owl Drug Company (owl motif), San Francisco
Teal-blue, 9½ inches, tooled top $75–125
American 1900–1908

The Owl Drug Company (owl motif), San Francisco
Teal-blue-green, 9⅜ inches, tooled top, smooth base............$60–100
American 1905–1910

The Owl Drug Company (owl motif)
Cobalt-blue, 9½ inches x 3 inches, tooled top $500–700
American 1892–1895 (rare and seldom seen owl bottle)

The Owl Drug Company, One Wing (owl motif)
Light amethyst, 9⅞ inches, tooled top $150–200
American 1895–1906 (rare misspelled "Gwl" in this size)

The Owl Drug Company—The Owl Drug Company
Aqua, 9⅛ inches, tooled top $100–200
American 1895–1905 (extremely rare)

The Owl Drug Company (owl motif), San Francisco, New York, Chicago
Emerald-green, 9¾ inches, crown top, citrate of magnesia......$45–65
American 1920–1930

Partenopea Chemical House; 12 ounces, Napoi, Italy, Allentown, PA, U.S.A.
Yellow with reddish hue, 7⅝ inches, tooled top, smooth base ...$40–80
American 1900–1910

Pepper Sauce
Aqua, 8 inches, applied top, open pontil................................$40–60
American 1850–1860

Phcie Cottin, 51 Ruede Seine, a Paris
Clear, 4⅞ inches, open pontil $20–40
French 1860–1910

Pioneer 1850 (mortar and pestle motif)
Pale green-aqua, 6⅛ inches, tooled top, smooth base $400–600
American 1861–1865 (first of the Dickey's Chemist San Francisco bottles, the only one known in this color)

Prepared by J.C. Wadleigh—Delights Spanish Lustral
Aqua, 5⅞ inches, applied top, open pontil $20–40
American 1850–1860

R.C. and A.—New York
Dark cobalt-blue, 9¼ inches, applied top, smooth base $100–150
American 1874–1880 (rare)

Redington Company, Ess Jamaica Ginger, San Francisco
Aqua, 5¾ inches, tooled top, smooth base.............................$20–40
American 1876–1880

Ricin, The P.S. Company Inc., Phila, PA
Emerald-green, 3½ inches, tooled top, smooth base $35–75
American 1890–1900

Rushton Clark and Company—Chemist's New York
Aqua, 9½ inches, applied top, open pontil $100–200
American 1847–1860

Searby's Florida Water
Dark aqua, 9¼ inches, applied top $30–60
American 1875–1885

**Simmons Hardware Company Inc., Sole Distributors,
St. Louis, MO (XXX oil monogram motif), U.S.A.**
Aqua, 5¼ inches, tooled top, smooth base, triangle shape $50–100
American 1895–1905

**Siphon Kumysgen Bottle for Preparing Kumyss from Kumysgen
(cross moon motif), Reed and Carnrick, NY, Water Mark,
Powder Mark**
Dark cobalt-blue, 8½ inches, tooled top, smooth base $100–200
American 1880–1890

Searby's
Florida Water,
1875–1885.

**Steinhauser and Eaton Prescription Druggists—S. and E.
(mortar and pestle motif), Watsonville, CA**
Emerald-green, 8¾ inches, tooled top, smooth base $100–150
American 1900–1910 (rare in this size)

Such's—California Cure for Asthma and Lung Diseases
Dark aqua, 8⅛ inches, applied top, smooth base $700–1,000
American 1865–1875 (highly sought after Western cure, fewer than
6 known, found only in northern California)

**Sun Drug Company, (winged mortar and pestle motif),
Los Angeles**
Amber, 8¾ inches, tooled top, smooth base, bitters or tonic..$500–700
American 1890–1905

**Sun Drug Company (winged mortar and pestle motif),
Los Angeles, CAL**
Light amber, 5¾ inches, tooled top, smooth base $75–150
American 1890–1905

**Sun Drug Company (winged mortar and pestle motif),
Los Angeles, CA**
Amber, 5⅞ inches, tooled top, smooth base $75–100
American 1890–1905

**Sutherland Sisters—7, Sutherland Sisters Hair Grower, NEW
YORK**
Clear, 6 inches, tooled top, smooth base $50–100
American 1886–1900

Swaim's—Panacea—Phila
Aqua, 8 inches, applied top, smooth base $60–100
American 1860–1870

Temple of Health
Aqua, 8⅞ inches, tooled top, (Western medicine) $50–100
American 1895–1910

Geog. C. Thaxter Druggist, Carson City, NEV
Clear, 4 inches, tooled top, smooth base $40–80
American 1874–1885

**The Blood, Dr. Kilmer's Ocean Weed Heart Remedy Specific—
Dr. Kilmer and Company, Binghamton, NY**
Aqua, 8⅝ inches, tooled top, smooth base..........................$100–150
American 1890–1900

The Carey Medical Corp'n—Dr. Carey's Marsh Root, Elmira, NY
Aqua, 9½ inches, tooled top $50–100
American 1890–1900

**The Cuticura System of Curing Constitutional Humors—
Potter Drug and Chemical Company, Boston, MASS, U.S.A.**
Aqua, 9⅛ inches, applied top $25–50
American 1880–1885

**The New York Pharmacal Association—Lactopeptine the Best
Digestive Agent in Dyspepsia and Indigestion—Lactopeptine
Syrup with Phosphates**
Cobalt-blue, 7⅜ inches, tooled top, smooth base.................$75–100
American 1880–1888

The Shaker Family Pills—Dose 2 to 4—A. J. White
Light amber, 2⅛ inches, tooled top, smooth base $30–50
American 1870–1880

**The Standard Tonic—The Sherry and Iron Company
("S I" monogram motif), Stockton, CAL, U.S.A.**
Aqua, 10¾ inches, tooled top, smooth base........................$175–275
American 1876–1882 (highly sought after Western tonic, fewer than
10 known)

Todco, Trademark (large owl motif)
Clear, 9⅝ inches, tooled top, smooth base..........................$200–300
American 1892–1895 (fewer than 3 known)

Two Wings (owl motif), Quinine Hair Tonic
Clear, 6 inches, stopper in embossed with "The Owl
Drug Co." $30–50
American 1925–1930

Two Wings (owl motif)
Amber, 8 inches, tooled top $100–150
American 1908–1910 (rare and seldom seen)

Turtle-ine, S.F., CALIFORNIA
Clear, 7¼ inches, open pontil $20–40
American 1860–1910

U.S.A. Hospital Department
Dark purple-puce, 3 inches, tooled top, smooth base.........$200–300
American 1861–1864 (extremely rare in this color)

U.S.A. Hospital Department
Dark forest-green, 5½ inches, smooth base............................$20–30
American 1861–1864

U.S.A. Hospital Department
Dark cobalt-blue, 5 inches, smooth base $20–30
American 1861–1864

U.S.A. Hospital Department,
6¾ inches, 5½ inches,
1861–1865.

U.S.A. Hospital Department,
6¾ inches, 2¾ inches,
1861–1865.

U.S.A. Hospital Department
Clear, 6¾ inches, tooled top $50–75
American 1861–1865

U.B.A. Hospital Department
Clear, 2¾ inches, flared top $50–75
American 1861–1865 ("U.B.A." is unique feature)

U.S.A. Hospital Department
Clear, 6¾ inches, tooled top, smooth base..........................$100–150
American 1861–1865 (rare in this color)

U.S.A. Hospital Department
Clear, 5½ inches, tooled top, smooth base..........................$100–150
American 1861–1865 (rare in this color)

U.S.A. Hospital Department
Aqua, 6⅜ inches, applied top, smooth base $75–150
American 1860–1865

U.S.A. Hospital Department
Cobalt-blue, 7¼ inches, tooled top, smooth base................$500–700
American 1861–1865 (extremely rare in this size and color)

U.S.A. Hospital Department (base: "S D S")
Bright yellow, 9 inches, applied top, smooth base..............$250–350
American 1861–1865 (extremely rare in this color)

U.S.A. Hospital Department
Red-strawberry-puce, 9 inches, applied top, smooth base....$600–1,000
American 1861–1865

U.S.A. Hospital Department (base has a dot)
Olive-green, 9 inches, applied top, smooth base $150–250
American 1861–1865

U.S.A. Hospital Department
Light olive-yellow, 9 inches, applied top, smooth base.......$200–300
American 1861–1865

U.S.A. Hospital Department
Medium strawberry-puce, 9⅛ inches, applied top,
smooth base...$400–600
American 1861–1865

U.S.A. Hospital Department
Dark emerald-green, 9¼ inches, applied top, smooth base....$200–400
American 1861–1865

U.S.A. Hospital Department
Yellow, 9¼ inches, applied top..$200–300
American 1861–1865

U.S.A. Hospital Department (base has a dot)
Light emerald-green with a hue of olive, 9¼ inches,
applied top, smooth base $200–400
American 1861–1865

U.S.A. Hospital Department (base has a six-point star)
Lime-green with a hue of olive, 9½ inches, applied top $200–300
American 1861–1865

U.S.A. Hospital Department
Olive-green, 9½ inches, applied top, smooth base.................$75–125
American 1861–1865

U.S.A. Hospital Department
Aqua, 9 inches, applied top, smooth base $100–150
American 1861–1865 (rare in this color)

U.S.A. Hospital Department
Emerald-green, 9½ inches, applied top, smooth base..........$200–300
American 1861–1865

U.S.A. Hospital Department (base has a six-point star)
Olive-amber, 9½ inches, applied top, smooth base.............$200–300
American 1861–1865

U.S.A. Hospital Department
Dark olive-green, 9½ inches, applied top, smooth base $200–400
American 1861–1865

U.S.A. Hospital Department (base: "S D S")
Yellow with an orange hue, 9⅜ inches, applied top,
smooth base..$250–450
American 1861–1865

Valentine Hassmer's Lung and Cough Syrup, "Price per Bottle $1.25, 5 Bottles to a Gallon, P.O. Box 1886"
Amber, 11⅞ inches, applied top, smooth base....................$300–400
American 1877–1880 (extremely rare, fewer than 10 known)

Vigor of Life
Aqua, 6½ inches, tooled top, smooth base..............................$15–25
American 1880–1910

Walt's Wild Cherry Tonic—The Great Tonic
Light amber, 8¾ inches, tooled top, smooth base $40–80
American 1912–1917

Wakelee's Camelline
Cobalt-blue, 4⅞ inches, applied top, smooth base................$50–100
American 1868–1875 (hard to find in an applied top)

Wakelee's Camelline
Light amber, 4¾ inches, tooled top, smooth base $20–30
American 1895–1905

Walfox Brand (running fox motif)
Cobalt-blue, 5¾ inches, tooled top, smooth base..................$60–100
American 1890–1900

W.H. Chedic Druggist, Carson City, NEV
Clear, 6 inches, tooled top, smooth base $20–30
American 1874–1891

M. Webster Druggist, Virginia City, NEVADA
Clear, 3½ inches, tooled top, smooth base............................$75–125
American 1861–1883 (extremely rare)

Common medicine
bottle, light blue,
1870–1890.

Williams S.L.K. Formula
Clear, 6 inches $10–15
American 1910–1940

Wm. J. Bryan Apothecary (monogram motif), San Francisco
Medium cobalt-blue, 6¼ inches, tooled top, smooth base.......$50–80
American 1870–1875

W.T. Wenzell, San Francisco
Aqua, 5⅝ inches, applied top...$50–75
American 1870–1875

Wyeth's Apothecary Jar
Amber, 8½ inches, tooled top..$20–30
American 1900–1920

Zerbe's Essence of Life
Aqua, 5¾ inches, tooled top $10–20
American 1890–1900

Milk
Bottles

Collecting milk bottles in recent years has taken on a renewed interest among many collectors. The first patent for a milk bottle was issued in January 1875 to the "Jefferson Co. Milk Assn." The bottle itself featured a tin top with a spring clamping device. The first known standard-shaped milk bottle (post 1930) had a patent date of March 1880 and was made by the Warren Glass Works of Cumberland, Maryland. In 1884, A. V. Whiteman patented a jar with a domed tin cap to be used along with the patent of the Thatcher and Barnhart fastening device for a glass lid. There is no trace, however, of a patent for the bottle itself. Among collectors today, the Thatcher milk bottle is one of the most prized. There are several variations on the original. Very early bottles were embossed with a picture of a Quaker farmer milking his cow while seated on a stool. "Absolutely Pure Milk" is stamped into the glass on the bottle's shoulder.

An important development in the design of the milk bottle was the patent issued to H. P. and S. L. Barnhart for their methods of capping and sealing. Their invention involved the construction of a bottle mouth adapted to receive and retain a wafer disk or cap. It was eventually termed the milk bottle cap and revolutionized the milk bottling industry. Between 1900 and 1920, there were not many new patents on bottles. With the introduction of the Owens Semiautomatic and Automatic Bottle Machines, milk bottles were mass-produced. Between 1921 and 1945, the greatest number of milk bottles were manufactured and used. After 1945, square milk bottles and paper cartons were commonly used.

Half-pint milk, Tonopah, NV, 1900–1920.

Milk bottles reflecting inset paper cap, 1930s.

Of all the milk bottles, there are two types that are of particular interest to the collector. These are the "baby-face," which had an embossed baby's face on the upper part of the neck, and the "cop-the-cream," which had a policeman's head and cap embossed into the neck. Both of these clear-colored bottles, along with their tin tops, are very rare and valuable.

Round Embossed Ambers

Rieck's Buttermilk
Half pint, C. 1900 ....$75

V.M. and I.C. Company—Milk-O
Half pint, C. 1920 ....$50

Harmony Creamery Buttermilk—The Best
10 ounces, Pittsburgh, PA, C.-1900 ....$150

Dolfinger, Phila, PA
Quart, C. 1900 ....$100

Featherstone Farms, Featherstone, VA
Quart, C. 1920 ....$100

Lang's Creamery, Inc., Buffalo, NY
Quart, C. 1930 ....$50

McJunkin's Straight Dairy Company, Pittsburgh, PA
Quart, C. 1910 ....$75

Pure Milk Corp. (Canadian Dairy)
Imperial quart, C. 1920 ....$100

Rieck's, Pittsburgh, PA
Quart, C. 1920 ....$75

Wm. H. Spindler, McKeesport, PA
Quart, C. 1920 ....$75

Wm. Weckerle and Sons, Inc., Buffalo, NY
Quart, C. 1900 ....$25

Peoples Milk Company, Buffalo, NY
Quart, C. 1910 ....$25–40

Service Milk Company, Inc., Buffalo, NY
Quart, C. 1925 ....$75

Rieck's Pure Milk and Cream
Half gallon, C. 1900 ....$200

Round Embossed Greens

Alta Crest Farm, Spencer, MASS
Quart, Henry Kart patent (cow's head), C. 1930 ....$400

Lang's Creamery, Buffalo, NY
Quart, C. 1930 ....$300

Assorted milk
bottles,
1880–1900.

Carrigan's Niagara Dairy Company, Niagara Falls, NY
Quart, C. 1930 ....$400

Weckerle, Buffalo, NY
Quart, C. 1930 ....$200

Cream Separator Milk Bottles

Union Dairy Company, Steubenville, OH
Half pint, C. 1935 ....$100

Lantz Bros Dairy Company, Follansbee, WV
Pint, C. 1935 ....$35–50

Nobles Dairy, Porterville, CA—5 cent Store Bottle
Quart, C. 1935 ....$60

Conrad and Graeber Smile A While Dairy, Sigourney, LA
Quart, C. 1935, embossed $50

Dairymen's League Coop. Assn., Inc.
Quart, C. 1935, embossed $35

Gillette and Sons, Watertown, NY
Quart, C. 1935, embossed $35

Oak Bend Dairy, Beloit, KANS
Quart, C. 1935, embossed..$50

Half-pint Babytops and Cop the Cream

Brookfield Dairy, Hellertown, PA
Half pint, C. 1940 ....$25

Blue-Bell Farm, Cop the Cream, Irvington, NJ
Half pint, C. 1940 ....$70

Flanders Dairy, MASS
Half pint, C. 1950 ....$25

Good-Rich Dairy Products, Mt. Carmel, PA
Half pint, C. 1945, embossed..$25

Quart Round Pyro Babytops

Old Homestead Dairy, Windsor, VT
Quart, C. 1940...$50

Store milk bottle,
1890.

Julius Anderson, Rockland, MA
Quart, C. 1945...$50

Dickson Dairy, Dickson, PA
Quart, C. 1945...$50

Quart Square Pyro Babytops

Fox Dairy, Fostoria, OH
Quart, C. 1950...$25

Sweets Dairy, Fredonia, NY
Quart, C. 1940...$50

Quart Round Embossed Cop the Cream

Highland Dairy, Rochester, NY
Quart, C. 1940...$50

Royal Farms Dairy, Baltimore, MD
Quart, C. 1945...$50

Quart Round Pyro Cop the Cream

Green Acre Dairy, Newport, RI
Quart, C. 1945...$50

Furman Brothers Quality Purity Service, Ithaca, NY
Quart, C. 1940...$50

Matuellas Dairy, Hazeltown, PA
Quart, C. 1940...$40

Roberts Jersey Farm, Norway, ME
Quart, C. 1945...$50

Quart Square Pyro Cop the Cream

Orchard Farm Dairy, Dallas, PA
Quart, C. 1947...$25

Half Gallon

**The Cream Whips Associated Dairies, Milk Cream—
Buttermilk, Los Angeles**
Half gallon, C. 1940 ....$400

Plain Milk Bottle
Half gallon rectangle, twin top, C. 1950 ....$20–50

Quarter Pint
These small bottles were used mostly for cream and sometimes milk for schools.

Biar Cliff Farm
C. 1910 ....$5–10

City Dairy, Ltd., Canadian Imperial
C. 1920 ....$5–20

Clover Farms
C. 1920 ....$5–10

Cloverland Dairy
C. 1940 ....$5–10

Assorted milk bottles,
1880–1900.

Dairymen's League
C. 1940 ....$5–10

Farmers Dairy
C. 1920 ....$5–10

H.E. Booth, Dunkirk, NY
C. 1940 ....$5–10

Haleaka Dairy, Makawaok, HI
C. 1935 ....$10–25

Hamilton Dairies, Ltd., Canadian Imperial
C. 1920 ....$5–20

M. Murry, Buffalo, NY
C. 1910 ....$5–10

Oakland Cream Depot, Oakland, CALIF
C. 1920 ....$20–50

Richmond Dairy, Richmond, VA
C.-1935...$5–10

Sterm and Shewin Dairy, Washington, DC
C. 1935 ....$5–10

Stiplis Willis—Jones
C. 1935 ....$5–10

Western Dairy, Alameda, CALIF
C. 1920 ....$5–10

Hospital Milk Bottles
The dairies did not want to mix the regular bottles with the hospital bottles, which caused these bottles to become quite uncommon, very valuable and collectible.

Baltimore City Hospital, Baltimore, MD
Half pint, C. 1935 ....$5–15

Assorted milk bottles, quarter- to half-pints,
1880–1900.

Johns Hopkins Hospital, Baltimore, MD
Half pint, C. 1935 ....$5–15

Johns Hopkins Hospital, Baltimore, MD
Quart, C. 1940 ....$5–15

Eastern State Hospital
Half pint, C. 1935 ....$5–15

Piedmont Sanatorium
Quart, C. 1930 ....$5–15

Union Memorial Hospital
Quart, C. 1935 ....$5–15

Square Amber
*The square amber milk bottle was used by dairies to contain a special
vitamin D milk. The quart size was the most common, with the pint,
half pint, and half gallon being more rare.*

Taylor's Dairy
Half pint, C. 1950 ....$10

Bellview Dairy, Syracuse, NY
C. 1947 ....$2–5

Borden's with Elsie
C. 1950 ....$5–10

Carnation
C. 1952 ....$5–15

Gratzer Dairy, Syracuse, NY
C. 1950 ....$2–5

Hopewell Dairy, Bellefontaine, OH
C. 1950 ....$5–15

Mohawk Farms, Newington, CONN
C. 1950 ....$5–15

Netherland, Rochester, NY
C. 1950 ....$5–10

Parkside Dairy, East Rochester, NY
C. 1945 ....$3–10

Sun Glo
C. 1950 ....$2–5

UVM
C. 1945 ....$10–30

University of Connecticut
C. 1950 ....$5–10

Creamtops

Lake View Dairy, Ithaca, NY
Pint, C. 1940...$10

Alamito, Omaha's Pioneer Dairy
Quart, C. 1945, two-color...$25

Amhurst Farm Dairy, Buffalo, NY
Quart, C. 1943...$12

Langs, Buffalo, NY
Quart, C. 1923...$8

Meridale Farms, Oneonta, NY
Quart, C. 1935...$10–20

Mountain Meadow Dairy, Bisbee, ARIZONA
Quart, C. 1945, two–color $25

Otto Milk Company, Pittsburgh, PA
Quart, C. 1935..$8

Sky Royal Dairy, Front Royal, VA
Quart, C. 1935...$5–15

The Graduate Milk Bottle
Quart, C. 1935..$10–20

Thompson Dairy, Washington, DC
Quart, C. 1945..$8

Union Dairy, Sacramento, CA
C. 1950, squat type $25

Miscellaneous Milk Bottles

Lester Milk Company
C. 1885..$200

Clermont Pure Milk, Columbia Co., NY
C. 1885..$200

Original Thatcher
Quart, C. 1884..$100

Chicago Sterilized Milk Company, Chicago, IL
Quart, C. 1880..$50

Condensed Milk Company, Property of New York
Quart, C. 1885..$75

Coffee creamers, clear and milk glass, 1890–1920.

Willowbrook Stock Farm
Quart, C. 1890 ....$75

John Coe, Winchester, VA
Quart, C. 1890 ....$75

Wards Alderney Milk Assn.
Pint, C. 1892 ....$500

A.G. Smalley, Pat. Apld. For
Half pint, C. 1895 ....$300

Dr. Brush's Farm, Milk for Infants
C. 1890 ....$150

McCann and Company, Right from the Churn Buttermilk
Two quarts, C. 1890 ....$200

McJunkin-Straight Dairy Company Buttermilk
Two quarts, C. 1890 ....$200

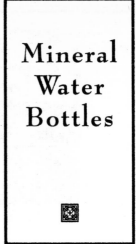

Mineral Water Bottles

The drinking of water from mineral springs was very popular for a full century, with the peak period falling between 1860 and 1900. The majority of collectible bottles were produced during these years. Although the shapes and sizes of mineral water bottles are not very creative, the lettering and design, both embossed and paper, are bold and interesting. Mineral bottles can range in size from 7 inches up to 14 inches. Most were cork stopped, manufactured in a variety of colors, and embossed with the name of the glasshouse manufacturer and an eagle.

B.R. Lippincott and Company, Stockton Superior Mineral Water, Union Glass Works
Cobalt-blue, 7⅜ inches, applied top, iron pontil.................$400–600
American 1852–1858 (extremely rare)

Buffalo Mineral Water, Springs Nature Materia Medica (motif of lady sitting on stool) Trademark
Yellow, 10½ inches..$50–100
American 1910–1920 (rare in this color)

C.A. Reiners and Company, 723 Turk Street, S.F.— Improved, Trademark (moon and stars motif), Mineral Water
Aqua, 7 inches, applied top, smooth base $50–100
American 1875–1882

Schweppes
Mineral Water,
1890.

C.A. Reiners and Company, S.F.—Improved Mineral Water, Trademark (moon and stars motif)

Light lime-green, 7 inches, applied top $200–400
American 1873–1875 only (fewer than 5 known without an address)

C.A. Reiners and Company, 723 Turk Street, S.F.— Improved, Trademark (moon and stars motif), Mineral Water

Green-aqua, 7 inches, applied top, smooth base $40–80
American 1875–1882

C.A. Reiners and Company, San Francisco—Improved Mineral Water (moon and three stars motif)

Aqua, 7⅛ inches, applied top, smooth base $200–300
American 1873–1875 only (fewer than 6 known without an address)

Clark and White, New York

Emerald-green, pint, applied top, smooth base $70–100
American 1856–1866

Clark and White, "C," New York

Dark olive-green, pint, applied top, smooth base $30–50
American 1860–1866

Clark and White, "C," New York

Olive-green, quart, applied top, smooth base $30–60
American 1860–1866

C.A. Reiners and Company,
723 Turk Street, S.F.,
Improved Mineral Water,
1875–1882.

Clark and White, NY, "N 1 1"
Olive-green, 7½ inches, applied top, pontiled $400–600
American 1856–1860 (extremely rare)

Congress Spring Company, "C," Saratoga, NY, Congress Water
Dark blue-green, pint, applied top, smooth base...................$30–60
American 1885–1889

D.A. Knowlton, Saratoga, NY
Olive-green, pint, applied top, smooth base........................$75–150
American 1861–1863

D.A. Knowlton, Saratoga, NY
Dark forest-green, quart, applied top, smooth base............$150–250
American 1861–1863

Excelsior Spring, Saratoga, NY
Emerald-green, pint, applied top, smooth base $65–100
American 1865–1870

Guilford Mineral ("G W & S W" in circle), Guilford, VT, Spring Water
Dark blue-green, quart, applied top, smooth base..............$100–150
American 1865–1875

Haas Brothers Natural Mineral Water—Napa Soda
Dark aqua, 7¼ inches, applied top, smooth base.................$75–100
American 1873–1890

Hathorn Spring, Saratoga, NY
Dark blue-green, pint, applied top, smooth base...................$40–80
American 1864–1889

Hathorn Spring, Saratoga, NY
Olive-amber, pint, applied top, smooth base.........................$40–80
American 1864–1889

Hathorn Spring, Saratoga, NY
Dark blue-green, quart, applied top, smooth base...............$50–100
American 1864–1889

Hathorn Spring, Saratoga, NY
Light golden amber, quart, applied top...............................$75–125
American 1864–1889

High Rock Congress Spring (rock motif), "C & W," Saratoga, NY
Emerald-green, pint, applied top, smooth base $75–150
American 1860–1870

J. Boardman—New York—Mineral Waters (star motif), This Bottle Is Never Sold
Sapphire-blue, 7½ inches, applied top, iron pontil.............$300–400
American 1850–1860 (rare in this color)

Lynde and Putnam Mineral Waters, San Francisco, CA, Union Glass Works, Philadelphia
Teal-blue, 7½ inches, applied top, iron pontil $175–225
American 1850–1851

Massena Spring Water (monogram, bird in frame motif)
Turquoise-blue, quart, applied top, smooth base $125–200
American 1875–1885 (extremely rare in this color)

McCauley Mineral Water, Phila
Dark blue-green, 7 inches, applied top, iron pontil............$150–250
American 1850–1860

Middletown Healing Springs, Gray and Clark, Middletown, VT
Orange-amber, quart, applied top, smooth base.....................$35–65
American 1865–1875

Mineral Waters
Emerald-green, 7¼ inches, applied top, iron pontil................$50–75
American 1844–1850

Napa Soda, Phil Caduc, Natural Mineral Water
Blue-aqua, 7 inches, applied top, smooth base.......................$40–70
American 1873–1881

Napa Soda—Natural Mineral Water, "T.A.W."
Dark blue-green, 7¼ inches, applied top, smooth base $125–175
American 1861–1862

Napa Soda, Phil Caduc, Natural Mineral Water
Green-aqua, 7½ inches, applied top, smooth base $40–60
American 1873–1881

Natural Mineral Water, "F.M.," Vallejo—Jackson's Napa Soda Spring's
Light aqua, 7 inches, applied top, smooth base $200–400
American 1873–1880 (fewer than 5 known)

Oak Orchard Acid Spring's—"Address G.W. Merchant," Lockport, NY
Dark blue-green, quart, applied top, smooth base................$50–100
American 1860–1870

Roussel's Mineral Water, Manufactured in Silver—Dyottville Glass Works, Phila., Silver Medal 1847 Awarded, This Bottle Is Never Sold
Dark blue-green, 7¼ inches, applied top, iron pontil..........$125–175
American 1847–1855

Samuel's Soda Spring's—Natural Mineral Water, "Trade a Mark"
Aqua, 7⅛ inches, applied top, smooth base $75–100
American 1873–1890

Stirling's Magnetic Mineral Spring, Eaton Rapids, MI
Light amber, quart, applied top, smooth base $75–125
American 1860–1865 (rare in this color)

Tahoe Soda Springs—Natural Mineral Water (base: "Registered"), Tahoe, CA
Aqua, 7 inches, tooled top $125–175
Amerian 1902–1906 (extremely rare)

Tolenas Soda Spring—Natural Mineral Water
Aqua, 7 inches, applied top, smooth base $30–60
European 1885–1910

W. Lant and Company, Coventry—Registery (monogram motif) Trademark
Aqua, 7½ inches, applied top, smooth base $30–60
American 1885–1910

Walter's Napa County Soda—Mineral Water from Walter's Soda Springs, Trademark (horseshoe motif) (base: "Herve Somps Agts")
Dark aqua, 6¾ inches, tooled top $50–100
American 1890–1891 (made for one year only)

White Pelican Water (acid etched), White Pelican (pelican holding bottle motif), Mineral Spring Company, Klamath Falls, OREGON
Clear, 12 inches, tooled top $75–125
Austrian 1900–1920 (rare)

Williams and Severance, San Francisco, CA—Soda and Mineral Waters
Green, 7⅞ inches, applied top, iron pontil $200–300
American 1852–1854

Zatembo Mineral Springs, ALASKA—Bottle Not to Be Sold
Aqua, 7½ inches, tooled top, smooth base.........................$150–250
American 1900–1910

W. Lant and Company, Coventry—Registery; Tolenas Soda Springs, Natural Mineral Water, 1885–1910.

Pattern-Molded Bottles

A pattern-molded bottle is one that is blown into a ribbed or otherwise patterned mold. This group includes globular and chestnut flasks. One of these, the Stiegel bottle, manufactured during the late eighteenth century, is considered very rare and valuable. The two types of Stiegel bottles manufactured at the Stiegel Glass Factory are the Diamond daisy and Hexagon designs.

Since pattern-molded bottles are among the more valuable and rare pieces, collectors need to familiarize themselves with the types, sizes, colors, and the various manufacturers of these bottles.

Beehive Bottle
Aqua, 8¾ inches, 16 swirled ribs $70–90

Beehive Bottle
Blue-aqua, 8¼ inches, 24 swirled ribs.................................$600–800

Beehive Bottle
Golden amber, 9⅞ inches, 26 vertical ribs...................$1,400–1,800

Beehive Bottle
Medium green, 9 inches, 31 vertical ribs......................$1,800–2,200

Chestnut Flask
Pink-amethyst, 5½ inches, 21–diamond pattern $250–350

Chestnut Flask
Medium golden amber, 5¾ inches, 10–diamond pattern....$2,500–3,000

Chestnut Flask
Tobacco yellow-amber, 6¼ inches, 14 ribs swirled to left ...$200–300

Chestnut Flask
Colorless, 6 inches, 16-expanded-diamond pattern $25–30

Chestnut Flask
Yellow-amber, 6½ inches, 18 swirled ribs...........................$250–350

Chestnut Flask
Light green, 6⅞ inches, 18 swirled ribs...............................$100–125

Chestnut Flask
Light green-aqua, 6 inches, 20 vertical ribs $90–100

Chestnut Flask
Red-amber, 5¼ inches, 24-rib broken-swirl pattern......$1,000–1,500

Chestnut Flask
Red-amber, 5½ inches, 24 swirled ribs $250–300

Chestnut Flask
Golden amber, 4¾ inches, 24 vertical ribs $225–250

Chestnut Flask
Light green, 7½ inches, 24 vertical ribs...............................$100–125

Chestnut Flask
Colorless, 3⅞ inches, 32 vertical ribs...................................$70–100

Chestnut Flask
Medium yellow-amber, 6⅞ inches, unpatterned $90–120

Club Bottle
Aqua, 8 inches, 16 vertical ribs $125–150

Club Bottle
Light green, 9 inches, 24 swirled ribs, flattened $350–450

Cruet
Colorless, 8 inches, 14 ribs, blown handle $125–150

Flask
Black glass with white spots, 4¾ inches, 13-rib mold $250–300

Flask
Clear green, two-piece mold, 18 vertical heavy ribs $125–150

Flask
Cobalt, 4 inches, 20 swirled ribs, flattened oval shape $200–300

Flask
Golden amber, 6⅛ inches, 24 vertical ribs..........................$350–450

Flask or Nurser
Green-aqua, 7½ inches, 12-diamond pattern..........................$50–75

Flask or Nurser
Pale green, 8 inches, teardrop shape, diamond pattern $60–90

Flask, Pocket
Golden amber, 4¾ inches, free-blown $90–120

Globular
Aqua, 7¾ inches, 16 swirled ribs...$80–100

Globular Bottle
Aqua, 7 inches, 18 vertical ribs $200–225

Globular Bottle
Light green, 7⅛ inches, 24 swirled ribs..................................$40–60

Globular Bottle
Medium citron, 7⅛ inches, 24 swirled ribs..................$2,500–3,000

Globular Bottle
Medium golden amber, 7¾ inches, 24 swirled ribs.............$450–650

Globular Bottle
Medium amber, 7⅛ inches, 24 swirled ribs $300–350

Globular Bottle
Aqua, 9⅛ inches, 24 swirled ribs...$20–30

Globular Bottle
Aqua, 7½ inches, 24 swirled ribs $100–125

Globular Bottle
Medium yellow-amber, 7⅜ inches, 24 swirled ribs.............$350–450

Grandfathers Flask
Deep orange-amber, 8 inches, 24 vertical ribs.................$800–1,000

Pinch Bottle
Cobalt-blue, 9¾ inches, 24 swirled ribs.............................$350–450

Pocket Bottle
Medium amethyst, 7⅞ inches, 16 vertical ribs $125–150

Pumpkin Flask
Deep olive-green, pint, 20 vertical ribs...............................$350–450

Ribbed Handled Jug
Aqua, 5⅜ inches, 16 ribs $175–225

Ribbed Toilet Water Bottle
Amethyst, 6 inches, 16 vertical ribs.............................$1,500–2,000

Stiegel Type
Deep amethyst, 5½ inches, 20 diamond cells over flutes...$3,000–4,000

Stiegel Type
Deep amethyst, 5½ inches, 12-diamond oval pattern....$3,500–4,500

Stiegel Type
Colorless with purple tint, 6 inches, daisy and hexagon
pattern $600–900

Stiegel Type
Medium red-amethyst, 5½ inches, diamond daisy........$3,000–4,000

Pickle Bottles

The pickle bottle is one of the largest of bottles, with a wide mouth and being square or cylindrical shape. While the pickle bottle was unique in design, its color was almost exclusively aqua, with occasional multicolored bottles. When looking through ghost town dumps and digging behind older pioneer homes, you're sure to find pickle bottles in great numbers since pickles were a common and well-liked food, especially in the mining communities.

One of the more common and popular types among collectors is the cathedral design, with Gothic-style window panels on the sides of the bottle.

Cathedral
Aqua, 6⅜ inches, square with lattice design..........................$75–125

Cathedral
Rich emerald-green, 8⅛ inches, rolled lip, iron pontil $400–600
American 1855–1865

Cathedral
Aqua, 8¾ inches, square...$30–50

Cathedral
Green-aqua, 8¾ inches, square with diamond lattice on three
panels $125–175

Cathedral
Deep aqua, 8⅞ inches, square with large star on panels......$350–450

Six-sided cathedral
pickle bottle,
1860–1870.

Cathedral
Deep aqua, 9 inches, six-sided $150–200

Cathedral
Aqua, 13 inches, six-sided $125–175

Cathedral
Deep emerald-green, 12 inches, rolled lip, iron pontil $500–800
American 1855–1865

G.P. Sanborn and Son/Union Brand, Boston Pickles
Yellow-amber, 5 inches...$110–140

G.P. Sanborn and Son/Union Brand, Boston Pickles
Aqua, 5 inches $50–60

Heinz and Noble, Pittsburgh, PA
Deep aqua, 7⅞ inches...$60–70
American 1870–1875

Heinz and Noble, Pittsburgh, PA
Aqua, 8¼ inches, applied mouth, smooth base.....................$100–150
American 1870–1875 (one of the earlier Heniz bottles)

JM Clark and Company—Louisville, KY
Yellow-amber, 8½ inches..$60–90

JM Clark and Company—Louisville, KY
Yellow-amber, 5¼ inches..$40–60

Milwaukee Pickle Company, Wauwatosa, WI
Orange-amber, 12⅝ inches...$200–250

Milwaukee Pickle Company, Wauwatosa, WI
Yellow-amber, 9⅝ inches..$100–125

Sanborn, Parker and Company, Union Brand, Boston Pickles
Yellow-olive, 8⅛ inches...$250–300

Skilton Foote and Company, Bunker Hill Pickles
Medium amber, 11¼ inches $350–450

Skilton Foote and Company, Bunker Hill Pickles
Olive-yellow, 7⅞ inches $100–125

Skilton Foote and Company, Bunker Hill Pickles
Aqua, 5⅜ inches $14–16

Sol Wangenheim and Company, San Francisco
Aqua, 11¼ inches $30–50

T.B. Smith and Company—Philad
Aqua, 10⅝ inches $40–60

T.B. Smith and Company—Philad
Emerald-blue-green, 8⅞ inches $650–750

W. Numsen and Son—Baltimore
Aqua, 10⅜ inches $350–450

Wells and Miller, New York
Medium emerald-green, 6⅜ inches......................................$250–350

Wells and Miller and Provost
Aqua, 11½ inches...$250–300

W.K. Lewis and Company—Boston, Cathedral
Bright green, 10¼ inches..$120–150

WM Underwood and Company, Boston
Medium emerald, 11½ inches...$500–750

WM Underwood and Company, Boston
Aqua, 11⅜ inches...$225–300

Poison
Bottles

Poison bottles are a unique category for collecting by the very nature of their contents. While most people assume that poison bottles are plain, the fact is that most are very decorative in order to make them easily identifiable as containers of toxic substances. Around 1853, the American Pharmaceutical Association recommended laws for identification of all poison bottles. In 1872, the American Medical Association also recommended that poison bottles be identified with a rough surface on one side and the word *poison* on the other. As so often happened during that era, passing of these laws was very difficult and the manufacturers were left to do whatever they wanted. Because a standard wasn't established, a varied group of bottle shapes, sizes, and patterns were manufactured, including the skull and crossbones, or skulls, leg bones, and coffins.

These bottles were manufactured with quilted or ribbed surfaces and diamond/lattice–type patterns for identification by touch. Colorless bottles are very rare since most poison bottles were produced in dark shades of blue and brown, another identification aid. When collecting these bottles, caution must be exercised since it is not uncommon to find a poison bottle with its original contents. If the bottle has the original glass stopper the value will greatly increase.

Ammonia, Manufactured by S.F. Gaslight Company
Aqua, 7¾ inches, tooled top..$20–40
American 1885–1895

Poison—Bowman's Drug Stores—Poison (base: "2/C.L.G. Co., Patent Appl'd For")
Dark cobalt-blue, 4 inches, tooled top $250–350
American 1900–1910 (extremely rare with label)

Poison—Bowman's Drug Stores—Poison (base: "4/C.L.G. Co., Patend Applied For")
Cobalt-blue, 5 inches, tooled top, smooth base $300–400
American 1895–1905, Oakland, CA

Gift (six-sided, skull and crossbones motif)
Light aqua, 8 inches, tooled top, smooth base......................$30–60
German 1900–1910

Guarantee Stamp Calvert's Extra Pure Carbolic Acid (arrow wheel motif)
Dark amber, 7¾ inches, tooled top $75–100
American 1890–1910

Gift—poison bottle (German), 1900–1910.

Poison—H.K. Mulford Company, Chemist, Philadelphia, cobalt-blue, 1900–1910.

Poison—H.K. Mulford Company Chemists, Philadelphia, Poison (skull and crossbones motif)
Cobalt-blue, 3⅛ inches, tooled top $100–150
American 1900–1910

Poison, Manufactured Only by the Merrimac Chemical Company, Boston, U.S.A. 5 pounds, Swift's Arseate of Lead
White and black, 6¼ inches...$75–125
American 1910–1920

The Owl Drug Company (owl motif), Poison
Cobalt-blue, 2¾ inches, tooled top $125–175
American 1892–1900 (owl motif is in the slug plate)

The Owl Drug Company (owl motif), Poison
Cobalt-blue, 2⅞ inches, tooled top, smooth base.................$60–100
American 1905–1915

The Owl Drug Company (owl motif), Poison
Cobalt-blue, 3¼ inches, tooled top $75–125
American 1892–1895

The Owl Drug Company (owl motif), Poison
Cobalt-blue, 4¼ inches, tooled top, smooth base...............$100–150
American 1895–1905

The Owl Drug Company (owl motif), San Francisco, Chicago, New York, Los Angeles—Poison
Clear, 9¾ inches, tooled top $50–100
American 1900–1935

The Owl Drug Company (owl motif), San Francisco, Chicago, New York, Los Angeles—Poison
Cobalt-blue, 3½ inches, tooled top $50–100
American 1900–1935

The Owl Drug Company (owl motif), Poison ˅
Cobalt-blue, 5 inches, two-wing poison............................$150–250
American 1910–1930 (extremely rare)

The Owl Drug Company (owl motif), Poison
Cobalt-blue, 5⅛ inches, tooled top $175–275
American 1895–1910 (this size hard to find)

The Owl Drug Company (owl motif), Poison
Cobalt-blue, 5⅛ inches, tooled top $400–500
American 1892–1900 (owl motif is in slug plate, hard to find in this size)

The Owl Drug Comapny (owl motif), Poison
Cobalt-blue, 7⅞ inches, tooled top $500–600
American 1895–1905

The Owl Drug Company (owl motif), San Francisco, Poison
Emerald-green, 9½ inches, tooled top $35–55
American 1900–1908

The Owl Drug Company (owl motif), San Francisco, Poison
Cobalt, 3¼ inches, tooled top $35–55
American 1900–1908

Poison (base: "E.R.S.& S.")
Cobalt-blue, 2¾ inches, tooled top, smooth base.................$75–125
American 1900–1910 (rare)

Poison (figural of a skeleton)
Brown, black, and white pottery, 6⅞ inches $150–250
Japanese 1915–1925

Poison—Poison
Light cobalt-blue, 3 inches..$40–60
American 1930–1940

Poison—Poison
Cobalt-blue, 3⅛ inches..$60–100
American 1920–1930

Poison—Poison
Cobalt-blue, 2⅝ inches..$60–100
American 1920–1930

Poison—Poison (base: "#4 C.L.G. Co. Patent Applied For")
Emerald-green, 5 inches, irregular hexagon $100–150
American 1900–1910

Poisonous, Not to Be Taken—"R D No 590540"
Dark cobalt-blue, 4¼ inches $30–60
European 1890–1910

Poisonous, Not to be Taken (base: "16")
Dark cobalt-blue, 8 inches, ground top, smooth base.........$100–150
European 1890–1910

Poison—Poison (base: "#8 C.L.G. Co. Patent Applied For")
Cobalt-blue, 6¼ inches, irregular hexagon..........................$150–250
American 1900–1910

Poison, Quilt Pattern (base: "U.S.P.H.S.")
Dark cobalt-blue, 4⅜ inches, tooled top $1,750–2,250
American 1880–1890 (possibly only one known in this size with
large mouth)

Quilted Poison
Cobalt-blue, 4¾ inches, tooled top, smooth base....................$20–40
American 1890–1910

Assortment of various poisons, 1900–1920.

Poison, Quilt Pattern (base: "U.S.P.H.S.")
Cobalt-blue, 5⅛ inches, tooled top $100–150
American 1880–1890 (rarer of the quilt pattern poisons)

Poison, Quilt Pattern (base: "U.S.P.H.S.")
Cobalt-blue, 5⅜ inches, tooled top $750–1,000
American 1880–1890 (extremely rare with wide mouth, fewer than 5 known)

Traveling Embalming Kit with Two Large Poisons, One Has "OZ" on It, Other Has "Champion Embalming Fluid, The Champion Chemical Company, Springfield Ohio, Poison" and "8 oz thru 56 oz."
Clear, 8¾ inches, tooled top $400–600
American 1900–1910

Sarsaparilla Bottles

Sarsaparilla was another "cure-all" elixir which actually fit into the group of the Cures or Bitters category. In the seventeenth century sarsaparilla was touted as a blood purifier and later as a cure for the dreaded disease of syphilis. The drink itself became popular in the United States in the 1820s as a cure-all for a number of different ailments. As time passed, sarsaparilla became nothing more than the "snake oil" sold at medicine shows. One of the most popular brands among collectors is Doctor Townsend, which was advertised as "The most extraordinary medicine in the World." Usually, these bottles are aqua or green. Blues and darker colors are rarer.

A.H. Bull—Extract of Sarsaparilla, Hartford, CONN
Aqua, 6¾ inches, applied top, open pontil $75–150
American 1845–1855

Bristol's—Genuine Sarsaparilla, New York
Aqua, 10⅜ inches, tooled top, smooth base..........................$50–100
American 1885–1895

Brown's Sarsaparilla for the Kidneys, Liver and Blood
Aqua, 9⅛ inches, tooled top $40–80
American 1884–1894

Dalton's Sarsaparilla and Nerve Tonic, Belfast, ME, U.S.A.
Aqua, 9 inches, tooled top $75–125
American 1893–1902

Dr. Cronk
Brown and tan pottery, 10¾ inches $75–125
American 1888–1894

**Dr. Guysott's—Yellow Dock and Sarsaparilla, B and P,
New York**
Aqua, 7⅞ inches, applied top, smooth base $100–150
American 1860–1870

**Dr. Myer's Vegetable Extract Sarsaparilla Wild Cherry
Dandelion, Buffalo, NY**
Dark aqua, 9½ inches, applied top, iron pontil...................$100–200
American 1850–1860

Dr. Townsend's Sarsaparilla, Albany, NY
Emerald-green, 9½ inches, tooled top, smooth base $75–100
American 1885–1895

Dr. Townsend's Sarsaparilla, Albany, NY
Dark blue-green, 9⅜ inches, applied top, open pontil $100–150
American 1845–1855

**Foley's Sarsaparilla, Mfd. by Foley and Company,
Chicago, U.S.A.**
Amber, 9¼ inches, tooled top..$75–100
American 1890–1895

John Bull—Extract of Sarsaparilla, Louisville, KY
Dark aqua, 9 inches, applied top, smooth base $100–150
American 1860–1865

Levings and Company's—Sarsaparilla and Rose Willow
Aqua, 7½ inches, tooled top, smooth base..........................$200–300
American 1892–1894 only, San Francisco

Log Cabin—Sarsaparilla, Rochester, NY (base: "Pat. Sept. 6, 87")
Olive-amber, 9 inches, applied top $125–175
American 1887–1892

Rush's Sarsaparilla and Iron, A.H. Flanders, M.D., New York
Aqua, 8⅝ inches, applied top, smooth base $40–80
American 1872–1882

Sands' Sarsaparilla—Genuine—New York
Pale aqua, 10 inches, applied top, open pontil $75–150
American 1840–1850

The Honduras Company's—Compound Extra Sarsaparilla—Abram's and Carrol Sole Agents, San Francisco
Aqua, 9⅝ inches, applied top, smooth base $100–150
American 1876–1880 (rare)

Wynkoop's Katharismic Sarsaparilla, New York
Cobalt-blue, 9¾ inches, applied top, iron pontil..............$500–1,000
American 1845–1855

Yager's Sarsaparilla
Amber, 8½ inches, tooled top, smooth base $75–125
American 1896–1900

Snuff Bottles

Snuff was basically comprised of tobacco mixed with ingredients of salt, different scents, and flavors such as cinnamon and nutmeg. It was usually mixed in a powder form, and inhaling snuff was much more fashionable than smoking or chewing tobacco. It was yet another substance touted as a cure-all, in this case for sinus problems, headaches, and numerous other problems.

Most of the snuff bottles from the eighteenth and early nineteenth centuries were embossed, dark brown or black, with straight sides. They were either square or rectangular in shape, with beveled edges and narrow bodies with wide mouths. In the latter part of the nineteenth century, the bottles were colorless or aqua and rectangular or cylindrical, with occasional embossing and possibly labels.

Doctor Marshall's Snuff
Aqua, 3⅓ inches, labeled $50–75

E. Roome, Troy, NEW YORK
Olive-green, 4½ inches...$150–175

E. Roome, Troy, NEW YORK
Olive-amber, 4½ inches...$150–200

E. Roome, Troy, NEW YORK
Pale blue-green, 4¼ inches $550–750

Garrett Snuff Company
Blown by mouth, 4 inches $5–7

Hockin, Duke Street, London
Dark olive-green, 4 inches, applied top, pontil...................$150–250
English 1840–1860

Levi Garrett and Sons
Amber, 4⅜ inches...$175–225

Otto Landsberg and Company, Celebrated Snuff
Cobalt, 5 inches $20–25

Railroad Mill Snuff
Amber, 4½ inches..$10–15

Rectangular, with Beveled Edges
Olive-amber, 6¼ inches..$30–40

Snuff
Medium olive-green, 4⅛ inches, sheared top, open pontil......$30–50
American 1850–1860

Square Snuff Bottle
Yellow-amber, 4 inches...$125–150

True Cephalic Snuff by the King's Patent
Aqua, 3¾ inches...$150–200

True Cephalic Snuff by the King's Patent
Deep aqua, 3½ inches...$150–175

Wyman's Copenhagen Snuff
Amber, quart...$60–80

Soda Bottles

After years of selling, buying, and trading, I think that the soda bottle supports one of the largest collector groups in the United States. Even collectors who don't normally seek out soda bottles always seem to have a few on their tables for sale (or under the table).

Soda bottles, as a rule, are not unique in design since the manufacturers had the task of producing bottles as cheaply as possible to keep up with demand. The only way to distinquish between bottles is by the lettering, logos, embossing, or labels (not very common).

Soda is basically artificially flavored or unflavored carbonated water. In 1772, an Englishman named Joseph Priestley succeeded in defining the process of carbonation. Small quantities of unflavored soda were sold by Professor Benjamin Silliman in 1806. By 1810, New York druggists were selling homemade seltzer as a cure-all for stomach problems. By 1881, flavoring was included in these seltzers.

The first commercially sold soda was Imperial Inca Cola, its name inspired by the Native American Indian, which promoted medical benefits. The first truly successful cola drink was developed in 1886 by Dr. John Styth Pemberton of Atlanta, Georgia. It's known today as Coca-Cola. Carbonated water was added to Coca-Cola in 1887. By 1894, bottled Coca-Cola was taking off. The familiar design of the Coke bottle as we now know it was designed in 1915 by Alex Samuelson. Numerous inventors attempted to ride on the coattails of Coke's success. The most successful of these inventors was Caleb Bradham, who started Brad's drink in 1890, and in 1896 changed its name to Pep-Kola. In 1898, it was changed to Pipi-Cola, and by 1906 to Pepsi-Cola. The taste war goes on today.

With the advent of the soda bottle and the use of carbonation, the age of closure inventions set in. Various entrepreneurs developed the Hutchinson-type wire stoppers, lighting stoppers, and cod stoppers.

A. Hubener, 97 and 99 West 24th Street, New York
Aqua, 7¼ inches, applied top, smooth base $40–60
American 1860–1865

A.J. Wintle and Sons, Bill Mills, N.R. Ross
Aqua, 9½ inches, applied top, smooth base $30–60
European 1880–1900

Chronology of the Coca-Cola bottles, 1894–1975.

(left to right) 1) Hutchinson-Style Bottle: Type unit in which Coca-Cola was first bottled in 1894 by Joseph A. Biedenharn, Vicksburg, Mississippi–the first Bottler of Coca-Cola. 2) Hutchinson-Style Bottle used 1899–1902: This style bottle was used briefly by Bottlers of Coca-Cola after November 1899 and before 1903. 3 and 4) Straight-sided bottle with the trade-mark Coca-Colar embossed in glass: Type unit designed for crown closures and distributed with the diamond-shaped label between 1900–1916, inclusive. Both flint and amber bottles were used by the Bottlers of Coca-Cola during this period. 5) The first glass package for Coca-Cola using classic contour design and introduced into the market in 1916. 6 and 7) Two successive designs with patent revisions used between 1923 (patent date: December 25, 1923) and 1951 when the 1937 patent (number D-105529) expired. In 1960, the contour design for the bottle was registered as a trademark. 8) Applied Color Label, for trade-mark Coca-Cola on panels, introduced on all sizes of classic contour bottles for Coca-Cola in 1957 and continued thereafter. 9) The no-return, or one-way glass bottle, first introduced in 1961; later modified for twist-top. 10) Experimental plastic 10-oz. package for Coca-Cola in classic contour design with twist-top cap; tested, 1970–1975. This package not in general circulation, Spring, 1975.

Coca-Cola
Bottling Works,
Petersburg, VA—
Trade Mark
Registered,
1900–1910.

A.J. Wintle and
Sons, Bill Mills,
N.R. Ross,
1880–1900.

A.J. Wintle and Sons, Bill Mills, N.R. Ross
Yellow, 6 inches, applied top, smooth base $25–50
European 1880–1900

A.W. Cudworth and Company, San Francisco
Blue-green, 7¼ inches, applied top, smooth base...................$40–60
American 1859–1861

A.W. Cudworth and Company, San Francisco
Green, 7 inches, applied top, iron pontil............................$150–250
American 1856–1860 (rarer of the pontiled Cudworths)

A.W. Cudworth and Company, San Francisco, CA
Green, 7¼ inches, applied top, iron pontil $125–175
American 1856–1860

A.W. Meyer, 1885, Savannah, GA
Blue-green, 7¼ inches, applied top, smooth base................$100–200
American 1885–1890

Flasks:
Hunter-Fisherman 1850–1860;
Eagle 1850–1860.

Label under glass whiskeys:
multi-colored lady
1900–1910; "A Merry
Christmas And Happy New
Year—Good Luck"
1900–1910; pink and brown
colored lady 1890–1910.

Flasks: Wormser Bros., San Francisco 1867–1872; WestFord Glass
Co., Sheaf of Grain 1860–1865; Cornucopia-Urn 1845–1855; Eagle-
Eagle 1840–1860; Washington-Jackson 1830–1850.

Collection of barber bottles: first three 1890–1910; last two 1900–1920.

Variety of medicine bottles: A.H. Smith & Co. 1880–1885; Caswell Mark & Co. 1861–1868; The New York Pharmacal Association 1880–1888; NY Pharmacal Association 1874–1880; NY Medical University 1870–1875; Farmers Horse Medicine 1880–1890; J & C Maguire, Chemist & Druggist 1860–1865; "Dr. J. J. Hogan, Next To Post Office" 1890–1895; Mayhew & Wenzell, San Francisco 1869–1874.

Assortment of Owl Drug Store bottles and lids 1890–1900.

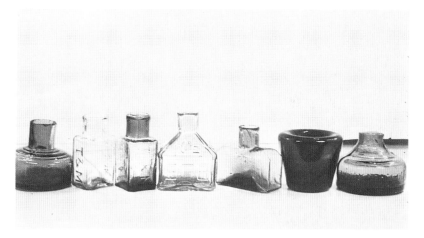

Assortment of various ink bottles 1850–1870.

Assortment of various medicine and poison bottles 1860–1910.

Assortment of soda and mineral waters: Heiss Philada, Union Glass Works 1850–1860; Mineral Waters 1844–1850, B.R. Lippincott & Co. 1852–1858; Safford Bottling Works, Safford Arizona, Distilled Soda Water Co. of Alaska 1890–1906; E.L. Billing's Sac City–Geyser Soda 1872–1879; Southwick & Tupper–New York 1845–1855.

Assortment of soda bottles 1850–1880.

Assortment of whiskey bottles and medicine bottles: Simmond's Nabob Trade 1879–1887; W.H. Spears & Co., Old Pioneer Whiskey 1875–1878; Valentine Hassmer's Lung & Cough Syrup 1877–1880; Wm. H. Spears & Co., Pioneer Whiskey 1882–1890; Thistle Dew Whiskey 1879–1885.

R.L. Higgins Master Ink, Virginia City, NV 1875.

R.L. Higgins Inks, Virginia City, NV 1875; Aqua Master Ink, Aqua Cone, and Amber Master Ink.

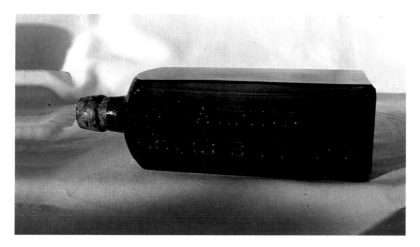

Alpine Herb Bitters, NV 1875.

W.S. Wright Sodas, Virginia City, NV 1861–1869.

Thos. Taylor & Co., Importers, Virginia City, NV 1867–1883.

G.P. Morrill, Virginia City, NV 1863–1874.

James Dwar Hutchinsons, Elko, NV 1872–1876.

Pearson Bros. Hutchinson, Bodie, CA 1870.

Almeda Soda Water Company (acid etched) (shaking hands motif) Oakland, CA
Clear, 12 inches, tooled top $50–100
Austrian 1895–1915 (rare)

Arizona Bottling Works, Phoenix, ARIZONA
Aqua, 6¾ inches, tooled top $10–20
American 1900–1920

Arizona Bottling Works, Phoenix, ARIZONA
Aqua, 7¾ inches, tooled top..$20–35
American 1900–1915

B.J. McGee Benicia
Dark blue-aqua, 7¼ inches, applied top, smooth base $75–125
American 1867

Babb and Company, San Francisco, CAL
Blue-green, 7⅜ inches, applied top, iron pontil $100–200
American 1852–1854

Barcal
Amber, quart, tooled top..$15–30
American 1902–1940

Bay City Soda Water Company (antler motif), S F (large star motif)
Cobalt-blue, 7¼ inches, applied top, smooth base $100–150
American 1871–1880

Bay City Soda Water Company (antler motif), S F (large star motif)
Medium cobalt-blue, 7¼ inches, applied top, smooth base $80–120
American 1871–1880

Boley and Company, Sasc City, CA—Union Glass Works, Philad
Cobalt-blue, 7¼ inches, applied top, iron pontil.................$150–250
American 1850–1862

T & H (soda), Sonoma, CA (gravitating stopper, extremely rare), 1864–1865.

Lancaster Glass Works, NY, 1850–1860.

Bremenkamph and Regli, Eureka, NEV
Aqua, 7 inches, tooled top, smooth base $150–250
American 1875–1900

Buffalo Bottling Company, Reno, NEV
Aqua, 7⅛ inches $125–175
American 1910–1915 (seldom seen)

**Carbonated Water Bottled by National Soda Works
(acid etched) (horseshoe motif), Stockton, CAL**
Clear, 11¾ inches, tooled top $50–100
Austrian 1900–1910

Champagne—Mead (8 sided)
Aqua, 7¼ inches, applied top, smooth base $60–100
American 1862–1872

Champagne—Mead (8 sided)
Dark aqua, 7⅜ inches, applied top, smooth base $40–80
American 1871–1872 only

City Bottling Works, Detroit, MI—C. Norris
Dark aqua, 7¼ inches, applied top, smooth base $75–150
American 1860–1865 (rare)

Clarke and White, New York
Dark green, 7¼ inches, applied top, smooth base $25–50
American 1860–1873

Clarke and White, New York (large C)
Dark green, 9½ inches, applied top, smooth base $40–70
American 1860–1873

Coca-Cola Bottling Works, Petersburg, VA—Trademark Registered
Dark amethyst, 7⅞ inches, tooled top, smooth base $75–125
American 1900–1910

Coca-Cola—Los Angeles
Dark amber, 7¾ inches, tooled top, smooth base...............$100–150
American 1900–1906 (West Coast ambers are rare)

Coca-Cola Bottling Company, Rome, GA, Trademark Registered, This Bottle Not to Be Sold
Amethyst, 7⅛ inches, tooled top, smooth base $50–100
American 1900–1910

Lahaina Ice Company Limited, Lahaina, Maui; Excelsior Soda Works Company Limited, Hilo, 1908–1910.

Coca-Cola Bottling Company (acid etched), Las Vegas, NEVADA
Clear, 12 inches $350–450
American 1915–1925 (extremely rare)

Concord Soda Works (acid etched) (eagle shield motif) "C.J. & H.H.T.," Concord, CA
Clear, 12 inches, tooled top $75–150
Austrian 1910–1920

Conolly and Brother—Geyser Soda
Aqua, 7¼ inches, applied top, smooth base $60–100
American 1862–1872

Crystal Soda Water Company—Patented November 12, 1872, "Taylor's U.S. PT."
Aqua, 7⅝ inches, applied top $75–125
American 1873–1886

D. S. and Company, San Francisco
Aqua, 7 inches, applied top, smooth base $60–100
American 1861–1864 only (rare)

Distilled Soda Water Company of Alaska
Aqua, 7¼ inches, tooled top, smooth base $400–600
American 1890–1906 (Alaskas are one of the hardest of the fifty states to find)

E and J Ludtman, Santa Cruz Company, CAL
Aqua, 7⅛ inches, applied top, smooth base $20–30
American 1864–1875

E.L. Billing's, Sac City—Geyser Soda
Sapphire-blue, 7¼ inches, applied top, smooth base $75–125
American 1872–1879

El Dorado
Dark blue-green, 7⅛ inches, applied top, smooth base $75–125
American 1860–1870 (rare in this color)

El Dorado
Blue-green, 7⅜ inches, applied top, smooth base $40–60
American 1865–1875

Coca-Cola Bottling Company, Rome, GA, Trademark Registered, This Bottle Not To Be Sold, 1900–1910.

J.D. Stellmenn, Palmyra, NY; Ashland Bottling Works, Ashland, WI; John Howell, Buffalo, NY; 1885–1900.

E.S. Hart—Canton, CT
Dark lime-green, 7⅛ inches, applied top, smooth base.........$50–100
American 1860–1870

E.Y. Cronk Root Beer, Chicago—Registered (E.Y.C. monogram motif) Trademark, Bode
Cobalt-blue, 7⅜ inches, tooled top, smooth base................$400–600
American 1865–1875 (extremely rare)

Eagle Works, Philad
Dark blue-green, 7⅜ inches, applied top, iron pontil..........$200–300
American 1845–1855 (rare)

Empire Soda Works (antler motif), Vallejo (eagle motif)
Dark blue-green 7¼ inches, applied top, smooth base........$100–200
American 1860–1870

Empire Soda Works (antler motif), Vallejo (large eagle motif)
Dark blue-aqua, 7¼ inches, applied top, smooth base..........$75–125
American 1870–1878

English Cod Soda Bottle
Aqua, 9 inches, tooled top, smooth base $10–40
American 1890–1910

English Cod Soda Bottle
Emerald-green, 7½ inches, applied top, smooth base $10–40
American 1890–1910

Fairmont Hotel (acid etched)
Clear, 12 inches, tooled top $40–60
Austrian 1900–1920

Frank O'Grady, Empire Soda Works, Vallejo, CA
Clear, 12 inches, tooled top $100–200
Austrian 1900–1920 (rare)

Ghirardelli's Branch Oakland
Medium cobalt, 7⅜ inches, applied top, smooth base.........$200–300
American 1863–1869 (only blob soda from Oakland, CA)

Golden—Gate
Dark blue-green, 7¼ inches, applied top, smooth base.......$100–150
American 1860–1865

**H. Brader and Company—Penalty for Selling This Bottle—
XLCR—Soda Works—738 Broadway, S. F. (8 sided)**
Aqua, 7¼ inches, applied top, smooth base $150–200
American 1863–1864 (extremely rare)

Hathorn Spring, Saratoga, NY
Medium green, 7½ inches, pint, applied top, smooth base $25–75
American 1860–1873

**Heiss, Philadelphia (star motif)—(large H), Union Glass Works,
Philad**
Dark cobalt-blue, 7⅜ inches, applied top, iron pontil.........$150–250
American 1850–1860

Henry, Winkle, Sac. City—XX
Aqua, 7½ inches, applied top, iron pontil............................$150–200
American 1852–1854 (aqua pontil California sodas are rare)

Hotel Del Monte
Clear, 12 inches, tooled top $40–60
Czechoslovakian 1900–1920

This Bottle Is The Property of O'Neill Brothers, Mark North Fitzroy; A.J. Wintle and Sons, Bill Mills, N.R. Ross, 1880–1900 (European).

Royal Crown Cola, 1936.

Imperial Ginger Ale and Soda Water Company Inc. (bear holding bottle motif), Oakland, CAL
Clear, 12 inches, tooled top $50–100
Austrian 1900–1920

Italian Soda Water Manufactor, San Francisco
Green 7¼ inches, applied top, iron pontil $200–300
American 1856–1863 (rare in green)

J.A. Lomax, 14 and 16 Charles Place, Chicago—A & D.H.C.
Cobalt-blue, 7 inches, applied top, smooth base $150–250
American 1860–1865 (rare)

J.F. Batterman, Brooklyn, NY
Lime-green, 6¾ inches, applied top, smooth base....................$40–80
American 1860–1870

J.L. Bliven and Company, Oakland, CAL
Aqua, 7⅛ inches, applied top, smooth base $20–40
American 1864–1875

J. Lake, Schenectady, NY
Cobalt-blue, 7¾ inches, applied top, round bottom, iron
pontil..$250–350
American 1857–1858 only (rare)

J. Leonard, Huntingdon, PA
Aqua, 7¼ inches, applied top, smooth base.......................$100–200
American 1860–1865 (extremely rare)

J.W. Harris'—Soda Water—New Haven, CONN (8 sided)
Cobalt-blue, 7½ inches, applied top, smooth base..............$250–350
American 1860–1863

Jackson's Napa Soda—A Natural Mineral Water, Jackson's
Lime-green, 7⅛ inches, tooled top..$40–80
American 1900–1906

Jackson's Napa Soda (label only)
Amber, quart, tooled top...$15–30
American 1902–1940

Jurgens and Price Bottlers, Helena, MONT
Aqua, hutch, tooled top, smooth base...................................$30–50
American 1888–1900

Jurgens and Price Bottlers, Helena, MONT
Aqua, blub, tooled top, smooth base.....................................$30–50
American 1888–1900

**Knicker Bocker Soda Water, 164. 18th Street, NY 1848, W.P.
(10 sided)**
Cobalt-blue, 7 inches, applied top, iron pontil...................$350–450
American 1850–1868

Knicker Bocker Soda Water, C.C. (10 sided)
Medium cobalt-blue, 7¼ inches, applied top, iron pontil.....$350–450
American 1850–1855 ("C.C." stands for "Carpenter and Cobb")

Knox Granatelli, (acid etched), Napa, Net Contents 32 Ozs.
Light amethyst, 12 inches $75–150
American 1910–1920 (extremely rare)

Variety of soda/pop
bottles, 1910–1936.

L and V
Green, 7⅛ inches, applied top, iron pontil $250–350
American 1852–1857

**Liberty Soda Works (acid etched), Trademark (Liberty Bell
motif), Oakland, CA, Contents 1 Quart 2 Ounces**
Amethyst, 11¾ inches $75–150
American 1910–1920 (extremely rare)

Lime Juice (arrow motif)
Dark olive-amber, 10¼ inches, applied top, smooth base ...$300–400
European 1840–1850

Livermore Soda Works (acid etched), Livermore, CALIF
Clear, 11¾ inches..$150–250
American 1910–1920 (extremely rare)

Luke Beard
Medium green, 7 inches, applied top, iron pontil...............$250–350
American 1848–1853

Luke Beard
Dark aqua, 7⅛ inches, applied top, smooth base $200–300
American 1860–1867 (rare in this color)

**Marin Bottling Works (acid etched), (M.B.W. monogram motif),
S.R. CA**
Clear, 11¾ inches, tooled top $100–150
Austrian 1900–1920 (rare)

Luke Beard,
1860–1867.

Nonpareil Soda Water Company
(rare), 1881–1887.

Merritt and Company, Helena, MT
Aqua, 7¼ inches, applied top, smooth base $100–200
American 1870–1880

Milch Bros. Bottlers, Helena, MONT
Amber, half pint beer, applied top, smooth base $30–50
American 1888–1900

Mills' Seltzer Springs
Aqua, 7½ inches, applied top, smooth base $40–60
American 1874–1885

Nonpareil Soda Water Company, S. F.
Aqua, 7 inches, applied top, smooth base $40–80
American 1881–1887 (rare)

This Bottle Is the Property of O'Neill Brothers, Trademark (monogram motif), Mark North Fitzroy
Aqua, 10 inches, applied top, smooth base $25–50
European 1880–1900

Owen Casey Eagle Soda Works—Sac City
Medium cobalt-blue, 7¼ inches, applied top, smooth base $75–125
American 1867–1871

Pacific Congress Water (deer motif)
Dark aqua, 7⅛ inches, applied top, smooth base $50–80
American 1869–1876

Pacific Congress Water—P. Caduc
Dark blue-aqua, 7¼ inches, applied top, smooth base $50–100
American 1868–1881

**Palace Hotel (acid etched) (monogram motif), San Francisco,
The Palace Hotel**
Clear, 11¾ inches, tooled top $50–100
Czechoslovakian 1900–1920

Petaluma Soda and Seltzer Works, (acid etched), Petaluma, CAL
Clear, 12 inches, tooled top $50–100
American 1910–1920 (rare)

**Philip Young and Company, Savannah, GA (eagle, shield, flag
motif)**
Dark blue-green, 7½ inches, applied top, smooth base $150–250
American 1860–1870

Phoenix Bottling Works, Phoenix, ARIZONA
Aqua, 8¼ inches, tooled top $10–20
American 1900–1920

Pacific Congress Water,
blob-top soda,
1867–1876.

Assortment of miscella-
neous soda/punch bottles:
Frost (Coca-Cola Bottling
Company); Payson Bottling
Company, Quality
Beverages, Payson, UT;
Delaware Punch, Non-
Alcoholic Imitation Punch;
Uncle Jo; 1900–1930.

Phoenix Bottling Works, Phoenix, ARIZONA
Aqua, 7⅝ inches, tooled top $10–20
American 1900–1920

Pioneer Soda Works (shield monogram motif), San Francisco
Aqua, 7½ inches, applied top $150–250
American 1866–1873 (extremely rare)

Registered Coca-Cola, Richmond, VA
Amber, 7¾ inches, tooled top, smooth base $50–80
American 1900–1910

Reno Bottling Works (acid etched) (star motif), Reno
Clear, 12 inches, tooled top $100–200
Austrian 1908–1914 (extremely rare)

**Rodgers (acid etched), Superior Quality Sparkling Artesian
Water, Carbonated from the Mountains of Napa County,
Rodgers Bottling Company, Vallejo, CALIF**
Vaseline glass, 12 inches, tooled top $100–200
Czechoslovakian 1900–1920 (extremely rare)

Rose City Soda Works (acid etched), Santa Rosa, CAL
Clear, 12 inches, tooled top $100–150
Austrian 1900–1920 (rare)

Ross's—Belfast
Yellow with a reddish hue, 6¼ inches, round bottom............$75-150
American 1880–1890

Safford Bottling Works, Safford, ARIZ
Dark amethyst, 7⅛ inches, tooled top................................$250–350
American 1885–1895

San Francisco Glass Works
Aqua, 7⅛ inches, applied top, smooth base $40–80
American 1870–1876

San Francisco Glass Works
Dark sapphire-blue, 7⅛ inches, applied top, smooth base....$400–600
American 1870–1876 (fewer than 10 known in this color)

Sanitary Soda Water Company, Phoenix, ARIZ
Aqua, 6¾ inches, tooled top $20–35
American 1900–1915

Salt River Bottling Works, Phoenix, ARIZ
Aqua, 6¾ inches, tooled top $20–35
American 1900–1915

San Francisco
Glass Works,
1870–1876.

Smith and Company, Philad—M
Blue-green, 7 inches, applied top, smooth base.....................$30–60
American 1860–1865

Southwick and Tupper, New York
Blue-green, 7½ inches, applied top, iron pontil $100–200
American 1850–1860

Southwick and Tupper, New York (10 sided)
Dark blue-green, 7⅝ inches, applied top, iron pontil $250–350
American 1845–1855

Sparks Bottling Company, Sparks, NEVADA (base)
Aqua, 7⅞ inches..$250–350
American 1905–1907 only (fewer than 8 known)

Star Soda Works (acid etched) (star motif), Sonoma, CA,
Net Contents 1 Quart
Clear, 11¾ inches, tooled top $100–200
Czechoslovakian 1900–1920 (rare)

Taylor and Company Soda Waters, San Francisco, Eureka
Medium cobalt-blue, 6¾ inches, applied top, iron pontil ...$200–300
American 1850–1854 (extremely rare and seldom seen California
soda)

Collection of Coca-Cola bottles, 1940–1955.

Thos Maher
Dark green, 7 inches, applied top, iron pontil...................$125–175
American 1850–1860

W.H. Burt, San Francisco
Green, 7⅜ inches, applied top, iron pontil.........................$150–250
American 1855–1860

W.H.H. Chicago, Never Sold (base), H
Cobalt-blue, 7 inches, applied top, smooth base...............$100–200
American 1860–1865

Wm. Eagle—New York—Premium Soda Water (8 sided)
Bright emerald-green, 7 inches, applied top, iron pontil....$300–400
American 1850–1860 (rare in this color)

W.S. Wright (base), Pacific Glass Works
Dark aqua, 7 inches, applied top, smooth base...................$75–125
American 1862–1867 (Wright was the first soda manufacturer in
Nevada, rare)

W.S. Wright (base), Pacific Glass Works
Dark aqua, 7⅛ inches, applied top, smooth base...............$150–250
American 1862–1867 (Wright was the first soda manufacturer in
Virginia City, Nevada; rare)

Hekelnkaemper Brothers,
Atchison, KN, 7¼ ounces,
1910–1940.

Hires Root Beer soda bottles,
1900–1940.

Collection of soda bottles, 1850–1860.

W.S. Wright (base), Pacific Glass Works

Medium emerald-green with an aqua hue, 7⅛ inches $100–200
American 1862–1867 (Wright was the first soda manufacturer in
Virginia City, Nevada; rare)

W.S. Wright (base), Pacific Glass Works

Dark blue-aqua, 7⅛ inches, applied top, smooth base $100–200
American 1862–1867 (Wright was the first soda manufacturer in
Virginia City, Nevada; rare)

W.S. Wright (base), Pacific Glass Works

Dark blue-green 7¼ inches, applied top, smooth base $300–400
American 1862–1867 (Wright was the first soda manufacturer in
Virginia City, Nevada; extremely rare in this color)

White Pine Soda Company (acid etched), Ely, NV (top), Elko Bottling Works

Clear, 10¾ inches, tooled top $200–400
German 1890–1900 (extremely rare)

Collection of soda bottles, 1850–1860.

Soda bottle, 1880.

Wielands Bottling Works, Reno, NEV
Aqua, 7⅛ inches, tooled top $125–175
American 1908–1919 (rare)

XLCR Soda Works (star shield motif), Martinez, CA,
Trademark Registered
Clear, 12 inches, tooled top $75–150
Austrian 1900–1920 (rare)

Young Blood
Green, 7¼ inches, applied top, smooth base..........................$30–60
American 1860–1870

Ziegler's Soda Works, Tucson, ARIZ
Aqua, 6½ inches, tooled top $200–300
American 1895–1906 (rare Arizona bottle)

Target Balls

Target balls, which are small rounded bottles, were filled with confetti, ribbon, and other items. They were used for target practice from the 1850s to the early 1900s. They gained considerable popularity during the 1860s and 1870s with the Buffalo Bill Cody and Annie Oakley Wild West shows. Around 1900, clay pigeons started to be used in lieu of target balls. Because they were made to be broken, they are unfortunately extremely difficult to find, and are very rare, collectible, and valuable.

Agnew and Brown, Corner of 27th and Smallman Sts., Pittsburgh, PA (motif of a pigeon in flight)
Medium amber, 2¼ inches diameter.............................$3,000–5,000
American 1875–1890 (one of the most desirable and sought after of the known target balls; only 2 or 3 known examples)

"Bogardus" Glass Ball, "Pat'd. Apr 10 1877"
Medium yellowish olive-green, 2¾ inches diameter............$350–450
American 1877–1890 (rare and desirable color for a Bogardus ball)

Bogardus, Quilted
Light yellow-olive, 2½ inches $300–350
American 1877–1890

Bogardus, Quilted
Cobalt-blue, 2½ inches..$500–600
American 1877–1890

Bogardus, Quilted
Amber, 2½ inches..$125–150
American 1877–1890

Jas. Brown and Son, 136 Wood St., Pitts'g, PA—Manufacturer and Dealers in Firearms
Medium amber, 2½ inches diameter, sheared lip,
smooth base...$2,500–3,500
American 1875–1890 (extremely rare)

L. Jones Gunmaker, Blackburn, Lancashire
Light cobalt-blue, 2¾ inches diameter $125–175
English 1875–1890

NB Glass Works, Perth
Cornflower blue, 2½ inches...$75–100

NB Glass Works, Perth
Cobalt-blue, 2½ inches...$75–100

Quilted Pattern, Man Shooting Gun
Colorless...$100–150

Quilted Pattern, Man Shooting Gun
Amethyst..$150–250

Unembossed
Medium amber, 2½ inches $45–55

Unembossed
Medium amber, 2½ inches $40–60

WW Greener St. Marys Works
Cornflower blue, 2½ inches..$60–90

WW Greener St. Marys Works
Amethyst, 2½ inches...$125–175

Warner Bottles

The Warner bottle was named for H. H. Warner, who sold a number of remedies developed by a Dr. Craig. Warner developed his bottle for those and other cures and began producing great volumes and varieties (over twenty) in 1879 in Rochester, New York.

Warner bottles can frequently be found with their original label and boxes giving additional value to these already expensive and rare bottles.

Log Cabin Cough and Consumption Remedy
Amber, 9¼ inches..$125–175

Log Cabin Extract, Rochester, NY
Amber, 8¼ inches..$80–100

Log Cabin Sarsaparilla, Rochester, NY
Amber, 9 inches..$125–150

Log Cabin Scalpine, Rochester, NY
Amber, 8¾ inches..$300–350

**12½ Fluid Ozs., Warner's Safe Remedies Co.
(safe motif), Rochester, NY, U.S.A.**
Clear, 9 inches, tooled top, smooth base $50–75
American 1905–1915

Warner's Safe Bitters
Amber, 9½ inches..$500–750

Warner's Safe Cure (safe motif), London
Yellow-amber, 9⅛ inches, applied top, smooth base...........$100–200
English 1883–1892

Warner's Safe Diabetes Cure
Amber, 9½ inches..$90–130

**Warner's Safe Kidney and Liver Cure (left-hand safe motif),
Rochester, NY**
Dark amber, 9¼ inches, tooled top, smooth base.................$75–100
American 1890–1900 (scarce left-hand variant)

**Warner's Safe Kidney and Liver Cure (safe motif), Rochester,
NY (base: "A. & D.H.C.")**
Amber, 9½ inches, applied top $75–125
American 1879–1886 (rare Warner's slug plate)

**Warner's Safe Kidney and Liver Cure (safe motif), Rochester,
NY**
Amber, 9¾ inches, applied top, smooth base.........................$20–30
American 1883–1890

**Warner's Safe Cure (safe motif); London, England; Toronto,
Canada; Rochester, NY**
Amber, 11 inches, tooled top, smooth base........................$300–400
American 1890–1900

Warner's Safe Nervine, (base: A & DHC)
Yellow, 9½ inches...$150–200

Warner's Safe Nervine
Medium amber, 7⅜ inches $25–30

Warner's Safe Nervine
Amber, 9¾ inches..$30–40

Warner's Safe Rheumatic Cure
Amber, 9½ inches...$50–70

Warner's Safe Tonic
Amber, 7½ inches...$400–550

Warner's Safe Tonic Bitters
Deep amber, 7⅜ inches $300–400

Whiskey Bottles

Whiskeys, sometimes referred to as spirits, come in an array of sizes, designs, shapes, and colors. The whiskey bottle dates back to the nineteenth century and the avid collector can acquire rare and valuable pieces.

In 1860, E. G. Booz manufactured a whiskey bottle in the design of a cabin embossed with the year 1840 and the words "Old Cabin Whiskey." One theory has it that the word booze was derived from his name to describe hard liquor. The Booz bottle is given the credit of being the first to emboss a name on whiskey bottles.

After the repeal of Prohibition in 1933, the only inscription that could be found on any liquor bottle was "Federal Law Forbids Sale or Re-use of This Bottle," which was continued through 1964.

A. Fenkausen and Company (monogram motif), San Francisco
Clear, 12 inches, applied top $250–350
American 1883–1890

Always Pure Old Elk Whiskey (back bar) (elk motif in horseshoe)
Emerald-green with white enamel, 11¼ inches, tied pontil....$650–750
American 1890–1910

Argonaut Trademark (shield motif), E. Martin and Company, San Francisco, CAL
Amber, 11¼ inches, tooled top..$50–75
American 1900–1906

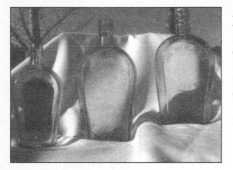

Assortment of Nevada whiskeys: Frank Adadie, Eureka, NV; Bartlett and Ostreicher, Gem Saloon, Elko, NV; Max Oberfelder, Eureka, NV (the Ostreicher and Oberfelder are the only 2 known in the Western states), 1878–1891.

**Atlas Bourbon (man holding globe motif),
Sole Controllers, Mohns and Kaltenback, San
Francisco**
Clear, 11½ inches, tooled top $200–300
American 1895–1901

**Barney Schow Wholesale and Retail Wines and Liquors,
Willits, CA**
Amber, 11 inches, tooled top...$200–300
American 1898–1905 (fewer than 10 known)

**Bear Grass Bourbon (bear head motif), Braunschweiger and
Company**
Clear, 10⅞ inches, tooled top...$350-450
American 1890–1895

**Belle of Anderson (star motif), Old Fashion Handmade Sour
Mash**
Milk glass, 8 inches, tooled top, smooth base......................$75–125
American 1890–1900

**Belle of Anderson (star motif), Old Fashion Handmade Sour
Mash**
Milk glass, 8¼ inches, tooled top, smooth base $75–125
American 1890–1900

Belmont (back bar)
Clear with white enamel, 11¼ inches, tooled top, smooth
base $75–100
American 1900–1910

Washington Bar, Coleman and Granger, Tonopah, NV (screw-top whiskey), 1905–1906.

Henry Campe and Company, Wholesale Liquor Dealers, San Francisco, CA, 1895–1900.

Back bar whiskey decanters (European), 1840–1860.

Booth and Company (anchor motif), Sacramento
Light amethyst, 12 inches, tooled top $700–1,000
American 1890–1894 (highly sought after picture whiskey)

Brown Forman Company, Louisville, KY
Dark amethyst, 4¼ inches, tooled top....................................$40–60
American 1895–1905

Brunswick Rye (back bar)
Clear, 11¼ inches, tooled top, smooth base.......................$150–250
American 1900–1910

Burwood (back bar)
Clear with white enamel, 10¾ inches, tooled top, smooth base $125–200
American 1900–1918

Cartan, McCarthy and Company (monogram motif), San Francisco
Light golden amber, 11½ inches, applied top, smooth base...$250–350
American 1882–1888

Cartan, McCarthy and Company (monogram motif),
San Francisco
Amber, 11⅞ inches, tooled top...$100–150
American 1885–1888

Catto's Whiskey (back bar) (covered in copper)
Copper, 9¾ inches, applied top..$150–250
American 1885–1895

Chapin and Gore Sour Mash 1867, Chicago (glass cap), Pat. Aug
6, 72, (base: H), Franks, Patd Aug 1872
Amber, 8½ inches, applied top, smooth base.....................$100–150
American 1882–1888 (glass screw cap)

Chevalier's Ginger Brandy, Trademark (monogram motif)
Amber, 11⅛ inches, applied top, smooth base....................$350–450
American 1884–1888

Crown Distilleries (sample) (crown motif), Company (in
wicker)
Amber, 5¾ inches, tooled top, smooth base $25–50
American 1900–1910 (has inside screw threads for stopper)

Patent whiskey flask,
1860–1870.

Dancing Lady,
1890–1900.

Dancing Lady
(reverse side of
bottle),
1890–1900.

Dancing Lady (label under glass), Compliments of John Quinn, 94 6th Ave., NY, Xmas 1902
Clear, 5½ inches, ground top, smooth base $350–450
American 1902

Dancing Lady (label under glass) (eagle motif)
Clear, black and white, 5½ inches, ground top, smooth
base $250–350
American 1890–1900

Davy Crockett Hey, Graverholz and Company, S. F., Sole Agents, Pure Gold Bourbon
Light amber, 11⅞ inches, tooled top $75–150
American 1890–1905

E Commins and Company (monogram motif), San Francisco, CAL
Red-amber, 11½ inches, applied top, smooth base $400–600
American 1885–1891

Ear of Corn
Light amber, 9¾ inches, applied top, smooth base $150–250
American 1860–1870

El Monte (sample) (monogram motif), Bourbon, Louisville, KY
Clear, 4 inches, tooled top, smooth base $50–100
American 1910–1918 (El Monte Distilling Company was based in San Francisco from 1910–1918)

A Merry Christmas
and Happy New
Year—Good Luck,
1900–1910.

Empire State Rye (back bar)
Clear with white enamel, 10 inches, tooled top, smooth
base..$100–150
American 1900–1918

**The F. Chevalier Company, Old (castle motif) Castle,
San Francisco, CA**
Amber, 11 inches, tooled top (has inside threads)..................$50–80
American 1905–1910

Finch's Golden Wedding Rye (back bar)
Clear with white enamel, 11¼ inches, tooled top, smooth
base $75–100
American 1900–1918

**GBL, Bottled by Goldberg Bowen and Lebenbaum, Importers of
Wines and Liquors, 426 to 432 Pine St., S. F.**
Clear, 11⅜ inches, applied top, smooth base......................$200–300
American 1882–1886 (flint glass)

Goldberg, Bowen and Company, San Francisco—Oakland
Clear, 11⅞ inches, tooled top $40–50
American 1900–1910

Goldberg, Bowen and Company, San Francisco—Oakland
Amber, 11⅞ inches, tooled top..$40–50
American 1900–1910

Collection of label-under-glass whiskeys: Dancing Lady, 1890– 1900; Multicolored Lady, 1900–1910; A Merry Christmas and Happy New Year—Good Luck, 1900–1910; Pink-and-Brown-Colored Lady, 1890–1910; Dancing Lady—Compliments of John Quinn, 1902.

Geo. S. Ladd and Company Wholesale Liquors, Stockton, CAL
Dark amber, 11 inches, tooled top $60–100
American 1905–1915 (seldom seen)

G.O. Blake's Kentucky Whiskey (two barrels motif), G.O. Blake's Bourbon Company, Kentucky Whiskey, Adam Taylor and Company, Proprietors, Boston and Louisville, G.O. Blake's Kentucky Whiskey
Amber, 11⅛ inches, tooled top..$200–300
American 1890–1900

Wicker pattern whiskey; Malcolm Fraser and Company, Ancient Liquer, 1900–1920.

Common whiskey, one style glob top, 1905–1915.

G.O. Blake's Bourbon Company, Kentucky Whiskey (two barrels), Miller and Stewart and Company, Louisville, KY— G.O. Blake's Whiskey
Dark amber, 11½ inches, applied top, smooth base............$250–350
American 1871–1876

G.O. Blake's Bourbon Company, Kentucky Whiskey, Pond, Reynolds and Company, Sole Agent's for Pacific Coast
Light olive with amber hue, 12 inches, applied top, smooth base $2,000–2,500
American 1868–1887 (fewer than 5 known in this color)

G.O. Blake's Rye and Sour Whiskey (two barrels motif), Adams Taylor and Company, Proprietors, Full Quart (label), Registered
Clear, 12⅝ inches, tooled top $75–150
American 1895–1905 (seldom seen with a label)

Bottled by Goldberg, Bowen and Company (monogram motif), Importers of Wines and Liquors, 426 to 432 Pine St., S. F.
Clear, 11⅜ inches, applied top $50–100
American 1890–1905

Bottled by Goldberg, Bowen and Company (monogram motif), Importers of Wines and Liquors, 426 to 432 Pine St., S. F.
Clear, 11½ inches, tooled top $40–60
American 1896–1905

Bottled by Goldberg, Bowen and Lebenbaum (monogram motif), Importers of Wines and Liquors, 426 to 432 Pine St., S. F.
Clear, 11½ inches, tooled top $75–125
American 1892–1895

Golden Eagle Distilleries Company (eagle motif), San Francisco, CAL
Amber, 11⅛ inches, tooled top...$500–750
American 1904–1910 (rare picture whiskey)

Grommes and Ullrich National Club (back bar)
Clear, 10¾ inches, tooled top, smooth base......................$100–150
American 1905–1906 only (San Francisco)

Gundlach—Bundschu Wine Company, Rhine Farm Sonoma (motif of man holding glass), Bacchus Brand, San Francisco, CAL
Light amber, 11⅜ inches, tooled top $150–250
American 1897–1903

Trademark, N. Vanbergen and Company (horse motif), Gold Dust Kentucky Bourbon, N. Vanbergen and Company Sole Propts
Dark amethyst, 11⅜ inches, tooled top.........................$1,500–2,500
American 1877–1883 (extremely rare in tooled top)

Trademark, Gold Dust (horse motif), Kentucky Bourbon, N. Vanbergen and Company, Sole Propts
Clear, 11⅞ inches, tooled top $300–500
American 1882–1892

Trademark, N. Vanbergen and Company (standing horse motif), Gold Dust Kentucky Bourbon, N. Vanbergen and Company Sole Propts
Aqua, 11¾ inches, applied top, smooth base $800–1,200
American 1877–1883

Hotel Donnelly, Tacoma (sample)
Clear, 3⅜ inches, ground top, smooth base $40–60
American 1895–1900 (rare)

Hotel Donnelly, Tacoma
(rare), 1895–1900.

Assortment of black
glass whiskey bottles,
1870–1890.

**J.H. Cutter Old Bourbon (J.H.C. barrel motif) (J.H. Cutter Old
Bourbon crown motif), Trademark (J.H. Cutter Pure Old Rye
crown motif), C.P. Moorman Manufacturer, Louisville, KY,
Cutter Whiskey**
Amber, 11 inches, tooled top $700–1,000
American 1885–1895 (fewer than 5 known)

**J.H. Cutter Old Bourbon (crown motif), Bottled by A.P.
Hotaling and Company**
Light olive with amber hue, 11½ inches, tooled top $50–75
American 1890–1895 (rare in this color)

J.H. Cutter Extra (star shield motif), Trademark, Old Bourbon
Olive-amber, 11¾ inches, applied top $150–250
American 1880–1885

**Cutter O.K. Whiskey, J.H. Cutter Old Bourbon (crown barrel
motif), Trademark, C.P. Moorman Manufacturer, Louisville, KY,
A.P. Hotaling's O.K. Cutter Whiskey**
Amber, 11¾ inches, tooled top...$80–120
American 1890–1900

**Cutter A No. 1 Whiskey, J.H. Cutter Old Bourbon Trademark
(crown barrel motif), C.P. Moorman Manufacturer, Louisville,
KY—A.P. Hotaling's A No. 1 Cutter Whiskey**
Light amber with olive hue, 11¾ inches, applied top..........$450–650
American 1874–1879 (rare)

J.H. Cutter Old Bourbon (crown motif), A.P. Hotaling and Company Sole Agents
Black-amber, 11¾ inches, applied top $60–100
American 1880–1885

J.H. Cutter Old Bourbon (bird motif, all in a circle), J.H. Cutter Old Bourbon (J.H.C. in a barrel motif), Trademark (crown motif), C.P. Moorman Manufacturer, Louisville, KY, A.P. Hotaling and Company, Sole Agents—Cutter OK Whiskey
Dark amber, 11⅞ inches, applied top $400–600
American 1873–1879

J.H. Cutter Old Bourbon (crown motif), E. Martin and Company Sole Agents
Light amber with olive hue, 11⅞ inches, applied top..........$200–300
American 1874–1879

J.H. Cutter Extra, Trademark (star motif), Old Bourbon
Medium olive-green, 11⅞ inches, applied top, smooth
base $750–1,000
American 1870–1875 (rare color, fewer than 10 known)

J.H. Cutter Extra (star shield motif), Trademark, Old Bourbon
Dark amber, 12 inches, applied top (star on base) $75–125
American 1885–1890

Collection of
whiskey bottles,
1860–1890.

J.H. Cutter Extra, Trademark (shield star motif), Old Bourbon
Medium amber, 12 inches, applied top,
smooth base (star on base) $50–75
American 1885–1890

Trademark (antler motif), J. Moore Old Bourbon, E. Chielovich and Company, Sole Agents
Dark olive-amber, 11⅞ inches, applied top, smooth base ...$600–800
American 1873–1876 (fewer than 5 known in this color)

James T. Y. Sons—Philadelphia
Dark blue-green, 10½ inches, applied top, iron pontil........$100–200
American 1845–1855 (very rare)

Jesse Moore (back bar)
Clear with white enamel, 11¼ inches, tooled top $250–350
American 1900–1917

Trademark (antlers motif), Jesse Moore and Company, Louisville, KY, C.H. Moore (star motif) Old Bourbon and Rye, Jesse Moore—Hunt Company, San Francisco
Red, 11⅜ inches, applied top...$450–650
American 1895–1900

Jno. H. Graves Old Kentucky Whiskey, San Jose, CAL
Amber, 11 inches, tooled top $60–100
American 1910–1915

Collection of whiskey bottles, 1860–1890.

Kentucky Club (monogram motif), Old Bourbon, W.M. Watson and Company, Oakland, CA
Clear, 12⅛ inches, applied top $100–150
American 1888–1895

Kohlberg and Cavagnaro (monogram motif), Wholesale Liquors, Stockton, CAL
Clear, 11¼ inches, applied top $300–600
American 1891–1894

La Feld Prot from La Feld Vineyard, Napa Co, CA
Amber, 11¼ inches, applied top, smooth base......................$50–100
American 1865–1875

Landregan and White Wholesale Liquor Merchants, Oakland, CA
Amber, 11 inches, tooled top...$40–60
American 1905–1912

Laurel Crown Old Bourbon (crown barrel motif with "W.H. & Co."), Wm. Hoelscher and Company Sole Agent, S. F.
Dark amber, 11⅝ inches, applied top, smooth base......$2,000–3,000
American 1879–1880 (rare, fewer than 5 known)

Lilienthal and Company (crown, shield monogram motif) Distillers
Light amber, 11⅞ inches, applied top................................$150–250
American 1874–1880 (oldest of Lilienthal's)

Assortment of whiskeys with applied lip and two types of glob tops, 1900–1920.

Louis Taussig and Company, Wholesale Liquor Dealers, San Francisco
Amber, 12 inches, inside threaded tooled top $100–150
American 1895–1902

M and W or XX and XX
Amber, 12½ inches, tooled top, smooth base $50–75
American 1900–1910

MacFarland and Company (monogram motif), Honolulu
Light amber, 11¾ inches, applied top............................. $600–1,000
American 1885–1895 (fewer than 10 known)

Major Special (back bar)
Clear with white enamel, 10¾ inches, tooled top $100–200
American 1895–1905 (ground round bottom)

Multicolored Lady (label under glass)
Clear, 5⅞ inches, ground top, smooth base $350–450
American 1900–1910

N. Grange Sole Agent, Pacific Coast
Amber, 11½ inches, applied top, smooth base................. $750–1,000
American 1882–1885 (fewer than 10 known)

Nabob
Amber, 11⅛ inches, applied top $75–125
American 1882–1884

Two different types of common whiskeys with applied lips, 1900–1920.

The F. Chevalier Company, Old Castle Whiskey (castle motif), San Francisco, CAL
Amber, 10¼ inches, tooled top, inside threads $50–100
American 1905–1910

Old Gilt Edge, O (crown motif) K, Bourbon Wichman, Lutgen and Company, Sole Agents, San Francisco
Light orange-amber, 11⅛ inches, applied top, smooth
base $350–550
American 1893–1895 only

Old Gilt Edge, O (crown motif) K, Bourbon Wichman, Lutgen and Company, Sole Agents, San Francisco
Amber, 11¾ inches, tooled top...$500–700
American 1893–1895 (rare tooled picture whiskey)

Distilled in 1848, Old Kentucky 1849 Reserve Bourbon, A.M. Bininger and Company, 338 Broadway, NY
Light amber, 8 inches, applied top, open pontil bottom.....$150–250
American 1849–1850

Old Kirk, A.P. Hotaling and Company Whiskey
Clear, 10⅞ inches, tooled top, pontiled $40–60
American 1900–1918

Old Kirk, A.P. Hotaling and Company, whiskey, 1900–1910.

Unembossed back bar whiskey barrel, 8⅜ inches, 1865–1875; Old Kentucky Reserve Bourbon, 8 inches, 1849–1850.

Old Kirk, A.P. Hotaling and Company Whiskey
Light amethyst, 11 inches, tooled top, tied pontil $100–150
American 1900–1910

Old Valley Whiskey (back bar) (cross motif)
Clear, 9 inches, tooled top $100–200
American 1870–1880 (rare Western back bar)

Label Under Glass, Our Candidates, William McKinley and Theodore Roosevelt Whiskey (base), E. Packham Jr., Patented July 13th 1897, Baltimore, MD
Multicolored, 10¾ inches, tooled top $1,500–2,500

Label Under Glass, Our Candidates, William Jennings Bryan and Adlai Ewing Stevenson (base), E. Packham Jr., Patented July 13th 1897, Baltimore, MD
Multicolored, 10¾ inches, tooled top $1,500–2,500
American 1901

Paul Jones (back bar)
Clear with multicolored enamel, tooled top, smooth base ...$200–300
American 1900–1918

Pepper Distillery Hand Made Sour Mash, Jas. E. Pepper and Company, Distillers Lexington, KY (shield motif) Trademark, Carroll and Carroll Sole Agents, San Francisco
Amber, 11¾ inches, tooled top...$200–300
American 1888–1905

Pink and Brown Colored Lady, Mary Jansen (label under glass)
Clear, 6 inches, ground top, smooth base $350–450
American 1890–1910

Pride of Kentucky Old Bourbon, Livingston and Company, Sole Agents
Amber, 12 inches, applied top, smooth base................$1,220–2,000
American 1874–1879 (fewer than 10 known)

Monogram Pure Rye (keystone motif), Alfred Greenebaum and Company, Sole Agents
Olive-yellow, 9¾ inches, applied top $300–500
American 1888–1892 (extremely rare in this color)

R G and Company
Dark amethyst, 4¾ inches, tooled top $30–60
American 1900–1910

Roth and Company (monogram motif), San Francisco
Amber, 11¾ inches, tooled top $40–70
American 1890–1900

Roth and Company (monogram motif), San Francisco
Aqua, 11¾ inches, tooled top (inside thread) $75–100
American 1902–1911 (rare with label)

The Rothenberg Company Old Judge Kentucky Whiskey (man holding glass motif), Trademark Registered, San Francisco, CA
Amber, 11¼ inches, tooled top $60–100
American 1907–1915

R.R. Dinnigan and Company, Wholesale Wine and Liquor Merchants, San Francisco, CA
Dark amber, 11 inches, tooled top $50–100
American 1904–1908

Assortment of various types of whiskey bottles, 1870–1920.

Silver Overlay Bourbon
(Pinch back bar),
1900–1918.

Siebe Brothers and Plaagemann, Rosedale OK Whiskey, Sole Agents
Amethyst, 11 inches, tooled top..$40–80
American 1890–1907

Silver Overlay Bourbon (Pinch back bar)
Dark purple, 9½ inches, tooled top, smooth base...............$125–175
American 1900–1918

Simmond's Nabob
Amber, 10½ inches, applied top...$75–125
American 1879–1885

Simmond's Nabob Pure KY Bourbon Whiskey (Arab being served by a servant motif) Trademark
Amber, 10⅝ inches, applied top, smooth base..............$1,200–1,500

Simmond's Nabob Pure KY Bourbon Whiskey (Arab being served by a servant motif), Trademark
Red-amber, 10¾ inches, applied top, smooth base.............$450–550
American 1879–1887

Spruance Stanley and Company 1869 (horseshoe motif), Liquor Dealers, San Francisco, CA
Amber, 11½ inches, tooled top (base: large star and "P.C.G.W.") $50–100
American 1902–1905

Teakettle Old Bourbon—Shea, Bocqueraz and McKee Agents, San Francisco, 1873–1885; J.H. Cutter Old Bourbon, C.P. Moorman Manufacturing, Louisville, KY, 1873–1879; Pure Rye Whiskey, Alfred Greenebaum and Company,

Common whiskey (glob top); The Hayner Distilling Company Distillers, 1900–1920.

Standard Old Bourbon Whiskey, Weil Bros., San Francisco, Sole Agents
Dark amber, 11⅞ inches, applied top, smooth base............$100–150
American 1878–1885

Tea Kettle Old Bourbon (teakettle motif), Trademark, Shea, Bocqueraz and McKee Agents, San Francisco
Black-amber, 12 inches, applied top, smooth base.............$450–650
American 1871–1887

Tea Kettle Old Bourbon (teakettle motif), Trademark, Shea, Bocqueraz and McKee Agents, San Francisco
Honey-amber, 12¼ inches, applied top $250–350
American 1873–1885

The Duffy Malt Whiskey Company (sample) (monogram motif), Rochester, NY, U.S.A.
Amber, 4 inches, tooled top $40–80
American 1895–1905

The Duffy Malt Whiskey Company (monogram motif),
Rochester, NY, U.S.A. (base: Patd Aug. 24 1886)
Amber, 8⅛ inches, tooled top...$60–100
American 1900–1910 (rare in this small size)

The Duffy Malt Whiskey Company (monogram motif),
Baltimore, MD, U.S.A.
Amber, 10¼ inches, applied top, smooth base.......................$30–60
American 1886–1890

The Placer Hotel Company, Helena, MONT
Clear, 11¾ inches, tooled top..$100–200
American 1905–1910 (extremely rare)

The Yosemite Wine Company, Oakland, CAL
Clear, 11¾ inches, tooled top...$50–100
American 1910–1912 only

Thistle Dew Whiskey
Medium amber, 10¾ inches, applied top, smooth base $350–450
American 1879–1885

Thos. Taylor and Company Importers, Virginia, N
Light amber, 11⅞ inches, applied top, smooth base $1,500–2,500
American 1870–1883 (fewer than 10 known, Nevada whiskey)

Tom Burke Bourbon (label only), G. Cohn and Company,
San Francisco (base: "667 H."—"H" stands for "Holt Glass
Works, West Berkeley, CA")
Aqua, 11½ inches, tooled top..$50–75
American 1893–1906

United Cal. and Montebello Wineyards Cons's, S. F., CAL
Amber, 11¼ inches, tooled top...$75–150
American 1911–1916

W.A. Lacey Whiskey (back bar)
Clear with inlaid gold, 10⅞ inches, tooled top, smooth base $100–150
American 1900–1948

Collection of whiskey bottles, 1860–1890.

Warren's Whiskey (back bar)
Reddish amber, 11⅛ inches, applied top $75–125
American 1892–1900 (Oakland, CA)

Weil Brothers and Sons (monogram motif), San Francisco
Light amber, 11½ inches, tooled top $350–550
American 1888–1889 only (fewer than 5 known in tooled top)

William H. Daly, New York
Dark emerald-green, 10 inches, applied top, smooth base.....$85–125
American 1866–1882

The Winedale Company, The W Company, Oakland, CAL
Amber, 9¾ inches, tooled top...$75–150
American 1905–1910

Wm.H. Spars and Company, Old Pioneer Whiskey (bear motif), A. Fenkhausen and Company, Sole Agents, San Francisco
Amber, 11¾ inches, applied top, smooth base.................$800–1,000
American 1875–1878

Wm. H. Spears and Company, Old Pioneer Whiskey (bear motif), Fenkhausen and Braunschweiger, Sole Agents, San Francisco
Honey-amber, 12 inches, applied top, smooth base $100–200
American 1878–1881 (extremely rare, fewer than 10 known)

Common whiskey,
one style applied
lip, 1900–1915.

Common whiskey,
one style glob top,
1905–1915.

Common whiskey
(clear), glob top,
1905–1915.

Wolters Brothers and Company, 115 and 117 Front St., S. F.
Amber, 11⅞ inches, applied top $300–500
American 1886–1895

**W.T. Ellis and Son, Trademark White Swan, Kentucky
Whiskey, Marysville, CAL**
Amethyst, 11¾ inches, tooled top.....................................$250–450
American 1900 only (extremely rare, fewer than 5 known in good
condition)

Yellowstone (back bar)
Clear with inlaid gold, 11 inches, tooled top, smooth base....$75–125
American 1900–1918

New Bottles

New Bottles: Post–1900

The bottles listed in this section have been broken down solely by characteristics of the bottles themselves. The contents of these groups hold little interest for the collector. New bottles covered in this section are valuable precisely for their decorative, appealing, and sometimes unique designs.

The goal of most new-bottle collectors is to collect a complete set of items designed and produced by a favorite manufacturer. As it is with the reproductions of old bottles such as Coca-Cola, or new items such as the Avon items, the right time to purchase is when the first issue comes out on the retail market, or prior to retail release if possible. As with the old bottles, I have provided a good cross section of new bottles in various price ranges and categories rather than listing only the rarest or most collectible pieces.

The pricing shown reflects the value of the particular item listed. Newer bottles are usually manufactured in limited quantities without any reissues. Since retail prices are affected by factors such as source, type of bottle, desirability, condition, and the possibility that the bottle was produced exclusively as a collectors' item, the pricing can fluctuate radically at any given time.

Bottle Grading

Pricing for new bottles is dependent upon a number of variables that break down into the following three categories:

1. Rarity and demand of the specific bottle
2. Type of bottle based on historical or event-oriented condition

3. Unique features
    Labeling
    Color
    Design
    Manufacturer's production errors

After the above variables have been determined, bottles are then categorized, just as the older bottles are, as falling into one of the following conditions:

1. **Mint**—An empty or full bottle (preferably full) with a label or embossing. Clear in color and clean, with no chips, scrapes, or evident wear. If there is a box, it must also be in good condition.

2. **Extra Fine**—An empty bottle with the label showing only slight wear, or embossing. Clear in color, clean, with no chips or scrapes, but some wear. Usually there is no box, or the box is not in very good condition.

3. **Very Good**—The bottle shows some wear and its label is usually missing or not very visible. Most likely there is no embossing and no box.

4. **Good**—Bottle reflects additional wear and label is completely absent. Color is usually faded and bottle is dirty. It's common to see some scrapes and minor chips, and most likely there will be no box.

5. **Fair or Average**—Bottle shows much wear, the label is missing, and there is no embossing. The color is very faded and the piece has numerous scrapes, chips, or even cracks. It will definitely come without an accompanying box.

Even with the preceding guidelines, it is important to have access to additional resources for grading rare and unusual bottles that present the collector with a real challenge—and a feeling of accomplishment when the collector does discover its origin. The bibliography of this book provides a listing of references I find very useful. Remember, too, that other collectors and dealers represent a wealth of unique information and experience. Use them!

Avon
Bottles

Avon began as the California Perfume Company, owned by D. H. McConnell, who as a door-to-door book salesman gave away perfume samples to stop the doors from slamming in his face. As time went on, McConnell gave up on book selling and went into perfume. Although located in New York, the name "Avon" was used in 1929 along with the name "California Perfume Company" or C.P.C. After 1939, the Avon name was used exclusively. The C.P.C. bottles are very rare and collectible due to the small quantities issued, many of which have not been well preserved.

Avon today offers the collector a wide range of unlimited items with shapes of cars, people, chess sets, trains, animals, sporting items (footballs and baseballs, for example), and numerous other objects. The most sought after and scarce are the pre-World War II figurals since very few of these items were well preserved.

Anything that is Avon related is also considered collectible. That includes the boxes, brochures, magazine ads, or anything else with the Avon name. Since many people who sell Avon items are unaware of their value, a collector can find great prices at swap meets, flea markets, and garage sales.

It doesn't stop there. Avon continues to issue new original bottles in a variety of sizes, colors, designs, and shapes. Although the new items are issued in limited editions, the issues are larger in order to accommodate not only the collector, but also the general public.

A Man's World, Globe on stand 1969................................$7–10

A Winner, Boxing gloves 1960...$20–25

Abraham Lincoln, Wild Country After-shave 1970–1972 .....$3–5

After-shave on Tap, Wild Country $3–5

Aladdin's Lamp 1971 ....$7–10

Alaskan Moose 1974 ....$5–8

Alpine Flask 1966–1967 ....$35–45

American Belle, Sonnet Cologne 1976–1978 ....$5–7

American Buffalo 1975 ....$6–8

American Eagle Pipe 1974–1975 ....$6–8

American Eagle, Windjammer After-shave 1971–1972 ....$3–4

American Ideal Perfume,
California Perfume Company 1911...............................$125–140

American Schooner, Oland After-shave 1972–1973 ....$4–5

Andy Capp Figural (England) 1970..................................$95–105

Angler, Windjammer After-shave 1970 ....$5–7

Apple Blossom Toilet Water 1941–1942 ....$50–60

Apothecary, Lemon Velvet Moist Lotion 1973–1976 ....$4–6

Apothecary, Spicy After-shave 1973–1974 ....$4–5

Aristocrat Kittens Soap (Walt Disney) $5–7

Armoire Decanter, Charisma Bath Oil 1973–1974 ....$4–5

Armoire Decanter, Elusive Bath Oil 1972–1975....................$4–5

Auto Lantern 1973..$6–8

Auto, Big Mack Truck, Windjammer After-shave 1973–1975...$5–6

Auto, Cord, 1937 Model, Wild Country After-shave 1974–1975...$7–8

Auto, Country Vendor, Wild Country After-shave 1973.......$7–8

Auto, Dusenberg, Silver, Wild Country After-shave 1970–1972...$8–9

Auto, Dune Buggy, Sports Rally Bracing Lotion 1971–1973 ..$4–5

Auto, Electric Charger, Avon Leather Cologne 1970–1972...$6–7

Auto, Hayes Apperson, 1902 Model, Avon Blend 7 After-shave
1973–1974...$5–7

Auto, Maxwell 23, Deep Woods After-shave 1972–1974 ......$5–6

Auto, MG, 1936, Wild Country After-shave 1974–1975 ....$4–5

Auto, Model A, Wild Country After-shave 1972–1974..........$4–5

Auto, Red Depot Wagon, Oland After-shave 1972–1973.......$6–7

Auto, Rolls Royce, Deep Woods After-shave 1972–1975 ......$6–8

Auto, Stanley Steamer, Windjammer After-shave 1971–1972....$6–7

Auto, Station Wagon, Tai Winds After-shave 1971–1973 .....$7–8

Auto, Sterling 6, Spicy After-shave 1968–1970.....................$6–7

Auto, Sterling 6 II, Wild Country After-shave 1973–1974....$4–5

Auto, Stutz Bearcat, 1914 Model, Avon Blend 7 After-shave
1974–1977...$5–6

Auto, Touring T, Tribute After-shave, 1969–1970.................$6–7

Auto, Volkswagen, Red, Oland After-shave 1972...................$5–6

Avon Calling, Phone, Wild Country After-shave 1969–1970...$15–20

Avon Dueling Pistol II, Black Glass 1972...........................$10–15

Avonshire Blue Cologne 1971–1974.....................................$4–5

Baby Grand Piano, Perfume Glace 1971–1972....................$8–10

Baby Hippo 1977–1980 ....$4–5

Ballad Perfume, 3 drams, ⅜ ounce 1939 ....$100–125

Bath Urn, Lemon Velvet Bath Oil 1971–1973 ....$4–5

Beauty Bound Black Purse 1964..$45–55

Bell Jar Cologne 1973 ....$5–10

Benjamin Franklin, Wild Country After-shave 1974–1976 ...$4–5

Big Game Rhino, Tai Winds After-shave 1972–1973.............$7–8

Big Whistle 1972..$4–5

Bird House Power Bubble Bath 1969 ....$7–8

Bird of Paradise Cologne Decanter 1972–1974......................$4–5

Blacksmith's Anvil, Deep Woods After-shave 1972–1973 .....$4–5

Bloodhound Pipe, Deep Woods After-shave 1976.................$5–6

Blue Blazer After-shave Lotion 1964.................................$25–30

Blue Blazer Deluxe 1965 ....$55–65

Blue Moo Soap on a Rope 1972...$5–6

Blunderbuss Pistol 1976...$7–10

Bon Bon Black, Field and Flowers Cologne 1973.................$5–6

Bon Bon White, Occur Cologne 1972–1973.........................$5–6

Bon Bon White, Topaze Cologne 1972–1973.......................$5–6

Boot Gold Top, Avon Leather After-shave 1966–1971 ....$3–4

Boot Western 1973 ....$4–5

Boots and Saddle 1968 ....$20–22

Brocade Deluxe 1967 ....$30–35

Buffalo Nickel, Liquid Hair Lotion 1971–1972 ....$4–5

Club Bottle, 5th Annual 1976 ....$25–30

Club Bottle, Bud Hastin 1974 ....$70–95

Club Bottle, CPC Factory 1974...$30–40

Collector's Pipe, Windjammer After-shave 1973–1974 ....$3–4

Colt Revolver 1851 1975–1976...$10–12

Corncob Pipe After-shave 1974–1975...................................$4–6

Corvette Stingray '65 1975..$5–7

Covered Wagon, Wild Country After-shave 1970–1971 ....$4–5

Daylight Shaving Time 1968–1970...$5–7

Defender Cannon 1966...$20–24

Dollar's 'N' Scents 1966–1967..$20–24

Dutch Girl Figurine, Somewhere 1973–1974.......................$8–10

Duck After-shave 1971 ....$4–6

Dueling Pistol 1760 1973–1974...$9–12

Dueling Pistol II 1975..$9–12

Eight Ball Decanter, Spicy After-shave 1973 ....$3–4

Electric Guitar, Wild Country After-shave 1974–1974..........$4–5

Enchanted Frog Cream Sachet, Sonnet 1973–1976 ....$3–4

Fashion Boot, Moonwind Cologne 1972–1976 ....$5–7

Fashion Boot, Sonnet Cologne 1972–1976............................$5–7

Fielder's Choice 1971–1972...$4–6

Fire Alarm Box 1975–1976 ....$4–6

First-Class Male, Wild Country After-shave 1970–1971 ....$3–4

First Down, Soap on a Rope 1970–1971 ....$7–8

First Down, Wild Country After-shave................................$3–4

First Volunteer, Tai Winds Cologne 1971–1972 ....$6–7

Fox Hunt 1966 ....$25–30

French Telephone, Moonwind Foaming Bath Oil 1971 .....$20–24

Garnet Bud Vase, To a Wild Rose Cologne 1973–1976.........$3–5

Gavel, Island Lime After-shave 1967–1968............................$4–5

George Washington, Spicy After-shave 1970–1972 ....$2–3

George Washington, Tribute After-shave 1970–1972............$2–3

Gold Cadillac 1969–1973...$7–10

Gone Fishing 1973–1974 ....$5–7

Grade Avon Hostess Soap 1971–1972 ....$6–8

Hearth Lamp, Roses, Roses, 1973–1976................................$6–8

Hobnail Decanter, Moonwind Bath Oil 1972–1974 ....$5–6

Hunter's Stein 1972 ....$10–14

Indian Chieftan, Protein Hair Lotion 1972–1975 ....$2–3

Indian Head Penny, Bravo After-shave 1970–1972................$4–5

Inkwell, Windjammer After-shave 1969–1970.......................$6–7

Iron Horse Shaving Mug, Avon Blend 7 After-shave
1974–1976...$3–4

Jack-in-the-Box, Baby Cream 1974.......................................$4–6

Jaguar Car 1973–1976..$6–8

Jolly Santa 1978 ....$6–7

Joyous Bell 1978 ....$5–6

King Pin 1969–1970 ....$4–6

Kodiak Bear 1977...$5–10

Koffee Klatch, Honeysuckle Foam Bath Oil 1971–1974 ....$5–6

Liberty Bell, Tribute After-shave 1971–1972 ....$4–6

Liberty Dollar, After-shave 1970–1972...............................$4–6

Lincoln Bottle 1971–1972 ....$3–5

Lip Pop Colas, Cherry 1973–1974.......................................$1–2

Lip Pop Colas, Cola 1973–1974...$1–2

Lip Pop Colas, Strawberry 1973–1974 ....$1–2

Longhorn Steer 1975–1976 ....$7–9

Looking Glass, Regence Cologne 1970–1972......................$7–8

Mallard Duck 1967–1968 ....$8–10

Mickey Mouse, Bubble Bath 1969.....................................$10–12

Mighty Mitt Soap on a Rope 1969–1972 ....$7–8

Ming Cat, Bird of Paradise Cologne 1971 ....$5–7

Minibike, Sure Winner Bracing Lotion 1972–1973 ....$3–5

Nile-Blue Bath Urn, Skin So Soft 1972–1974 ....$4–6

No Parking 1975–1976 ....$5–7

Old Faithful, Wild Country After-shave 1972–1973..............$4–6

One Good Turn, Screwdriver 1976.......................................$5–6

Opening Play, Dull Golden, Spicy After-shave 1968–1969...$8–10

Opening Play, Shiny Golden, Spicy After-shave 1968–1969..$14–17

Owl Fancy, Roses, Roses 1974–1976....................................$3–4

Owl Soap Dish and Soaps 1970–1971 ....$8–10

Packard Roadster 1970–1972..$4–7

Pass Play Decanter 1973–1975..$6–8

Peanuts Gang Soaps 1970–1972 ....$8–9

Pepperbox Pistol 1976..$5–10

Perfect Drive Decanter 1975–1976 ....$7–9

Pheasant 1972–1974..$7–9

Piano Decanter, Tai Winds After-shave 1972........................$3–4

Pipe, Full, Decanter, Brown, Spicy After-shave 1971–1972 ...$3–4

Pony Express, Avon Leather After-shave 1971–1972 ....$3–4

Pony Post "Tall" 1966–1967 ....$7–9

Potbelly Stove 1970–1971 ....$5–7

President Lincoln, Tai Winds After-shave 1973....................$6–8

President Washington, Deep Woods After-shave 1974–1976 ...$4–5

Quail 1973–1974..$7–9

Rainbow Trout, Deep Woods After-shave 1973–1974...........$3–4

Road Runner, Motorcycle $4–5

Rook, Spicy After-shave 1973–1974 ....$4–5

Royal Coach, Bird of Paradise Bath Oil 1972–1973..............$4–6

Scent with Love, Elusive Perfume 1971–1972 ....$9–10

Scent with Love, Field Flowers Perfume 1971–1972...........$9–10

Scent with Love, Moonwind Perfume 1971–1972...............$9–10

Side-wheeler, Tribute After-shave 1970–1971 ....$4–5

Side-wheeler, Wild Country After-shave 1971–1972.............$3–4

Small World Perfume Glace, Small World 1971–1972..........$3–4

Snoopy Soap Dish Refills 1968–1976....................................$3–4

Snoopy's Bubble Tub 1971–1972...$3–4

Spark Plug Decanter 1975–1976 ....$2–5

Spirit of Saint Louis, Excalibur After-shave 1970–1972........$6–8

Stagecoach, Wild Country After-shave 1970–1977................$5–6

Tee Off, Electric Pre-Shave, 1973–1975 ....$2–3

Ten-Point Buck, Wild Country After-shave 1969–1974 ....$5–7

Twenty-Dollar Gold Piece, Windjammer After-shave
1971–1972...$4–6

Uncle Sam Pipe, Deep Woods After-shave 1975–1976..........$4–5

Viking Horn 1966 ....$12–16

Western Boot, Wild Country After-shave 1973–1975 ....$2–3

Western Saddle 1971–1972...$7–9

Wild Turkey 1974–1976...$6–8

World's Greatest Dad Decanter 1971 ....$4–6

Ballantine Bottles

Ballantine bottles, which are brightly colored and ceramic, contain imported Scotch whiskey and usually read "Blended Scotch Whiskey, 14 Years Old." The majority of these bottles' designs are based on sporting or outdoor themes, such as ducks or fishermen with their head represented by the bottle cap. The more collectible items, however, are the older bottles (1930), which are nonfigural and very decorative.

Charioteer...$5–10

Discus Thrower..$5–10

Duck $8–10

Fisherman..$10–12

Gladiator..$5–10

Golf Bag...$8–10

Mallard Duck...$6–8

Mercury $5–10

Old Crow Chessman..$9–10

Scottish Knight..$10–12

Seated Fisherman..$10–12

Silver Knight $12–15

Zebra..$12–15

Barsottini Bottles

The Barsottini bottle, which is manufactured in Italy, does not use any American or nongeographic themes for the U.S. marketplace. These bottles are ceramic and come in gray and white to represent the brickwork of buildings, and usually represent European subjects such as the Eiffel Tower or the Florentine Steeple.

Alpine Pipe, 10 inches $8–12

Antique Automobile, Ceramic, Coupe $6–9

Antique Automobile, Open Car $6–9

Clock, with Cherub $30–40

Clowns, Ceramic, 12 inches Each $9–12

Eiffel Tower, Gray and White, 15 inches $8–12

Florentine Cannon, "L," 15 inches $14–20

Florentine Steeple, Gray and White $9–12

Monastery Cask, Ceramic, 12 inches $14–20

Paris Arc de Triomphe, 7½ inches $10–12

Pisa's Leaning Tower, Gray and White $10–12

Roman Coliseum, Ceramic $7–10

Trivoli Clock, Ceramic, 15 inches $12–15

Jim Beam Bottles

The James B. Beam distilling company was founded in 1778 by Jacob Beam in Kentucky and now bears the name of Colonel James B. Beam, Jacob Beam's grandson. Beam whiskey was very popular in the South during the nineteenth and early twentieth centuries but not produced on a large scale. Because of low production, the early Beam bottles are very rare, collectible, and valuable.

In 1953, the Beam company packaged bourbon in a special Christmas/New Year ceramic decanter, which was a rarity for any distiller. When the decanters sold well, Beam decided to redevelop its method of packaging, which led to production of a wide variety of different series in the 1950s. The first of these were the ceramics of 1953. In 1955 the executive series was issued to commemorate the 160th anniversary of the corporation. In 1955, Beam introduced the Regal China series to honor significant people, places, and events with a concentration on America and contemporary situations. In 1956, political figures were introduced with the elephant and the donkey as well as special productions for customer specialties, which were made on commission. In 1957, the trophy series came along to signify various achievements within the liquor industry. And, in 1958, the state series was introduced to commemorate the admission of Alaska and Hawaii into the union. The practice has continued with Beam still producing decanters commemorating all fifty states.

In total, over 500 types of Beam bottles have been issued since 1953.

AC Spark Plug 1977
Replica of a spark plug in white, green, and gold $22–26

Ahepa 50th Anniversary 1972
Regal China bottle designed in honor of AHEPA's (American
Hellenic Education Progressive Association) 50th anniversary.....$4–6

Aida 1978
Figurine of character from the opera *Aida* $140–160

Akron Rubber Capital 1973
Regal China bottle honoring Akron, OH $15–20

Alaska 1958
Regal China, 9½ inches, star-shaped bottle............................$55–60

Alaska 1964–1965
Reissue of the 1958 bottle...$40–50

Alaska Purchase 1966
Regal China, 10 inches, blue and gold bottle.............................$4–6

American Samoa 1973
Regal China, reflects the seal of Samoa......................................$5–7

American Veterans..$4–7

Antique Clock $35–45

Antioch 1967
Regal China, 10 inches, commemorates diamond jubilee of Regal..$5–7

Antique Coffee Grinder 1979
Replica of a box coffee mill used in mid-nineteenth century...$10–12

Antique Globe 1980
Represents the Martin Behaim globe of 1492 ....$7–11

Antique Telephone (1897) 1978
Replica of an 1897 desk phone, second in a series $50–60

Antique Trader 1968
Regal China, 10½ inches, represents Antique Trader newspaper ...$4–6

Appaloosa 1974
Regal China, 10 inches, represents favorite horse of the
Old West $12–15

Arizona 1968
Regal China, 12 inches, represents the State of Arizona..............$4–6

Armadillo..$8–12

Armanetti Award Winner 1969
Honor's Aramnetti, Inc. of Chicago as "Liquor Retailer of
the Year"...$6–8

Armanetti Shopper 1971
Reflects the slogan "It's fun to Shop Armanetti—Self-Service Liquor
Store," 11¾ inches...$6–8

Armanetti Vase 1968
Yellow-toned decanter embossed with flowers...........................$5–7

Bacchus 1970
Issued by Armanetti Liquor Stores of Chicago, IL, 11¾ inches ...$6–9

Barney's Slot Machine 1978
Replica of the world's largest slot machine $14–16

Barry Berish 1985
Executive series..$110–140

Barry Berish 1986
Executive series, bowl $110–140

Bartender's Guild 1973
Commemorative honoring the International Bartenders
Association...$4–7

Baseball 1969
Issued to commemorate the 100th anniversary of baseball.....$18–20

Beam Pot 1980
Shaped like a New England bean pot, club bottle for the New
England Beam Bottle and Specialties Club.............................$12–15

Beaver Valley Club 1977
A club bottle to honor the Beaver Valley Jim Beam Club of
Rochester $8–12

Bell Scotch 1970
Regal China, 10½ inches, in honor of Arthur Bell and Sons........$4–7

Beverage Association, NLBA $4–7

The Big Apple 1979
Apple-shaped bottle with "The Big Apple" over the top............$8–12

Bing's 31st Clambake Bottle 1972
Commemorates 31st Bing Crosby National Pro-Am Golf
Tournament in January 1972 ....$25–30

Bing Crosby National Pro-Am 1970...$4–7

Bing Crosby National Pro-Am 1971 ....$4–7

Bing Crosby National Pro-Am 1972....................................$15–25

Bing Crosby National Pro-Am 1973....................................$18–23

Bing Crosby National Pro-Am 1974....................................$15–25

Bing Crosby National Pro-Am 1975....................................$45–65

Bing Crosby 36th 1976..$15–25

Bing Crosby National Pro-Am 1977....................................$12–18

Bing Crosby National Pro-Am 1978....................................$12–18

Black Katz 1968
Regal China, 14½ inches...$7–12

Blue Cherub Executive 1960
Regal China, 12½ inches...$70–90

Blue Daisy 1967
Also known as Zimmerman Blue Daisy $10–12

Blue-gill, Fish $12–16

Blue Goose Order...$4–7

Blue Jay 1969...$4–7

Blue Goose 1979
Replica of blue goose, authenticated by Dr. Lester Fisher, director of
Lincoln Park Zoological Gardens in Chicago $7–9

Blue Hen Club $12–15

Blue Slot Machine 1967 ....$10–12

Bobby Unser Olsonite Eagle 1975
Replica of the racing car used by Bobby Unser $40–50

Bob DeVaney $8–12

Bob Hope Desert Classic 1973
First genuine Regal China bottle created in honor of the Bob Hope
Desert Classic...$8–9

Bob Hope Desert Classic 1974 ....$8–12

Bohemian Girl 1974
Issued for the Bohemian Café in Omaha, NB, to honor the Czech
and Slovak immigrants in the United States, 14¼ inches $10–15

Bonded Gold $4–7

Bonded Mystic 1979
Urn-shaped bottle, burgundy-colored $4–7

Bonded Silver $4–7

Boris Godinov, with Base 1978
Second in opera series...$350–450

Bourbon Barrel $18–24

Bowling Proprietors $4–7

Boys Town of Italy 1973
Created in honor of the Boys Town of Italy $7–10

Bowl 1986
Executive series...$20–30

Broadmoor Hotel 1968
To celebrate the 50th anniversary of this famous hotel in Colorado
Springs, CO, "1918—The Broadmoor—1968" $4–7

Buffalo Bill 1971
Regal China, 10½ inches, commemorates Buffalo Bill.................$4–7

Bulldog 1979
Honors the 204th anniversary of the United States Marine
Corps...$15–18

Cable Car 1968
Regal China, 4½ inches..$4–6

Caboose 1980...$50–60

California Mission 1970
This bottle was issued for the Jim Beam Bottle Club of Southern
California in honor of the 20th anniversary of the California
Missions, 14 inches...$10–15

California Retail Liquor Dealers Association 1973
Designed to commemorate the 20th anniversary of the California
Retail Liquor Dealers Association $6–9

Cal-Neva 1969
Regal China, 9½ inches..$5–7

Camellia City Club 1979
Replica of the cupola of the State Capitol Building in
Sacramento $18–23

Cameo Blue 1965
Also known as the Shepherd Bottle $4–6

Cannon 1970
Bottle issued to commemorate the 175th anniversary of the Jim
Beam Company. Some of these bottles have a small chain shown on
the cannon and some do not. Those without the chain are harder to
find and more valuable, 8 inches
    Chain $2–4
    No chain $9–13

Canteen 1979
Replica of the exact canteen used by the armed forces..............$8–12

Captain and Mate 1980...$10–12

Cardinal (Kentucky Cardinal) 1968 ....$40–50

Carmen 1978
Third in the opera series $140–180

Carolier Bull 1984
Executive series...$18–23

Catfish $16–24

Cathedral Radio 1979
Replica of one of the earlier dome-shaped radios $12–15

Cats 1967
Trio of cats: Siamese, Burmese, and Tabby.............................$6–9

Cedars of Lebanon 1971
This bottle was issued in honor of the Jerry Lewis Muscular
Dystrophy Telethon in 1971 ....$5–7

Charisma 1970
Executive series...$4–7

Charlie McCarthy 1976
Replica of Edgar Bergen's puppet from the 1930s $20–30

Cherry Hills Country Club 1973
Commemorating 50th anniversary of Cherry Hills Country
Club...$4–7

Cheyenne, Wyoming 1977 ....$4–6

Chicago Cubs, Sports Series $30–40

Chicago Show Bottle 1977
Commemorates 6th annual Chicago Jim Beam Bottle Show ...$10–14

Christmas Tree..$150–200

Churchill Downs—Pink Roses 1969
Regal China, 10¼ inches...$5–7

Churchill Downs—Red Roses 1969
Regal China, 10¼ inches $9–12

Circus Wagon 1979
Replica of a circus wagon from the late nineteenth century $24–26

Civil War North 1961
Regal China, 10¼ inches..$10–15

Civil War South 1961
Regal China, 10¼ inches..$25–35

Clear Crystal Bourbon 1967
Clear glass, 11½ inches..$5–7

Clear Crystal Scotch 1966 ....$9–12

Clear Crystal Vodka 1967 ....$5–8

Cleopatra Rust 1962
Glass, 13¼ inches $3–5

Cleopatra Yellow 1962
Glass, 13¼ inches, rarer than Cleopatra Rust $8–12

Clint Eastwood 1973
Commemorating Clint Eastwood Invitational Celebrity Tennis
Tournament in Pebble Beach $14–17

Cocktail Shaker 1953
Glass, Fancy Disp. Bottle, 9¼ inches...$2–5

Coffee Grinder $8–12

Coffee Warmers 1954
Four types are known: red, black, gold, and white...................$7–12

Coffee Warmers 1956
Two types with metal necks and handles $2–5

Coho Salmon 1976
Official seal of the National Fresh Water Fishing Hall of Fame
is on the back..$10–13

Colin Mead...$180–210

Cobalt 1981
Executive series...$18–23

Collector's Edition 1966
Set of six glass famous paintings: *The Blue Boy, On the Terrace, Mardi
Gras, Austide Bruant, The Artist Before His Easel*, and *Laughing
Cavalier* (each) $2–5

Collector's Edition Volume II 1967
A set of six flask-type bottles with famous pictures: *George Gisze,
Soldier and Girl, Night Watch, The Jester, Nurse and Child*, and *Man on
Horse* (each) $2–5

Collector's Edition Volume III 1968
A set of eight bottles with famous paintings: *On the Trail, Indian
Maiden, Buffalo, Whistler's Mother, American Gothic, The Kentuckian,
The Scout*, and *Hauling in the Gill Net* (each)................................$2–5

Collector's Edition Volume IV 1969
A set of seven bottles with famous paintings: *Balcony, The Judge, Fruit
Basket, Boy with Cherries, Emile Zola, The Guitarist Zouave*, and
Sunflowers (each)..$2–5

Collector's Edition Volume V 1970
A set of six bottles with famous paintings: *Au Cafe, Old Peasant,
Boaring Party, Gare Saint Lazare, The Jewish Bride*, and *Titus at Writing
Desk* (each) $2–5

Collector's Edition Volume VI 1971
A set of three bottles with famous art pieces: *Charles I, The Merry
Lute Player*, and *Boy Holding Flute* (each) $2–5

Collector's Edition Volume VII 1972
A set of three bottles with famous paintings: *The Bag Piper, Prince
Baltasor*, and *Maidservant Pouring Milk* (each)..............................$2–5

Collector's Edition Volume VIII 1973
A set of three bottles with famous portraits: Ludwig van Beethoven,
Wolfgang Mozart, and Frederic Francis Chopin (each)................$2–5

Collector's Edition Volume IX 1974
A set of three bottles with famous paintings: *Cardinal, Ring-Neck
Pheasant*, and *The Woodcock* (each)..$3–6

Collector's Edition Volume X 1975
A set of three bottles with famous pictures: *Sailfish, Rainbow Trout*,
and *Largemouth Bass* (each) $3–6

Collector's Edition Volume XI 1976
A set of three bottles with famous paintings: *Chipmunk, Bighorn
Sheep*, and *Pronghorn Antelope* (each)..$3–6

Collector's Edition Volume XII 1977
A set of four bottles each with a different reproduction of James
Lockhart on the front (each) $3–6

Collector's Edition Volume XIV 1978
A set of four bottles with James Lockhart paintings: *Raccoon,
Mule Deer, Red Fox*, and *Cottontail Rabbit* (each) $3–6

Collector's Edition Volume XV 1979
A set of three flasks with Frederic Remington paintings: *The Cowboy*
(1902), *The Indian Trapper* (1902), and *Lieutenant S. C. Robertson*
(1890) (each) $2–5

Collector's Edition Volume XVI 1980
A set of three flasks depicting duck scenes: *The Mallard,
The Redhead*, and *The Canvasback* (each) $3–6

Collector's Edition Volume XVII 1981
A set of three flask bottles with Jim Lockhart paintings: *Great Elk,
Pintail Duck*, and *The Horned Owl* (each)....................................$3–6

Colorado 1959
Regal China, 10¾ inches..$20–25

Colorado Centennial 1976
Replica of Pike's Peak...$8–12

Colorado Springs $4–7

Computer, Democrat 1984..$12–18

Computer, Republican 1984..$12–18

Convention Bottle 1971
Commemorates the first national convention of the National
Association of Jim Beam Bottle and Specialty Clubs hosted by the
Rocky Mountain Club, Denver, CO $5–7

Convention Number 2, 1972
Honors the second annual convention of the National Association
of Jim Beam Bottle and Specialty Clubs in Anaheim, CA $20–30

Convention Number 3, Detroit 1973
Commemorates the third annual convention of Beam Bottle
Collectors in Detroit, MI $10–12

Convention Number 4, Pennsylvania 1974
Commemorates the annual convention of the Jim Beam Bottle Club
in Lancaster, PA $80–100

Convention Number 5, Sacramento 1975
Commemorates the annual convention of the Camellia City Jim
Beam Bottle Club in Sacramento, CA $5–7

Convention Number 6, Hartford 1976
Commemorates the annual convention of the Jim Beam Bottle Club
in Hartford, CT $5–7

Convention Number 7, Louisville 1978
Commemorates the annual convention of the Jim Beam Bottle Club
in Louisville, KY..$5–7

Convention Number 8, Chicago 1978
Commemorates the annual convention of the Jim Beam Bottle Club
in Chicago, IL $8–12

Convention Number 9, Houston 1979
Commemorates the annual convention of the Jim Beam Bottle Club
in Houston, TX...$20–30
    Cowboy, beige..$35–45
    Cowboy, in color...$35–45

Convention Number 10, Norfolk 1980
Commemorates the annual convention of the Jim Beam Bottle Club
at the Norfolk Naval Base, VA $18–22
    Waterman, pewter $35–45
    Waterman, yellow $35–45

Convention Number 11, Las Vegas 1981
Commemorates the annual convention of the Jim Beam Bottle Club
in Las Vegas, NV $20–22
    Showgirl, blond $45–55
    Showgirl, brunette $45–55

Convention Number 12, New Orleans 1982
Commemorates the annual convention of the Jim Beam Bottle Club
in New Orleans, LA $30–35
    Buccaneer, gold $35–45
    Buccaneer, in color $35–45

Convention Number 13, Saint Louis 1983 (stein)
Commemorates the annual convention of the Jim Beam Bottle Club
in Saint Louis, MO $55–70
    Gibson girl, blue $65–80
    Gibson girl, yellow $65–80

Convention Number 14, Florida, King Neptune 1984
Commemorates the annual convention of the Jim Beam Bottle Club
in Florida $15–20
    Mermaid, blond $35–45
    Mermaid, brunette $35–45

Convention Number 15, Las Vegas 1985
Commemorates the annual convention of the Jim Beam Bottle Club
in Las Vegas, NV $40–50

Convention Number 16, Pilgrim Woman, Boston 1986
Commemorates the annual convention of the Jim Beam Bottle Club
in Boston, MA $35–45
    Minuteman, color $85–105
    Minuteman, pewter $85–105

Convention Number 17, Louisville 1987
Commemorates the annual convention of the Jim Beam Bottle Club
in Louisville, KY...$55–75
   Kentucky Colonel, blue $85–105
   Kentucky Colonel, gray $85–105

Convention Number 18, Bucky Beaver 1988....................$30–40
   Portland rose, red..$30–40
   Portland rose, yellow...$30–40

Convention Number 19, Kansas City 1989
Commemorates the annual convention of the Jim Beam Bottle Club
in Kansas City, MO $40–50

Cowboy 1979
Awarded to collectors who attended the 1979 convention for the
International Association of Beam Clubs $35–50

CPO Open $4–7

Crappie 1979
Commemorates the National Fresh Water Fishing Hall of Fame ..$10–14

Dark Eyes Brown Jug 1978..$4–6

D-Day..$12–18

Delaware Blue Hen Bottle 1972
Commemorates the State of Delaware $4–7

Delco Freedom Battery 1978
Replica of a Delco battery..$18–22

Delft Blue 1963 ....$3–5

Delft Rose 1963..$4–6

Del Webb Mint 1970
   Metal stopper $10–12
   China stopper...$50–60

Devil Dog..$15–25

Dial Telephone 1980
Fourth in a series of Beam telephone designs $40–50

Dodge City 1972
Issued to honor the centennial of Dodge City...........................$5–6

Doe 1963
Regal China, 13½ inches..$10–12

Doe—Reissued 1967...$10–12

Dog 1959
Regal China, 15¼ inches..$20–25

Don Giovanni 1980
The fifth in the opera series...$140–180

Donkey and Elephant Ashtrays 1956
Regal China, 12 inches (pair) $12–16

Donkey and Elephant Boxers 1964 (pair) $14–18

Donkey and Elephant Clowns 1968
Regal China, 12 inches (pair) $4–7

Donkey and Elephant Football Election Bottles 1972
Regal China, 9½ inches (pair)...$6–9

Donkey New York City 1976
Commemorates the National Democratic Convention in
New York City $10–12

Duck 1957
Regal China, 14¼ inches..$15–20

Ducks and Geese 1955 ....$5–8

Ducks Unlimited Mallard 1974..$40–50

Ducks Unlimited Wood Duck 1975 ....$45–50

Ducks Unlimited 40th Mallard Hen 1977 ....$40–50

Ducks Unlimited Canvasback Drake 1979 ....$30–40

Ducks Unlimited Blue-winged Teal 1980
The sixth in a series, 9½ inches $40–45

Ducks Unlimited Green-winged Teal 1981 ....$35–45

Ducks Unlimited Wood Ducks 1982 ....$35–45

Ducks Unlimited American Wigeon PR 1983 ....$35–45

Ducks Unlimited Mallard 1984..$55–75

Ducks Unlimited Pintail PR 1985 ....$30–40

Ducks Unlimited Redhead 1986 ....$15–25

Ducks Unlimited Blue Bill 1987..$40–60

Ducks Unlimited Black Duck 1989 ....$50–60

Eagle 1966
Regal China, 12½ inches...$10–13

Eldorado 1978..$7–9

Election, Democrat 1988 ....$30–40

Election, Republican 1988...$30–40

Elephant and Donkey Supermen 1980 (pair)....................$10–14

Elephant Kansas City 1976
Commemorates the National Republican Convention in
Kansas City $8–10

Elks...$4–7

Elks National Foundation..$8–12

Emerald Crystal Bourbon 1968
Green glass, 11½ inches $3–5

Emmett Kelly 1973
Likeness of Emmett Kelly as sad-faced Willie the Clown........$18–22

Emmett Kelly, Native Son...$50–60

Ernie's Flower Cart 1976
In honor of Ernie's Wines and Liquors of Northern California..$24–28

Evergreen, Club Bottle..$7–10

Expo 1974
Issued in honor of the World's Fair held at Spokane, WA..........$5–7

Falstaff 1979
Second in Australian opera series, limited edition of
1,000 bottles...$150–160

Fantasia Bottle 1971 ....$5–6

Father's Day Card $15–25

Female Cardinal 1973..$8–12

Fiesta Bowl, Glass..$8–12

Fiesta Bowl 1973
The second bottle created to honor the Fiesta Bowl $9–11

Figaro 1977
Character Figaro from the opera *Barber of Seville*................$140–170

Fighting Bull..$12–18

Figi Islands $4–6

First National Bank of Chicago 1964
Commemorates the 100th anniversary of the First National Bank of
Chicago. Approximately 130 were issued, with 117 being given as
mementos to the bank directors and none for public distribution.
This is the most valuable Beam bottle known. Also, beware of
reproductions $1,900–2,400

Fish 1957
Regal China, 14 inches...$15–18

Fish Hall of Fame $25–35

Five Seasons 1980
Club bottle for the Five Seasons Club of Cedar Rapids honors the
State of Iowa $10–12

Fleet Reserve Association 1974
Issued by the Fleet Reserve Association to honor the Career Sea
Service on its 50th anniversary...$5–7

Florida Shell 1968
Regal China, 9 inches..$4–6

Floro de Oro 1976...$10–12

Flower Basket 1962
Regal China, 12¼ inches...$30–35

Football Hall of Fame 1972
Reproduction of the new Professional Football Hall of Fame
Building $14–18

Foremost—Black and Gold 1956
First Beam bottle issued for a liquor retailer, Foremost Liquor
Store of Chicago...$225–250

Foremost—Speckled Beauty 1956
The most valuable of the Foremost bottles $500–600

Fox 1967, Blue Coat $65–80

Fox 1971, Gold Coat..$35–50

Fox, Green Coat...$12–18

Fox, White Coat $20–30

Fox, on a Dolphin $12–15

Fox, Uncle Sam $5–6

Fox, Kansas City, Blue, Miniature $20–30

Fox, Red Distillery...$1,100–1,300

Franklin Mint $4–7

French Cradle Telephone 1979
Third in the Telephone Pioneers of America series $20–22

Galah Bird 1979 ....$14–16

Gem City, Club Bottle $35–45

George Washington Commemorative Plate 1976
Commemorates the U.S. Bicentennial, 9½ inches $12–15

German Bottle—Weisbaden 1973 ....$4–6

German Stein $20–30

Germany 1970
Issued to honor the American armed forces in Germany $4–6

Glen Cambell 51st 1976
Honors the 51st Los Angeles Open at the Riviera Country Club
in February 1976 ....$7–10

Golden Chalice 1961 ....$40–50

Golden Jubilee 1977
Executive series...$8–12

Golden Nugget 1969
Regal China, 12½ inches...$35–45

Golden Rose 1978...$15–20

Grand Canyon 1969
Honors the Grand Canyon National Park's 50th Anniversary.....$7–9

Grant Locomotive 1979 ....$55–65

Gray Cherub 1958
Regal China, 12 inches..$240–260

Great Chicago Fire Bottle 1971
Commemorates the great Chicago fire of 1871 and salutes Mercy
Hospital, which helped the fire victims $18–22

Great Dane 1976 ....$7–9

Green China Jug 1965
Regal Glass, 12½ inches...$4–6

Hank Williams, Jr. $40–50

Hannah Dustin 1973
Regal China, 14½ inches..$10–12

Hansel and Gretel Bottle 1971 ....$4–6

Harley Davidson 85th Anniversary Decanter $110–150

Harley Davidson 85th Anniversary Stein........................$180–220

Harolds Club—Man-in-a-Barrel 1957
First in a series made for Harolds Club in Reno, NV $380–410

Harolds Club—Silver Opal 1957
Commemorates the 25th anniversary of Harolds Club $20–22

Harolds Club—Man-in-a-Barrel 1958 ....$140–160

Harolds Club—NV (gray) 1963
Created for the "Nevada Centennial—1864–1964." This is a rare
and valuable bottle..$90–110

Harolds Club—NV (silver) 1964 ....$90–110

Harolds Club—Pinwheel 1965..$40–45

Harolds Club—Blue Slot Machine 1967 ....$10–14

Harolds Club—VIP Executive 1967
Limited quantity issued...$50–60

Harolds Club—VIP Executive 1968....................................$55–65

Harolds Club—Gray Slot Machine 1968 ....$4–6

Harolds Club—VIP Executive 1969
This bottle was given as a Christmas gift to the casino's
executives $260–285

Harolds Club—Covered Wagon 1969–1970 ....$4–6

Harolds Club 1970 .... $40–60

Harolds Club 1971 .... $40–60

Harolds Club 1972 .... $18–25

Harolds Club 1973 .... $18–24

Harolds Club 1974 .... $12–16

Harolds Club 1975 .... $12–18

Harolds Club VIP 1976 .... $18–22

Harolds Club 1977 .... $20–30

Harolds Club 1978 .... $20–30

Harolds Club 1979 .... $20–30

Harolds Club 1980 .... $25–35

Harolds Club 1982 .... $110–145

Harp Seal $12–18

Harrahs Club, Nevada—Gray 1963
This is the same bottle used for the Nevada Centennial and
Harolds Club $500–550

Harry Hoffman $4–7

Harveys Resort Hotel at Lake Tahoe $6–10

Hatfield 1973
The character of Hatfield from the story of the Hatfield and
McCoy feud $15–20

Hawaii 1959
Tribute to the 50th state $35–40

Hawaii—Reissued 1967 .... $40–45

Hawaii 1971 .... $6–8

Hawaii Aloha 1971 .... $6–10

Hawaiian Open Bottle 1972
Honors the 1972 Hawaiian Open Golf Tournament....................$6–8

Hawaiian Open 1973
Second bottle created in honor of the United Hawaiian Open Golf
Classic..$7–9

Hawaiian Open 1974
Commemorates the 1974 Hawaiian Open Golf Classic $5–8

Hawaiian Open Outrigger 1975 ....$9–11

Hawaiian Paradise 1978
Commemorates the 200th anniversary of the landing of
Captain Cook...$15–17

Hemisfair 1968
Commemorates "Hemisfair 68—San Antonio" $8–10

Herre Brothers..$22–35

Hobo, Australia $10–14

Hoffman 1969...$4–7

Holiday—Carolers $40–50

Holiday—Nutcracker $40–50

Home Builders 1978
Commemorates the 1979 convention of the Home Builders...$25–30

Hone Heke $200–250

Honga Hika 1980
First in a series of Maori warrior bottles. Honga Hika was a war-chief
of the Ngapuke tribe $220–240

Horse (Appaloosa) $8–12

Horse (black)..$18–22

Horse (black), reissued 1967...$10–12

Horse (brown) $18–22

Horse (brown), reissued 1967 ....$10–12

Horse (mare and foal) $35–45

Horse (Oh, Kentucky) $70–85

Horse (pewter) $12–17

Horse (white) $18–20

Horse (white), reissued 1967 ....$12–17

Horseshoe Club 1969 ....$4–6

Hula Bowl 1975 ....$8–10

Hyatt House—Chicago $7–10

Hyatt House—New Orleans $8–11

Idaho 1963 ....$30–40

Illinois 1968
Honors the Sesquicentennial 1818–1968 of Illinois $4–6

Indianapolis Sesquicentennial $4–6

Indianapolis 500 ....$9–12

Indian Chief 1979 ....$9–12

International Chili Society 1976 ....$9–12

Italian Marble Urn 1985
Executive series $12–17

Ivory Ashtray 1955 ....$8–10

Jackalope 1971
Honors the Wyoming jackalope $5–8

Jaguar $18–23

Jewel Tea Man—50th Anniversary $35–45

John Henry 1972
Commemorates the legendary "steel-drivin' man" $18–22

Joliet Legion Band 1978
Commemorates the 26th national championship $15–20

Kaiser International Open Bottle 1971
Commemorates the 5th Annual Kaiser International Open Golf
Tournament $5–6

Kangaroo 1977 .... $10–14

Kansas 1960
Commemorates the "Kansas 1861–1961 Centennial" $35–45

Kentucky Black Head—Brown Head 1967
    Black head $12–18
    Brown head $20–28
    White head $18–23

Kentucky Derby 95th, Pink, Red Roses 1969 .... $4–7

Kentucky Derby 96th, Double Rose 1970 .... $15–25

Kentucky Derby 97th 1971 .... $4–7

Kentucky Derby 98th 1972 .... $4–6

Kentucky Derby 100th 1974 .... $7–10

Key West 1972
Honors the 150th anniversary of Key West, FL $5–7

King Kamehameha 1972
Commemorates the 100th anniversary of King Kamehameha
Day $8–11

King Kong 1976
Commemorates Paramount's movie release in December 1976 ... $8–10

Kiwi 1974 .... $5–8

Koala Bear 1973 .... $12–14

Laramie 1968
Commemorates the "Centennial Jubilee Laramie Wyo.
1868–1968" $4–6

Largemouth Bass Trophy Bottle 1973
Honors the National Fresh Water Fishing Hall of Fame $10–14

Las Vegas 1969
Bottle used for customer specials, casino series $4–6

Light Bulb 1979
Honors Thomas Edison...$14–16

Lombard 1969
Commemorates "Village of Lombard, Illinois—1869
Centennial 1969" $4–6

London Bridge...$4–7

Louisville Downs Racing Derby 1978...................................$4–6

Louisiana Superdome $8–11

LVNH Owl...$20–30

Madame Butterfly 1977
Figurine of Madame Butterfly, music box plays "One Fine Day"
from the opera $340–370

The Magpies 1977
Honors an Australian football team $18–20

Maine 1970 ....$4–6

Majestic 1966...$20–24

Male Cardinal $18–24

Marbled Fantasy 1965 ....$38–42

Marina City 1962
Commemorates modern apartment complex in Chicago........$10–15

Marine Corps $25–35

Mark Antony 1962 ....$18–20

Martha Washington 1976 ....$5–6

McCoy 1973
Character of McCoy from the story of the Hatfield
and McCoy feud...$14–17

McShane—Mother-of-pearl 1979
Executive series..$85–105

McShane—Titans 1980..$85–105

McShane—Cobalt 1981
Executive series..$115–135

McShane—Green Pitcher 1982
Executive series..$80–105

McShane—Green Bell 1983
Executive series..$80–110

Mephistopheles 1979
Figurine depicts Mephistopheles from the opera *Faust*, music box
plays "Soldier's Chorus" $160–190

Michigan Bottle 1972..$7–9

Milwaukee Stein..$30–40

Minnesota Viking 1973..$9–12

Mint 400 1970..$80–105

Mint 400 1970
Commemorates the annual Del Webb Mint 400 ....$5–6

Mint 400 1971...$5–6

Mint 400 1972
Commemorates the 5th annual Del Webb Mint 400 ....$5–7

Mint 400 1973
Commemorates the 6th annual Del Webb Mint 400 ....$6–8

Mint 400 1974...$4–7

Mint 400 7th Annual 1976 ....$9–12

Mississippi Fire Engine 1978...$120–130

Model A Ford 1903 (1978)..$38–42

Model A Ford 1928 (1980)...$65–75

Montana 1963
Tribute to "Montana, 1864 Golden Years Centennial 1964"...$50–60

Monterey Bay Club 1977
Honors the Monterey Bay Beam Bottle and Specialty Club.......$9–12

Mortimer Snerd 1976 ....$24–28

Mother-of-pearl 1979 ....$10–12

Mount Saint Helens 1980
Depicts the eruption of Mount Saint Helens...........................$20–22

Mr. Goodwrench 1978...$24–28

Musicians on a Wine Cask 1964 ....$4–6

Muskie 1971
Honors the National Fresh Water Fishing Hall of Fame $14–18

National Tobacco Festival 1973
Commemorates the 25th anniversary of the National Tobacco
Festival $7–8

Nebraska 1967 ....$7–9

Nebraska Football 1972
Commemorates the University of Nebraska's national championship
football team of 1970–1971 ....$5–8

Nevada 1963..$34–38

New Hampshire 1967 ....$4–8

New Hampshire Eagle Bottle 1971 ....$18–23

New Jersey 1963 ....$40–50

New Jersey Yellow 1963..$40–50

New Mexico Bicentennial 1976..$8–12

New Mexico Statehood 1972
Commemorates New Mexico's sixty years of statehood $7–9

New York World's Fair 1964..$5–6

North Dakota 1965 ....$45–55

Northern Pike 1977
The sixth in a series designed for the National Fresh Water Fishing
Hall of Fame $14–18

Nutcracker Toy Soldier 1978 ....$90–120

Ohio 1966..$5–6

Ohio State Fair 1973
In honor of the 120th Ohio State Fair $5–6

Olympian 1960...$2–4

One Hundred First Airborne Division 1977
Honors the division known as the Screaming Eagles...............$8–10

Opaline Crystal 1969...$4–6

Oregon 1959
Honors the centennial of the state $20–25

Oregon Liquor Commission $25–35

Osco Drugs $12–17

Panda 1980..$20–22

Paul Bunyan $4–7

Pearl Harbor Memorial 1972
Honoring the Pearl Harbor Survivors Association $14–18

Pearl Harbor Survivors Association 1976..............................$5–7

Pennsylvania 1967 ....$4–6

Pennsylvania Dutch, Club Bottle $8–12

Permian Basin Oil Show 1972
Commemorates the Permian Basin Oil Show in Odessa, TX.......$4–6

Petroleum Man $4–7

Pheasant 1960 ....$14–18

Pheasant 1961, reissued; also 1963, 1966, 1967, 1968.......$8–11

Phi Sigma Kappa (centennial series) 1973
Commemorates the 100th anniversary of this fraternity.............$3–4

Phoenician 1973...$6–9

Pied Piper of Hamlin 1974 ....$3–6

Ponderosa 1969
A replica of the Cartwrights of "Bonanza" TV series fame $4–6

Ponderosa Ranch Tourist 1972
Commemorates the millionth tourist to the Ponderosa Ranch ...$14–16

Pony Express 1968..$9–12

Poodle—Gray and White 1970 ....$5–6

Portland Rose Festival 1972
Commemorates the 64th Portland, OR, Rose Festival $5–8

Portola Trek 1969
Issued to celebrate the 200th anniversary of San Diego.............$3–6

Poulan Chain Saw 1979..$24–28

Powell Expedition 1969
Depicts John Wesley Powell's survey of the Colorado River $3–5

Preakness 1970
Issued to honor the 100th anniversary of the running of the
Preakness...$5–6

Preakness Pimlico 1975..$4–7

Presidential 1968
Executive series..$4–7

Prestige 1967
Executive series...$4–7

Pretty Perch 1980
Eighth in a series, this fish is used as the official seal of the National
Fresh Water Fishing Hall of Fame...$13–16

Prima Donna 1969 ....$4–6

Professional Golf Association.............................$4–7

Queensland 1978 ....$20–22

Rabbit $4–7

Rainbow Trout 1975
Produced for the National Fresh Water Fishing Hall of Fame....$12–15

Ralph Centennial 1973
Commemorates the 100th anniversary of the Ralph Grocery
Company $10–14

Ralph's Market...$8–12

Ram 1958...$40–55

Ramada Inn 1976 ....$10–12

Red Mile Racetrack $8–12

Redwood 1967 ....$6–8

Reflections 1975
Executive series...$8–12

Regency 1972 ....$7–9

Reidsville 1973
Issued to honor Reidsville, NC, on its centennial $5–6

Renee the Fox 1974
Represents the companion for the International Association of Jim
Beam Bottle and Specialties Club's mascot $7–9

Rennie the Runner 1974.......................................$9–12

Rennie the Surfer 1975 ....$9–12

Reno 1968
Commemorates "100 Years—Reno" $4–6

Republic of Texas 1980 ....$12–20

Republican Convention 1972 ....$500–700

Republican Football 1972 ....$350–450

Richard Hadlee $110–135

Richards—New Mexico 1967
Created for Richards Distributing Company of
Albuquerque, NM $8–10

Robin 1969 ....$5–6

Rocky Marciano 1973 ....$14–16

Rocky Mountain, Club Bottle $10–15

Royal Crystal 1959 ....$3–6

Royal Di Monte 1957 ....$45–55

Royal Emperor 1958 ....$3–6

Royal Gold Diamond 1964 ....$30–35

Royal Gold Round 1956 ....$80–90

Royal Opal 1957 ....$5–7

Royal Porcelain 1955 ....$380–420

Royal Rose 1963 ....$30–35

Ruby Crystal 1967 ....$6–9

Ruidoso Downs 1968
Pointed ears...$24–26
Flat ears..$4–6

Sahara Invitational Bottle 1971
In honor of the Del Webb 1971 Sahara Invitational Pro-Am Golf
Tournament $6–8

San Bear—Donkey 1973
Political series $1,500–2,000

Samoa $4–7

San Diego 1968
Issued by the Beam Company for the 200th anniversary of its
founding in 1769 ....$4–6

San Diego—Elephant 1972 ....$15–25

Santa Fe 1960 ....$120–140

SCCA, etched $15–25

SCCA, smoothed $12–18

Screech Owl 1979 ....$18–22

Seafair Trophy Race 1972
Commemorates the Seattle Seafair Trophy Race $5–6

Seattle World's Fair 1962 ....$10–12

Seoul, Korea 1988 ....$60–75

Sheraton Inn $4–6

Short Dancing Scot 1963 ....$50–65

Short-Timer 1975 ....$15–20

Shriners 1975 ....$10–12

Shriners—Indiana $4–7

Shriners Pyramid 1975
Issued by the El Kahir Temple of Cedar Rapids, IA $10–12

Shriners Rajah 1977 ....$24–28

Shriners Temple 1972 ....$20–25

Shriners Western Association $15–25

Sierra Eagle $15–22

Sigma Nu Fraternity 1977 ....$9–12

Sigma Nu Fraternity—Kentucky...$8–12

Sigma Nu Fraternity—Michigan $18–23

Smith's North Shore Club 1972
Commemorating Smith's North Shore Club, at Crystal Bay,
Lake Tahoe $10–12

Smoked Crystal 1964...$6–9

Snow Goose 1979 ....$8–10

Snowman $125–175

South Carolina 1970
In honor of its tricentennial 1670–1970....................................$4–6

South Dakota—Mount Rushmore 1969 ....$4–6

South Florida—Fox on Dolphin 1980
Bottle sponsored by the South Florida Beam Bottle and Specialties
Club...$14–16

Sovereign 1969
Executive series..$4–7

Spenger's Fish Grotto 1977 ....$18–22

Sports Car Club of America $5–7

Statue of Liberty 1975 ....$8–12

Statue of Liberty 1985 ....$18–20

Saint Bernard 1979 ....$30–35

Saint Louis, Club Bottle..$10–15

Saint Louis Arch 1964 ....$10–12

Saint Louis Arch—reissue 1967 ....$16–18

Saint Louis Statue 1972......................................$8–10

Sturgeon 1980
Exclusive issue for a group that advocates the preservation of
sturgeons $14–17

Stutz Bearcat 1914, 1977.....................................$45–55

Submarine—Diamond Jubilee...............................$35–45

Submarine Redfin 1970
Issued for Manitowoc Submarine Memorial Association.............$5–7

Superdome 1975
Replica of the Louisiana Superdome...........................$5–8

Swagman 1979
Replica of an Australian hobo called a swagman who roamed that
country looking for work during the Depression...................$10–12

Sydney Opera House 1977 ....$9–12

Tall Dancing Scot 1964..$9–12

Tavern Scene 1959...$45–55

Telephone No. 1 1975
Replica of a 1907 phone of the magneto wall type $25–30

Telephone No. 2 1976
Replica of an 1897 desk set....................................$30–40

Telephone No. 3 1977
Replica of a 1920 cradle phone................................$15–20

Telephone No. 4 1978
Replica of a 1919 dial phone...................................$40–50

Telephone No. 5 1979
Replica of a pay phone...$25–35

Telephone No. 6 1980
Replica of a battery phone..$20–30

Telephone No. 7 1981
Replica of a digital dial phone $35–45

Tenpin 1980..$8–11

Texas Hemisfair...$7–11

Texas Rose 1978
Executive series..$14–18

Thailand 1969...$4–6

Thomas Flyer 1907, 1976B $60–70

Tiffany Poodle 1973
Created in honor of Tiffiny, the poodle mascot of the National
Association of the Jim Beam Bottle and Specialties Clubs $20–22

Tiger—Australian $14–18

The Tigers 1977
Issued in honor of an Australian football team $20–24

Titian 1980..$9–12

Tobacco Festival $8–12

Tombstone...$4–7

Travelodge Bear $4–7

Treasure Chest 1979..$8–12

Trout Unlimited 1977
To honor the Trout Unlimited conservation organization.......$14–18

Truth or Consequences Fiesta 1974
Issued in honor of Ralph Edwards's radio and television show $14–18

Turquoise China Jug 1966...$4–6

Twin Bridges Bottle 1971
Commemorates the largest twin bridge between Delaware and
New Jersey $40–42

Twin Cherubs 1974
Executive series..$8–12

Twin Doves 1987
Executive series..$18–23

U.S. Open 1972
Honors the U.S. Open Golf Tourney at Pebble Beach, CA........$9–12

Vendome Drummers Wagon 1975
Honors the Vendomes of Beverly Hills, CA $60–70

VFW Bottle 1971
Commemorates the 50th anniversary of the Department of
Indiana VFW $5–6

Viking 1973 ....$9–12

Volkswagen Commemorative Bottle—Two Colors 1977
Commemorates the Volkswagen Beetle $40–50

Vons Market $28–35

Walleye Pike 1977
Designed for the National Fresh Water Fishing Hall of Fame ...$12–15

Walleye Pike 1987 ....$17–23

Washington 1975
A state series bottle to commemorate the Evergreen State $5–6

Washington—The Evergreen State 1974
The club bottle for the Evergreen State Beam Bottle and
Specialties Club..$10–12

Washington State Bicentennial 1976 ....$10–12

Waterman 1980...$100–130

Western Shrine Association 1980
Commemorates the Shriners convention in Phoenix, AZ........$20–22

West Virginia 1963 ....$130–140

White Fox 1969
Issued for the 2nd anniversary of the Jim Beam Bottle and
Specialties Club in Berkeley, CA $25–35

Wisconsin Muskie Bottle 1971...$15–17

Woodpecker 1969..$6–8

Wyoming 1965..$40–50

Yellow Katz 1967
Commemorates the 50th anniversary of the Katz Department
Stores...$15–17

Yellow Rose 1978
Executive series...$7–10

Yellowstone Park Centennial..$4–7

Yosemite 1967...$4–6

Yuma Rifle Club...$18–23

Zimmerman—Art Institute...$5–8

Zimmerman Bell 1976
Designed for Zimmerman Liquor Store of Chicago....................$6–7

Zimmerman Bell 1976 ....$6–7

Zimmerman—Blue Beauty 1969 ....$9–12

Zimmerman—Blue Daisy...$4–6

Zimmerman—Cherubs 1968..$4–6

Zimmerman—Chicago..$4–6

Zimmerman—Eldorado $4–7

Zimmerman—Glass 1969...$7–9

Zimmerman—Oatmeal Jug...$40–50

Zimmerman—The Peddler Bottle 1971...............................$4–6

Zimmerman Two-Handled Jug 1965...................................$45–60

Zimmerman Vase, Brown $6–9

Zimmerman Vase, Green $6–9

Zimmerman—50th Anniversary $35–45

Automobile and Transportation Series

Chevrolet

1957 Convertible, Black, New...$85–95

1957 Convertible, Red, New..$75–85

1957, Black $70–80

1957, Dark Blue, PA...$70–80

1957, Red $80–90

1957, Sierra Gold $140–160

1957, Turquoise $50–70

1957, Yellow Hot Rod $65–75

Camaro 1969, Blue...$55–65

Camaro 1969, Burgundy...$120–140

Camaro 1969, Green $100–120

Camaro 1969, Orange $55–65

Camaro 1969, Pace Car $60–70

Camaro 1969, Silver...$120–140

Camaro 1969, Yellow, PA $55–65

Corvette 1986, Pace Car, Yellow, New..........................$60–85

Corvette 1984, Black...$70–80

Corvette 1984, Bronze $100–200

Corvette 1984, Gold..$100–120

Corvette 1984, Red...$55–65

Corvette 1984, White..$55–65

Corvette 1978, Black...$140–170

Corvette 1978, Pace Car $135–160

Corvette 1978, Red...$50–60

Corvette 1978, White..$40–50

Corvette 1978, Yellow...$40–50

Corvette 1963, Black, PA $75–85

Corvette 1963, Blue, NY $90–100

Corvette 1963, Red...$60–70

Corvette 1963, Silver $50–60

Corvette 1955, Black, New $110–140

Corvette 1955, Copper, New $90–100

Corevette 1955, Red, New $110–140

Corvette 1954, Blue, New..$90–100

Corvette 1953, White, New $100–120

Dusenburg

Convertible, Cream $130–140

Convertible, Dark blue $120–130

Convertible, Light blue $80–100

Convertible Coupe, Gray $160–180

Ford

International Delivery Wagon, Black $80–90

International Delivery Wagon, Green $80–90

Fire Chief 1928..$120–130

Fire Chief 1934 ....$60–70

Fire Pumper Truck 1935..$45–60

Model A, Angelo's Liquor $180–200

Model A Parkwood Supply $140–170

Model A 1903, Black $35–45

Model A 1903, Red..$35–45

Model A 1928 ....$60–80

Model A Fire Truck 1930..$130–170

Model T 1913, Black $30–40

Model T 1913, Green $30–40

Mustang 1964, Black..$100–125

Mustang 1964, Red..$35–45

Mustang 1964, White..$25–35

Paddy Wagon 1930 ....$100–200

Phaeton 1929..$40–50

Pickup Truck 1935..$20–30

Police Car 1929, Blue..$75–85

Police Car 1929, Yellow..$350–450

Police Patrol Car 1934 ....$60–70

Police Tow Truck 1935..$20–30

Roadster 1934, Cream, PA, New $80–90

Thunderbird 1956, Black $60–70

Thunderbird 1956, Blue, PA..$70–80

Thunderbird 1956, Gray ....,........$50–60

Thunderbird 1956, Green...$60–70

Thunderbird 1956, Yellow $50–60

Woodie Wagon 1929...$50–60

Mercedes

1974, Blue..$30–40

1974, Gold $60–80

1974, Green $30–40

1974, Mocha $30–40

1974, Red..$30–40

1974, Sand beige, PA..$30–40

1974, Silver, Australia..$140–160

1974, White $35–45

Trains

Baggage Car $40–60

Boxcar, Brown $50–60

Boxcar, Yellow..$40–50

Bumper...$5–8

Caboose, Gray $45–55

Caboose, Red..$50–60

Casey Jones with Tender $65–80

Casey Jones Caboose...$40–55

Casey Jones Accessory Set...$50–60

Coal Tender, No Bottle $20–30

Combination Car..$55–65

Dining Car $75–90

Flatcar $20–30

General Locomotive $60–70

Grant Locomotive...$50–65

Log Car...$40–55

Lumber Car..$12–18

Observation Car $15–23

Passenger Car $45–53

Tank Car..$15–20

Track $4–6

Turner Locomotive...$80–100

Water Tower $20–30

Wood Tender..$40–45

Wood Tender, No Bottle $20–25

Other

Ambulance..$18–22

Army Jeep $18–20

Bass Boat...$12–18

Cable Car $25–30

Circus Wagon $20–30

Ernie's Flower Cart $20–30

Golf Cart $20–30

HC Covered Wagon 1929 ....$10–20

Jewel Tea $70–80

Mack Fire Truck 1917..$120–135

Mississippi Pumper Fire Truck 1867 ....$115–140

Oldsmobile 1903 ....$25–35

Olsonite Eagle Racer...$35–40

Police Patrol Car 1934, Yellow $110–140

Space Shuttle $20–30

Stutz 1914, Gray...$40–50

Stutz 1914, Yellow..$40–50

Thomas Flyer 1909, Blue $60–70

Thomas Flyer 1909, Ivory...$60–70

Vendome Wagon...$40–50

Volkswagen, Blue...$40–50

Volkswagen, Red..$40–50

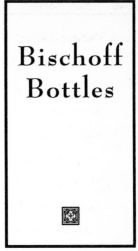

Bischoff Bottles

Bischoffs, which was founded in Trieste, Italy, in 1777, issued decorative figurals in the eighteenth century, long before any other company. The early bottles are rare because of the limited production and the attrition of extent bottles over the years. Modern-day Bischoffs were imported into the United States beginning in 1949. Collectors haven't shown intense interest in modern imports and since sales have not been made often enough to have establish values, prices are not included in this book. Three other types of Bischoffs will be covered: Kord Bohemian decanters, Venetian glass figurals, and ceramic decanters and figurals.

Kord Bohemian Decanters

These decanters were hand-blown and hand-painted glass bottles created in Czechoslovakia by the Kord Company, with a tradition of Bohemian cut, engraved, etched, and flashed glass. Stoppers and labels with the bottles are considered very rare and valuable today. The cut-glass and ruby-etched decanters were imported to the United States in the early 1950s. The ruby-etched is considered rare only if complete with the stopper.

In addition, most of these decanters have a matching set of glasses, which increases the value if the entire set is intact.

Amber Flowers 1952
A two-toned glass decanter, 15½ inches, dark amber
stopper...$30–40

Amber Leaves 1952
Multitoned bottle with long neck, 13½ inches........................$30–40

Anisette 1948–1951
Clear glass bottle with ground glass stopper, 11 inches..........$20–30

Bohemian Ruby-Etched 1949–1951
Round decanter, tapered neck, etched stopper, 15½ inches....$30–40

Coronet Crystal 1952
A round tall bottle, multitoned, with a broad band of flowers, leaves,
and scroll circles, 14 inches $30–40

Cut-Glass Decanter (blackberry) 1951
A geometric design, hand-cut overall, ground stopper,
10½ inches $32–42

Czech Hunter 1958
Round thick clear glass, heavy round glass base, 8½ inches....$18–26

Czech Hunter's Lady 1958
"Mae West"–shaped decanter of cracked clear glass, 10 inches $18–26

Dancing—Country Scene 1950
Clear glass hand-blown decanter with peasant boy and girl doing a
country dance beside a tree, 12¼ inches..................................$25–35

Dancing—Peasant Scene 1950
Decanter of pale and amber glass, peasants in costume dancing to
music of bagpipes, 12 inches $25–35

Double—Dolphin 1949–1969
Fish-shaped twin bottles joined at the bellies, hand-blown clear
glass...$20–30

Flying Geese Pitcher 1952
Green glass handle and stopper, glass base, 9½ inches............$15–25

Flying Geese Pitcher 1957
Clear crystal handled pitcher, gold stopper, 9½ inches...........$15–25

Horse Head 1947–1969
Pale amber-colored bottle in the shape of a horse's head, round
pouring spout on top, 8 inches $15–25

Jungle Parrot—Amber Glass 1952
Hand-etched jungle scenes with a yellow-amber color,
15½ inches $25–35

Jungle Parrot—Ruby Glass 1952
Hand-etched jungle scenes with a ruby-colored body,
15½ inches $20–30

Old Coach Bottle 1948
Pale amber color, round glass stopper, 10 inches...................$25–35

Old Sleigh Bottle 1949
Glass decanter, hand-painted, signed, 10 inches....................$22–32

Wild Geese—Amber Glass 1952
Tall round decanter with tapering etched neck, flashed with a
yellow-amber color, 15½ inches..$25–35

Wild Geese—Ruby Glass 1952
Tall round decanter with tapering etched neck, flashed with a
ruby-red color, 15½ inches...$25–35

Venetian Glass Figurals
*These figurals are produced in limited editions by the Serguso Glass
Company in Morano, Italy, and are unique in design and color, with
birds, fish, cats, and dogs.*

Black Cat 1969
Glass black cat with curled tail, 12 inches long $18–25

Dog—Alabaster 1966
Seated alabaster glass dog, 13 inches..................................$33–45

Dog—Dachshund 1966
Alabaster dog with brown tones, 19 inches long................$40–50

Duck 1964
Alabaster glass tinted pink and green, long neck, upraised wings,
11 inches long...$42–52

Fish—Multicolor 1964
Round fat fish; alabaster glass; green, rose, yellow $18–25

Fish—Ruby 1969
Long, flat, ruby glass fish, 12 inches long $25–35

Ceramic Decanters and Figurals
These are some of the most interesting, attractive, and valuable of the Bischoff collection and are made of ceramic, stoneware, and pottery. Decanters complete with handles, spouts, and stoppers demand the highest value.

African Head 1962...$15–18

Bell House 1960 ....$30–40

Bell Tower 1960 ....$15–30

Boy (Chinese) Figural 1962................................$30–40

Boy (Spanish) Figural 1961 ....$25–35

Clown with Black Hair 1963...............................$30–40

Clown with Red Hair 1963 ....$15–25

Deer Figural 1969...$20–25

Egyptian Dancing Figural 1961 ....$12–17

Egyptian Pitcher—Two Musicians 1969 ....$15–24

Egyptian Pitcher—Three Musicians 1959..............$20–28

Floral Canteen 1969..$18–22

Fruit Canteen 1969 ....$13–19

Girl in Chinese Costume 1962 ....$30–40

Girl in Spanish Costume 1961 ....$30–40

Greek Vase Decanter 1969.................................$13–19

Mask—Gray Face 1963......................................$16–26

Oil and Vinegar Cruets—Black and White 1959..........$18–25

Vase—Black and Gold 1959...............................$19–22

Watchtower 1960 ....$12–16

Borghini Bottles

Borghini bottles, ceramics of modernistic style with historical themes, are manufactured in Pisa, Italy. These bottles vary greatly in price depending on distribution points. The lowest values are in areas closest to the point of distribution or near heavy retail sales. Recent bottles are stamped "Borghini Collection Made In Italy."

Cats
Black with red ties, 6 inches...$11–15

Cats
Black with red ties, 12 inches...$10–15

Female Head
Ceramic, 9½ inches $11–15

Penguin
Black and white, 6 inches...$8–11

Penguin 1969
Black and white, 12 inches...$12–16

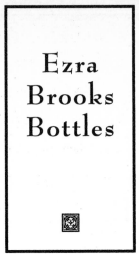

Ezra Brooks Bottles

The Ezra Brooks Distilling Company did not start to issue figurals until 1964, ten years after the Jim Beam company, and quickly became a strong rival due to effective distribution, promotion techniques, original designs, and choice of subjects.

While many of the Brooks bottles depict the same themes as the Jim Beam series (sports and transportation), they also produced bottles based on original subjects. The Maine lobster looks good enough to put on anyone's dinner table. The most popular series depict antiques such as an Edison phonograph and a Spanish cannon. Yearly new editions highlight American historical events and anniversaries. One of my favorites is the Bucket of Blood (1970)—from the Virginia City, Nevada, saloon by the same name—in a bucket-shaped bottle.

While these bottles are still filled with Kentucky bourbon, most purchases of these figural bottles are made by collectors.

Alabama Bicentennial 1976 ....$12–14

American Legion 1971
Distinguished embossed star emblem from World War I $20–30

American Legion 1972
Salutes the Illinois American Legion's 54th National Convention....$45–55

American Legion 1973
Salutes Hawaii, which hosted the American Legion's 54th National
Convention $10–12

American Legion—Denver 1977 ....$19–22

American Legion—Miami Beach 1973................................$8–12

Amvets—Dolphin 1974......................................$8–10

Amvets—Polish Legion 1973..............................$14–18

Antique Cannon 1969..$6–9

Antique Phonograph 1970....................................$8–12

Arizona 1969
Man with burro in search of Lost Dutchman Mine....................$4–8

Auburn 1932 Classic Car 1978..........................$18–20

Badger No. 1 Boxer 1973....................................$9–11

Badger No. 2 Football 1974...............................$10–14

Badger No. 3 Hockey 1974.................................$9–12

Baltimore Oriole Wildlife 1979.........................$20–30

Bare-Knuckle Fighter 1971.................................$5–7

Baseball Hall of Fame 1973...............................$20–22

Baseball Player 1974..$14–16

Bear 1968..$5–9

Bengal Tiger Wildlife 1979................................$20–30

Betsy Ross 1975..$8–12

Big Bertha
Nugget Casino's very own elephant with a raised trunk........$10–13

Big Daddy Lounge 1969
Salute to South Florida's state liquor chain and Big Daddy Lounges....$4–6

Bighorn Ram 1973...$14–18

Bird Dog 1971..$12–14

Bordertown
Salutes the Borderline Club, on the border of California
and Nevada $5–10

Bowler 1973 .... $4–6

Bowling Tenpins 1973 .... $9–12

Brahma Bull 1972 .... $10–12

Bucket of Blood 1970
Salutes the famous Virginia City, NV, saloon; bucket-shaped bottle....$5–7

Bucking Bronco, Rough Rider 1973 .... $7–9

Bucky Badger, Football $20–25

Bucky Badger, Hockey 1975 .... $18–24

Bucky Badger No. 1 Boxer 1973 .... $9–12

Buffalo Hunt 1971 .... $5–7

Bulldog 1972
Mighty canine mascot and football symbol $10–14

Bull Moose 1973 .... $12–15

Busy Beaver $4–7

Cabin Still $20–35

Cable Car 1968 .... $5–6

California Quail 1970 .... $8–10

Canadian Honker 1975 .... $9–12

Canadian Loon Wildlife 1979 .... $25–35

Cardinal 1972 .... $20–25

Casey at the Bat 1973 .... $6–10

Ceremonial Indian 1970 .... $15–18

CB Convoy Radio 1976..$5–9

Charolais Beer 1973...$10–14

Cheyenne Shootout 1970
Honoring the Wild West and its Cheyenne Frontier Days........$6–10

Chicago Fire 1974...$20–30

Chicago Water Tower 1969..$8–12

Christmas Decanter 1966...$5–8

Christmas Tree 1979 ....$13–17

Churchill 1970
Commemorating the "Iron Curtain" speech at Westminster College
by Churchill...$5–9

Cigar Store Indian 1968 ....$4–6

Classic Firearms 1969
Embossed gun set consisting of derringer, Colt .45, Peacemaker,
over-and-under flintlock, and pepperbox..............................$15–19

Clowns, Imperial Shrine 1978..$9–11

Clown Bust No. 1 Smiley 1979 ....$22–28

Clown Bust No. 2 Cowboy 1979..$20–25

Clown Bust No. 3 Pagliacci 1979 ....$15–22

Clown Bust No. 4 Keystone Kop $30–40

Clown Bust No. 5 Cuddles $20–30

Clown Bust No. 6 Tramp..$20–30

Clown with Accordion 1971...$15–18

Clown with Balloon 1973 ....$20–32

Club Bottle, Birthday Cake..$9–12

Elk
Salutes those organizations that practiced benevolence
and charity $20–28

English Setter—Bird Dog 1971 ....$14–17

Equestrienne 1974 ....$7–10

Esquire, Ceremonial Dancer $10–16

Farthington Bike 1972 ....$6–8

Fire Engine 1971 ....$14–18

Fireman 1975 ....$18–23

Fisherman 1974 ....$8–12

Flintlock 1969 (two versions: Japanese and Heritage)
Japanese $7–9
Heritage $12–16

Florida "Gators" 1973
Tribute to the University of Florida Gators football team $9–11

Foe Eagle 1978 ....$15–20

Foe Flying Eagle 1979 ....$20–25

Foe Eagle 1980 ....$25–40

Foe Eagle 1981 ....$18–28

Football Player 1974 ....$10–14

Ford Mustang $20–30

Ford Thunderbird—1956, 1976 ....$70–80

Foremost Astronaut 1970
Tribute to a major liquor supermart, Foremost Liquor Store $5–7

Fresno Decanter $5–12

Fresno Grape with Gold $48–60

Fresno Grape 1970 ....$6–11

Gamecock 1970...$9–13

Go Big Red, Football-Shaped Bottle
No. 1 with football 1972......................................$20–28
No. 2 with hat 1971..$18–22
No. 3 with rooster 1972.......................................$10–14

Golden Antique Cannon 1969
Symbol of Spanish power...$5–7

Golden Eagle 1971 ....$18–22

Golden Grizzly Bear 1970 ....$4–6

Golden Horseshoe 1970
Salute to Reno's Horseshoe Club $7–9

Golden Rooster No. 1
Replica of solid-gold rooster on display at Nugget Casino
in Reno, NV $35–50

Gold Prospector 1969 ....$5–9

Gold Seal 1972..$12–14

Gold Turkey $35–45

Go Tiger Go 1973 ....$10–14

Grandfather Clock 1970 ....$5–7

Grandfather Clock 1970 ....$12–20

Greater Greensboro Open 1972 ....$16–19

Greater Greensboro Open 1972 ....$15–20

Greater Greensboro Open Golfer 1973 ....$17–24

Greater Greensboro Open Map 1974.........................$29–36

Greater Greensboro Open Cup 1975 ....$25–30

Greater Greensboro Open Club and Ball 1977 ....$20–25

Great Stone Face—Old Man of the Mountain 1970 ....$10–14

Great White Shark 1977 ....$8–14

Hambletonian 1971 ....$13–16

Happy Goose 1975 ....$12–15

Harolds Club Dice 1968 ....$8–12

Hereford 1971 ....$12–15

Hereford 1972 ....$12–15

Historical Flask Eagle 1970 ....$3–5

Historical Flask Flagship 1970 ....$3–5

Historical Flask Liberty 1970 ....$3–5

Historical Flask Old Ironsides 1970 ....$3–5

Historical Flask 1970 ....$3–5

Hollywood Cops 1972 ....$12–18

Hopi Indian 1970
Kachina doll $15–20

Hopi Kachina 1973 ....$50–75

Idaho—Ski the Potato 1973
Salutes the State of Idaho $8–10

Indianapolis 500 ....$30–35

Indian Ceremonial $13–18

Indian Hunter 1970 ....$12–15

Iowa Farmer 1977 ....$55–65

Iowa Grain Elevator 1978 ....$25–34

Iron Horse Locomotive $8–14

Jack O'Diamonds 1969 ....$4–6

Jayhawk 1969 ....$6–8

Jester 1971 ....$6–8

Jug, Old-time 1.75 Liters $9–13

Kachina Doll No. 1 1971 ....$80–100

Kachina Doll No. 2 1973 ....$10–60

Kachina Doll No. 3 1974 ....$50–60

Kachina Doll No. 4 1975 ....$20–25

Kachina Doll No. 5 1976 ....$30–40

Kachina Doll No. 6 1977 ....$25–35

Kachina Doll No. 7 1978 ....$35–45

Kachina Doll No. 8 1979 ....$50–60

Kansas Jayhawk 1969 ....$4–7

Katz Cats 1969
Siamese cats are symbolic of Katz Drug Company of
Kansas City, KS $8–12

Katz Cats Philharmonic 1970
Commemorating its 27th annual Star Night $6–10

Keystone Kops 1980 ....$32–40

Keystone Kops 1971 ....$25–35

Killer Whale 1972 ....$15–20

King of Clubs 1969 ....$4–6

King Salmon 1971 ....$18–24

Liberty Bell 1970..$5–6

Lincoln Continental Mark I 1941.....................................$20–25

Lion on the Rock 1971..$5–7

Liquor Square 1972 ....$5–7

Little Giant 1971
Replica of the first horse-drawn steam engine to arrive at the
Chicago fire in 1871 ....$11–16

Maine Lighthouse 1971 ....$18–24

Maine Lobster 1970 ....$15–18

Man-o-War 1969 ....$10–16

M&M Brown Jug 1975B $15–20

Map, U.S.A. Club Bottle 1972 ....$7–9

Masonic Fez 1976 ....$12–15

Max "The Hat" Zimmerman 1976....................................$20–25

Military Tank 1971 ....$15–22

Minnesota Hockey Player 1975..$18–22

Minuteman 1975...$10–15

Missouri Mule, Brown 1972 ....$7–9

Moose 1973 ....$20–28

Motorcycle $10–14

Mountaineer 1971
One of the most valuable Ezra Brooks figural bottles..............$40–55

Mr. Foremost 1969 ....$7–10

Mr. Maine Potato 1973 ....$6–10

Mr. Merchant 1970 ....$6–10

Mule..$8–12

Mustang Indy Pace Car 1979...............................$20–30

Nebraska—Go Big Red!.......................................$12–15

New Hampshire State House 1970.........................$9–13

North Carolina Bicentennial 1975........................$8–12

Nugget Classic
Replica of golf pin presented to golf tournament participants...$7–12

Oil Gusher $6–8

Old Capital 1971..$30–40

Old EZ No. 1 Barn Owl 1977 ....$25–35

Old EZ No. 2 Eagle Owl 1978 ....$40–55

Old EZ No. 3 Show Owl 1979 ....$20–35

Old Man of the Mountain 1970............................$10–14

Old Water Tower 1969
Famous landmark, survived the Chicago fire of 1871 ....$12–16

Oliver Hardy Bust $12–18

Ontario 500 1970..$18–22

Overland Express 1969...$17–20

Over-Under Flintlock Flask 1969...........................$6–9

Panda—Giant 1972..$12–17

Penguin 1972 ....$8–10

Penny Farthington High-wheeler 1973 ....$9–12

Pepperbox Flask 1969 ....$4–6

Phoenix Bird 1971 ....$20–26

Phoenix Jaycees 1973 ....$10–14

Phonograph $15–20

Piano 1970 ....$12–13

Pirate 1971...$6–10

Polish Legion American Vets 1978 ....$18–26

Portland Head Lighthouse 1971
Honors the lighthouse that has guided ships safely into Maine
Harbor since 1791 ....$18–24

Potbellied Stove 1968...$5–6

Queen of Hearts 1969
Playing card symbol with royal flush in hearts on front
of the bottle $4–6

Raccoon Wildlife 1978..$30–40

Ram 1973..$13–18

Razorback Hog 1969 ....$12–18

Razorback Hog 1979 ....$20–30

Red Fox 1979..$30–40

Reno Arch 1968
Honoring the "Biggest Little City in the World," Reno, NV $4–8

Sailfish 1971...$7–11

Salmon, Washington King 1971..$20–26

San Francisco Cable Car 1968 ....$4–8

Sea Captain 1971 ....$10–14

Sea Lion—Gold 1972...$11–14

Senators of the U.S. 1972
Honors the senators of the United States of America.............$10–13

Setter 1974...$10–15

Shrine King Tut Guard 1979 ....$16–24

1804 Silver Dollar 1970..$5–8

Silver Saddle 1973 ....$22–25

Silver Spur Boot 1971
Cowboy-boot-shaped bottle with silver spur buckled on; "Silver
Spur—Carson City Nevada" embossed on side of boot $7–11

Simba 1971...$9–12

Ski Boot 1972 ....$5–7

Slot Machine 1971
A replica of the original nickel Liberty Bell slot machine invented by
Charles Fey in 1895 ....$18–24

Snowmobiles 1972 ....$8–11

South Dakota Air National Guard 1976 ....$18–22

Spirit of '76 1974 ....$5–7

Spirit of Saint Louis 1977, 50th Anniversary $6–11

Sprint Car Racer $30–40

Stagecoach 1969...$10–12

Stan Laurel Bust 1976..$10–16

Stock Market Ticker 1970
A unique replica of a ticker-tape machine $8–11

Stonewall Jackson 1974..$22–28

Strongman 1974...$8–12

Sturgeon 1975...$20–28

John L. Sullivan 1970 ....$15–20

Syracuse, NY 1973 ....$11–16

Tank Patton 1972
Reproduction of a U.S. Army tank $16–20

Tecumseh 1969
Figurehead of the U.S.S. *Delaware*; this decanter is an embossed
replica of the statue of the United States Naval Academy $5–6

Telephone 1971
Replica of the old-time upright handset telephone $16–19

Tennis Player 1972 ....$8–12

Terrapin, Maryland 1974 ....$14–16

Texas Longhorn 1971 ....$18–22

Ticker Tape 1970 ....$8–12

Tiger on Stadium 1973
Commemorates college teams who have chosen the tiger
as their mascot $12–17

Tom Turkey $18–24

Tonopah 1972 ....$12–15

Totem Pole 1972 ....$10–14

Tractor 1971
A model of the 1917 Fordson made by Henry Ford $9–11

Trail Bike Rider 1972 ....$10–12

Trojan Horse 1974 ....$15–18

Trojans—USC Football 1973 ....$10–14

Trout and Fly 1970 ....$7–11

Truckin' and Vannin' 1977 ....$7–12

Vermont Skier 1972 ....$10–12

VFW—Veterans of Foreign Wars 1973 ....$6–10

Virginia—Red Cardinal 1973 ....$15–20

Walgreen Drugs 1974 ....$16–24

Weirton Steel 1973 ....$15–18

Western Rodeos 1973 ....$17–23

West Virginia—Mountaineer 1971 ....$65–75

West Virginia—Mountain Lady 1972 ....$14–20

Whale 1972 ....$14–20

Wheat Shocker 1971
The mascot of the Kansas football team in a fighting pose $5–7

Whiskey Flask 1970
Reproduction of collectible American patriotic whiskey flask of the
1800s: Old Ironsides, Miss Liberty, American Eagle, Civil War
Commemorative $12–14

Whitetail Deer 1947 ....$18–24

White Turkey 1971 ....$20–25

Wichita $4–8

Wichita Centennial 1970 ....$4–6

Winston Churchill 1969 ....$6–10

Zimmerman's Hat 1968
A salute to "Zimmerman's—World's Largest Liquor Store" $5–6

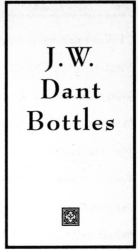

J.W. Dant Bottles

J.W. Dant Distilling Company also produces bottles similar to the Brooks and
Beam bottles, and they likewise have
strong collector appeal. These bottles usu-
ally depict American themes such as patriotic events and folklore in
addition to various animals.

Because Dant has such a liking for American history and tradi-
tions, most of these bottles are decorated with historical scenes in full
color. Some bottles carry an embossed American eagle and shield
with stars. These bottles are all limited editions and the molds are not
reused.

Alamo..$4–6

American Legion..$3–7

Atlantic City..$4–6

Bobwhite..$6–8

Boeing 747...$5–8

Boston Tea Party, Eagle to Left..............................$4–6

Boston Tea Party, Eagle to Right.........................$9–12

Bourbon...$3–5

Paul Bunyan..$5–7

California Quail...$7–9

Chukar Partridge $7–9

Clear Tip Pinch..$7–9

Constitution and Guerriere $5–7

Duel Between Burr and Hamilton $8–10

Eagle $6–9

Fort Sill Centennial 1969 ....$7–11

Patrick Henry...$4–7

Indianapolis 500 ....$7–11

Mountain Quail $7–9

Mount Rushmore $5–9

Prairie Chicken $5–7

Reverse Eagle $5–8

Ring-necked Pheasant $7–9

Ruffed Grouse $4–7

San Diego..$4–6

Speedway 500 ....$6–9

Stove—Potbelly..$9–11

Washington Crossing Delaware $5–7

Woodcock..$6–9

Wrong-Way Charlie $15–20

Garnier
Bottles

Garnet Et Cie, a French firm founded in 1858, has long been given credit as the pioneer of the modern collectible liquor bottle and introduced the Garnier figural bottles in 1899. During Prohibition and World War II, there was a temporary halt in production but they quickly resumed manufacturing in the 1950s.

Those bottles manufactured prior to World War II are the most rare and valuable but are not listed in this book due to the difficulty of establishing valid price levels. Among them are the Cat (1930), Clown (1910), Country Jug (1937), Greyhound (1930), Penguin (1930), and Marquise (1931).

Aladdin's Lamp 1963 ....$40–50

Alfa Romeo 1913, 1970 ....$20–30

Alfa Romeo 1929, 1969 ....$20–30

Alfa Romeo Racer 1969 ....$20–30

Antique Coach 1970 ....$25–30

Apollo 1969
Apollo spaceship, 13½ inches..$17–22

Aztec Vase 1965...$15–20

Baby Foot—Soccer Shoe 1963
Black with white trim, 3¾ inches x 8½ inches.........................$10–20
1962 soccer shoe, large $7–11

Baby Trio 1963...$7–10

Baccus Figural 1967...$20–25

Bahamas
Black policeman, white jacket and hat, black pants, red stripe,
gold details $15–24

Baltimore Oriole 1970 ....$10–16

Bandit Figural 1958...$10–14

Bedroom Candlestick 1967 ....$20–25

Bellows 1969 ....$14–21

Bird Ashtray 1958..$3–4

Bluebird 1970...$12–18

Bouquet 1966 ....$15–25

Bull (and matador), Animal Figural 1963.......................$17–23

Burmese Man Vase 1965..$15–25

Canada..$11–14

Candlestick 1955 ....$25–35

Candlestick Glass 1965 ....$15–25

Cannon 1964 ....$50–60

Cardinal State Bird—Illinois 1969.................................$12–15

Cat—Black 1962 ....$15–25

Cat—Gray 1962 ....$15–25

Chalet 1955 ....$40–50

Chimney 1956...$55–65

Chinese Dog 1965...$15–25

Chinese Statuette—Man 1970...$15–25

Chinese Statuette—Woman 1970 ....$15–25

Christmas Tree 1956 ....$60–70

Citroën 1922, 1970..$20–30

Classic Ashtray 1958 ....$20–30

Clock 1958 ....$20–30

Clown Holding Tuba 1955 ....$15–25

Coffee Mill 1966 ....$20–30

Columbine Figural 1968
Female partner..$20–30
Harlequin...$30–40

Drunkard—Drunk on Lamppost...$15–20

Duckling Figural 1956 ....$18–26

Duo 1954
Two clear glass bottles stacked, two pouring spouts..............$12–18

Egg Figural 1956..$70–80

Eiffel Tower 1951
13½ inches..$15–25
12½ inches..$14–20

Elephant Figural 1961 ....$20–30

Empire Vase 1962..$10–18

Fiat 500 1913, 1970
Yellow body..$20–30

Fiat Nuevo 1913, 1970
Blue body..$20–30

Flask Garnier 1958...$9–12

Flying Horse Pegasus 1958 ....$50–60

Ford 1913, 1970 ....$20–30

Fountain 1964 ....$25–35

Giraffe 1961 ....$20–35

Goldfinch 1970 ....$12–16

Goose 1955 ....$14–24

Grenadier 1949 ....$55–65

Harlequin Standing 1968 ....$13–19

Harlequin with Mandolin 1958 ....$30–40

Horse Pistol 1964 ....$15–25

Hunting Vase 1964 ....$25–35

Hussar 1949
French Cavalry soldier of the 1800s $25–35

India $10–15

Indian 1958 ....$15–20

Jockey 1961 ....$25–35

Lancer 1949 ....$15–22

Locomotive 1969 ....$15–25

Log—Round 1958 ....$20–30

London—Bobby $12–18

Loon 1970 ....$10–18

Maharajah 1958 ....$70–80

MG 1933, 1970 ....$15–25

Mockingbird 1970 ....$8–14

Montmartre Jug 1960...$12–18

Monuments 1966
A cluster of Parisian monuments..$15–25

Napoleon on Horseback 1969 ....$20–30

Nature Girl 1959...$10–15

New York Policeman..$9–13

Packard 1930, 1970 ....$20–30

Painting 1961 ....$25–35

Paris, French Policeman $10–15

Paris Taxis 1960..$20–30

Partridge 1961 ....$25–35

Pheasant 1969...$25–35

Pigeon—Clear Glass 1958 ....$10–15

Pony 1961 ....$25–35

Poodle 1954 ....$12–15

Renault 1911, 1969...$20–30

Road Runner 1969 ....$10–15

Robin 1970 ....$10–15

Rocket 1958 ....$10–15

Rolls Royce 1908, 1970 ....$20–30

Rooster 1952..$15–25

Saint Tropez Jug 1961B $20–30

Scarecrow 1960..$25–35

Sheriff 1958..$15–25

Hoffman Bottles

The Hoffman bottles are considered limited editions since each issue is restricted in terms of quantity produced. When this set number is reached, the molds are destroyed, which quickly establishes these designs as very collectible, rare, and valuable.

While these bottles often reflect European figures in various occupations, they have also focused on American subjects. These include the 1976 Bicentennial bottle and the 1976 Hippie bottle.

Occupation Series

Mr. Bartender with Music Box
"He's a Jolly Good Fellow"...$25–30

Mr. Charmer with Music Box
"Glow Little Glow Worm" $10–15

Mr. Dancer with Music Box
"The Irish Washerwoman"...$18–22

Mr. Doctor with Music Box
"As Long as He Needs Me" $20–25

Mr. Fiddler with Music Box
"Hearts and Flowers"...$20–22

Mr. Guitarist with Music Box
"Johnny Guitar"...$20–22

Mr. Harpist with Music Box
"Do-Re-Mi"..$10–15

Mr. Lucky with Music Box
"When Irish Eyes Are Smiling" $15–20

Mrs. Lucky with Music Box
"The Kerry Dancer" $12–15

Mr. Policeman with Music Box
"Don't Blame Me" $30–35

Mr. Sandman with Music Box
"Mr. Sandman"..$10–20

Mr. Saxophonist with Music Box
"Tiger Rag" $15–20

Mr. Shoe Cobbler with Music Box
"Danny Boy"...$15–20

Bicentennial Series 4/5–Quart Size

Betsy Ross with Music Box
"The Star-Spangled Banner"..$30–40

Majestic Eagle with Music Box
"America the Beautiful"...$60–80

C.M. Russell Series 4/5–Quart Size

Buffalo Man $20–25

Flathead Squaw $15–20

Last of Five Thousand $14–18

Red River Breed...$23–30

The Scout..$30–40

The Stage Drive $20–30

Trapper $20–30

Japanese Bottles

While bottle making in Japan is an ancient art, the collectible bottles now produced are mainly for export purposes. Greater numbers of these bottles, now available in the American marketplace, have kept prices reasonable.

Daughter $12–18

Faithful Retainer $25–35

Golden Pagoda $12–18

"Kiku" Geisha, Blue, 13¼ inches $20–30

Maiden..$12–18

Noh Mask $12–18

Okame Mask...$50–70

Playboy $14–24

Princess...$14–24

Red Lion Man...$40–60

Sake God, Colorful Robe, Porcelain, 10 inches $20–30

Sake God, White, Bone China, 10 inches $12–15

White Lion Man..$35–50

White Pagoda $15–20

"Yuri" Geisha, Pink, Red Sash, 13¼ inches........................$35–45

House of Koshu

Angel, with Book, 7 ounces $5–10

Angel, Sitting on a Barrel, 17 ounces $5–10

Beethoven Bust, 7 ounces..$5–10

Centurian Bust, 7 ounces $5–10

Children, 7 ounces $7–10

Declaration of Independence $4–6

Geisha, Blue $40–45

Geisha, Cherry Blossom $30–35

Geisha, Lily...$25–35

Geisha, Violet $30–40

Geisha, Wisteria $30–40

Geisha, Lavender with Fan $45–50

Geisha, Reclining..$60–70

Geisha, Sitting..$45–50

Lion Man, Red $40–45

Lion Man, White $80–95

Pagoda, Green $25–30

Pagoda, White...$20–25

Pagoda, Gold...$15–20

Sailor with a Pipe $6–10

Kamotsuru Bottles

Daokoru, God of Wealth...$9–13

Ebisu, God of Fishermen $10–15

Goddess of Art..$10–12

Hotei, God of Wealth $7–10

Kentucky Gentlemen Bottles

These bottles are similar in design to the Beam and Brooks bottles but are released less frequently. As a rule, these bottles reflect clothing of various periods of American history, most notably around the Civil War time frame.

Confederate Infantry
In gray uniform with sword, 13½ inches $10–15

Frontiersman (1969)
Coonskin cap, fringed buckskin, power horn, long rifle,
14 inches $12–15

Kentucky Gentlemen (1969)
Figural bottle, frock coat, top hat and cane; "Old Colonel," gray
ceramic, 14 inches $12–15

Pink Lady (1969)
Long bustle skirt, feathered hat, pink parasol, 13¼ inches......$20–32

Revolutionary War Officer
In dress uniform and boots, holding sword, 14 inches...........$12–16

Union Army Sergeant
In dress uniform with sword, 14 inches $9–13

Lionstone Bottles

Lionstone bottles, manufactured by Lionstone Distillery, reflect a great deal of realism in their designs in terms of components and details. Their "Shootout at O.K. Corral" work, for example, consists of three bottles with nine figures and two horses.

The Lionstone bottles are issued in series form and include a sport, circus, and bicentennial series. The most popular among collectors is the Western series. Since prices of these bottles have continued to be firm in the market, the collector should always be on the lookout for old, uncirculated stock.

Bar Scene No. 1 ....$125–140

Bartender $18–22

Belly Robber..$12–16

Blacksmith $20–30

Molly Brown $18–25

Buffalo Hunter...$25–35

Calamity Jane..$18–23

Camp Cook $13–17

Camp Follower $9–12

Canadian Goose $45–55

Casual Indian..$8–12

Cavalry Scout $8–12

Cherry Valley Club..$50–60

Chinese Laundryman...$12–15

Annie Christmas $10–15

Circuit Judge...$8–12

Corvette, 1.75 Liters..$60–75

Country Doctor..$12–18

Cowboy..$8–10

Frontiersman...$14–16

Gambels Quail...$8–12

Gentleman Gambler..$25–35

God of Love...$17–22

God of War..$17–22

Gold Panner $25–35

Highway Robber...$15–20

Jesse James $18–23

Johnny Lightning $50–65

Judge Roy Bean $20–30

Lonely Luke...$45–60

Lucky Buck..$18–24

Mallard Duck...$35–45

Miniatures—Western (six)..$85–110

Mint Bar with Frame $700–900

Mint Bar with Nude and Frame $1,000–1,250

Mountain Man $15–20

Annie Oakley $14–16

Pintail Duck $40–55

Proud Indian $10–14

Railroad Engineer $15–18

Renegade Trader $15–18

Riverboat Captain $10–15

Roadrunner $28–36

Saturday Night Bath $60–70

Sheepherder $25–35

Sheriff $10–12

Sodbuster $13–16

Squawman $20–30

Stagecoach Driver $45–60

STP Turbocar $40–50

STP Turbocar with Gold and Platinum (pair) $150–185

Telegrapher $15–20

Tinker $25–35

Tribal Chief $25–35

Al Unser No. 1 .... $15–20

Wells Fargo Man $8–12

Woodhawk $15–17

Bicentennial Series

Firefighters No. 1 ....$110–120

Mail Carrier..$23–29

Molly Pitcher $10–12

Paul Revere..$10–12

Betsy Ross $15–25

Sons of Freedom...$25–34

George Washington...$15–25

Winter at Valley Forge..$16–20

Bicentennial Westerns

Barber...$30–40

Firefighter No. 3...$60–70

Indian Weaver $20–24

Photographer $34–40

Rainmaker...$22–28

Saturday Night Bath $50–65

Trapper...$30–36

Bird Series (1972–1974)

Bluebird—Eastern $18–24

Bluebird—Wisconsin $20–30

Bluejay $20–25

Peregrine Falcon...$15–18

Meadowlark $15–20

Mourning Doves $50–70

Swallow $15–18

Circus Series (miniatures)

The Baker $10–15

Burmese Lady $10–15

Fat Lady...$10–15

Fire-eater $10–15

Giant with Midget $10–15

Giraffe-Necked Lady..$10–14

Snake Charmer...$10–15

Strong Man $10–15

Sword Swallower..$10–15

Tattooed Lady $10–15

Dog Series (miniatures)

Boxer $10–15

Cocker Spaniel $9–12

Collie..$10–15

Pointer..$10–15

Poodle $10–15

European Worker Series

The Cobbler..$20–25

The Horseshoer $20–35

The Potter $20–35

The Silversmith $25–35

The Watchmaker $20–35

The Woodworker $20–35

Oriental Worker Series

Basket Weaver..$25–35

Egg Merchant...$25–35

Gardener...$25–35

Sculptor..$25–35

Tea Vendor...$25–35

Timekeeper...$25–35

Sports Series

Baseball $22–30

Basketball...$22–30

Boxing $22–30

Football $22–30

Hockey $22–30

Tropical Bird Series (miniatures)

Blue-Crowned Chlorophonia $12–16

Emerald Toucanet $12–16

Northern Royal Flycatcher $12–16

Painted Bunting..$12–16

Scarlet Macaw...$12–16

Yellow-headed Amazon $12–16

Miscellaneous Lionstone Bottles

Buccaneer	$25–35
Cowgirl	$45–55
Dance Hall Girl	$50–55
Falcon	$15–25
Firefighter No. 2	$80–100
Firefighter No. 3	$25–35
Firefighter No. 5, 60th Anniversary	$22–27
Firefighter No. 6, Fire Hydrant	$40–45
Firefighter No. 6, Gold or Silver	$250–350
Firefighter No. 7, Helmet	$60–90
Firefighter No. 8, Fire Alarm Box	$45–60
Firefighter No. 8, Gold or Silver	$90–120
Firefighter No. 9, Extinguisher	$55–60
Firefighter No. 10, Trumpet	$55–60
Firefighter No. 10, Gold	$200–260
Firefighter No. 10, Silver	$125–175
Indian Mother and Papoose	$50–65
"The Perfesser"	$40–45
Roses on Parade	$60–80
Screech Owls	$50–65
Unser-Olsonite Eagle	$35–45

Miscellaneous Miniatures

Bartender $12–15

Cliff Swallow Miniature $9–12

Dance Hall Girl Miniature $15–22

Firefighter Emblem $24–31

Firefighter Engine No. 8 ....$24–31

Firefighter Engine No. 10 ....$24–31

Horseshoe Miniature $14–20

Kentucky Derby Racehorse, Cannanade $35–45

Lucky Buck $10–12

Rainmaker $10–15

Sahara Invitational No. 1 ....$35–45

Sahara Invitational No. 2 ....$35–45

Sheepherder $12–15

Shootout at O.K. Corral, (set of 3) $250–300

Woodpecker $10–15

Luxardo Bottles

The Girolamo Luxardo bottle is made in Torreglia, Italy, and was first imported into the United States in 1930. The Luxardo bottle usually contained wine or liquors, as Luxardo also produces wine.

Luxardo bottles are well designed and meticulously colored, adding to the desirability of this line. Most of these bottles are figural and consist of historical subjects and classical themes. The most popular bottle, the Cellini, was introduced in the early 1950s and is still used. The names and dates of many of the earlier bottles are not known due to lack of owners' records. Bottles in mint condition with the original label, and with or without contents, are very rare, collectible, and valuable. One of the rarer and more valuable of these bottles is the Zara, which was made prior to World War II.

Alabaster Fish Figural (1960–1968) $30–40

Alabaster Goose Figural (1960–1968)
Green and white, wings $25–35

Ampulla Flask (1958–1959) $20–30

Apothecary Jar (1960)
Hand-painted multicolor, green and black $20–30

Assyrian Ashtray Decanter (1961)
Gray, tan, and black $15–25

Autumn Leaves Decanter (1952)
Hand-painted, two handles $35–45

Autumn Wine Pitcher (1958)
Hand-painted country scene, handled pitcher......................$30–40

Babylon Decanter (1960)
Dark green and gold $16–23

Bizantina (1959)
Gold-embossed design, wide body.........................$28–38

Blue-and-Gold Amphora (1968)
Blue and gold with pastoral scene in white oval $20–30

Blue Fimmetta or Vermillian (1957)
Decanter $20–27

Brocca Pitcher (1958)
White background pitcher with handle, multicolor flowers,
green leaves...$28–37

Buddha Goddess Figural (1961)
 Goddess head in green-gray stone.........................$14–19
 Miniature $11–16

Burma Ashtray Specialty (1960)
Embossed white dancing figure, dark green background $20–25

Burma Pitcher Specialty (1960)
Green and gold, white embossed dancing figure $14–19

Callypso Girl Figural (1962)
Black West Indian girl, flower headdress in bright color $20–25

Candlestick Alabaster (1961) $30–35

Cellini Vase (1958–1968)
Glass-and-silver decanter, fancy.............................$14–19

Cellini Vase (1957)
Glass-and-silver-handled decanter with serpent handle..........$14–19

Ceramic Barrel (1968)
Barrel-shaped with painted flowers $14–19

Cherry Basket Figural (1960)
White basket, red cherries......................................$14–19

Classical Fragment Specialty (1961)
Roman female figure and vase..$25–33

Cocktail Shaker (1957)
Glass-and-silver decanter, silver-painted top.........................$14–19

Coffee Carafe Specialty (1962)
Old-time coffeepot, white with blue flowers..........................$14–19

Curva Vaso Vase (1961)
Green, green and white, ruby-red $22–29

Deruta Amphora (1956)
Colorful floral design on white..$11–16

Deruta Cameo Amphora (1959)
Colorful floral scrolls and cameo head on eggshell white $25–35

Deruta Pitcher (1953)
Multicolor flowers on base perugia $11–16

Diana Decanter (1956)
White figure of Diana with deer on black..............................$11–16

Dogal Silver and Green Decanter (1952–1956)
Hand-painted gondola $14–19

Dogal Silver Ruby (1952–1956)
Hand-painted gondola $14–18

Dogal Silver Ruby Decanter (1956)
Hand-painted Venetian scene and flowers............................$17–22

Dogal Silver Smoke Decanter (1952–1955)
Hand-painted gondola $14–19

Dogal Silver Smoke Decanter (1953–1954)
Hand-painted gondola $11–16

Dogal Silver Smoke Decanter (1956)
Hand-painted silver clouds and gondola $11–16

Dogal Silver Smoke Decanter (1956)
Hand-painted gondola, buildings, flowers............................$14–18

Dolphin Figural (1959)
Yellow, green, blue..$42–57

"Doughnut" Bottle (1960) $15–20

Dragon Amphora (1953)
Two-handled white decanter with colorful dragon and flowers $10–15

Dragon Amphora (1958)
One handle, white pitcher, color dragon................................$14–18

Duck-Green Glass Figural (1960)
Green-and-amber duck, clear glass base................................$35–45

Eagle (1970) $45–55

Egyptian Specialty (1960)
Two-handled amphora, Egyptian design on tan and gold.......$14–19

Etruscan Decanter (1959)
Single-handled black greek design on tan background...........$14–19

Euganean Bronze (1952–1955) $14–19

Euganean Coppered (1952–1955).......................$13–18

Faenza Decanter (1952–1956)
Colorful country scene on white single-handled decanter $21–28

Fighting Cocks (1962)
Combination decanter and ashtray................................$14–19

Fish—Green and Gold Glass Figural (1960)
Green, silver, and gold, clear glass base................................$30–40

Fish—Ruby Murano Glass Figural (1961)
Ruby-red tone of glass..$30–40

Florentine Majolica (1956)
Round-handled decanter, painted pitcher $20–30

Gambia (1961)
Black princess, kneeling, holding tray $8–12

Golden Fakir, Seated Snake Charmer with Flute and Snakes
1961 gold $26–37
1960 black and gray $26–37

Gondola (1959)
Highly glazed abstract gondola and gondolier in black...........$21–27

Gondola (1960)..$14–19

Grapes, Pear Figural $25–40

Mayan (1960)
Mayan temple godhead mask..$15–25

Mosaic Ashtray (1959), Combination Decanter Ashtray
Black, yellow, green, 11½ inches $15–25
Black, green; miniature, 6 inches $10–14

Nubian
Kneeling black figure $14–19

Opal Majolica (1957)
Two gold handles, translucent top $14–19

Penguin Murano Glass Figural (1968)
Black-and-white penguin...$25–30

Pheasant Murano Glass Figural (1960)
Red and clear glass on a crystal base $35–45

Pheasant Red and Gold Figural (1960)
Red-and-gold glass bird $40–60

Primavera Amphora (1958)
Two-handled vase shape..$14–19

Puppy Cucciolo Glass Figural (1961)
Amber and green glass...$26–37

Puppy Murano Glass Figural (1960)
Amber glass $26–37

Silver Blue Decanter (1952–1955)
Hand-painted silver flowers and leaves $22–28

Silver Brown Decanter (1952–1955)
Hand-painted silver flowers and leaves $26–37

Sir Lancelot (1962)
Figure of English knight in full armor $14–19

Springbok Amphora (1952)
Leaping African deer $14–19

Squirrel Glass Figural (1968)
Amethyst colored squirrel on crystal base $40–50

Sudan (1960)
African motif in browns, blue, yellow, and gray $14–19

Torre Rosa (1962)
Rose-tinted tower of fruit $16–24

Torre Tinta (1962)
Multicolor tower of fruit..$18–22

Tower of Fruit (1968)
Various fruit in natural colors $16–24

Tower of Fruit Majolica Torre Bianca (1962)
White-and-gray tower of fruit $16–24

McCormic Bottles

These pieces, like Kentucky Gentlemen and others, are similar in design to the Beam and Brooks bottles but are released in limited numbers.

The McCormic bottles, which originally or still contain McCormick Irish Whiskey, are manufactured in different series, including cars, famous Americans, frontiermen decanters, and gunfighters. The famous Americans series has been produced most often and represents celebrities from colonial times to the twentieth century.

Barrel Series

Barrel, with Stand and Shot Glasses 1958	$25–30
Barrel, with Stand and Plain Hoops 1968	$15–20
Barrel, with Stand and Gold Hoops 1968	$20–25

Bird Series

Blue Jay 1971	$20–25
Canadian Goose, Miniature	$18–25
Gambel's Quail 1982	$45–55
Ring-neck Pheasant 1982	$45–55
Wood Duck 1980	$30–35

Car Series

Packard 1937	$25–35

The Pony Express...$20–25

The Sand Buggy Commemorative Decanter..................$35–50

Confederate Series

Jeb Stuart $25–35

Jefferson Davis..$25–30

Robert E. Lee $25–35

Stonewall Jackson...$25–35

Country and Western Series

Hank Williams, Sr., 1980...$50–55

Hank Williams, Jr., 1980 ....$70–80

Tom T. Hall 1980 ....$32–42

Elvis Presley Series

Elvis '55 1979..$40–50

Elvis '55 Mini $25–35

Elvis '55 Mini 1980 ....$20–30

Elvis '68 1980..$40–50

Elvis '68 Mini 1980 ....$25–35

Elvis '77 1978 ....$65–80

Elvis '77 Mini 1979 ....$32–40

Elvis Bust 1978..$24–35

Elvis Designer I
Music box plays "Are You Lonesome Tonight?"...............$85–100

Elvis Designer II
Music box plays "It's Now or Never" $140–160

Elvis Gold 1979 ....$180–220

Elvis Karate $100–130

Elvis Sergeant $190–210

Elvis Silver 1980..$120–135

Famous American Portrait Series

Abe Lincoln with Law Book in Hand............................$35–45

Alexander Graham Bell with Apron $10–15

Captain John Smith $12–20

Charles Lindbergh..$24–28

Eleanor Roosevelt...$12–20

George Washington Carver $28–40

Henry Ford $20–25

Lewis Meriwether..$16–20

Pocahontas $30–42

Robert E. Perry $25–35

Thomas Edison...$35–45

Ulysses S. Grant with Coffeepot and Cup....................$15–25

William Clark..$15–20

Football Mascots

Alabama Bamas $26–34

Arizona Sun Devils...$39–48

Arizona Wildcats...$21–27

Arkansas Hogs 1972...$42–48

Auburn War Eagles $16–24

Baylor Bears 1972...$24–30

California Bears...$20–25

Drake Bulldogs, Blue Helmet and Jersey 1974..............$15–20

Georgia Bulldogs, Black Helmet and Red Jersey............$12–19

Georgia Tech Yellowjackets $15–25

Houston Cougars 1972..$20–30

Indiana Hoosiers 1974 ....$15–25

Iowa Cyclones 1974..$45–55

Iowa Hawkeyes 1974...$60–70

Iowa Purple Panthers $32–42

Louisiana State Tigers 1974...$15–20

Michigan State Spartans...$15–20

Michigan Wolverines 1974...$15–25

Minnesota Gophers 1974 ....$8–12

Mississippi Rebels 1974..$8–12

Mississippi State Bulldogs, Red Helmet and Jersey 1974..$12–18

Nebraska Cornhuskers 1974 ....$12–18

Nebraska Football Player $35–45

Nebraska, Johnny Rogers, No. 1................................$230–260

New Mexico Lobo..$32–40

Oklahoma Sooners Wagon 1974 ....$20–28

Oklahoma Souther Cowboy 1974 ....$14–18

Oregon Beavers 1974...$10–18

Oregon Ducks 1974...$12–18

Purdue Boilermaker 1974...$15–25

Rice Owls 1972..$20–30

Smu Mustangs 1972 ....$17–24

TCU Horned Frogs 1972 ....$25–30

Tennessee Volunteers 1974 ....$8–12

Texas A & M Aggies 1972...$22–30

Texas Tech Raiders 1972 ....$20–26

Texas Horns 1972 .... $23–33

Washington Cougars 1974 .... $20–25

Washington Huskies 1974 .... $15–25

Wisconsin Badgers 1974 .... $15–25

Frontiersmen Commemorative Decanters 1972

Daniel Boone $15–22

Davy Crockett $17–25

Jim Bowie $12–15

Kit Carson $14–18

General

A&P Wagon $50–55

Airplane, Spirit of Saint Louis 1969 .... $60–80

American Bald Eagle 1982 .... $30–40

American Legion Cincinnati 1986 .... $25–35

Buffalo Bill 1979 .... $70–80

Cable Car $25–30

Car, Packard 1980 .... $30–40

Chair, Queen Anne $20–30

Ciao Baby 1978 .... $20–25

Clock, Cuckoo 1971 .... $25–35

De Witt Clinton Engine 1970 .... $40–50

French Telephone 1969 .... $20–28

Globe, Angelica 1971 .... $25–32

Henry Ford 1977 .... $20–24

Hutchinson Kansas Centennial 1972 .... $15–25

Jester 1972 .... $20–28

Jimmy Durante 1981
With music box, plays "Inka Dinka Doo" $31–40

Joplin Miner 1972 ....$15–25

J.R. Ewing 1980
With music box, plays theme song from "Dallas" $22–27

J.R. Ewing, Gold-colored $50–55

Julia Bulette 1974 ....$140–160

Lamp, Hurricane..$13–18

Largemouth Bass 1982 ....$20–28

Lobsterman 1979..$20–30

Louis Armstrong..$60–70

Mark Twain 1977 ....$18–22

Mark Twain, Mini...$13–18

McCormick Centennial 1956 ....$80–120

Mikado 1980...$60–80

Missouri Sesquicentennial China 1970...............................$5–7

Missouri Sesquicentennial Glass 1971................................$3–7

Ozark Ike 1979 ....$22–27

Paul Bunyan 1979 ....$25–30

Pioneer Theater 1972 ....$8–12

Pony Express 1972 ....$20–25

Renault Racer 1969 ....$40–50

Sam Houston 1977 ....$22–28

Stephen F. Austin 1977..$14–18

Telephone Operator $45–55

Thelma Lu 1982 ....$25–35

U.S. Marshal 1979 ....$25–35

Will Rogers 1977...$18–22

Yacht Americana 1971 ....$30–38

Gunfighter Series

Bat Masterson $20–30

Billy the Kid $25–30

Black Bart..$26–35

Calamity Jane $25–30

Doc Holiday $25–35

Jesse James..$20–30

Wild Bill Hickok...$21–30

Wyatt Earp..$21–30

Jug Series

Bourbon Jug..$62–70

Gin Jug..$6–10

Old Holiday Bourbon 1956...$6–18

Platte Valley 1953 ....$3–6

Platte Valley, Half Pint...$3–4

Vodka Jug..$6–10

King Arthur Series

King Arthur on Throne..$30–40

Merlin the Wizard with His Wise Old Magical Robe 1979...$25–35

Queen Guinevere, The Gem of Royal Court..................$12–18

Sir Lancelot of the Lake in Armor, A Knight of the Round
Table $12–18

The Literary Series

Huck Finn 1980...$20–25

Tom Sawyer 1980...$22–26

Miniatures

Charles Lindbergh Miniature 1978 ....$10–14

Confederates Miniature Set (4) 1978 ....$40–50

Henry Ford Miniature 1978...$10–14

Mark Twain Miniature 1978 ....$12–18

Miniature Gunfighters (8) 1977 ....$110–140

Miniature Noble 1978 ....$14–20

Miniature Spirit of '76 1977...$15–25

Patriot Miniature Set (8) 1976................................$250–350

Pony Express Miniature 1980 ....$15–18

Will Rogers Miniature 1978 ....$12–16

The Patriots

Benjamin Franklin 1975...$13–17

Betsy Ross 1975..$20–25

George Washington 1975 ....$20–27

John Paul Jones 1975 ....$15–20

Patrick Henry 1975 ....$14–18

Patrick Henry, Miniature...$12–15

Paul Revere 1975...$20–25

Spirit of '76 1976...$50–60

Thomas Jefferson 1975 ....$14–18

Pirate Series

Pirate No. 1 1972...$10–12

Pirate No. 2 1972 ....$10–12

Pirate No. 3 1972...$8–12

Pirate No. 4 1972..$8–12

Pirate No. 5 1972..$8–12

Pirate No. 6 1972 ....$8–12

Pirate No. 7 1972 ....$8–12

Pirate No. 8 1972..$8–12

Pirate No. 9 1972..$8–12

Pirate No. 10 1972 ....$20–28

Pirate No. 11 1972 ....$20–28

Pirate No. 12 1972 ....$20–28

Rural Americana Series

Woman Feeding Chickens 1980...................................$25–35

Woman Washing Clothes 1980 ....$30–40

Shrine Series

Circus...$20–35

Dune Buggy 1976 ....$25–35

Imperial Council $20–25

Jester (Mirth King) 1972...$30–40

The Noble 1976..$25–32

Sports Series

Air Race Propeller 1971 ....$15–20

Air Race Pylon 1970...$10–15

Johnny Rodgers No. 1 1972..$160–195

Johnny Rodgers No. 2 1973...$70–85

K.C. Chiefs 1969 ....$18–25

K.C. Royals 1971 ....$10–15

Muhammad Ali 1980 ....$20–30

Nebraska Football Player 1972 ....$33–45

Skibob 1971 ....$10–11

Train Series

Jupiter Engine 1969..$20–25

Mail Car 1970...$25–28

Passenger Car 1970...$35–45

Wood Tender 1969 ....$14–18

Old Blue Ribbon Bottles

These bottles, like other figurals, are manufactured to contain Old Blue Ribbon liquor.

The Blue Ribbon bottles are noted for distinct realism of historical themes and depictions of railroad cars from the nineteenth century. In addition, Blue Ribbon is the only manufacturer to produce a hockey series with each bottle commemorating a different hockey team.

Air Race Decanter	$18–26
Blue Bird	$14–19
Caboose	$20–30
Eastern Kentucky University	$15–21
Jupiter '60 Mail Car	$13–17
Jupiter '60 Passenger Car	$16–23
Jupiter '60 Wood Tender	$13–17
Jupiter '60 Locomotive	$15–22
K.C. Royals	$19–26
Pierce Arrow	$13–15
***Santa Maria* Columbus' Ship**	$15–20
***Titanic* Ocean Liner**	$35–45

Transportation Series

Balloon $9–12

Fifth Avenue Bus..$14–21

Prairie Schooner...$10–11

River Queen $10–15

River Queen, Gold...$20–25

Hockey Series

Boston Bruins $14–18

Chicago Black Hawks...$14–18

Detroit Red Wings...$14–18

Minnesota North Stars $14–18

New York Rangers...$14–18

Saint Louis Blues...$14–18

Old Commonwealth Bottles

The Old Commonwealth brand, produced by J.P. Van Winkle and Son, is one of the newer companies (1974) to produce whiskey in collectible decanters. The ceramic decanters themselves are manufactured in the Orient, while the whiskey is made and the bottling is done at the Hoffman Distilling Company in Lawrenceburg, Kentucky.

Today, the majority of the decanters are produced in regular and miniature sizes. The titles of most pieces appear on the bottle's front plaque.

Alabama Crimson Tide 1981
University of Alabama symbol...$23–30

Bulldogs 1982
The mascot of the University of Georgia Bulldogs $20–30

Chief Illini No. 1 1979
The mascot for the University of Illinois................................$70–85

Chief Illini No. 2 1981
The mascot for the University of Illinois................................$55–65

Chief Illini No. 3 1979
The mascot for the University of Illinois................................$65–75

Coal Miner No. 1 1975
Standard size..$80–100
Mini 1980 ....$20–30

Coal Miner No. 2 1976
Standard size...$20–30
Mini 1982 ....$19–23

Coal Miner No. 3 1977
Standard size...$28–36
Mini 1981 ....$20–25

Coal Miner—Lunchtime—No. 4 1980
Standard size...$33–43
Mini $15–20

Cottontail 1981 ....$25–35

Elusive Leprechaun 1980 ....$24–30

Fisherman, "A Keeper" 1980....................$20–30

Golden Retriever 1979...............................$30–40

Kentucky Thoroughbreds 1976 ....$30–40

Kentucky Wildcat $32–42

LSU Tiger 1979..$45–55

Lumberjack..$15–25

Missouri Tiger $35–45

Old Rip Van Winkle No. 1 1974 ....$40–50

Old Rip Van Winkle No. 2 1975 ....$35–45

Old Rip Van Winkle No. 3 1977.................$30–40

Pointing Setter Decanter 1965 ....$16–23

Quail on the Wing Decanter 1968 ....$7–12

Rebel Yell Rider 1970 ....$23–32

Rip Van Winkle Figurine 1970 ....$32–40

Sons of Ireland 1972.................................$15–20

Sons of Erin 1969......................................$6–9

South Carolina Tricentennial 1970 ....$12–19

Tennessee Walking Horse 1977 ....$24–35

USC Trojans 1980
Standard size...$45–55
Mini $11–16

Weller Masterpiece 1963...$26–35

Western Boot Decanter 1982
Standard size...$20–25
Mini $8–12

Western Logger 1980..$25–34

Wildcats 1982 ....$40–46

Wings Across the Continent 1972 ....$16–23

Yankee Doodle $25–32

Modern Firefighters Series

Modern Hero No. 1 1982
Standard size $25–35
Mini $8–12

The Nozzleman No. 2 1982
Standard size $30–40
Mini $17–24

On Call No. 3 1982
Standard size $45–55
Mini $15–24

Fallen Comrade No. 4 1982
Standard size $30–40
Mini $17–25

Waterfowler Series

Waterfowler No. 1 1979...$40–50

Here They Come No. 2 1980 ....$32–42

Good Boy No. 3 1981 ....$32–42

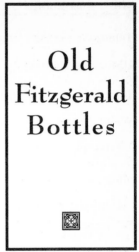

Old Fitzgerald Bottles

These bottles are manufactured by the Old Fitzgerald Distilling Company to package its whiskey and bourbon. These bottles are often called Old Cabin Still bottles, for one of the brand names under which they were distributed and sold.

These bottles are issued in both decanter and figural designs in various types and colors portraying different Irish and American subjects. Runs are produced in very limited quantities.

Americas Cup Commemorative 1970 .... $15–22

Blarney Castle 1970 .... $12–19

Browsing Deer Decanter 1967 .... $15–22

California Bicentennial 1970 .... $15–22

Candelite Decanter 1955 .... $9–12

Colonial Decanter 1969 .... $4–7

Crown Decanter $5–9

Gold Coast Decanter 1954 .... $10–15

"Golden Bough" Decanter 1971 .... $4–9

Gold Web Decanter 1953 .... $10–16

Hillbilly 1969, Pint $13–18

Hillbilly Bottle 1954, Pint...$13–18

Hillbilly Bottle 1954, Quart..$13–18

Hillbilly Bottle 1954, Gallon (very rare)............................$60–85

Jewel Decanter 1951–1952..$9–15

Leaping Trout Decanter 1969..$11–16

Leprechaun Bottle 1968..$25–32

LSU Alumni Decanter 1970..$25–32

Man O' War Decanter 1969 ....$5–9

Memphis Commemorative 1969 ....$8–12

Nebraska 1971...$27–32

Nebraska 1972 ....$18–25

Ohio State Centennial 1970 ....$12–18

Old Cabin Still Decanter 1958 ....$16–23

Pilgrim Landing Commemorative 1970.............................$14–24

Ski-Country Bottles

These bottles are produced in limited editions and offer a variety of subjects such as Indians, owls, game birds, Christmas themes, and customer specialties. Due to the limited editions and high quality of detailing, these bottles are rated high on the wish lists of most collectors.

Animals

Badger Family
Standard size $35–45
Mini $16–24

Bobcat Family
Standard size $45–60
Mini $16–25

Coyote Family
Standard size $37–48
Mini $17–23

Kangaroo
Standard size $22–32
Mini $18–28

Koala $20–28

Raccoon
Standard size $36–45
Mini $25–30

Skunk Family
Standard size $40–50
Mini $22–26

Snow Leopard
Standard size $36–43
Mini $30–35

Birds

Blackbird
Standard size $34–40
Mini $29–30

Black Swan
Standard size $30–35
Mini $18–24

Blue Jay
Standard size $50–60
Mini $42–49

Cardinal
Standard size $55–70
Mini $35–45

Condor
Standard size $45–55
Mini $25–30

Gamecocks
Standard size $120–130
Mini $40–46

Gila Woodpecker
Standard size $55–65
Mini $26–32

Peace Dove
Standard size $50–60
Mini $20–26

Peacock
Standard size $80–100
Mini $45–60

Penguin Family
Standard size $45–55
Mini $21–27

Wood Duck
Standard size $175–200
Mini $125–150

Christmas

Bob Cratchit
Standard size $40–50
Mini $25–30

Mrs. Cratchit
Standard size $40–50
Mini $25–30

Scrooge
Standard size $40–50
Mini $15–20

Circus

Clown
Standard size $44–52
Mini $27–33

Elephant on Drum
Standard size $35–45
Mini $35–45

Jenny Lind, Blue Dress
Standard size $55–75
Mini $48–60

Lion on Drum
Standard size $31–36
Mini $23–28

Palomino Horse
Standard size $40–48
Mini $30–40

P. T. Barnum
Standard size $32–40
Mini $20–25

Ringmaster
Standard size $20–25
Mini $15–18

Tiger on Ball
Standard size $35–44
Mini $31–37

Tom Thumb
Standard size $20–25
Mini $16–21

Customer Specialties

Ahrens-Fox Engine $140–180

Bonnie and Clyde (pair)
Standard size $60–70
Mini $55–62

Caveman
Standard size $16–23
Mini $18–22

Mill River Country Club $38–47

Olympic Skier, Gold $85–110

Olympic Skier, Red
Standard size $22–30
Mini $30–35

Olympic Skier, Blue
Standard size $25–32
Mini $35–40

Political Donkey and Elephant $50–60

Domestic Animals

Basset Hound
Standard size $45–55
Mini $26–32

Holstein Cow $45–60

Eagles, Falcons, and Hawks

Birth of Freedom
Standard size $85–95
Mini $65–75

Eagle on the Water
Standard size $90–110
Mini $38–45

Easter Seals Eagle
Standard size $48–60
Mini $22–29

Falcon, Gallon $350–425

Gyrfalcon
Standard size $54–60
Mini $27–34

Happy Eagle
Standard size $85–105
Mini $80–95

Mountain Eagle
Standard size $130–150
Mini $100–120

Osprey Hawk
Standard size $140–160
Mini $100–120

Peregrine Falcon
Standard size $75–85
Mini $18–25

Prairie Falcon
Standard size $65–80
Mini $35–48

Red-Shoulder Hawk
Standard size $60–70
Mini $34–40

Redtail Hawk
Standard size $75–95
Mini $33–40

White Falcon
Standard size $68–75
Mini $30–40

Fish

Muskellunge
Standard size $30–37
Mini $17–21

Rainbow Trout
Standard size $40–50
Mini $24–30

Salmon
Standard size $30–35
Mini $18–22

Trout $27–32

Game Birds

Banded Mallard $50–60

Chukar Partridge
Standard size $33–40
Mini $16–21

King Eider Duck $50–60

Mallard 1973 ....$50–60

Pheasant, Mini $52–62

Pheasant, Golden
Standard size $40–45
Mini $24–30

Pheasant in the Corn
Standard size $50–60
Mini $30–39

Pheasants Fighting
Standard size $70–80
Mini $35-45

Pheasants Fighting, Half Gallon $145–165

Pintail $76–85

Prairie Chicken..$55–65

Ruffed Grouse
Standard size $40–50
Mini $22–28

Turkey
Standard size $80–100
Mini $100–120

Grand Slam

Desert Sheep
Standard size $75–90
Mini $25–30

Mountain Sheep
Standard size $50–60
Mini $24–30

Stone Sheep
Standard size $50–65
Mini $27–34

Horned and Antlered Animals

Antelope..$45–60

Bighorn Ram
Standard size...$65–75
Mini $25–31

Mountain Goat
Standard size...$30–45
Mini $38–48

Mountain Goat, Gallon $525–600

Whitetail Deer
Standard size...$30–95
Mini $34–40

Indians

Ceremonial Antelope Dancer
Standard size...$52–62
Mini $36–45

Ceremonial Buffalo Dancer
Standard size...$150–185
Mini $32–38

Ceremonial Deer Dancer
Standard size...$85–100
Mini $40–48C

Ceremonial Eagle Dancer
Standard size...$185–205
Mini $24–34

Ceremonial Falcon Dancer
Standard size...$85–100
Mini $34–45

Ceremonial Wolf Dancer
Standard size...$50–60
Mini $32–40

Chief No. 1
Standard size $105–125
Mini $14–20

Chief No. 2
Standard size $105–125
Mini $14–20

Cigar Store Indian $32–40

Dancers of the Southwest, Set
Standard size $250–300
Mini $140–175

Owls

Barn Owl
Standard size $48–55
Mini $20–24

Great Gray Owl
Standard size $48–55
Mini $20–25

Horned Owl
Standard size $60–70
Mini $70–80

Horned Owl, Gallon $700–800

Saw Whet Owl
Standard size $40–45
Mini $20–25

Screech Owl Family
Standard size $80–90
Mini $68–75

Spectacled Owl
Standard size $70–85
Mini $58–68

Rodeo

Barrel Racer

Standard size $58–68

Mini $20–26

Bull Rider

Standard size $42–49

Mini $22–28

Wyoming Bronco

Standard size $48–66

Mini $25–35

Trademarks

T he words and letters in bold are abbreviations of the trademark as it appeared on the bottle. Each is followed by the complete name and location of the company and the approximate period of time in which the trademark was used.

Domestic Trademarks

A   John Agnew & Son, Pittsburgh, PA, 1854–1866.

A IN A CIRCLE   American Glass Works, Richmond, VA, and Paden City, WV, 1909–1936.

A & B TOGETHER (AB)   Adolphus Busch Glass Manufacturing Co, Belleville, IL, and Saint Louis, MO, 1904–1907.

AB Co.   American Bottle Co., Chicago IL, 1905–1930.

A B G M Co.   Adolphus Busch Glass Manufacturing Co, Belleville, IL, and Saint Louis, MO, 1886–1928.

A & Co.   John Agnew and Co., Pittsburgh, PA, Indian Queen, Ear of Corn and other flasks, 1854–1892.

A C M E   Acme Glass Co., Olean, NY, 1920–1930.

A & D H C   A. & D.H. Chambers, union flasks, Pittsburgh, PA, 1842–1886.

AGEE AND AGEE IN SCRIPT   Hazel Atlas Glass Co., Wheeling, WV, 1921–1925.

A.G.W. Co.,   American Glass Works Ltd., 1860–1905.

AGW   American Glass Works, 1880.

ANCHOR FIGURE WITH H IN CENTER   Anchor Hocking Glass Corp., Lancaster, OH, 1955.

A. R. S.   A.R. Samuels Glass Co., Philadelphia, PA, 1855–1872.

A S F W W VA.   A.S. Frank Glass Co., Wellsburg, WV, 1859.

ATLAS   Atlas Glass Co., Washington, PA, and later Hazel Atlas Glass Co., 1896–1965.

BALL AND BALL IN SCRIPT   Ball Bros. Glass Manufacturing Co., and later Ball Corporation, Muncie, IN, 1887–1973.

BERNARDIN IN SCRIPT   W.J. Latchford Glass Co., Los Angeles, CA, 1932–1938.

THE BEST   Gillender & Sons, Philadelphia, PA, 1867–1870.

B F B Co.   Bell Fruit Bottle Co., Fairmount, IN, 1910.

B. G. Co.   Belleville Glass Co., Belleville, IL, 1882.

BISHOP'S   Bishop and Co., San Diego and Los Angeles, CA, 1890–1920.

BK   Benedict Kimber, Bridgeport & Brownsville, PA, 1822–1840.

BOYDS IN SCRIPT   Illinois Glass Co., Alton, IL, 1900–1930.

BRELLE (IN SCRIPT) JAR   Brelle Fruit Jar Manufacturing Co., San Jose, CA, 1912–1916.

BRILLIANTE   Jefferis Glass Co., Fairton, NJ, and Rochester, PA, 1900–1905.

C IN A CIRCLE   Chattanooga Bottle & Glass Co. and later Chattanooga Glass Co., 1927–present.

C in a square   Crystal Glass Co., Los Angeles, CA, 1921–1929.

C IN A STAR   Star City Glass Co., Star City, WV, 1949–present.

CANTON DOMESTIC FRUIT JAR   Canton Glass Co., Canton, OH, 1890–1904.

C & Co. or C Co   Cunninghams & Co., Pittsburgh, PA, 1880–1907.

CCCo   C. Conrad & Co. (beer), St. Louis, MO, 1876–1883.

C C Co.   Carl Conrad & Co., Saint Louis, MO, 1876–1883.

C C G Co.   Cream City Glass Co., Milwaukee, WI, 1888–1893.

C.F.C.A.   California Fruit Canners Association, Sacramento, CA, 1899–1916.

C G M Co   Campbell Glass Manufacturing Co., West Berkeley, CA, 1885.

C G W   Campbell Glass Works, West Berkeley, CA, 1884–1885.

C & H   Coffin & Hay, Winslow, NJ, 1838–1842.

C L G Co.   Carr-Lowrey Glass Co., Baltimore, MD, 1889–1920.

Clyde, N. Y.   Clyde Glass Works, Clyde, NY, 1870–1882.

Clyde in script   Clyde Glass Works, Clyde, NY, 1895.

C Milw   Chase Valley Glass Co., Milwaukee, WI, 1880.

Cohansey   Cohansey Glass Manufacturing Co., Philadelphia, PA, 1870–1900.

C.V.Co. No. 1 and No. 2   Milwaukee, WI, 1880–1881.

DB   Du Bois Brewing Co., Pittsburgh, PA, 1918.

Dexter   Franklin Flint Glass Works, Philadelphia, PA, 1861–1880.

Diamond (plain)   Diamond Glass Co., 1924-present.

The Dictator   William McCully & Co., Pittsburgh, PA, 1855–1869.

Dictator   William McCully & Co., Pittsburgh, PA, 1869–1885.

D & O   Cumberland Glass Mfg. Co., Bridgeton, NJ, 1890–1900.

D O C   D.O. Cunningham Glass Co., Pittsburgh, PA, 1883–1937.

D S G Co.   De Steiger Glass Co., LaSalle, IL, 1867–1896.

Duffield   Duffield, Parke & Co., Detroit, MI, 1866–1875.

Dyottsville   Dyottsville Glass Works, Philadelphia, PA, 1833–1923.

ECONOMY (IN SCRIPT) TRADEMARK   Kerr Glass Manufacturing Co., Portland, OR, 1903–1912.

ELECTRIC TRADEMARK IN SCRIPT   Gayner Glass Works, Salem, NJ, 1910.

ELECTRIC TRADEMARK   Gayner Glass Works, Salem, NJ, 1900–1910.

ERD & CO., E R DURKEE   E.R. Durkee & Co., New York, NY, post-1874.

E R DURKEE & CO   E.R. Durkee & Co., New York, NY, 1850–1860.

EUREKA 17   Eurkee Jar Co., Dunbar, WV, 1864.

EUREKA IN SCRIPT   Eurkee Jar Co., Dunbar, WV, 1900-1910.

EVERLASTING (IN SCRIPT) JAR   Illinois Pacific Glass Co., San Francisco, CA, 1904.

F INSIDE A JAR OUTLINE   C.L. Flaccus Glass Co., Pittsburgh, PA, 1900–1928.

F & A   Fahnstock & Albree, Pittsburgh, PA, 1860–1862.

FL OR FL & Co.   Frederick Lorenz & Co., PIttsburgh, PA, 1819–1841.

G E M   Hero Glass Works, Philadelphia, PA, 1884–1909.

G & H   Gray and Hemingray, Cincinnati, OH, 1848–1864.

GILBERDS   Gilberds Butter Tub Co., Jamestown, NY, 1883–1890.

GREENFIELD   Greenfield Fruit Jar & Bottle Co., Greenfield, IN, 1888–1912.

H (WITH VARYING NUMERALS)   Holt Glass Works, West Berkeley, CA, 1893–1906.

HAZEL   Hazel Glass Co., Wellsburg, WV, 1886–1902.

HELME   George W. Helme Co., Jersey City, NJ, 1870–1895.

HEMINGRAY   Hemingray Brothers & Co. and later Hemingray Glass Company, Covington, KY, 1864–present.

H.J. HEINZ   H.J. Heinz Co., Pittsburgh, PA, 1860–1869.

HEINZ & NOBLE   H.J. Heinz Co., Pittsburgh, PA, 1869–1872.

F.J. HEINZ   H.J. Heinz Co., Pittsburgh, PA, 1876–1888.

H.J. HEINZ CO.   H. J. Heinz Co., Pittsburgh, PA, 1888–present.

HS IN A CIRCLE   Twitchell & Schoolcraft, Keene, NH, 1815–1816.

I G Co.   Ihmsen Glass Co., Pittsburgh, PA, 1870–1898.

I. G. Co.   Ihmsen Glass Co., 1895.

I. G. Co.   Monogram, III, Glass Co. on fruit jar, 1914.

I. P. G.   In diamond, III, Pacific Glass Corp., 1925–1930.

IG   Illinois Glass, F inside of a jar outline, C.L. Flaccus ½ glass ½ Co., Pittsburgh, PA, 1900–1928.

III. GLASS CO.   1916–1929.

I G   Illinois Glass Co., Alton, IL, before 1890.

I G CO. IN A DIAMOND   Illinois Glass Co., Alton, IL, 1900–1916.

IMPROVED G E M   Hero Glass Works, Philadelphia, PA, 1868.

I P G   Illinois Pacific Glass Co., San Francisco, CA, 1902–1932.

JAF & CO., PIONEER AND FOLGER   J.A. Floger & Co., San Francisco, CA, 1850–present.

J D 26 S   John Ducan & Sons, New York, NY, 1880–1900.

J R   Stourbridge Flint Glass Works, Pittsburgh, PA, 1823–1828.

JBS MONOGRAM   Joseph Schlitz Brewing Co., Milwaukee, WI, 1900.

JT   Mantua Glass Works and later Mantua Glass Co., Mantua, OH, 1824.

JT & Co   Brownsville Glass Works, Brownsville, PA, 1824–1828.

KENSINGTON GLASS WORKS   Kensington Glass Works, Philadelphia, PA, 1822–1932.

KERR IN SCRIPT   Kerr Glass Manufacturing Co. and later Alexander H. Kerr Glass Company, Portland, OR; Sand Spring, OK; Chicago, IL; Los Angeles, CA; 1912–present.

K H & G   Kearns, Herdman & Gorsuch, Zanesville, OH, 1876–1884.

K & M   Knoz & McKee, Wheeling, WV, 1824–1829.

K Y G W AND KYGW Co.   Kentucky Glass Works Company, Louisville, KY, 1849–1855

LAMB   Lamb Glass Co., Mount Vernon, OH, 1855–1964.

L & W   Lorenz & Wightman, PA, 1862–1871.

L G Co   Louisville Glass Works, Louisville, KY, 1880.

LIGHTNING   Henry W. Putnam, Bennington, VT, 1875–1890.

L K Y G W   Louisville Kentucky Glass Works, Louisville, KY, 1873–1890.

"MASCOT," "MASON" AND M F G Co.   Mason Fruit Jar Co., Philadelphia, PA, 1885–1890.

MASTADON   Thomas A. Evans Mastadon Works and later Wm. McCully & Co., Pittsburgh, PA, 1855–1887.

MG IN SLANT LETTERS   Maywood Glass, Maywood, CA, 1930–1950.

M.G. CO.   Missouri Glass Co., 1900.

M.G. Co.   Modes Glass Co., IN, 1895–1904.

M. G. W.   Middletown Glass Co., NY, 1889.

MOORE BROS.   Moore Bros., Clayton, NJ, 1864–1880.

N B B G Co   North Baltimore Bottle Glass Co., North Baltimore, OH, 1885–1930.

O   Owen Bottle Company

O-D-1-O & DIAMOND & I   Owens III Pacific Coast Co., CA, 1932–1943. Mark of Owen-III. Glass Co. merger in 1930.

P F W   Pacific Glass Works, San Francisco, CA, 1862–1876.

PREMIUM   Premium Glass Co., Coffeyville, KS, 1908–1914.

PUTNAM GLASS WORKS IN A CIRCLE   Putnam Flint Glass Works, Putnam, OH, 1852–1871.

P & W   Perry & Wood and later Perry & Wheeler, Keene, NH, 1822–1830.

QUEEN (IN SCRIPT) TRADE MARK, ALL IN A SHIELD   Smalley, Kivian & Onthank, Boston, MA, 1906–1919.

RAU'S   Fairmount Glass Works, Fairmount, IN, 1898–1908.

R & C Co   Roth & Co., San Francisco, CA, 1879–1888.

RED WITH A KEY THROUGH IT   Safe Glass Co., Upland, IN, 1892–1898.

R G Co.   Renton Glass Co., Renton, WA, 1911.

ROOT   Root Glass Co., Terre Haute, IN, 1901–1932.

S IN ONE SIDE OF A STAR   Southern Glass Co., Los Angeles, CA, 1920–1929.

S.B. & G. Co.   Stretor Bottle & Glass Co., IL, 1881–1905.

S. F. & P.G.W.   John Wieland's extra pale Cac. Bottling Works, S.F.

S & C   Stebbins & Chamberlain or Coventry Glass Works, Coventry, CT, 1825–1830.

S F G W   San Francisco Glass Works, San Francisco, CA, 1869–1876.

SQUIBB   E. R. Squibb, M.D., Brooklyn, NY, 1858–1895.

STANDARD (IN SCRIPT, MASON)   Standard Coop. Glass Co. and later Standard Glass Company, Marion, IN, 1894–1932.

STAR GLASS CO   Star Glass Co., New Albany, IN, 1860–1900.

SWAYZEE   Swayzee Glass Co., Swayzee, IN, 1894–1906.

T C W   T.C. Wheaton Co., Millville, NJ, 1888–present.

T S   Coventry Glass Works, Coventry, CT, 1820–1824.

W & CO   Thomas Wightman & Co., Pittsburgh, PA, 1880–1889.

W C G Co   West Coast Glass Co., Los Angeles, CA, 1908–1930.

WF & S MILW   William Franzen & Son, Milwaukee, WI, 1900–1929.

W G W   Woodbury Glass Works, Woodbury, NJ, 1882–1900.

W T & Co   Whitail-Tatum & Co., Millville, NJ, 1857–1935.

Foreign Trademarks

A IN A CIRCLE   Alembic Glass Industries, Bangalore, India.

BIG A, IN CENTER OF IT GM   Australian Glass Mfg. Co., Kilkenny, So. Australia.

A.B.C.   Albion Bottle Co. Ltd., Oldbury, North Birmingham, England.

A.G.W.   Alloa Glass Limited, Alloa, Scotland.

A G B Co.   Albion Glass Bottle Co., England (trademark is found under Lea and Perrins), 1880–1900.

AVH.A.   Van Hoboken & Co., Rotterdam, the Netherlands, 1800–1898.

B & C Co. L   Bagley & Co. Ltd., Est. 1832 and still operating, England.

BEAVER   Beaver Flint Glass Co., Toronto, Ontario, Canada, 1897–1920.

BOTTLE IN FRAME   Veb Glasvoerk Drebkau, Drebkau, N.L. Germany.

CROWN WITH THREE DOTS   Crown Glass, Waterloo, N.S., Wales.

CS & Co.   Cannington, Shaw & Co., St. Helens, England, 1872–1916.

CROWN WITH FIGURE OF A CROWN   Excelsior Glass Co., Saint John's, Canada, and later Diamond Glass Co., Montreal, Quebec, Canada, 1879–1913.

D IN CENTER OF A DIAMOND   Cominion Glass Co., Montreal, Quebec.

D.B. IN A BOOK FRAME   Dale Brown & Co., Ltd., Mesborough, York, England.

EXCELSIOR   Excelsior Glass Co., Saint John's, Canada, 1878–1883.

FISH   Veb Glasvoerk Stralau, Berlin.

HH   Werk Hermannshutte, Czechoslovakia.

HAMILTON   Hamilton Glass Works, Hamilton, Ontario, Canada, 1865–1872.

HAT   Brougba (Bulgaria).

HUNYADI JANOS   Andreas Saxlehner, Buda–Pesth, Austria–Hungary, 1863–1900.

IYGE ALL IN A CIRCLE   The Irish Glass Bottle, Ltd., Dublin, Ireland.

KH   Kastrupog Holmeqaads, Copenhagen, Denmark.

L ON A BELL   Lanbert S.A., Belgium.

LIP   Lea & Perrins, London, England, 1880–1900.

LS IN A CIRCLE   Lax & Shaw, Ltd., Leeds, York, England.

M IN A CIRCLE   Cristales Mexicanos, Monterey, Mexico.

N IN A DIAMOND   Tippon Glass Co., Ltd., Tokyo, Japan.

NAGC   North American Glass Co., Montreal, Quebec, Canada, 1883–1890.

PG   Verreries De Puy De Dome, S.A., Paris, France.

R   Louis Freres & Co., France, 1870–1890.

S IN A CIRCLE   Vetreria Savonese, A. Voglienzone, S.A., Milano, Italy.

S.A.V.A. ALL IN A CIRCLE   Asmara, Ethiopia.

S & M   Sykes & Macvey, Castleford, England, 1860–1888.

T IN A CIRCLE   Tokyo, Seibin, Ltd., Tokyo, Japan.

vFo   Vidreria Ind. Figuerras Oliveiras, Brazil.

VT   Ve.Tri S.p.a., Vetrerie Trivemta Vicenza, Italy.

VX   Usine de Vauxrot, France.

WECK IN A FRAME   Weck Glaswerk G. mb.H, ofigen, in Bonn, Germany.

Y IN A CIRCLE   Etaria Lipasmaton, Athens, Greece.

Bottle Clubs

Bottle clubs are one of the best sources of bottles for beginners, and offer a great opportunity to meet old-timers, and get information, not to mention have a good time. The bottle clubs listed here reflect the latest information available at the time of publication and are subject to change. The list represents a good cross section of clubs across the United States.

ALABAMA

Alabama Bottle Collectors Society
2768 Hanover Circle
Birmingham, AL 35205
(205) 933-7902

Azalea City Beamers Bottle and
Specialty Club
100 Bienville Avenue
Mobile, AL 36606
(205) 473-4251

Bama Beamers Bottle and
Specialty Club
Route 1, P.O. Box 72
Sheffield, AL 35660
(205) 383-6884

Choctaw Jim Beam Bottle and
Specialty Club
218 South Hamburg Street
Butler, AL 36904
(205) 459-3140

Heart of Dixie Beam Bottle and
Specialty Club
2136 Rexford Road
Montgomery, AL 36116

Mobile Bottle Collectors Club
8844 Lee Circle
Irvington, AL 36544
(205) 957-6725

Mobile Bottle Collectors Club
Route 4, P.O. Box 28
Theodore, AL 36582

Montgomery, Alabama, Bottle Club
1940A Norman Bridge Court
Montgomery, AL 36104

Montgomery Bottle and Insulator Club
2021 Merrily Drive
Montgomery, AL 36111
(205) 288-7937

North Alabama Bottle and Glass Club
P.O. Box 109
Decatur, AL 35601

Tuscaloosa Antique Bottle Club
1617 11th Street
Tuscaloosa, AL 35401

*Southern Beamers Bottle and
Specialty Club*
1400 Greenbrier Road, Apartment
G-3
Anniston, AL 36201
(205) 831-5151

*Vulcan Beamers Bottle and
Specialty Club*
5817 Avenue Q
Birmingham, AL 35228
(205) 831-5151

ALASKA

Alaska Bottle Club
8510 East 10th
Anchorage, AK 99504

ARIZONA

Avon Collectors Club
P.O. Box 1406
Mesa, AZ 86201

*Fort Smith Area Bottle Collectors
Association*
4618 South "Q"
Fort Smith, AZ 72901

Kachina Ezra Brooks Bottle Club
3818 West Cactus Wren Drive
Phoenix, AZ 85021

Phoenix A.B.C. Club
1939 West Waltann Lane
Phoenix, AZ 85023
(602) 933-9757

Pick and Shovel A.B.C. of Arizona, Inc.
P.O. Box 7020
Phoenix, AZ 85011

*Southern AZ Historical Collector's
Association, Limited*
6211 Piedra Seca
Tucson, AZ 85718

Tri-City Jim Beam Bottle Club
2701 East Utopia Road, Sp. #91
Phoenix, AZ 85024
(602) 867-1375

*Valley of the Sun Bottle and
Specialty Club*
212 East Minton
Tempe, AZ 85281

*White Mountain Antique Bottle
Collectors Association*
P.O. Box 503
Eager, AZ 85925

*Wildcat Country Beam Bottle and
Specialty Club*
2601 South Blackmoon Drive
Tucson, AZ 85730
(602) 298-5943

ARKANSAS

*Fort Smith Area Bottle Collectors
Association*
2201 South 73rd Street
Fort Smith, AR 72903

Hempsted County Bottle Club
710 South Hervey
Hope, AR 71801

Indian Country A.B. and Relic Society
3818 Hilltop Drive
Jonesboro, AR 72401

Little Rock Antique Bottle Club
#7 Rockwood
Cabot, AR 72023
(501) 843-9127

Madison County Bottle Collectors Club
Route 2, Box 304
Huntsville, AR 72740

Razorback Jim Beam Bottle and
Specialty Club
2609 South Taylor
Little Rock, AR 72204
(501) 664-1335

Southwest Arkansas Bottle Club
Star Route
Delight, AR 71940

CALIFORNIA

Amethyst Bottle Club
3245 Military Avenue
Los Angeles, CA 90034

Antique Bottle Club Association
of Fresno
P.O. Box 1932
Fresno, CA 93718

Antique Bottle Collectors of
Orange County
223 East Pomona
Santa Ana, CA 92707

A-OK Beamers
7650 Balboa Boulevard
Van Nuys, CA 91406
(213) 787-2674

Argonaut Jim Beam Bottle Club
8253 Citadel Way
Sacramento, CA 95826
(916) 383-0206

Avon Bottle and Specialties Collectors
Southern California Division
9233 Mills Avenue
Montclair, CA 91763

Bay Area Vagabonds Jim Beam Club
224 Castleton Way
San Bruno, CA 94066
(415) 355-4356

Beach Cities Beamers
3111 Highland Avenue
Manhattan Beach, CA 90266

Beam Bottle Club of Southern
California
3221 North Jackson
Rosemead, CA 91770

Beaming Beamers Jim Beam Bottle and
Specialty Club
3734 Lynhurst Way
North Highlands, CA 95660
(916) 482-0359

Beam's Orange County Bottle and
Specialty Club
1516 East Harmony Lane
Fullerton, CA 92631
(714) 526-5137

Bidwell Bottle Club
Box 546
Chico, CA 95926

Bishop Belles and Beaux Bottle Club
P.O. Box 1475
Bishop, CA 93514

Blossom Valley Jim Beam Bottle and
Specialty Club
431 Grey Ghost Avenue
San Jose, CA 95111
(408) 227-2759

Bodfish Beamers Jim Beam Bottle Club
19 Dow Drive
P.O. Box 864-A
Bodfish, CA 93205
(714) 379-3280

Bytown Bottle Seekers
P.O. Box 375
Ontario, CA 91761
(613) 838-5802

California Ski Country Bottle Club
212 South El Molino Street
Alhambra, CA 91801

Camellia City Jim Beam Bottle Club
3734 Lynhurst Way
North Highlands, CA 95660

Central California Avon Bottle and
Collectible Club
P.O. Box 232
Amador City, CA 95601

Cherry Valley Beam Bottle and
Specialty Club
6851 Hood Drive
Westminster, CA 92683

Chief Solano Bottle Club
4-D Boynton Avenue
Sulsun, CA 94585

Curiosity Bottle Association
Box 103
Napa, CA 94558

Fiesta City Beamers
329 Mountain Drive
Santa Barbara, CA 93103

First Double Springs Collectors Club
13311 Illinois Street
Westminster, CA 92683

Five Cities Beamers
756 Mesa View Drive, Sp. 57
Arroyo Grande, CA 93420

Fresno Raisin Beamers
3850 East Ashian #A
Fresno, CA 93726
(209) 224-3086

Glass Belles of San Gabriel
518 West Neuby Avenue
San Gabriel, CA 91776

Glasshopper Figural Bottle Association
P.O. Box 6642
Torrance, CA 90504

Golden Bear Ezra Brooks Bottle Club
8808 Capricorn Way
San Diego, CA 92126

Golden Bear Jim Beam Bottle and
Specialty Club
8808 Capricorn Way
San Diego, CA 92126

Golden Gate Beam Club
35113 Clover Street
Union City, CA 94587
(415) 487-4479

Golden Gate Historical Bottle Society
6019 Arlington Boulevard
Richmond, CA 94805

Greater California Antique Bottle
Collectors
P.O. Box 55
Sacramento, CA 95801

Grizzly Guzzlers Jim Beam Bottle Club
40080 Francis Way
P.O. Box 3725
Big Bear Lake, CA 92351

High Desert Bottle Hunters
P.O. Box 581
Ridgecrest, CA 93558

Highland Toasters Beam Bottle and
Specialty Club
1570 East Marshall
San Bernardino, CA 92404
(714) 883-2000

Hoffman's Mr. Lucky Bottle Club
2104 Rhoda Street
Simi Valley, CA 93065

Hollywood Stars—Ezra Brooks
Bottle Club
2200 North Beachwood Drive
Hollywood, CA 90028

Humboldt Antique Bottle Club
P.O. Box 6012
Eureka, CA 95501

Jewels of Avon
2297 Maple Avenue
Oroville, CA 95965

Jim Beam Bottle Club
139 Arlington
Berkeley, CA 94707

Jim Beam Bottle Club of Southern
California
1114 Coronado Terrace
Los Angeles, CA 90066

Juniper Hills Bottle Club
Route 1, Box 18
Valyerma, CA 93563

Kern County Antique Bottle Club
P.O. Box 6724
Bakersfield, CA 93306

Lilliputian Bottle Club
5119 Lee Street
Torrance, CA 90503

Lionstone Bottle Collectors of America
P.O. Box 75924
Los Angeles, CA 90075

Livermore Avon Club
6385 Claremont Avenue
Richmond, CA 94805

Lodi Jim Beam Bottle Club
429 East Lodi Avenue
Lodi, CA 95240

Los Angeles Historical Bottle Club
P.O. Box 60762
Terminal Annex
Los Angeles, CA 90060
(213) 332-6751

Mission Bells (Beams)
1114 Coronada Terrace
Los Angeles, CA 90026

Mission Tesore Jim Beam Bottle and
Specialty Club
7701 East Zayante Road
Felton, CA 95018
(408) 335-4317

Mission Trail Ezra Brooks Bottles and
Specialties Club, Inc.
4923 Bel Canto Drive
San Jose, CA 95124

Mission Trail Historical Bottle Club
P.O. Box 721
Seaside, CA 93955
(408) 394-3257

Modesto Beamers
1429 Glenwood Drive
Modesto, CA 95350
(209) 523-3440

Modesto Old Bottle Club (MOBC)
P.O. Box 1791
Modesto, CA 95354

Monterey Bay Beam Bottle and
Specialty Club
P.O. Box 258
Freedom, CA 95019

Motherlode Bottle Club
P.O. Box 337
Angels Camp, CA 95222

M. T. Bottle Club
P.O. Box 608
Solana Beach, CA 92075

Mt. Bottle Club
422 Orpheus
Encinitas, CA 92024

Mount Diablo Bottle Club
4166 Sandra Circle,
Pittsburg, CA 94565

Mount Diablo Bottle Society
1699 Laguna #110
Concord, CA 94520

Mount Whitney Bottle Club
P.O. Box 688
Lone Pine, CA 93545

Napa-Solano Bottle Club
1409 Delwood
Vallejo, CA 94590

National Jim Beam Bottle and
Specialty Club
5005 Cochrane Avenue
Oakland, CA 94618
(415) 655-5005

Northern California Jim Beam Bottle
and Specialty Club
P.O. Box 186
Montgomery Creek, CA 96065

Northwestern Bottle Club
P.O. Box 1121
Santa Rosa, CA 95402

Northwestern Bottle Collectors
Association
1 Keeler Street
Petaluma, CA 94952

Ocean Breeze Beamers
4841 Tacayme Drive
Oceanside, CA 92054
(714) 757-9081

Original Sippin' Cousins Ezra Brooks
Specialties Club
12206 Malone Street
Los Angeles, CA 90066

Palomar Jim Beam Club
246 South Las Posas
P.O. Box 125
San Marcos, CA 92069
(714) 744-2924

Pebble Beach Jim Beam Bottle Club
419 Alvarado Street
Monterey, CA 93940
(408) 373-5320

Painted Soda Bottle Collectors
Association
9418 Hilmer Drive
LaMesa, CA 92165
(619) 461-4354

Peninsula Bottle Club
P.O. Box 886
Belmont, CA 94002

Petaluma Bottle and Antique Club
P.O. Box 1035
Petaluma, CA 94952

Quail Country Jim Beam Bottle and
Specialty Club
625 Pleasant
Coalinga, CA 93210

Queen Mary Beam and Specialty Club
P.O. Box 2054
Anaheim, CA 92804

Relic Accumulators
P.O. Box 3513
Eureka, CA 95501

Santa Barbara Beam Bottle Club
5307 University Drive
Santa Barbara, CA 93111

Santa Barbara Bottle Club
P.O. Box 30171
Santa Barbara, CA 93105

San Bernardino County Historical
Bottle and Collectible Club
P.O. Box 6759
San Bernardino, CA 92412
(619) 244-5863

San Diego Antique Bottle Club
P.O. Box 5137
San Diego, CA 92165
(619) 274-5519

San Diego Jim Beam Bottle Club
2620 Mission Village Drive
San Diego, CA 92112

San Francisco Bay Area Bottle Club
160 Lower Via Casitas #8
Kentfield, CA 94904

San Joaquin Valley Jim Beam Bottle
and Specialties Club
4085 North Wilson Avenue
Fresno, CA 93704

San Jose Historical Bottle Club
Association
P.O. Box 5432
San Jose, CA 95150
(408) 259-7564

San Luis Obispo Antique Bottle Club
124-21 Street
Paso Robles, CA 93446
(805) 238-1848

Santa Maria Beam and Specialty Club
528 East Harding
San Maria, CA 93454
(805) 922-1238

Sequoia Antique Bottle Society
1900 4th Avenue
Kingsburg, CA 93631

*Sequoia Antique Bottle and Collectors
Society*
P.O. Box 3695
Visalia, CA 93278
(209) 686-1873

*Shasta Antique Bottle Collectors
Association*
Route 1, Box 3147-A
Anderson, CA 96007

Sierra Gold Ski Country Bottle Club
5081 Rio Vista Avenue
San Jose, CA 95129

*Ski-Country Bottle Club of Southern
California*
3148 North Walnut Grove
Rosemead, CA 91770

Solar Country Beamers
940 Kelly Drive
Barstow, CA 92311
(714) 256-1485

South Bay Antique Bottle Club
2589½ Valley Drive
Manhattan Beach, CA 90266

*Southern California Miniature
Bottle Club*
5626 Corning Avenue
Los Angeles, CA 90056

Southern Wyoming Avon Bottle Club
301 Canyon Highlands Drive
Oroville, CA 95965

Stockton Historical Bottle Society, Inc.
P.O. Box 8584
Stockton, CA 95204

*Sunnyvale Antique Bottle Collectors
Association*
613 Torrington
Sunnyvale, CA 94087

Superior California Bottle Club
P.O. Box 555
Anderson, CA 96007

Taft Antique Bottle Club
P.O. Box 334
Taft, CA 93268

Teen Bottle Club
Route 1, Box 60-TE
Eureka, CA 95501

Tehama County Antique Bottle Club
Route 1, Box 775
Red Bluff, CA 96080
(916) 527-1680

Tinseltown Beam Club
4117 East Gage Avenue
Bell, CA 90201
(213) 699-8787

Western World Collectors Association
P.O. Box 409
Ontario, CA 91761
(714) 984-0614

*Wildwind Jim Beam Bottle and
Specialty Club*
905 Eaton Way
Sunnyvale, CA 94087
(408) 739-1558

World Wide Avon Collectors Club
44021 Seventh Street
East Lancaster, CA 93534
(805) 948-8849

'49er Historical Bottle Association
P.O. Box 561
Penryn, CA 95663
(916) 663-3681

COLORADO

Alamosa Bottle Collectors
Route 2, Box 170
Alamosa, CO 81101

Antique Bottle Club of Colorado
P.O. Box 245
Littleton, CO 80160

Avon Club of Colorado Springs, CO
707 North Farragut
Colorado Springs, CO 80909

Colorado Mile-High Ezra Brooks Bottle
Club
7401 Decatur Street
Westminster, CO 80030

Foot-Hills Jim Beam Bottle and
Specialty Club
1303 Kilkenny Street
Boulder, CO 80303
(303) 665-3957

Four Corners Bottle and Glass Club
P.O. Box 45
Cortez, CO 81321

Horsetooth Antique Bottle Collectors,
Inc.
P.O. Box 944
Fort Collins, CO 80521

Lionstone Western Figural Club
P.O. Box 2275
Colorado Springs, CO 80901

Mile-Hi Jim Beam Bottle and
Specialty Club
13196 West Green Mountain Drive
Lakewood, CO 80228
(303) 986-6828

National Ski Country Bottle Club
1224 Washington Avenue
Golden, CO 80401
(303) 279-3373

Northeastern Colorado Antique
Bottle Club
P.O. Box 634
Fort Morgan, CO 80701

Northern Colorado Antique
Bottle Club
227 West Beaver Avenue
Fort Morgan, CO 80701

Northern Colorado Beam Bottle and
Specialty Club
3272 Gunnison Drive
Fort Collins, CO 80526
(303) 226-2301

Ole Foxie Jim Beam Club
P.O. Box 560
Westminster, CO 80020

Peaks and Plains Antique Bottle Club
P.O. Box 814
Colorado Springs, CO 80901

Pike's Peak Antique Bottle and
Collectors Club
P.O. Box 2012
Colorado Springs, CO 80901
(719) 574-6976

Rocky Mountain Jim Beam Bottle and
Specialty Club
Alcott Station
P.O. Box 12162
Denver, CO 80212

Southern Colorado Antique Bottle Club
843 Ussie Avenue
Canon City, CO 81212
(719) 275-3719

Telluride Antique Bottle Collectors
P.O. Box 344
Telluride, CO 80143

Western Figural and Jim Beam
Specialty Club
P.O. Box 4431
Colorado Springs, CO 80930

Western Slope Bottle Club
P.O. Box 354
Palisade, CO 81526
(303) 464-7727

CONNECTICUT

Connecticut Specialty Bottle Club, Inc.
P.O. Box 624
Stratford, CT

The National Association of Milk Bottle Collectors
4 Ox Bow Road
Westport, CT 06880
(203) 227-5244

Somers Antique Bottle Club
Somers, CT 06071
(203) 487-1071

Southern Connecticut Antique Bottle Collectors Association
34 Dartmouth Drive
Huntington, CT 06484
(203) 929-5197

Western Connecticut Jim Beam Bottle and Specialty Club
Route 1, Box 442
Old Hawleyville Road
Bethel, CT 06081
(203) 744-6118

DELAWARE

Blue Hen Jim Beam Bottle and Specialty Club
303 Potomac Drive
Wilmington, DE 19803
(302) 652-6378

Mason-Dixon Bottle Collectors Association
P.O. Box 505
Lewes, DE 19958

Tri-State Bottle Collectors and Diggers Club
730 Paper Mill Road
Newark, DE 19711
(302) 738-7523

FLORIDA

Antique Bottle Collectors Association of Florida
5901 Southwest 16th Street
Miami, FL 33144

Antique Bottle Collectors of Florida, Inc.
2512 Davie Boulevard
Fort Lauderdale, FL 33312

Antique Bottle Collectors of North Florida
P.O. Box 14796
Jacksonville, FL 32238
(904) 284-1499

Association of Florida Antique Bottle Collectors
P.O. Box 3105
Sarasota, FL 34230
(813) 923-6550

Bay Area Historical Bottle Collectors
P.O. Box 3454
Apollo Beach, FL 32210

Central Florida Insulator Collectors Club
707 Northeast 113th Street
Miami, FL 33161
(305) 895-0843

Central Florida Jim Beam Bottle Club
1060 West French Avenue
Orange City, FL 32763
(904) 775-7392

Crossarms Collectors Club
1756 Northwest 58th Avenue
Lauderhill, FL 33313

Deep South Jim Beam Bottle and
Specialty Club
16100 Southwest 278th Street
Homestead, FL 33031
(305) 248-7301

Everglades Antique Bottle Club
6981 Southwest 19th Street
Pompano, FL 33068

Everglades Antique Bottle and
Collectors Club
400 South 57 Terrace
Hollywood, FL 33023
(305) 962-3434

Florida Panhandle Jim Beam Bottle
and Specialty Club
706 James Court
Fort Walton Beach, FL 32548
(904) 862-3469

Gateway of the Palms Beam Bottle and
Specialty Club
6621 Katherine Road
West Palm Beach, FL 33406
(305) 683-3900

Gold Coast Collectors Club
Joseph I. Frakes
P.O. Box 10183
Wilton Manors, FL 33305

Halifax Historical Society
224½ South Beach Street
Daytona Beach, FL 32018

Harbor City Bottle Collectors Club
1232 Causeway
Eau, FL 32935

Longwood Bottle Club
P.O. Box 437
Longwood, FL 32750

Mid-State Antique Bottle Collectors
88 Sweetbriar Branch
Longwood, FL 32750
(407) 834-8914

Mid-State Antique Bottle Collectors
3400 East Grant Avenue
Orlando, FL 32806
(407) 896-8915

M.T. Bottle Collectors Association, Inc.
P.O. Box 1581
Deland, FL 32720

Northwest Florida Regional Bottle Club
P.O. Box 282
Port Saint Joe, FL 32456

Original Florida Keys Collectors Club
P.O. Box 212
Islamorada, FL 33036

Pensacola Bottle and Relic Collectors
Association
1004 Freemont Avenue
Pensacola, FL 32505

Ridge Area Antique Bottle Collectors
1219 Carlton
Lake Wales, FL 33853

Sanford Antique Bottle Collectors
2656 Grandview Avenue
Sanford, FL 33853
(305) 322-7181

Sarasota-Manatee Antique Bottle
Collectors Association
Route 1, Box 74-136
Sarasota, FL 33583

South Florida Jim Beam Bottle and
Specialty Club
7741 Northwest 35th Street
West Hollywood, FL 33024

Suncoast Antique Bottle Club
P.O. Box 12712
Saint Petersburg, FL 33733

Suncoast Antique Bottle Club
Association, Inc.
5305 8th Avenue South
Gulfport, FL 33707
(813) 866-0263

Suncoast Jim Beam Bottle and
Specialty Club
P.O. Box 5067
Sarasota, FL 33579

Tampa Antique Bottle Collectors
P.O. Box 4232
Tampa, FL 33607

West Coast Florida Ezra Brooks Bottle
Club
1360 Harbor Drive
Sarasota, FL 33579

GEORGIA

Bulldog Double Springs Bottle Collector
Club of Augusta, Georgia
1916 Melrose Drive
Augusta, GA 30906

Coastal Empire Bottle Club
P.O. Box 3714
Station B
Savannah, GA 31404

The Desoto Trail Bottle Collectors Club
406 Randolph Street
Cuthbert, GA 31740

Flint Antique Bottle and Coin Club
c/o Cordele-Crisp Company
Recreation Department
204 2nd Street North
Cordele, GA 31015

Flint River Jim Beam Bottle Club
Route 3
P.O. Box 6
Camilla, GA 31730
(912) 336-7034

Georgia Bottle Club
2996 Pangborn Road
Decatur, GA 30033

Georgia-Carolina Empty Bottle Club
P.O. Box 1184
Augusta, GA 30903

Macon Antique Bottle Club
P.O. Box 5395
Macon, GA 31208

Macon Antique Bottle Club
c/o 5532 Jane Run Circle
Macon, GA 31206

The Middle Georgia Antique Bottle Club
2746 Alden Street
Macon, GA 31206

Peachstate Bottle and Specialty Club
5040 Vallo Vista Court
Atlanta, GA 30342

Peachtree Jim Beam Bottlers Club
Lakeshore Drive
Daluth, GA 30136
(404) 448-9013

Peanut State Jim Beam Bottle and
Specialty Club
767 Timberland Street
Smyrna, GA 30080
(404) 432-8482

Southeastern Antique Bottle Club
P.O. Box 657
Decatur, GA 30033

Southeastern Antique Bottle Club
1546 Summerford Court
Dunwoody, GA 30338
(404) 394-6664

HAWAII

Hauoli Beam Bottle Collectors Club of
Hawaii
45-027 Ka-Hanahou Place
Kaneohe, HI 96744

Hawaii Historic Bottle Collectors Club
P.O. Box 90456
Honolulu, HI 96835
(808) 955-2130

IDAHO

Buhl Antique Bottle Club
500 12th
North Buhl, ID 83316

Eagle Rock Beam and Specialty Club
3665 Upland Avenue
Idaho Falls, ID 83401
(208) 522-7819

Em Tee Bottle Club
P.O. Box 62
Jerome, ID 83338

Fabulous Valley Antique Bottle Club
P.O. Box 8051
Boise, ID 83707

Idaho Beam and Specialty Club
2312 Burrell Avenue
Lewiston, ID 83501
(208) 743-5997

Inland Empire Jim Beam Bottle and Collectors' Club
1117 10th Street
Lewiston, ID 83501

Rock and Bottle Club
Route 1
Fruitland, ID 83619

Treasure Valley Beam Bottle and Specialty Club
2324 Norcrest Drive
Boise, ID 83705
(208) 343-6207

ILLINOIS

Antique Bottle Club of Northern Illinois
P.O. Box 23
Ingleside, IL 60041
(815) 338-2567

Alton Area Bottle Club
2448 Alby Street
Alton, IL 62002
(618) 462-4285

Blackhawk Jim Beam Bottle and Specialty Club
2003 Kishwaukee Street
Rockford, IL 61101

Central Illinois Jim Beam Bottle and Specialty Club
3725 South Sand Creek Road
Decatur, IL 62521

Central and Midwestern States Beam and Specialty Club
44 South Westmore
Lombard, IL 60148

Chicago Ezra Brooks Bottle and Specialty Club
3635 West 82nd Street
Chicago, IL 60652

Chicago Jim Beam Bottle and Specialty Club
1305 West Marion Street
Joliet, IL 60436

Dreamers Beamers
5721 Vial Parkway
La Grange, IL 60525
(312) 246-4838

Eagle Jim Beam Bottle and Specialty Club
1015 Hollycrest
P.O. Box 2084 CFS
Champaign, IL 61820
(217) 352-4035

1st Chicago Antique Bottle Club
P.O. Box A3382
Chicago, IL 60690
(708) 541-5788

Heart of Illinois Antique Bottle Club
2010 Bloomington Road
East Peoria, IL 61611

Illinois Jim Beam Bottle and Specialty Club
P.O. Box 13
Champaign, IL 61820

Illinois Bottle Club
P.O. Box 181
Rushville, IL 62681

International Association of Jim Beam
4338 Saratoga Avenue
Downers Grove, IL 60515

Kelly Club
147 North Brainard Avenue
La Grange, IL 60525

Land of Lincoln Bottle Club
2515 Illinois Circle
Decatur, IL 62526

Lewis and Clark Jim Beam Bottle and Specialty Club
P.O. Box 451
Wood River, IL 62095

Lionstone Bottle Collectors of America
P.O. Box 2418
Chicago, IL 60690

Little Egypt Jim Beam Bottle and Specialty Club
Route 2
Flat Rock, IL 62427
(618) 584-3338

Louis Joliet Bottle Club
12 Kenmore
Joilet, IL 60433

Metro East Bottle and Jar Association
309 Bellevue Drive
Delleville, IL 62223
(618) 233-8841

Metro East Bottle and Jar Association
1702 Keesler
Collinsville, IL 62234

Metro East Bottle and Jar Association
P.O. Box 185
Mascoutah, IL 62234

National Ezra Brooks Club
645 North Michigan Avenue
Chicago, IL 69611

North Shore Jim Beam Bottle Specialty Club
542 Glendale Road
Glenview, IL 60025

Pekin Bottle Collectors Association
P.O. Box 372
Pekin, IL 61554
(309) 347-4441

Rock River Valley Jim Beam Bottle and Specialty Club
1107 Avenue A
Rock Falls, IL 61071
(815) 625-7075

Starved Rock Jim Beam Bottle and Specialty Club
P.O. Box 177
Ottawa, IL 61350
(815) 433-3269

Sweet Corn Capital Bottle Club
1015 West Orange
Hoopeston, IL 60942

Tri-County Jim Beam Bottle Club
3702 West Lancer Road
Peoria, IL 61615
(309) 691-8784

INDIANA

American Collectors of Infant Feeders
5161 West 59th Street
Indianapolis, IN 46254
(317) 291-5850

City of Bridges Jim Beam Bottle and Specialty Club
1017 North 6th Street
Logansport, IN 46947
(219) 722-3197

Crossroads of America Jim Beam Bottle Club
114 South Green Street
Brownsburg, IN 46112
(317) 852-5168

Fort Wayne Historical Bottle Club
5124 Roberta Drive
Fort Wayne, IN 46306

Fort Wayne Historical Bottle Club
6793 C.R. 55
Spencerville, IN 46788
(219) 238-4842

Hoosier Jim Beam Bottle and
Specialty Club
P.O. Box 24234
Indianapolis, IN 46224

Indiana Ezra Brooks Bottle Club
P.O. Box 24344
Indianapolis, IN 46224

Jelly Jammers
R.R. 1, Box 23
Boggstown, IN 46110
(317) 835-7121

Lafayette Antique Bottle Club
3664 Redondo Drive
Lafayette, IN 47905

Michiana Jim Beam Bottle and
Specialty Club
58955 Locust Road
South Bend, IN 46614

Mid-West Antique Fruit Jar and
Bottle Club
P.O. Box 38
Flat Rock, IN 47234
(812) 587-5560

The Ohio Valley Antique Bottle and
Jar Club
214 John Street
Aurora, IN 47001

Steel City Ezra Brooks Bottle Club
Route 2, Box 32A
Valparaiso, IN 46383

Three Rivers Jim Beam Bottle and
Specialty Club
Route 4,Winchester Road
Fort Wayne, IN 46819
(219) 639-3041

We Found 'Em Bottle and
Insulator Club
P.O. Box 578
Bunker Hill, IN 46914

IOWA

Five Seasons Beam and Specialty Club
of Iowa
609 32nd Street, NE
Cedar Rapids, IA 52402
(319) 365-6089

Gold Dome Jim Beam Bottle and
Specialty Club
2616 Hull
Des Moines, IA 50317
(515) 262-8728

Hawkeye Jim Beam Bottle Club
658 Kern Street
Waterloo, IA 60703
(319) 233-9168

Iowa Antique Bottleers
Route 1, Box 145
Milton, IA 52570
(515) 675-3740

Iowa Great Lakes Jim Beam Bottle and
Specialty Club
Green Acres Mobile Park, Lot 88
Estherville, IA 51334
(712) 362-2759

Larkin Bottle Club
107 West Grimes
Red Oak, IA 51566

Midlands Jim Beam Bottle and
Specialty Club
Route 4
Harlan, IA 51537
(712) 744-3686

Quad Cities Jim Beam Bottle and
Specialty Club
2425 West 46th Street
Davenport, IA 52806
(319) 391-4319

Shot Tower Beam Club
284 North Booth Street
Dubuque, IA 52001
(319) 583-6343

KANSAS

Air Capital City Jim Beam Bottle and
Specialty Club
3256 Euclid
Wichita, KS 67217
(316) 942-3162

Bud Hastin's National Avon Collector's
Club
P.O. Box 12088
Overland Park, KS 66212

Cherokee Strip Ezra Brooks Bottle and
Specialty Club
P.O. Box 631
Arkansas City, KS 67005

Flint Hills Beam and Specialty Club
201 West Pine
El Dorado, KS 67402

Jayhawk Bottle Club
7919 Grant
Overland Park, KS 66212

Kansas City Antique Bottle Collectors
5528 Aberdeen
Shawnee Mission, KS 66205
(816) 433-1398

North-Central Kansas Antique Bottle
and Collectors Club
336 East Wisconsin
Russell, KS 67665
(913) 483-4380

Southeast Kansas Bottle and Relic Club
115 North Lafayette
Chanute, KS 66720
(316) 431-1643

Walnut Valley Jim Beam Bottle and
Specialty Club
P.O. Box 631
Arkansas City, KS 67005
(316) 442-0509

Wichita Ezra Brooks Bottle and
Specialty Club
8045 Peachtree Street
Wichita, KS 67207

KENTUCKY

Derby City Jim Beam Bottle Club
4105 Spring Hill Road
Louisville, KY 40207

Gold City Jim Beam Bottle Club
286 Metts Court
Apartment 4
Elizabethtown, KY 42701
(502) 737-9297

Kentuckiana Antique Bottle and
Outhouse Society
5801 River Knolls Drive
Louisville, KY 40222
(502) 969-8367

Kentucky Bluegrass Ezra Brooks
Bottle Club
6202 Tabor Drive
Louisville, KY 40218

Kentucky Cardinal Beam Bottle Club
428 Templin
Bardstown, KY 41104

Land by the Lakes Beam Club
Route 6, Box 320
Cadiz, KY 42211
(502) 522-8445

Louisville Bottle Collectors
11819 Garrs Avenue
Anchorage, KY 40223

Pegasus Jim Beam Bottle and
Specialty Club
9405 Cornflower Road
Valley Station, KY 40272
(502) 937-4376

LOUISIANA

Ark-La-Tex Jim Beam Bottle and
Specialty Club
1902 Carol Street
Bossier City, LA 71112
(318) 742-3550

Bayou Bottle Bugs
216 Dahlia
New Iberia, LA 70560

"Cajun Country Cousins" Ezra Brooks
Bottle and Specialty Club
1000 Chevis Street
Abbeville, LA 70510

Cenia Bottle Club
c/o Pam Tullos
Route 1, Box 463
Dry Prong, LA 71423

Crescent City Jim Beam Bottle and
Specialty Club
733 Wright Avenue
Gretna, LA 70053
(504) 367-2182

Dixie Diggers Bottle Club
P.O. Box 626
Empire, LA 70050

Historical Bottle Association of
Baton Rouge
1843 Tudor Drive
Baton Rouge, LA 70815

Ken Tally Jim Beam Bottle Club
110 Ken Tally Estates
Hammond, LA 70401
(504) 345-6186

New Albany Glass Works Bottle Club
732 North Clark Boulevard
Parksville, LA 47130

Northeast Louisiana Antique Bottle
Club
P.O. Box 4192
Monroe, LA 71291
(318) 322-8359

Red Stick Jim Beam Bottle Club
2127 Beaumont
Suite 4
Baton Rouge, LA 70806

Sanford's Night Owl Beamers
Route 2, Box 102
Greenwell Springs, LA 70739
(504) 261-3658

Shreveport Antique Bottle Club
1157 Arncliffe Drive
Shreveport, LA 71107
(504) 221-0089

MAINE

Dirigo Bottle Collectors Club
R.F.D. 3
Dexter, ME 04473
(207) 924-3443

Dover Foxcroft Bottle Club
50 Church Street
Dover Foxcroft, ME 04426

The Glass Bubble Bottle Club
P.O. Box 91
Cape Neddick, ME 03902

Jim Beam Collectors Club
10 Lunt Road
Falmouth, ME 04105

Kennebec Valley Bottle Club
9 Glenwood Street
Augusta, ME 04330

Mid-Coast Bottle Club
c/o Miriam Winchenbach
Waldoboro, ME 04572

New England Antique Bottle Club
P.O. Box 897
Rockport, ME 04856
(207) 236-9044

New England Bottle Club
45 Bolt Hill Road
Eliot, ME 03903

Paul Bunyan Bottle Club
237 14th Street
Bangor, ME 04401

Pine Tree Antique Bottle Club
Buxton Road
Saco, ME 04072

Pine Tree State Beamers
15 Woodside Avenue
Saco, ME 04072
(207) 284-8756

Tri-County Bottle Collectors
Association
R.F.D. 3
Dexter, ME 04930

Waldo County Bottlenecks Club
Head-of-the-Tide
Belfast, ME 04915

MARYLAND

Blue and Gray Ezra Brooks Bottle Club
2106 Sunnybrook Drive
Frederick, MD 21201

Catoctin Jim Beam Bottle Club
c/o Ron Danner
1 North Chatham Road
Ellicott City, MD 21063
(410) 465-5773

Mason-Dixon Bottle Collectors
Association
601 Market Street
Denton, MD 21629

Mid-Atlantic Miniature Whiskey
Bottle Club
208 Gloucester Drive
Glen Burnie, MD 21061
(410) 766-8421

South County Bottle Collector's Club
Bast Lane
Shady Side, MD 20867

MASSACHUSETTS

Baystate Beamers Bottle and
Specialty Club
27 Brookhaven Drive
Ludlow, MA 01056
(413) 589-0446

Berkshire Antique Bottle Association
R.D. 1, Hill Road
W. Stockbridge, MA 01266
(413) 298-3232

The Cape Cod Antique Bottle Club
c/o Mr. John Swanson
262 Setucket Road
Yarmouth, MA 02675

Merrimack Valley Antique Bottle Club
c/o M. E. Tarleton
Hillside Road
Boxford, MA 02675

New England Beam and Specialty Club
1104 Northampton Street
Holyoke, MA 01040

Scituate Bottle Club
54 Cedarwood Road
Scituate, MA 02066

Yankee Pole Cat Insulator Club
105 Richards Avenue
North Attleboro, MA 02760

MICHIGAN

Central Michigan Krazy Korkers
Bottle Club
Mid-Michigan Community College
Clare Avenue
Harrison, MI 48625

Chief Pontiac Antique Bottle Club
c/o Larry Blascyk
13880 Neal Road
Davisburg, MI 48019
(313) 634-8469

Dickinson Country Bottle Club
717 Henford Avenue
Iron Mountain, MI 49801

Flint Antique Bottle
Collectors Association
450 Leta Avenue
Flint, MI 48507

Flint Antique Bottle and
Collectors Club
3201 Lapeer Street
Flint, MI 48503
(313) 744-1135

Flint Eagles Ezra Brooks Club
1117 West Remington Avenue
Flint, MI 48507

Grand Valley Bottle Club
31 Dickinson Southwest
Grand Rapids, MI 49507

Great Lakes Jim Beam Bottle Club
of Michigan
1010 South Harvey
Plymouth, MI 48170
(313) 453-0579

Great Lakes Miniature Bottle Club
P.O. Box 245
Fairhaven, MI 48023

Huron Valley Bottle Club
12475 Saline-Milan Road
Milan, MI 48160

Huron Valley Bottle and
Insulator Club
6349 West Silver Lake Road
Linden, MI 48451
(313) 735-7381

Kalamazoo Antique Bottle Club
204 Monroe
Kalamazoo, MI 49007
(616) 349-3988

Lionstone Collectors Bottle and
Specialty Club of Michigan
3089 Grand Blanc Road
Swartz Creek, MI 48473

Manistee Coin and Bottle Club
207 East Piney Road
Manistee, MI 49660

Metro and East Bottle and
Jar Association
309 Bellevue Park Drive
Fairview Heights, MI 49660

Metro Detroit Antique Bottle Club
465 Moran Road
Grosse Pointe Farms, MI 48236
(313) 885-0912

Michigan Bottle Collectors Association
144 West Clark Street
Jackson, MI 49203

Michigan's Vehicle City Beam Bottles
and Specialty Club
907 Root Street
Flint, MI 48503

Mid-Michee Pine Beam Club
609 Webb Drive
Bay City, MI 48706

Northern Michigan Bottle Club
P.O. Box 421
Petoskey, MI 49770

Old Corkers Bottle Club
Route 1
Iron River, MI 49935

Red Run Jim Beam Bottle and
Specialty Club
172 Jones Street
Mount Clemens, MI 48043
(313) 465-4883

Traverse Area Bottle and
Insulator Club
P.O. Box 205
Acme, MI 49610

West Michigan Avon Collectors
331 Bellevue Southwest
Wyoming, MI 49508

W.M.R.A.C.C.
331 Bellevue Southwest
Grand Rapids, MI 49508

Wolverine Beam Bottle and
Specialty Club of Michigan
36009 Larchwood
Mount Clemens, MI 48043

World Wide Avon Bottle Collectors
Club
22708 Wick Road
Taylor, MI 48180

MINNESOTA

Arnfalt Collectors Beam Club
New Richard, MN 56072

Golpher State Jim Beam Bottle and Specialty Club
1216 Sheridan Avenue North
Minneapolis, MN 55411
(612) 521-4150

Heartland Jim Beam Bottle and Specialty Club
Box 633
245 Elm Drive
Foley, MN 56329
(612) 968-6767

Hey! Rube Jim Beam Bottle Club
1506 6th Avenue Northeast
Austin, MN 55912
(507) 433-6939

Lake Superior Antique Bottle Club
P.O. Box 67
Knife River, MN 55609

Minnesota 1st Antique Bottle Club
5001 Queen Avenue North
Minneapolis, MN 55430
(612) 521-9874

North-Star Historical Bottle Association Inc.
3308-32 Avenue South
Minneapolis, MN 55406
(612) 721-4165

Paul Bunyan Jim Beam Bottle and Specialty Club
Route 8, Box 656
Bemidji, MN 56601
(218) 751-6635

Truman, Minnesota, Jim Beam Bottle and Specialty Club
Truman, MN 56088
(507) 776-3487

Viking Jim Beam Bottle and Specialty Club
8224 Oxborough Avenue South
Bloomington, MN 55437
(612) 831-2303

MISSISSIPPI

Gum Tree Beam Bottle Club
104 Ford Circle
Tupelo, MS 38801

Magnolia Beam Bottle and Specialty Club
2918 Larchmont
Jackson, MS 39209
(601) 354-1350

Middle Mississippi Antique Bottle Club
P.O. Box 233
Jackson, MS 39205

Oxford Antique Bottlers
128 Vivian Street
Oxford, MS 38633

South Mississippi Antique Bottle Club
203 South 4th Avenue
Laurel, MS 39440

MISSOURI

Antique Bottle Club of Central Missouri
726 West Monroe
Mexico, MO 65265
(314) 581-1391

Antique Bottle and Relic Club of Central Missouri
c/o Ann Downing
Route 10
Columbia, MO 65210

Arnold, Missouri, Jim Beam Bottle and Specialty Club
1861 Jean Drive
Arnold, MO 63010
(314) 296-0813

Barnhart, Missouri, Jim Beam Bottle
and Specialty Club
2150 Cathlin Court
Barnhart, MO 63012

Bud Hastin's National Avon Club
P.O. Box 9868
Kansas City, MO 64134

Chesterfield Jim Beam Bottle and
Specialty Club
2066 Honey Ridge
Chesterfield, MO 63017

"Down in the Valley" Jim Beam
Bottle Club
528 Saint Louis Avenue
Valley Park, MO 63088

The Federation of Historical
Bottle Clubs
10118 Schuessler
Saint Louis, MO 63128
(314) 843-7573

Festus, Missouri, Jim Beam Bottle and
Specialty Club
Route 3, Box 117H
Frederick Road
Festus, MO 63028

First Capital Jim Beam Bottle and
Specialty Club
731 McDonough
Saint Charles, MO 63301

Florissant Valley Jim Beam Bottle and
Specialty Club
25 Cortez
Florissant, MO 63031

Greater Kansas City Jim Beam Bottle
and Specialty Club
P.O. Box 6703
Kansas City, MO 64123

Kansas City Antique Bottle Collectors
Association
1131 East 77 Street
Kansas City, MO 64131

Maryland Heights Jim Beam Bottle and
Specialty Club
2365 Wesford
Maryland Heights, MO 63043

Mineral Area Bottle Club
Knob Lick, MO 63651

Missouri Arch Jim Beam Bottle and
Specialty Club
2900 North Lindbergh
Saint Ann, MO 63074
(314) 739-0803

Mound City Jim Beam Decanter
Collectors
42 Webster Acres
Webster Groves, MO 63119

North-East County Jim Beam Bottle
and Specialty Club
10150 Baron Drive
Saint Louis, MO 63136

Northwest Missouri Bottle and
Relic Club
3006 South 28th Street
Saint Joseph, MO 64503

Rock Hill Jim Beam Bottle and
Specialty Club
9731 Graystone Terrace
Saint Louis, MO 63119
(314) 962-8125

Sho Me Jim Beam Bottle and
Specialty Club
Route 7, Box 314-D
Springfield, MO 65802
(417) 831-8093

Saint Charles Missouri, Jim Beam
Bottle and Specialty Club
122 South Cardinal
Saint Charles, MO 63301

Saint Louis Antique Bottle Collectors
Association
10118 Schuessler
Saint Louis, MO 63128
(314) 843-7573

Saint Louis Jim Beam Bottle and
Specialty Club
2900 Lindbergh
Saint Ann, MO 63074
(314) 291-3256

Troy, Missouri, Jim Beam Bottle and
Specialty Club
121 East Pershing
Troy, MO 63379
(314) 528-6287

Valley Bank Park Jim Beam Bottle and
Specialty Club
614 Benton Street
Valley Park, MO 63088

Walnut Park Jim Beam Bottle and
Specialty Club
5458 North Euclid
Saint Louis, MO 63114

West County Jim Beam Bottle and
Specialty Club
11707 Momarte Lane
Saint Louis, MO 63141

NEBRASKA

Cornhusker Jim Beam Bottle and
Specialty Club
5204 South 81st Street
Ralston, NE 68127
(402) 331-4646

Mini-Seekers
"A" Acres, Route 8
Lincoln, NE 68506

Nebraska Antique Bottle and
Collectors Club
14835 Drexel
Saint Omaha, NE 68137

Nebraska Big Red Bottle and
Specialty Club
N Street Drive-in
200 South 18th Street
Lincoln, NE 68508

NEVADA

Jim Beam Bottle Club of Las Vegas
212 North Orland Street
Las Vegas, NV 89107

Las Vegas Antique Bottle and
Collectibles Club
3901 East Stewart #16
Las Vegas, NV 89110
(702) 452-1263

Las Vegas Bottle Club
2632 East Harman
Las Vegas, NV 89121
(702) 731-5004

Lincoln County Antique Bottle Club
P.O. Box 191
Caliente, NV 89008
(702) 726-3655

Nevada Beam Club
P.O. Box 426
Fallon, NV 89406

Reno/Sparks Antique Bottle Club
P.O. Box 1061
Verdi, NV 89439

Southern Nevada Antique Bottle Club
431 North Spruce Street
Las Vegas, NV 89101

Virginia and Truckee Jim Beam Bottle
and Specialty Club
P.O. Box 1596
Carson City, NV 89701

Wee Bottle Club International
P.O. Box 1195
Las Vegas, NV 89101

NEW HAMPSHIRE

Bottlers of New Hampshire
125A Central Street
Farmington, NH 03835

Granite State Bottle Club
R.F.D. 1
Belmont, NH 03220

Yankee Bottle Club
P.O. Box 702
Keene, NH 03431
(603) 352-2959

Merrimack Valley Antique Bottle Club
776 Harvey Road
Manchester, NH 03103
(503) 623-4101

NEW JERSEY

Antique Bottle Collectors Club of Burlington County
18 Willow Road
Bordentown, NJ 08505

Artifact Hunters Association Inc.
c/o 29 Lake Road
Wayne, NJ 07470

The Jersey Devil Bottle Diggers Club
14 Church Street
Mount Holly, NJ 08060

Jersey Jackpot Jim Beam Bottle and Specialty Club
197 Farley Avenue
Fanwood, NJ 07023
(201) 322-7287

Jersey Shore Bottle Club
P.O. Box 995
Toms River, NJ 08754
(908) 240-5247

Lakeland Antique Bottle Club
18 Alan Lane
Mill Hill
Dover, NJ 07801
(201) 366-7482

Lionstone Collectors Club of Delaware Valley
R.D. 3, Box 93
Sewell, NJ 08080

Meadowland Beamers
413 24th Street
Union City, NJ 07087
(201) 865-3684

New Jersey Ezra Brooks Bottle Club
South Main Street
Cedarville, NJ 08311

North Jersey Antique Bottle Club Association
251 Vista View Drive
Mahwah, NJ 07430

South Jersey Heritage Bottle and Glass Club, Inc.
P.O. Box 122
Glassboro, NJ 08028
(609) 423-5038

Sussex County Antique Bottle Collectors
Division of Sussex County Historical Society
82 Main Street
Newton, NJ 07860

Trenton Jim Beam Bottle Club, Inc.
17 Easy Street
Freehold, NJ 07728

Twin Bridges Beam Bottle and Specialty Club
P.O. Box 347
Pennsville, NJ 08070

West Essex Bottle Club
76 Beaufort Avenue
Livingston, NJ 07039

NEW MEXICO

Cave City Antique Bottle Club
Route 1, Box 155
Carlsbad, NM 88220

Roadrunner Bottle Club of New Mexico
2341 Gay Road Southwest
Albuquerque, NM 87105

NEW YORK

Auburn Bottle Club
297 South Street Road
Auburn, NY 13021

*Big Apple Beamers Bottle and
Specialty Club*
2901 Long Branch Road
Oceanside, NY 11572
(516) 678-3414

*Catskill Mountains Jim Beam
Bottle Club*
6 Gardner Avenue
Middletown, NY 10940

*Chautauqua County Bottle
Collectors Club*
Morse Motel, Main Street
Sherman, NY 14781

Eastern Monroe County Bottle Club
c/o Bethelem Lutheran Church
1767 Plank Road
Webster, NY 14580

Empire State Bottle Club Association
P.O. Box 3421
Syracuse, NY 13220

Empire State Jim Beam Bottle Club
P.O. Box 561
Main Street
Farmingdale, NY 11735

Finger Lakes Bottle Collectors Association
399 Dubois Road
Ithaca, NY 14850
(607) 272-1995

*Genessee Valley Bottle Collectors
Association*
P.O. Box 7528
Rochester, NY 14615
(716) 872-4015

Greater Catskills Antique Bottle Club
P.O. Box 411
Liberty, NY 12754

*Hudson River Jim Beam Bottle and
Specialty Club*
48 College Road
Monsey, NY 10952

Hudson Valley Bottle Club
144 County Route 1
Warwick, NY 10990

Long Island Antique Bottle Association
P.O. Box 147
Bayport, NY 11705

National Bottle Museum
P.O. Box 621
Ballston Spa, NY 12020
(518) 885-7589

*Niagara Frontier Beam Bottle and
Specialty Club*
17 Ravensbrook Court
Getzville, NY 14066
(716) 688-6624

*North Country Bottle Collectors
Association*
Route 1
Canton, NY 13617

Rensselaer County Antique Bottle Club
P.O. Box 792
Troy, NY 12180

Rochester, New York, Bottle Club
7908 West Henrietta Road
Rush, NY 14543

Saratoga Type Bottle Collectors Society
531 Route 42
Sparrow Bush, NY 12780
(914) 856-1766

*Southern Tier Bottle and Insulator
Collectors Association*
47 Dickinson Avenue
Port Dickinson, NY 13901

*Suffolk County Antique Bottle
Association of Coney Island, Inc.*
P.O. Box 943
Melville, NY 11746

Tryon Bottle Badgers
P.O. Box 146
Tribes Hill, NY 12177

Twin Counties Old Bottle Club
Don McBride
Star Route, Box 242
Palenville, NY 12463
(518) 943-5399

Upper Susquehanna Bottle Club
P.O. Box 183
Milford, NY 13807

Warwick Valley Bottle Club
P.O. Box 393
Warwick, NY 10990

Western New York Bottle Club
Association
62 Adams Street
Jamestown, NY 14701
(716) 487-9645

Western New York Bottle Collectors
87 South Bristol Avenue
Lockport, NY 14094

West Valley Bottleique Club
P.O. Box 204
Killbuck, NY 14748
(716) 945-5769

NORTH CAROLINA

Blue Ridge Bottle and Jar Club
Dogwood Lane
Black Mountain, NC 28711

Carolina Bottle Club
c/o Industrial Piping Company
Anonwood
Charlotte, NC 28210

Carolina Jim Beam Bottle Club
1014 North Main Street
Burlington, NC 27215

Catawba Valley Jim Beam Bottle and
Specialty Club
265 5th Avenue
Northeast Hickory, NC 28601
(704) 322-5268

Goldsboro Bottle Club
2406 East Ash Street
Goldsboro, NC 27530

Greater Greensboro Moose Ezra
Brooks Bottle Club
217 South Elm Street
Greensboro, NC 27401

Kinston Collectors Club, Inc.
325 East Lenoir
Kinston, NC 28501

Pelican Sand Dunners Jim Beam Bottle
and Specialty Club
Lot 17-J
Paradise Bay Mobile Home Park
P.O. Box 344
Salter Path, NC 28575
(919) 247-3290

Tar Heel Jim Beam Bottle and
Specialty Club
6615 Wake Forest Road
Fayetteville, NC 20301
(919) 488-4849

Wilmington Bottle and Artifact Club
183 Arlington Drive
Wilmington, NC 28401
(919) 763-3701

Wilson Antique Bottle and
Artifact Club
Route 5
P.O. Box 414
Wilson, NV 27893

Yadkin Valley Bottle Club
General Delivery
Gold Hill, NC 28071

OHIO

Beam on the Lake Bottle and
Specialty Club
9151 Mentor Avenue, F 15
Mentor, OH 44060
(216) 255-0320

Buckeye Bottle Club
229 Oakwood Street
Elyria, OH 44035

Buckeye Bottle Diggers
Route 2
P.O. Box 77
Thornville, OH 44035

Buckeye Jim Beam Bottle Club
1211 Ashland Avenue
Columbus, OH 43212

Carnation City Jim Beam Bottle Club
135 West Virginia
Sebring, OH 44672
(216) 938-6817

Central Ohio Bottle Club
931 Minerva Avenue
Columbus, OH 43229

Diamond Pin Winners Avon Club
5281 Fredonia Avenue
Dayton, OH 45431

The Federation of Historical Bottle Clubs
c/o Gary Beatty, Treasurer
9326 Court Road 3C
Galion, OH 44833

Findlay Antique Bottle Club
407 Cimarron Court
Findlay, OH 45840
(419) 422-3183

First Capitol Bottle Club
c/o Maxie Harper
Route 1, Box 94
Laurelville, OH 43135

Gem City Beam Bottle Club
1463 East Stroop Road
Dayton, OH 45429

Greater Cleveland Jim Beam Club
5398 West 147th Street
Brook Park, OH 44142
(216) 267-7665

Heart of Ohio Bottle Club
P.O. Box 353
New Washington, OH 44854
(419) 492-2829

Jeep City Beamers
531A Durango
Toledo, OH 43609
(419) 382-2515

Jefferson County Antique Bottle Club
1223 Oakgrove Avenue
Steubenville, OH 43952

Lakeshore Beamers
2681 Douglas Road
Ashtabula, OH 44004
(216) 964-3457

Maple Leaf Beamers
8200 Yorkshire Road
Mentor, OH 44060
(216) 255-9118

Northern Ohio Jim Beam Bottle Club
43152 Hastings Road
Oberlin, OH 44074
(216) 775-2177

Northeastern Ohio Bottle Club
P.O. Box 57
Madison, OH 44057
(614) 282-8918

Northwest Ohio Bottle Club
104 West Main
Norwalk, OH 44857

Ohio Bottle Club
P.O. Box 585
Barberton, OH 44203
(216) 753-2115

Ohio Ezra Brooks Bottle Club
8741 Kirtland Chardon Road
Kirtland Hills, OH 44094

Pioneer Beamers
38912 Butternut Ridge
Elyria, OH 44035
(216) 458-6621

Queen City Jim Beam Bottle Club
4327 Greenlee Avenue
Cincinnati, OH 45217
(513) 641-3362

Rubber Capitol Jim Beam Club
151 Stephens Road
Akron, OH 44312

Sara Lee Bottle Club
27621 Chagrin Boulevard
Cleveland, OH 44122

Southwestern Ohio Antique Bottle and Jar Club
273 Hilltop Drive
Dayton, OH 45415
(513) 836-3353

OKLAHOMA

Bar-Dew Antique Bottle Club
817 East 7th Street
Dewey, OK 74029

Frontier Jim Beam Bottle and Specialty Club
P.O. Box 52
Meadowbrook Trailer Village, Lot 101
Ponca City, OK 74601
(405) 765-2174

Green County Jim Beam Bottle and Specialty Club
Route 2
P.O. Box 233
Chouteau, OK 74337
(918) 266-3512

McDonnell Douglas Antique Club
5752 East 25th Place
Tulsa, OK 74114

Oklahoma Territory Bottle and Relic Club
1300 South Blue Haven Drive
Mustang, OK 73064
(405) 376-1045

Ponca City Old Bottle Club
2408 Juanito
Ponca City, OK 74601

Sooner Jim Beam Bottle and Specialty Club
5913 Southeast 10th
Midwest City, OK 73110
(405) 737-5786

Southwest Oklahoma Antique Bottle Club
35 South 49th Street
Lawson, OK 73501

Tri-State Historical Bottle Club
817 East 7th Street
Dewey, OK 74029

Tulsa Antique and Bottle Club
P.O. Box 4278
Tulsa, OK 74159
(918) 622-8062

OREGON

Central Oregon Bottle and Relic Club
671 Northeast Seward
Bend, OR 97701

Central Oregon Bottle and Relic Club
1545 Kalama Avenue
Redmond, OR 97756

Central South Oregon Antique Bottle Club
708 South F Street
Lakeview, OR 97630

Emerald Empire Bottle Club
P.O. Box 292
Eugene, OR 97401

Frontier Collectors
504 Northwest Bailey
Pendleton, OR 97801

Gold Diggers Antique Bottle Club
1958 South Stage Road
Medford, OR 97501

Lewis and Clark Historical Bottle and
Collectors Society
8018 Southeast Hawthorne
Boulevard
Portland, OR 97501

Lewis and Clark Historical Bottle
Society
4828 Northeast 33rd
Portland, OR 97501

Molalla Bottle Club
Route 1
P.O. Box 205
Mulino, OR 97042

Oregon Antique Bottle Club
Route 3
P.O. Box 23
Molalla, OR 97038

Oregon Beamers Beam Bottle and
Specialty Club
P.O. Box 7
Sheridan, OR 97378

Oregon Botyle Collectors Association
3661 Southeast Nehalem Street
Portland, OR 97202

Pioneer Fruit Collectors Association
P.O. Box 175
Grand Ronde, OR 97347

Siskiyou Antique Bottle Collectors
Association
P.O. Box 1335
Medford, OR 97501

PENNSYLVANIA

Anthracite Jim Beam Bottle Club
406 Country Club Apartments
Dallas, PA 18612

Antique Bottle Club of
Burlington County
8445 Walker Street
Philadelphia, PA 19136

Beaver Valley Jim Beam Club
1335 Indiana Avenue
Monaca, PA 15061

Bedford County Bottle Club
P.O. Box 116
Loysburg, PA 16659
(814) 766-3215

Camoset Bottle Club
P.O. Box 252
Johnstown, PA 15901

Christmas Valley Beamers
150 Second Street
Richlandtown, PA 18955
(215) 536-4636

Classic Glass Bottle Collectors
RD# 2
Cogan Station, PA 17728

Cumberland Valley Jim Beam Club
P.O. Box 132
Middletown, PA 17057
(717) 944-5376

Delaware Valley Bottle Club
12 Belmar Road
Halboro, PA 19040

Del-Val Bottle Club
Route 152 and Hilltown Pike
Hilltown, PA 19040

East Coast Double Springs Specialty
Bottle Club
P.O. Box 419
Carlisle, PA 17013

East Coast Ezra Brooks Bottle Club
2815 Fiddler Green
Lancaster, PA 17601

Endless Mountain Antique Bottle Club
P.O. Box 75
Granville Summit, PA 16926

Erie Bottle Club
P.O. Box 373
Erie, PA 16512

Flood City Jim Beam Bottle Club
231 Market Street
Johnstown, PA 15901

Forks of the Delaware Bottle Club Association
2996 Georgetown Road
Nazareth, PA 18064
(215) 837-6800

Friendly Jim's Beam Club
508 Benjamin Franklin Highway East
Douglasville, PA 19518

Indiana Bottle Club
240 Oak Street
Indiana, PA 15701

Keystone Flyers Jim Beam Bottle Club
288 Hogan Boulevard
Box 42
Lock Haven, PA 17745
(717) 748-6741

Kiski Mini Beam and Specialty Club
816 Cranberry Drive
Monroeville, PA 15146

Laurel Valley Bottle Club
P.O. Box 131
Ligonier, PA 15658
(412) 238-9046

Ligonier Historic Bottle Club
P.O. Box 188
Ligonier, PA 15658
(412) 238-4590

Middletown Area Bottle Collectors Association
P.O. Box 1
Middletown, PA 17057
(717) 939-0288

Pagoda City Beamers
735 Florida Avenue
Riverview Park
Reading, PA 19605
(215) 929-8924

Penn Beamers' 14th
15 Gregory Place
Richboro, PA 18954

Pennsylvania Bottle Collectors
251 Eastland Avenue
York, PA 17402
(717) 854-4965

Pennsylvania Dutch Jim Beam Bottle Club
812 Pointview Avenue
Ephrate, PA 17522

Philadelphia Bottle Club
8203 Elberon Avenue
Philadelphia, PA 19111

Philadelphia Collectors Club
8445 Walker Street
Philadelphia, PA 19111

Pittsburgh Antique Bottle Club
209 Palomino Drive
Oakdale, PA 15701
(412) 788-4304

Pittsburgh Bottle Club
P.O. Box 401
Ingomar, PA 15127

Pittsburgh Bottle Club
1528 Railroad Street
Sewickley, PA 15143

Susquehanna Valley Jim Beam Bottle and Specialty Club
64 East Park Street
Elizabethtown, PA 17022
(717) 367-4256

Tri-County Antique Bottle and Treasure Club
R.D. 2
P.O. Box 30
Reynoldsville, PA 15851

Valley Forge Jim Beam Bottle Club
1219 Ridgeview Drive
Phoenixville, PA 19460
(215) 933-5789

*Washington County Antique
Bottle Club*
R.D. 2, Box 342
Carmichaela, PA 15320
(412) 966-7996

Whitetail Deer Jim Beam Bottle Club
94 Lakepoint Drive
Harrisburg, PA 17111
(717) 561-2517

RHODE ISLAND

*Seaview Jim Beam Bottle and
Specialty Club*
362 Bayview Avenue
Cranston, RI 02905
(401) 461-4952

SOUTH CAROLINA

Greer Bottle Collectors Club
P.O. Box 142
Greer, SC 29651

Lexington County Antique Bottle Club
201 Roberts Street
Lexington, SC 29072

Palmetto State Beamers
908 Alton Circle
Florence, SC 29501
(803) 669-6515

Piedmont Bottle Collectors
c/o R. W. Leizear
Route 3
Woodruff, SC 29388

South Carolina Bottle Club
1119 Greenbridge Lane
Columbia, SC 29210

Union Bottle Club
107 Pineneedle Road
Union, SC 29379

TENNESSEE

Cotton Carnival Beam Club
P.O. Box 17951
Memphis, TN 38117

Memphis Bottle Collectors Club
4098 Faxon Avenue
Memphis, TN 38122
(901) 323-7319

*Middle Tennessee Bottle
Collectors Club*
2405 Pennington Bend Road
Nashville, TN 37214
(313) 883-2457

Music City Beam Bottle Club
2008 June Drive
Nashville, TN 37214
(615) 883-1893

TEXAS

*Alamo Chapter Antique Bottle Club
Association*
701 Castano Avenue
San Antonio, TX 78209

*Alamo City Jim Beam Bottle and
Specialty Club*
5785 FM 1346
P.O. Box 20442
San Antonio, TX 78220

*Austin Bottle and Insulator
Collectors Club*
1614 Ashberry Drive
Austin, TX 78723
(512) 453-7900

Cowtown Jim Beam Bottle Club
2608 Roseland
Fort Worth, TX 76103
(817) 536-4335

El Paso Insulator Club
Martha Stevens, Chairman
4556 Bobolink
El Paso, TX 79922

The Exploration Society
603 9th Street NAS
Corpus Christi, TX 78419
(210) 922-2902

Foard C. Hobby Club
P.O. Box 625
Crowell, TX 79227

Fort Concho Bottle Club
1703 West Avenue
North San Angelo, TX 76901

Foursome (Jim Beam)
1208 Azalea Drive
Longview, TX 75601

Golden Spread Jim Beam Bottle and Specialty Club
1104 South Maddox
Dumas, TX 79029
(806) 935-3690

Gulf Coast Beam Club
128 West Bayshore Drive
Baytown, TX 77520

Gulf Coast Bottle and Jar Club
P.O. Box 1754
Pasadena, TX 77501
(713) 592-3078

Oil Patch Beamers
1300 Fairmont 112
Longview, TX 75604
(214) 758-1905

Republic of Texas Jim Beam Bottle and Specialty Club
616 Donley Drive
Euless, TX 76039

San Antonio Antique Bottle Club
c/o 3801 Broadway
Witte Museum Auditorium
San Antonio, TX 78209

UTAH

Utah Antique Bottle and Relic Club
517 South Hayes
Midvale, UT 84047
(801) 561-0438

Utah Antique Bottle Club
P.O. Box 15
Ogden, UT 84402

VIRGINIA

Apple Valley Bottle Collectors Club
P.O. Box 2201
Winchester, VA 22601

Bottle Club of the Virginia Peninsula
P.O. Box 5456
Newport News, VA 23605

Buffalo Beam Bottle Club
P.O. Box 434
Buffalo Junction, VA 24529
(804) 374-2041

Chesapeake Bay Beam Bottle and Specialty Club
515 Briar Hill Road
Norfolk, VA 23502
(804) 461-3763

Country Cousins Beam Bottle and Specialty Club
Route 2, Box 18C
Dinwiddie, VA 23841
(804) 469-7414

Dixie Beam Bottle Club
Route 4, Box 94-4
Glen Allen, VA 23060

Hampton Roads Area Bottle Collector's Association
4848 Virginia Beach Boulevard
Virginia Beach, VA 23462

Historical Bottle Diggers of Virginia
145 3rd Street
Broadway, VA 22815
(703) 896-7200

Merrimac Beam Bottle and Specialty Club
433 Tory Road
Virginia Beach, VA 23462
(804) 497-0969

Metropolitan Antique Bottle Club
109 Howard Street
Dumfries, VA 22026
(804) 221-8055

National Privy Diggers Association
614 Park Drive
Mechanicsville, VA 23111
(804) 746-9854

*Old Dominion Beam Bottle and
Specialty Club*
624 Brandy Creek Drive
Mechanicsville, VA 23111
(804) 746-7144

Potomac Bottle Collectors
8411 Porter Lane
Alexandria, VA 22308
(703) 360-8181

Richmond Area Bottle Club Association
524 Bayliss Drive
Richmond, VA 23235
(804) 320-5160

*Shenandoah Valley Beam Bottle and
Specialty Club*
11 Bradford Drive
Front Royal, VA 22630
(703) 743-6316

*Tidewater Beam Bottle and
Specialty Club*
P.O. Box 14012
Norfolk, VA 23518

Ye Old Bottle Club
General Delivery
Clarksville, VA 23927

WASHINGTON

Antique Bottle and Glass Collectors
P.O. Box 163
Snohomish, WA 98290

*Apple Capital Beam Bottle and
Specialty Club*
300 Rock Island Road
East Wenatchee, WA 98801
(509) 884-6895

*Blue Mountain Jim Beam Bottle and
Specialty Club*
P.O. Box 147
Russet Road
Walla Walla, WA 99362
(509) 525-1208

Capitol Collectors and Bottle Club
P.O. Box 202
Olympia, WA 98507

Cascade Treasure Club
254 Northeast 45th
Seattle, WA 98105

Chinook Ezra Brooks Bottle Club
233 Kelso Drive
Kelso, WA 98626

*Evergreen State Beam Bottle and
Specialty Club*
P.O. Box 99244
Seattle, WA 98199

*Inland Empire Bottle and
Collectors Club*
7703 East Trent Avenue
Spokane, WA 99206

Klickital Bottle Club Association
Goldendale, WA 98620

Mount Rainer Ezra Brooks Bottle Club
P.O. Box 1201
Lynwood, WA 98178

*Northwest Jim Beam Bottle Collectors
Association*
P.O. Box 7401
Spokane, WA 99207

Northwest Treasure Hunter's Club
East 107 Astor Drive
Spokane, WA 99208

Pacific Northwest Avon Bottle Club
25425 68th South
Kent, WA 98031

Seattle Jim Beam Bottle Collectors Club
8015 15th Avenue, Northwest
Seattle, WA 98107

Skagit Bottle and Glass Collectors
1314 Virginia
Mount Vernon, WA 98273

South Whedley Bottle Club
c/o Juanita Clyde
Langley, WA 98260

*Washington Bottle Collectors
Association*
P.O. Box 80045
Seattle, WA 98108

WEST VIRGINIA

Blennerhassett Jim Beam Club
Route 1
26 Poplar Street
Davisville, WV 26142
(304) 428-3184

*Wild Wonderful West Virginia
Jim Beam Bottle and Specialty Club*
3922 Hanlin Way
Weirton, WV 26062
(304) 748-2675

WISCONSIN

Badger Bottle Diggers
1420 McKinley Road
Eau Claire, WI 54701

Badger Jim Beam Club of Madison
P.O. Box 5612
Madison, WI 53705

Belle City Jim Beam Bottle Club
8008 104th Avenue
Kenosha, WI 53140
(414) 694-3341

*Bucken Beamers Bottle Club of
Milwaukee, WI*
North 95th Street, West
16548 Richmond Drive
Menomonee Falls, WI 53051
(414) 251-1772

Cameron Bottle Diggers
P.O. Box 276
314 South 1st Street
Cameron, WI 54822

Central Wisconsin Bottle Collectors
1608 Main Street
Stevens Point, WI 54481

*Heart of the North Beam Bottle and
Bottle Club*
1323 Eagle Street
Rhinelander, WI 54501
(715) 362-6045

Hooten Beamers
2511 Needles Lane
Wisconsin Rapids, WI 54494
(715) 423-7116

Indianhead Jim Beam Club
5112 Berry Street
Route 7
Menomonee, WI 54751
(715) 235-5627

Lumberjack Beamers
414 North 5th Avenue
Wausau, WI 54401
(715) 842-3793

Milwaukee Antique Bottle Club
North 88th Street West
15211 Cleveland Avenue
Menomonee Falls, WI 53051

Milwaukee Antique Bottle Club, Inc.
2343 Met-To-Wee Lane
Wauwatosa, WI 53226
(414) 257-0158

*Milwaukee Jim Beam Bottle and
Specialty Club, Ltd.*
North 95th Street West
16548 Richmond Drive
Menomonee Falls, WI 53051

Packerland Beam Bottle and
Specialty Club
1366 Avondale Drive
Green Bay, WI 54303
(414) 494-4631

Shot Tower Jim Beam Club
818 Pleasant Street
Mineral Point, WI 53565

South Central Wisconsin Bottle Club
c/o Dr. T. M. Schwartz
Route 1
Arlington, WI 53911

Sportsman's Jim Beam Bottle Club
6821 Sunset Strip
Wisconsin Rapids, WI 54494
(715) 325-5285

Sugar River Beamers
Route 1, Box 424
Brodhead, WI 53520
(608) 897-2681

WYOMING

Cheyenne Antique Bottle Club
4417 East 8th Street
Cheyenne, WY 82001

Insubott Bottle Club
P.O. Box 34
Lander, WY 82520

Bottle Dealers

Domestic

ARKANSAS

Ashdown
Buddy's Bottles
610 Park Avenue, 71822
(501) 898-5877
Hutchinson Sodas and Medicines

Jacksonville
Charles and Mary Garner
620 Carpenter Drive, 72076
(501) 982-8381

Rison
Rufus Buie
P.O. Box 226, 71665
(501) 325-6816

CALIFORNIA

Aromas
Bobbie's Country Store
1000 El Camino Real Highway 101
P.O. Box 1761
Carmel, CA 93921
(408) 394-3257

Beverly Hills
Alex Kerr
9584 Wilshire Boulevard, 90212
(213) 762-6320

Buena Park
Walter Yeargain
6222 San Lorenzo Drive, 90620
(714) 826-5264

Butler
Wayne Hortman
P.O. Box 183, 31006
(912) 862-3699

Chico
Randy Taylor
566 East 12th Street, 31006
(916) 342-4928

Citrus Heights
Duke Jones
P.O. Box 642, 95610
(916) 725-1989
California Embossed Beers

Concord
Stoney and Myrt Stone
1925 Natoma Drive, 94519
(415) 685-6326

Corona
Russell Brown
P.O. Box 441, 91720
(714) 737-7164

Cypress
Gary and Harriet Miller
5034 Oxford Drive, 90630
(714) 828-4778

Fillmore
Mike and Joyce Amey
625 Clay Street, 93015
(805) 524-3364

Gilroy
Vincent Madruga
P.O. Box 1261, 95021
(408) 847-0639
Bitters, Whiskeys, Historicals

Grand Terrace
Gary and Sheran Johnston
22853 De Berry, 92324
(714) 783-4101
Fruit Jars

Hesperia
Gene and Phyllis Kemble
14733 Poplar Street, 92345
(714) 244-5863

Huntington Beach
Larry Caddell
15881 Malm Circle, 92647
(714) 897-8133

Kingsburg
Jim Lindholm
2001 Sierra, 93631
(209) 897-1582

Los Altos
Louis and Cindy Pellegrini
1231 Thurston, 94022
(415) 965-9060

Marietta
John and Estelle Hewitt
366 Church Street, 30060
(404) 422-5525

Nevada City
John I. Hiscox
10457 Newton Road, P.O. Box 704,
95959
(916) 265-0386

Pasadena
Tony Gray
P.O. Box 467, 91102
(213) 564-3115
Unusual Colors, Pontiled Sodas,
American Codd Bottles

Gary Frederick
1030 Mission Street, 91030
(818) 799-1917
Soda Pop Bottles, Owls, Medicines

Penryn
Pat and Shirley Patocka
P.O. Box 326, 95663
(916) 663-3681
Insulators

Pollock Pines
Mel and Barbara De Mello
P.O. Box 186, 95726
(916) 644-6133

Redding
Byrl and Grace Rittenhouse
3055 Birch Way, 96002
(916) 243-0320

Ralph Hollibaugh
2087 Gelnyose Drive, 96001
(916) 243-4672

Doug Hansen
865 Commerce, 96002
(916) 547-3152

Tom Aldama
15245 Fawndale Road #2, 96003
(916) 275-1048
Painted Label Sodas

Redondo Beach
Shawn McAlister
333 Calle Miramar #C, 90277
(310) 791-0440
Whiskeys, Bitters, Colored Sodas

Sacramento
George and Rose Reidenbach
2816 "P" Street, 95816
(916) 451-0063

Sacto
Peck and Audie Markota
4627 Oakhallow Drive, 95842
(916) 334-3260

San Bernardino
Dwayne and Ofelia Anthony
1066 Scenic Drive, 92408
(714) 888-6417
Insulators, Fruit Jars, Poison Bottles

San Francisco
Bill Groves
2620 Sutter Street, 94115
(415) 922-6248

Randolph M. Haumann
415 Amherst Street, 94134
(415) 239-5807
Colored Figural Bitters

San Jose
Terry and Peggy Wright
6249 Lean Avenue, 95123
(408) 578-5580

Santa Maria
Valvern and Mary Kille McLuff
214 South Ranch Road, 93454
(805) 925-7014

Derek Abrams
129 East El Camino, 93454
(805) 922-4208
Whiskeys

Santa Rosa
Lewis Lambert
(707) 527-5724

Solana Beach
T. R. Schweighart
1123 Santa Luisa Drive, 92075

Stockton
Frank and Judy Brockman
104 West Park, 95202
(209) 948-0746

Sutter Creek
The Glass Bottle
22 Main Street, Sutter Creek,
Highway 49
(209) 267-0122
Figurals, Perfumes, Whiskeys, Milks

Westwood
Whitman's Bookeeping Service
219 Fir Street
P.O. Drawer KK, 96147
(916) 256-3437
Sodas

Windsor
Betty and Ernest Zumwalt
5519 Kay Drive, 95492
(707) 545-8670

Yreka
Sleep's Siskiyou Specialties
217 West Miner, P.O. Box 689,
96097

COLORADO

Aurora
Dan Anderson
(303) 690-9117

Snowmass Village
Jim Bishop
Box 5554, 81615
(303) 923-2348
Miniature Liquors

CONNECTICUT

Ashford
Woodland Antiques
P.O. Box 277, Mansfield Center,
06250
(203) 429-2983
Flasks, Bitters, Inks

Fairfield
Stephen Link
953 Post Road, 06430

Hartford
B'Thea's Cellar
31 Kensington Street, 06112
(203) 249-4686

Lime Rock
Mary's Old Bottles
White Hollow Road
Lakeville, CT 06039
(203) 435-2961

Mystic
Bob's Old Bottles
656 Noank Road, Route 215, 06355
(203) 536-8542

New Haven
Gerald "J" Jaffee and Lori Waldeck
P.O. Box 1741, 06507
(203) 787-4232
Poisons and Insulators

Newtown
Time In A Bottle
Gail Quick
Route 25, Hawleyville, CT 06440
(203) 426-0031

Niantic
Albert Corey
153 West Main Street, 06357
(203) 739-7493

Saybrook
Bill Stankard
61 Old Post Road, 06475
(203) 388-2435

Watertown
George E. Johnson
2339 Litchfield Road, 06795
(203) 274-1785

Woodstock
Norman and Elizabeth Heckler
06282
(203) 974-1634

FLORIDA

Brooksville
E. S. and Romie Mackenzie
Box 57, 33512
(904) 796-3400

Fort Meade
M and S Bottles and Antiques
421 Wilson Street
Mailing address: Route 2,
Box 84B3, 33841
(904) 285-9421

Fort Pierce
Gore's Shoe Repair
410 Orange Avenue, 33450
Florida Bottles and Black Glass

Hollister
This-N-That Shop
Albert B. Coleman
P.O. Box 185, 32047
(904) 328-3658

Hollywood
Hickory Stick Antiques
400 South 57-Terrace, 33023
(904) 962-3434
Canning Jars, Black Glass,
Household Bottles

Jacksonville
The Browns
6512 Mitford Road, 32210
(904) 771-2091
Sodas, Mineral Waters, Milks, Black
Glass

Key Largo
Dwight Pettit
33 Sea Side Drive, 33037
(305) 852-8338

New Port Richey
Garae and Lynn McLarty
6705 Dogwood Court, 33552
(813) 849-7166

Ormond
Mike Kollar
50 Sylvania Place, 32074

Palmetto
Jon Vander Schouw
P.O. Box 1151, 33561
(813) 722-1375

Sanford
Hidden Bottle Shop
2656 Grandview, 32771
(813) 322-7181

Tallahassee
Harry O. Thomas
2721 Parson's Rest, 32308
(904) 893-3834

Titusville
L. L. Linscott
3557 Nicklaus Drive, 32780
(305) 267-9170
Fruit Jars and Porcelain Insulators

GEORGIA

Butler
Wayne's Bottles
Box 183, 31006
(912) 862-3699
Odd Colors and Shapes

Dunwoody
Carlo and Dot Sellari
Box 888553, 30338
(404) 451-2483

Eatonton
James T. Hicks
Route 4, Box 265, 31024
(404) 485-9280

Laurenceville
Dave and Tia Janousek
2293 Mulligan Circle, 30245

Macon
Schmitt House Bottle Diggers
5532 Jane Rue Circle, 31206
(912) 781-6130

Newnan
Bob and Barbara Simmons
152 Greenville Street, 30263
(404) 251-2471

HAWAII

Honolulu
The Hawaiian Antique Bottle Shop
Kahuku Sugar Mill, P.O. Box 495,
96731
(808) 293-5581
Hawaiian Sodas, Whiskeys,
Medicines, and Milks

The Hawaii Bottle Museum
1044 Kalapaki Street
P.O. Box 25153, 96825
(808) 395-4671
Hawaiian Bottles, Oriental Bottles
and Pottery

IDAHO

Buhl
John Cothern
Route 1, 83316
(208) 543-6713

Silver City
Idaho Hotel
Jordan Street, Box 75, Murphy, ID
86350
(208) 495-2520

ILLINOIS

Addison
Ronald Selcke
4N236 8th Avenue, 60101
(312) 543-4848

Alton
Sean Mullikin
5014 Alicia Drive, 62002
(312) 466-7506

Mike Spiiroff
1229 Alton Street, 62002
(618) 462-2283

Belleville
Wayne and Jacqueline Brammer
309 Bellevue Drive, 62223
(618) 213-8841

Cerro Gordo
Marvin and Carol Ridgeway
450 West Cart, 61818
(217) 763-3271

Champaign
Casad's Antiques
610 South State Street, 61820
(217) 356-8455
Milk Bottles

Chicago
Tom and Gladys Bartels
5315 West Warwick, 60641
(312) 725-2433

Ernest Brooks
9023 South East End, 60617
(312) 375-9233

1st Chicago Bottle Club
P.O. Box A3382, 60690

Jerry McCann
5003 West Berwyn, 60630
(312) 777-0443
Fruit Jars

Joe Healy
3421 West 76th Street, 60652

William Kiggans
7747 South Kedzle, 60652
(312) 925-6148

Carl Malik
8655 South Keeler, 60652
(312) 767-8568

Jerry and Aryliss McCann
5003 West Berwyn, 60630
(312) 777-0443

Louis Metzinger
4140 North Mozart, 60618
(312) 478-9043

L. D. and Barbara Robinson
1933 South Homan, 60623
(312) 762-6096

Paul R. Welko
5727 South Natoma Avenue, 60638
(312) 582-3564
Blob Tops and Hutchinson Sodas

Al and Sue Verley
486 Longwood Court, 60411
(312) 754-4132

Deerfield
Jim Hall, 445 Patridge Lane, 60014
(312) 541-5788

John and Claudia Panek
816 Holmes, 60015
(312) 945-5493

Dieterich
Ray's and Betty Antiques
62424
(217) 925-5449
Bitters

Elmwood Park
Keith and Ellen Leeders
1728 North 76th Avenue, 60635
(312) 453-2085

Godfrey
Jeff Cress
3403 Morkel Drive, 62035
(618) 466-3513

Hickory Hills
Doug and Eileen Wagner
9225 South 88th Avenue, 60457
(312) 598-4570

Hillsboro
Jim and Perry Lang
628 Mechanic, 62049
(217) 532-2915

Ingelside
Art and Pat Besinger
611 Oakwood, 60041
(312) 546-2367

La Grange
John Murray
301 Hillgrove, 60525
(312) 352-2199

Lake Villa
Lloyd Bindscheattle
P.O. Box 11, 60046

Lemont
Russ and Lynn Sineni
1372 Hillcrest Road, 60439
(312) 257-2648

Mokena
Neal and Marianne Vander Zande
18830 Sara Road, 60448
(312) 479-5566

Morrison
Emma's Bottle Shop
Emma Rosenow
Route 3, 61270
(815) 778-4596
Beers, Inks, Bitters, Sodas

O'Fallon
Tom and Ann Feltman
425 North Oak Street, 62269
(618) 632-3327

Park Forest
Vern and Gloria Nitchie
300 Indiana Street, 60466
(312) 748-7198

Park Ridge
Ken's Old Bottles
119 East Lahon, 60068
(312) 823-1267
Milks, Inks, Sodas, Whiskeys

Pekin
Harry's Bottle Shop
612 Hillyer Street, 61555
(309) 346-3476
Pottery, Beers, Sodas, Medicines

Oertel's Bottle House
Box 682, 61555
(309) 347-4441
Peoria Pottery, Embossed Picnic
Beer Bottles, Fruit Jars

Quincy
Bob Rhinberger
Route 7, 62301
(217) 223-0191

Riverdale
Bob and Barbara Harms
14521 Atlantic, 60627
(312) 841-4068

Sauk Village
Ed McDonald
3002 23rd, 60511
(312) 758-0373

Trenton
Jon and Char Granada
631 South Main, 62293
(618) 224-7308

Wheaton
Ben Crane
1700 Thompson Drive, 60187
(312) 665-5662

Scott Garrow
2 South 338 Orchard Road, 60187

Wheeling
Hall
940 East Old Willow Road, 60090
(312) 541-5788

Steve Miller
623 Ivy Court, 60090
(312) 398-1445

Woodstock
Michael Davis
1652 Tappan, 66098
(815) 338-5147

Mike Henrich
402 McHenry Avenue, 66098
(815) 338-5008

INDIANA

Boggstown
Ed and Margaret Shaw
Route 1, Box 23, 46110
(317) 835-7121

Clinton
Tony and Dick Stringfellow
714 Vine, 47842
(317) 832-2355

Flora
Bob and Morris Wise
409 East Main, 46929
(219) 967-3713

Fort Wayne
Annett's Antiques
6910 Lincoln Highway East, 46803
(219) 749-2745

Goshen
Gene Rice
61935 CR37, Route 1, 46526

Wayne Wagner
23558 Creek Park Drive, 46526

Greenfield
George and Nancy Reilly
Route 10, Box 67, 46140
(317) 462-2441

Indianapolis
John and Dianna Atkins
3168 Beeler Avenue, 46224
(317) 299-2720

Nobelsville
Ricky and Becky Norton
Route G, Box 166, 46060
(317) 844-1772

Peru
Herrell's Collectibles
265 East Canal Street, 46970
(317) 473-7770

Scottsburg
Fort Harrod Glass Works
160 North Gardner Road, 47170
(812) 752-5170

Terre Haute
Harry and Dorothy Frey
5210 Clinton Road, 47805
(812) 466-4642

Westfield
Doug Moore
9 Northbrook Circle, 46074
(317) 896-3015

IOWA

Elkader
The Bottle Shop
206 Chestnut, 52043
(319) 245-2359
Sarsaparillas and Bitters

Storm Lake
Ralph and Helen Welch
804 Colonial Circle, 50588
(712) 732-4124

KANSAS

Halstead
Donald Haury
Route 2, 67056
(316) 283-5876

Lawrence
Mike Elwell
Route 2, Box 30, 66044
(913) 842-2102

Merriam
Dale Young
9909 West 55th Street, 66203
(913) 677-0175

Paola
Stewart and Sons Old Bottle Shop
610 East Kaskaskia, 66071
(913) 294-3434
Drugstore Bottles, Blob-Top Beers

Topeka
Joe and Alyce Smith
4706 West Hills Drive, 66606
(913) 272-1892

KENTUCKY

Alexandria
Michael and Kathy Kolb
6 South Jefferson, 41001
(606) 635-7121

Jeffersontown
Paul Van Vactor
100004 Cardigan Drive, 40299

Louisville
Gene Blasi
5801 River Knolls Drive, 40222
(502) 425-6995

Jerry and Joyce Phelps
6013 Innes Trace Road, 40222

Paul and Paulette Van Vactor
300 Stilz Avenue, 40299
(502) 895-3655

Paducah
Earl and Ruth Cron
808 North 25th Street, 42001
(502) 443-5005

LOUISIANA

Baton Rouge
Sidney and Eulalle Genius
1843 Tudor Drive, 70815
(504) 925-5774

Bobby and Ellen Kirkpatrick
7313 Meadowbrook Avenue, 70808

Sheldon L. Ray, Jr.
P.O. Box 17238, LSU, 70893
(504) 388-3814

Jennings
Cajun Pop Factory
P.O. Box 1113, 70546
(318) 824-7078
Hutchinsons, Blob Tops, Pontil
Sodas

Monroe
Everett L. Smith
100 Everett Drive, 71202
(318) 325-3534
Embossed Whiskeys

Natchitoches
Ralph and Cheryl Green
515 Elizabeth Street, 71457

New Orleans
Bep's Antiques
3923 Magazine Street, 70115
(504) 891-3468
Import Bottles

Dr. Charles and Jane Aprill
484 Chestnut, 70118
(504) 899-7441

Ruston
The Dirty Digger
1804 Church Street, 71270
(318) 255-6112

Bob and Vernell Willett
1804 Church Street, 71270
(318) 255-6112

MAINE

Bethel
F. Barrie Freeman, Antiques
Paradise Hill Road, 04217
(207) 824-3300

Bryant Pond
John and Althea Hathaway
04219

East Wilton
Don McKeen Bottles
McKeen Way, P.O. Box 5A, 04234

Milford
Spruce's Antiques
Main Street, P.O. Box 295, 04461
(207) 827-4756

Searsport
Morse and Applebee Antiques
U.S. Route 1, Box 164, 04974
(207) 548-6314
Early American Glass

Waldoboro
Wink's Bottle Shop
Route 235, 04572
(207) 832-4603

Daniel R. Winchenbaugh
R.F.D. 4, Box 21, 04572
(207) 832-7702

MARYLAND

North East
Pete's Diggins
Route 40 West, R.R. 3, Box 301, 21901
(410) 287-9245

Sudlersville
Fran and Bill Lafferty
Box 142, 21668

MASSACHUSETTS

Duxbury
Joe and Kathy Wood
49 Surplus Street, 02332
(617) 934-2221

Leverett
Metamorphosis
46 Teewaddle, R.F.D. 3, 01002
Hair Tonics and Medicines

Littleton
The Thrift and Gift Shop
Littleton Common, Box 21
(617) 486-4464

Mansfield
Shop In My Home
211 East Street, 02048
(617) 339-6086
Historic Flasks

North Easton
The Applied Lip Place
26 Linden Street, 02356
(617) 238-1432
Medicines, Whiskeys

Wellesley
Carlyn Ring
59 Livermore Road, 02181
(617) 235-5675

West Springfield
Leo A. Bedard
62 Craig Drive, Apartment 7A,
01089
Bitters, Whiskeys, Medicines

Yarmouth
Gloria Swanson Antiques
262 Setucket Road, 02675
(617) 398-8848
Inks

MICHIGAN

Ann Arbor
John Wolfe
1622 East Stadium Boulevard,
48104
(313) 665-6106

Bloomfield Hills
Jim and Robin Meehan
25 Valley Way, 48013
(313) 642-0176

Buchanan
Old Chicago
316 Ross Drive, 49107
(616) 695-5896
Hutchinson Sodas, Blob-Top Beers

Clarklake
Fred and Shirley Weck
8274 South Jackson, 49234
(517) 529-9631

Davisburg
Chief Pontiac Antique Bottle Shop
13880 Neal Road, 48019
(313) 634-8469

Detroit
Michael and Christina Garrett
19400 Stout, 48219
(313) 534-6067

Dundee
Ray and Hillaine Hoste
366 Main Street, 48131
(313) 529-2193

Gaines
E and E Antiques
9441 Grand Blanc Road, 48436
(517) 271-9063
Fruit Jars, Beer Bottles, Milks

Grand Rapids
Dewey and Marilyn Heetderks
21 Michigan Northeast, 49503
(616) 774-9333

Iron River
Sarge's
111 East Hemlock, 49935
(906) 265-4223
Old Mining Town Bottles,
Hutchinsons

Kalamazoo
Mark and Marty McNee
1009 Vassar Drive, 49001
(616) 343-9393

Lew and Leon Wisser
2837 Parchmount, 49004
(616) 343-7479

Lathrup
The Jar Emporium
Ralph Finch
19420 Saratoga, 48076
(313) 569-6749
Fruit Jars

Manistee
Chris and Becky Batdorff
516 Maple Street, 49660
(616) 723-7917

Monroe
Don and Glennie Burkett
3942 West Dunbar Road, 48161
(313) 241-6740

Stambaugh
Cooper Corner Rock and Bottle Shop
4th and Lincoln, 49964
(906) 265-3510
Beers, Hutchinsons, Medicines

Saint Joseph
Anvil Antiques
3439 Hollywood Road, 49085
(616) 429-5132
Insulators

Stugis
John and Kay Petruska
21960 Marathon Road, 49091
(616) 651-6400

Wuchanan
James Clengenpeel
316 Ross Drive, 49107
(616) 695-5896

MINNESOTA

Excelsior
Jim Conley
P.O. Box 351, 55331
(612) 935-0964

Minneapolis
Steve Ketcham
P.O. Box 24114, 55424
(612) 920-4205

Neal and Pat Sorensen
132 Peninsula Road, 55441
(612) 545-2698

Richfield
Ron and Vernie Feldhaus
6904 Upton Avenue, 55423
(612) 866-6013

Saint Paul
J and E
1000 Arcade Street, 55106
(612) 771-9654

MISSISSIPPI

Biloxi
Vieux Beloxie Pottery Factory
Restaurant
U.S. 90 East, 39530
(601) 374-0688
Mississippi Bottles

Columbia
Robert A. Knight
516 Dale Street, 39429
(601) 736-4249
Mississippi Bottles and Jugs

McComb
Robert Smith
623 Pearl River Avenue, 39648
(601) 684-1843

Starkville
Jerry Drott
710 Persimmon Drive,
P.O. Box 714, 39759
(601) 323-8796
Liniments, Drugstore Bottles

Vicksburg
Ted and Linda Kost
107 Columbia, 39180
(601) 638-8780

MISSOURI

Elsberry
Dave Hausgen
Route 1, 63343
(314) 898-2500

Glencoe
Sam and Eloise Taylor
3002 Woodlands Terrace, 63038
(314) 273-6244

Hannibal
Bob and Debbi Overfield
2318 Chestnut Street, 63401
(314) 248-9521

Independence
Mike and Carol Robinson
1405 North River, 64050
(816) 836-2337

Kansas City
Donald Kimrey
1023 West 17th Street, 64108
(816) 741-2745

Robert Stevens
1131 East 77th, 64131
(816) 333-1398

Linn Creek
The Bottle House
Route 1, Box 111, 65052
(314) 346-5890

Saint Louis
Gene and Alberta Kelley
1960 Cherokee, 63126
(314) 664-7203

Jerry Mueller
4520 Langtree, 63128
(314) 843-8357

Terry and Luann Phillips
1014 Camelot Gardens, 63125
(314) 892-6864

Hal and Vern Wagner
10118 Schuessler, 63128
(314) 843-7573
Historical Flasks, Colognes, Early
Glass

Taylor
Barkely Museum
U.S. 61
(314) 393-2408

Tipton
Joseph and Jean Reed
237 East Morgan, 65081
(816) 433-5937

Westphalia
Randy and Jan Haviland
American Systems Antiques, 65085
(314) 455-2525

NEBRASKA

Omaha
Born Again Antiques
1402 Williams Street, 68108
(402) 341-5177

Karl Person
10210 "W" Street, 68127
(402) 331-2666

Fred Williams
5712 North 33rd Street, 68111
(402) 453-4317

NEVADA

Carson City
Doug Southerland
Box 1345, 89702

Fallon
Don and Opal Wellman
P.O. Box 521, 89406
(702) 423-3490

Las Vegas
William V. Wright
220 South Bruce Street, 89101

Montello
Allen Wilson
P.O. Box 29, 89830
(702) 776-2511

Reno
Larry and Jann Shoemaker
P.O. Box 50546, 89513
(702) 747-6095

Sparks
Don and Bonnie McLane
1846 F Street, 89431
(702) 359-2171

NEW HAMPSHIRE

Amherst
Dave and Carol Waris
Boston Post Road, 03031
(603) 882-4409

Dover
Bob and Betty Morin
R.D. 3, Box 280, 03820

Exeter
Lucille Stanley
9 Oak Street, 03833
(603) 772-2296

Hampstead
Murray's Lakeside Bottle Shop
Benson Shores, P.O. Box 57, 03841
(603) 329-6969

Manchester
Jim and Joyce Rogers
Harvey Road, Route 10, 03103
(603) 623-4101

Troy
House of Glass
25 High Street, 03465
(603) 242-7947

NEW JERSEY

Branchville
Richard and Lesley Harris
Box 400, 07826
(201) 948-3935

Califon
Phil and Flo Alvarez
P.O. Box 107, 07830
(201) 832-7438

Englewood
Ed and Carole Clemens
81 Chester Place, Apartment D-2,
07631
(201) 569-4429

Flemington
John Orashen
R.D. 6, Box 345-A, 08822
(201) 782-3391

Hopewell
Tom and Marion McCandless
62 Lafayette Street, 08525
(609) 466-0619

Howell
Howell Township
Bruce and Pat Egeland
3 Rustic Drive, 07731
(201) 363-0556

Mickleton
Sam Fuss, Harmony Road, 08056
(609) 423-5038

Salem
Old Bottle Museum
4 Friendship Drive, 08079
(609) 935-5631

NEW MEXICO

Albuquerque
Irv and Ruth Swalwell
8826 Fairbanks, 87112
(505) 299-2977

Deming
Krol's Rock City and Mobile Park
Star Route 2, Box 15A, 88030
Hutchinson Sodas, Inks, Avons

NEW YORK

Auburn
Brewster Bottle Shop
297 South Street, 13021
(315) 252-3246
Milk Bottles

Ballston Lake
Tom and Alice Moulton
88 Blue Spruce Lane, R.D. 5, 12019

Binghamton
Jim Chamberlain
R.D. 8, 607 Nowland Road, 13904
(607) 772-1135

Jo Ann's Old Bottles
R.D. 2, Box 638
Port Crane, NY 13833
(607) 648-4605

Blodgett Mills
Edward Petter
P.O. Box 1, 13738
(607) 756-7891
Inks

Blooming Grove
Old Bottle Shop
Horton Road, P.O. Box 105, 10914
(914) 496-6841

Central Valley
J.J.'s Pontil Place
1001 Dunderberg Road
(914) 928-9144

Clifton Park
John Kovacik
11 Juniper Drive, 12065
(518) 371-4118

Richard Strunk
R.D. 4, Grooms Road, 12065
Flasks, Bitters, Saratogas

Cranberry Lake
The Bottle Shop Antiques
P.O. Box 503
(315) 848-2648

Elmira
Leonard and Joyce Blake
1220 Stolle Road, 14059
(716) 652-7752

Leroy
Kenneth Cornell
78 Main, 14482
(716) 768-8919

Lock Sheldrake
The Bottle Shop
P.O. Box 24, 12759
(914) 434-4757

Monticello
Manor House Collectibles
Route 42, South Forestburg
R.D. 1, Box 67, 12701
(914) 794-3967
Whiskeys, Beers, Sodas

Newark
Chris Davis
522 Woodhill, 14513
(315) 331-4078

New Windsor
David Byrd
43 East Kenwood Drive, 12550
(914) 561-7257

New York City
Chuck Moore
3 East 57th Street 10022

Bottles Unlimited
245 East 78th Street, 10021
(212) 628-8769
Eighteenth- and Nineteenth-
Century Bottles

Rochester
Burton Spiller
169 Greystone Lane, Apartment 13,
14618
(716) 244-2229

Robert Zorn
23 Knickerbocker Avenue, 14615
(716) 254-7470

Webster
Dick and Evelyn Bowman
1253 LaBaron Circle, 14580
(716) 872-4015

NORTH CAROLINA

Blowing Rock
Vieve and Luke Yarbrough
P.O. Box 1023, 28605
(704) 963-4961

Charlotte
Bob Morgan
P.O. Box 3163, 28203
(704) 527-4841

Durham
Clement's Bottles
5234 Willowhaven Drive, 27712
(919) 383-2493
Commemorative Soft Drink Bottles

Gold Hill
Howard Crowe
P.O. Box 133, 28071
(704) 279-3736

Goldsboro
Vernon Capps
Route 5, Box 529, 27530
(919) 734-8964

Raleigh
Rex D. McMillan
4101 Glen Laurel Drive, 27612
(919) 787-0007
North Carolina Blobs, Saloon
Bottles, Colored Drugstore Bottles

NORTH DAKOTA

Mandan
Robert Barr
102 North 9th Avenue, 58554

OHIO

Akron
Don and Barb Dzuro
5113 West Bath Road, 44313
(216) 666-8170

Jim Salzwimmer
3391 Tisen Road, 44312
(216) 699-3990

Beachwood
Allan Hodges
25125 Shaker Boulevard, 44122
(216) 464-8381

Bluffton
Schroll's Country Shop
3 Miles East of County Line on
County Road 33
(419) 358-6121

Byesville
Albert and Sylvia Campbell
R.D. 1, Box 194, 43723
(614) 439-1105

Cincinnati
Kenneth and Dudie Roat
7775 Kennedy Lane, 45242
(513) 791-1168

Cleveland
Joe and Mary Miller
2590 North Moreland Boulevard,
44120
(216) 721-9919

Dayton
Don and Paula Spangler
2554 Loris Drive, 45449
(513) 435-7155

Dublin
Roy and Barbara Brown
8649 Dunsinane Drive, 43017
(614) 889-0818

Frankfort
Roger Durflinger
P.O. Box 2006, 45628
(614) 998-4849

Hannibal
Gilbert Nething
P.O. Box 96, 43931
Hutchinson Sodas

Lancaster
R. J. and Freda Brown
125 South High Street, 43130
(614) 687-2899

Lewistown
Sonny Mallory
P.O. Box 134, 43333
(513) 686-2185

North Hampton
John and Margie Bartley
160 South Main, 45319
(513) 964-1080

Powhatan Point
Bob and Dawn Jackson
107 Pine Street, 43942
(614) 795-5565

Reynoldsburg
Bob and Phyllis Christ
1218 Creekside Place, 43068
(614) 866-2156

Springfield
Ballentine's Bottles
710 West First Street, 45504
(513) 399-8359

Larry R. Henschen
3222 Delrey Road, 45504
(513) 399-1891

Steubenville
Tom and Deena Caniff
1223 Oak Grove Avenue, 43952
(614) 282-8918

Bob and Mary Ann Willamagna
711 Kendall Avenue, 43952
(614) 282-9029

Stow
Doug and Joann Bedore
1483 Ritchie Road, 44224
(216) 688-4934

Toronto
Bob Villamagna
1518 Madison Avenue, P.O. Box 56,
43964
(614) 537-4503
Tri-State-Area Bottles, Stoneware

Warren
Michael Cetina
3272 Northwest Boulevard, 44485
(216) 898-1845

Washingtonville
Al and Beth Bignon
480 High Street, 44490
(216) 427-6848

Waynesville
The Bottleworks
70 North Main Street,
P.O. Box 446, 45068
(513) 897-3861

Wellington
Elvin and Cherie Moody
Trails End, 44090
(216) 647-4917

Xenia
Bill and Wanda Dudley
393 Franklin Avenue, 45385
(513) 372-8567

OKLAHOMA
Enid
Ronald and Carol Ashby,
831 East Pine, 73701
Rare and Scarce Fruit Jars

Oklahoma City
Joe and Hazel Nagy
3540 Northwest 23, 73107
(405) 942-0882

Sandsprings
Larry and Linda Shope
310 West 44th, 74063
(918) 363-8481

OREGON
Gladstone
Tom and Bonnie Kasner
380 East Jersey Street, 97027
(503) 655-9127
Insulators, Marbles, Bottles, Jars

Hillsboro
Robert and Marquerite Ornduff
Route 4, Box 236-A, 97123
(503) 538-2359

Lakeview
R. E. Barnett
P.O. Box 109, 97630
(503) 947-2415
Western Whiskey Bottles

Portland
Alan Amerman
2311 Southeast 147th, 97233
(503) 761-1661

The Glass House
4620 Southeast 104th, 97266
(503) 760-3346
Fruit Jars

PENNSYLVANIA

Alburtis
R. S. Riovo
686 Franklin Street, 18011
(215) 965-2706
Milk Bottles, Dairy Go-Withs

Bradford
Ernest Hurd
5 High Street, 16701
(814) 362-9915

Dick and Patti Mansour
458 Lambert Drive, 16701
(814) 368-8820

Claude and Ethel Lee
643 Bolivar Drive, 16701
(814) 362-3663
Jars

Canonsburg
John and Mary Schultz
R.D. 1, Box 118, 15317
(412) 745-6632

Coudersport
The Old Bottle Corner
508 South Main Street, 16915
(814) 274-7017
Fruit Jars, Blob Tops

East Greenville
James A. Hagenbach
102 Jefferson Street, 18041
(215) 679-5849

East Petersburg
Jere and Betty Hambleton
5940 Main Street, 17520
(717) 569-0130

Hatboro
Al and Maggie Duffield
12 Belmar Road, 19040
(215) 675-5175
Hutchinsons, Inks

Lancaster
Barry and Mary Hogan
3 Lark Lane, 17603

Levittown
Ed Lasky
43 Nightingale, 19054
(215) 945-1555

Marienville
Harold Bauer Antique Bottles
136 Cherry Street, 16239

McKees Rocks
Chuck Henigin
3024 Pitch Fork Lane, 15136
(412) 331-6159

Muncy
Harold Hill
161 East Water Street, 17756
(717) 546-3388

Pipersville
Allen Holtz
R.D. 1, 18947
(215) 847-5728

Pittsburgh
Carl and Gail Onufer
210 Newport Road, 15221
(412) 371-7725
Milk Bottles

Roulette
R. A. and Ester Heimer
P.O. Box 153, 16746
(814) 544-7713

Strongstown
Butch and Gloria Kim
R.D. 2, Box 35, 15957

RHODE ISLAND

Kenyon
Wes and Diane Seemann
Box 49, 02836
(203) 599-1626

SOUTH CAROLINA

Eashey
Bob Durham
704 West Main Street, 29640

Marion
Tony and Marie Shank
P.O. Box 778, 29571
(803) 423-5803

TENNESSEE

Knoxville
Ronnie Adams
7005 Charlotte Drive, 37914
(615) 524-8958

McMinnville
Terry Pennington
415 North Spring Street, 37110
Jack Daniels, Amber Coca-Cola

Memphis
Bluff City Bottlers
4630 Crystal Springs Drive, 38123
(901) 353-0541
Common American Bottles

Larry and Nancy McCage
3772 Hanna Drive, 38128
(901) 388-9329

Tom Phillips
2088 Fox Run Cove, 38138
(901) 754-0097

TEXAS

Amarillo
Robert Snyder
4235 West 13th, 79106

Euless
Mack and Alliene Landers
P.O. Box 5, 76039
(817) 267-2710

Houston
Bennie and Harper Leiper
2800 West Dallas, 77019
(713) 526-2101

Pasadena
Gerald Welch
4809 Gardenia Trail, 77505
(713) 487-3057

Port Isabel
Jimmy and Peggy Galloway
P.O. Drawer A, 78578
(512) 943-2437

Richardson
Chuck and Retaa Bukin
1325 Cypress Drive, 75080
(214) 235-4889

San Antonio
Sam Greer
707 Nix Professional Building, 78205
(512) 227-0253

UTAH

Salt Lake City
Dave Emett
1736 North Star Drive, 84116
(801) 596-2103
Utah Crocks and Jugs

VERMONT

Brattleboro
Kit Barry
88 High Street, 05301
(802) 254-2195

VIRGINIA

Alexandria
A. E. Steidel
6167 Cobbs Road, 22310

Arlington
Dick and Margie Stockton
2331 North Tuckahoe Street, 22205
(703) 534-5619

Chesterfield
Tom Morgan
3501 Slate Court, 23832

Fredericksburg
White's Trading Post
Boutchyards Olde Stable
Falmouth, VA 22401
(703) 371-6252
Fruit Jars

Hinton
Vic and Betty Landis
Route 1, Box 8A, 22801
(703) 867-5959

Huntly
Early American Workshop
Star Route, 22640
(703) 635-8252
Milk Bottles

Marshall
John Tutton
Route 1, Box 261, 22115
(703) 347-0148

Richmond
Lloyd and Carrie Hamish
2936 Woodworth Road, 23234
(804) 275-7106

Jim and Connie Mitchell
5106 Glen Alden Drive, 23234

WASHINGTON

Aberdeen
Kent Beach
1001 Harding Road, 98520
(206) 532-8556
All Owl Bottles/Items

Bellevue
Don and Dorothy Finch
13339 Newport Way, 98006
(206) 746-5640

Bremerton
Ron Flannery
423 Northeast Conifer Drive, 98310
(206) 692-2619

Federal Way
Pete Hendricks
3005 South 302nd Place, 98023
(206) 874-6345
Owl Bottles

Seattle
John W. Cooper
605 Northeast 170th Street, 96155
(206) 364-0858

WISCONSIN

Arlington
Mike and Carol Schwartz
Route 1, 53911
(608) 846-5229

Mequon
Jeff Burkhardt
12637 North River Forest Circle,
53092
(414) 243-5643

Bor Markiewicz
11715 West Bonniwell Road, 53092
(414) 242-3968

Oskosh
Richard Schwab
65-6 Lareen Road, 54901
(414) 235-9962

Stevens Point
Bill and Kathy Mitchell
703 Linwood Avenue, 55431
(715) 341-1471

Wautoma
George and Ruth Hansen
Route 2, Box 26, 54962
(414) 787-4893

Foreign

ENGLAND
New Milton Hants
Rob Goodacre
44 Arundel Close, BH 25 SUH
Tel: 0425 620794
Bitters, Whiskeys, Pictorial Gins

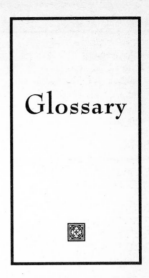

Glossary

Amethyst-colored Glass A clear glass that when exposed to the sun or bright light for a long period of time will turn various shades of purple. Only glass that contains manganese is subject to this process.

Amber-colored Glass Nickel was added in the glass production to obtain this common bottle color. It was believed that the resulting dark color would prevent the sun from damaging the contents of the bottle.

Annealing The gradual cooling of hot glass in a cooling chamber or annealing oven.

Applied Lip On bottles manufactured before 1880 the lip was applied after removal from the blowpipe. This may be only a ring of glass trailed around the bottle neck.

Automatic Bottle Machine Invented in 1903, revolutionized the bottle industry.

Aqua-colored glass The natural color of glass. The particular shade produced was dependent on the iron oxide used in the glass production. It was commonly produced until the 1930s.

Barber Bottle In the 1880s these colorful bottles decorated the shelves of barbershops and usually were filled with bay rum.

Batch A mixture of the ingredients necessary for the manufacture of glass.

Battledore A wooden paddle used by a glassblower to flatten the bottom or sides of a bottle.

Bitters An herbal, purportedly medicinal, mixture and flavoring, which contained a great quantity of alcohol, usually corn whiskey.

Black Glass This type of glass, produced between 1700 and 1875, is actually a dark olive-green color created by the carbon used in the glass production.

Blob Seal   A way of identifying an unembossed bottle. Manufacturers applied a molten coin-shaped blob of glass to the shoulder of this bottle, into which a seal with the logo, name of the distiller, date, or product name was impressed.

Blob Top   A large thick blob of glass that was placed around the lip of soda or mineral water bottles. A wire held the stopper, which was seated below the blob and anchored the wire when the stopper was closed, to prevent the carbonation from escaping.

Blown-in Mold   Process by which the gather of glass is blown into a mold to take the shape of the mold. The lips on these types of bottles were added later and the bases often have open pontil scars.

Blowpipe   A hollow iron tube wider and thicker at the gathering end than at the blowing end. Glassblowers used them to pick up the molten glass, which was then blown in a mold or free-blown outside the mold. Pipes vary from two and a half to six feet in length.

Cobalt-colored Glass   This color was used with patented medicines and poisons to distinguish them from other bottles. Excessive amounts resulted in the familiar "cobalt blue" color.

Crown Cap   A metal cap formed from a circular tin plate crimped on its edge to fit tightly over the rolled lip of a bottle. The inside of the cap was filled with a cork disk which created an airtight seal.

Cullet   Cleansed and broken glass added to the batch to bring about rapid fusion.

Date Line   The mold seam or mold line on a bottle. The length of this line provides collectors with a clue to the bottle's approximate age.

Decolorizer   A compound that is added to natural aquamarine bottle glass to render the glass clear.

Dip Mold   A one-piece mold open at the top.

Embossed Lettering   Raised print denoting the name of the product or manufacturer on the bottle.

Fire Polishing   The reheating of glass to eliminate unwanted blemishes.

Flared Lip   Bottles produced prior to 1900 have lips that have been worked out or flared out to reinforce the strength of the opening.

Flint Glass   Glass composed of a silicate of potash and lead.

Free-blown Glass   Items of this nature are produced with a blowpipe and do not utilize a mold.

Gaffer   The word for the master blower in the early glass houses.

Gather   The gob of molten glass adhering to the blowpipe in the first stage of the free-blown process.

Glory Hole   The small furnace used for the frequent reheatings necessary during the making of a bottle. The glory hole was also used in fire polishing.

Green Glass Refers to a composition of glass and not a color. The green color was caused by the iron impurities in the sand, which could not be controlled by the glassmakers.

Ground Pontil Refers to the smooth circle that remains when a rough pontil scar has been gound off.

Imperfections Include bubbles or tears of all sizes and shapes, bent shapes and necks, imperfect seams, and errors in spelling and embossing.

Improved Pontil Bottles having an improved pontil appear as reddish or blackish on the base.

Kick-up The deep indentation in the bottom of many bottles. This is formed by placing a projected piece of wood or metal in the base of the mold while the glass is still hot. Wine bottles are usually indented.

Laid-on Ring A bead of glass that has been trailed around the neck opening to reinforce the opening.

Lady's Leg Bottles that are shaped like long curving necks.

Manganese Utilized as a decolorizer between 1850 and 1910. Will also cause glass to turn purple under extreme heat.

Melting Pot This was a clay pot used to melt silicate in the glass making process.

Metal The molten glass.

Milk Glass Tin is added in glass production to obtain this colored glass, which was primarily used for cosmetic bottles.

Mold, Full-Height, Three-piece The entire bottle was formed in the mold, and two seams run the height of the bottle to the lip on both sides.

Mold, Three-piece Dip In this mold the bottom part of the bottle mold was one piece and the top, from the shoulder up, was two separate pieces. Mold seams appear circling the bottle at the shoulder and on each side of the neck.

Opalescence This is seen on the frosty bottle or variated-color bottle that has been buried in mud or silt; the minerals in these substances have interacted with the glass to create these effects.

Paste Mold These were made of two or more pieces of iron and were coated with a paste to prevent scratches on the glass. The seams were eliminated as the glass was turned in the mold.

Pontil, Puntee, or Punty Rod The iron rod attached to the base of a bottle by a gob of glass to hold the bottle during the finishing.

Pontil Marks To remove the bottle from the blowpipe, an iron rod with a small amount of molten glass was applied to the bottom of the bottle for handling while the neck and lip were finished. A sharp tap removed the bottle from the pontil, leaving a jagged glass scar.

Pressed Glass   Glass that has been pressed into a mold to take the shape of the mold or the pattern within the mold.

Pucellas   Called "the tool" by glassmakers. This tool is essential in shaping both the body and opening in blown bottles.

Pumpkinseed   A small round flat flask, often found in Western areas. Generally made of clear glass, the shape resembled the seed of the grown pumpkin. These bottles are also known as "Mickies," "Saddle Flasks," and "Two-Bit Ponies."

Round Bottom   A soda bottle made of heavy glass designed in the shape of a torpedo. This enabled the bottle to lie on its side, keeping the liquid in contact with the cork, and preventing the cork from drying and popping out of the bottle.

Sheared Lip   After the bottle was blown, a pair of scissorlike shears clipped the hot glass from the blowpipe. No top was applied and sometimes a slight flange was created.

Sick Glass   Glass bearing a superficial decay or deterioration that takes on a grayish tinge caused by erratic firing.

Slug Plate   A metal plate about two by four inches with a firm's name on it, that was inserted into a mold and customized bottles for a glasshouse's clients. By simply exchanging plates the glasshouse could use the same mold for many companies.

Snap Case   Also called a "snap tool." This tool replaced the pontil rod and enabled the worker to hold the bottle with a tool that had vertical arms curving out from a central stem. The snap case gripped the bottle and held it firmly during finishing of the neck and lip. The use of the snap case eliminated the pontil scars or marks, however, it did at times produce grip marks on the sides of the finished bottle.

Whittle Marks   Bottles formed in carved-wood molds have these distinctive marks. A similar effect was produced when forming hot glass on cold molds early in the morning. "Goose pimples" resulted on the surface of these bottles. As the day progressed and the mold warmed, later bottles were smooth.

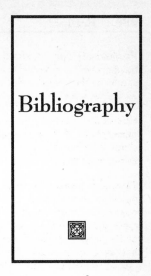

Bibliography

Books

Agee, Bill. *Collecting All Cures*. East Greenville, PA.: Antique Bottle & Glass Collector, 1973.

Barnett, R. E. *Western Whiskey Bottles*, Bend, OR.: Maverick Publishing, 1992.

Beck, Doreen. *The Book of Bottle Collecting*. Gig Harbor, WA.: Hamlin Publishing Group, Ltd., 1973.

Creswick, Alice M. *Redbook Number 6: The Collectors Guide to Old Fruit Jars*. Privately published. 0-8525 Kewowa SW. Grand Rapids, MI 49504, 1992.

DeGrafft, John. *American Sarsaparilla Bottles*. East Greenville, PA.: Antique Bottle & Glass Collector, 1980.

Diamond, Freda. *Story of Glass*. New York: Harcourt, Brace and Company, 1953.

Dumbrell, Roger. *Understanding Antique Wine Bottles*. Ithaca, N.Y.: Antique Collectors Club, 1983.

Eilelberner, George, and Agadjanian, Serge. *The Compleat American Glass Candy Containers Handbook*. Adele Bowden, 1986.

Ferraro, Pat and Ferraro, Bob. *A Bottle Collector's Book*. Sparks, NV.: Western Printing and Publishing Company, 1970.

Field, Anne E. *On the Trail of Stoddard Glass*. Dublin, NH.: William L. Bauhan, 1975.

Gardner, Paul Vickens. *Glass*. Smithsonian Illustrated Library of Antiques. N.Y.: Crown Publishers, 1979.

Holiner, Richard. *Collecting Barber Bottles*. Paducah, KY.: Collector Books, 1986.

Hudson, Paul. "Seventeenth-Century Glass Wine Bottles and Seals Excavated at Jamestown." *Journal of Glass Studies*, vol. 3, 1961.

Holabird, Fred and Haddock, Jack. *The Nevada Bottle Book*. Reno, NV.: R. F. Smith, 1981.

Hudgeons, Thomas E., III. *Official Price Guide to Bottles Old and New*. Orlando, FL.: House of Collectibles, 1983.

Hunter, Frederick William. *Stiegel Glass*. New York.: Dover Publications, 1950.

Innes, Lowell. *Pittsburgh Glass 1797–1891*. Boston, MA.: Houghton Mifflin Company, 1976.

Jackson, Barbara and Jackson, Sonny. *American Pot Lids*. East Greenville, PA.: Antique Bottle & Glass Collector, 1992.

Jarves, Deming. *Reminiscences of Glass Making*. New York: Hurd and Houghton, 1865.

Kendrick, Grace. *The Antique Bottle Collector*. Ann Arbor, MI.: Edwards Brothers Inc., 1971.

Ketchum, William C., Jr., *A Treasury of American Bottles*. Los Angeles: Rutledge Publishing, 1975.

Klesse, Brigitt and Mayr, Hans. "European Glass from 1500-1800." *The Ernesto Wolf Collection*. Germany: Kremayr and Scheriau, 1987.

Knittle, Rhea Mansfield. *Early American Glass*. Long Island, N.Y.: Garden City Publishing Company, 1948.

Kovel, Terry and Kovel, Ralph. *The Kovels' Bottle Price List*. New York: Crown Publishers, Inc., 1992.

Kovill, William E., Jr. *Ink Bottles and Ink Wells*. Taunton, MA: William L. Sullwold, 1971.

Lee, Ruth Webb. *Antique Fakes and Reproductions*. Privately published. North Borough, MA: 1971.

Maust, Don. *Bottle and Glass Handbook*. Uniontown, PA: E. G. Warman Publishing Co., 1956.

McKearin, Helen and McKearin, George S. *Two Hundred Years of American Blown Glass*, New York: Crown Publishers, 1950.

————.*American Glass*. New York: Crown Publishers, 1956.

McKearin, Helen and Wilson, Kenneth M. *American Bottles and Flasks and Their Ancestry*. New York: Crown Publishers, 1978.

Megura, Jim. *Official Price Guide Bottles*. New York: House of Collectibles, 1991.

Munsey, Cecil. *The Illustrated Guide to Collecting Bottles*. New York: Hawthorn Books, Inc., 1970.

Namiat, Robert. *Barber Bottles with Prices*. Randor, PA.: Wallace Homestead Book Company, 1977.

Nielsen, Frederick. *Great American Pontiled Medicines*. Cherry HIll, N.J.: The Cortech Corporation, 1978.

Northend, Mary Harrod. *American Glass*. New York: Tudor Publishing Company, 1940.

Ostrander, Diane. *A Guide to American Nursing Bottles*. York, PA.: ACIF Publications, 1992.

Pepper Adeline. *The Glass Gaffers of New Jersey*. New York: Charles Scribners Sons, 1971.

Ring, Carlyn. *For Bitters Only*. Concord, MA.: The Nimrod Press, Inc., 1980.

Schwartz, Marvin D. "American Glass." *Antiques*, vol. 1 (1974).

Seeliger, Michael. *H. H. Warner: His Company and His Bottles*. East Greenville, PA.: Antique Bottle & Glass Collector, 1974.

Skinner's, Inc. *Bottle Sale Catalogs*, Route 117, Bolton, MA 01740.

Sloan, Gene. *Perfume and Scent Bottle Collecting*. Randor, PA.: Wallace Homestead Book Company, 1986.

Spillman, Jane Shadel. *Glass Bottles, Lamps and Other Objects*. New York: Alfred A. Knopf, 1983.

Thompson, J. H. *Bitters Bottles*. Watkins Glen, N.Y.: Century House, 1947.

Toulouse, Julian Harrison. *Bottle Makers and Their Marks*. Camden, N.H.: Thomas Nelson Incorporated, 1971.

Tyson, Scott. *Glass Houses of the 1800s*. East Greenville, PA.: Antique Bottle & Glass Collector, 1971.

Tucker, Donald. *Collectors Guide to the Saratoga-Type Mineral Water Bottles*. East Greenville, PA.: Antique Bottle & Glass Collector, 1986.

Tutton, John. *Udderly Delightful*. Stephens City, VA: Commercial Press, Inc., 1989.

Umberger, Joe and Umberger, Arthur L. *Collectible Character Bottles*. Tyler, TX: Corker Book Company, 1969.

Von Spiegel, Walter. *Glass*. Battenberg Verlag, Munchen: 1979.

Watkins, Laura Woodside. *American Glass and Glassmaking*. New York: Chanticleer Press, 1950.

Watson, Richard. *Bitters Bottles*. New York: Thomas Nelson & Sons, 1965.

———. *Supplement to Bitters Bottles*. New York: Thomas Nelson & Sons, 1968.

Western Glass Auctions. *Bottle Sales Catalogs*, 1288 W. 11th Street, Suite #230, Tracy, CA 95376.

Wilson, Kenneth M. *New England Glass and Glass Making*. New York: Thomas Y. Crowell Company, 1972.

Zumwalt, Betty. *Ketchup, Pickles, Sauces*. SandPoint, ID: Mark West Publishers, 1980.

Periodicals

Armans of Newport. *Bottle Sales Catalogs.* 207 High Point Avenue, Portsmouth, RI 02871.

Bottles & Extra Magazine, P.O. Box 154, Happy Camp, CA 96039.

FJN Publishers. *Fruit Jar Newsletter,* 364 Gregory Avenue, West Orange, N.H. 07052-3743 (published monthly).

Garths Auctions, Inc. *Bottle Sale Catalogs,* 2690 Stratford Road, Delaware, OH 43015.

Glass Works Auctions. *Bottle Sale Catalogs,* P.O. Box 187, East Greenville, PA 18041.

Hagenbuch, Jim. *Antique Bottle & Glass Collector,* 102 Jefferson Street, P.O. Box 187, East Greenville, PA 18041 (published monthly).

Harmer Rooke Galleries. *Bottle Sale Catalogs,* 3 East 57th Street, New York, N.Y. 10022.

Heckler, Norman. *Bottle Sale Catalogs,* Bradford Corner Road, Woodstock Valley, CT 06282.

McDougald, Carol. *Crown Jewels of the Wire,* P.O. Box 1003, St. Charles, IL 60174-1003.

Shot Glass Exchange. *Glass Sales Catalogs,* Box 219AB, Western Springs, IL 60558.

The ⓒNFIDENT ⓒOLLECTOR™

KNOWS THE FACTS

Each volume packed with valuable information that no collector can afford to be without

THE OVERSTREET COMIC BOOK
GRADING GUIDE, 1st Edition
by Robert M. Overstreet and Gary M. Carter   76910-7/$12.00 US/$15.00 Can

THE OVERSTREET COMIC BOOK
PRICE GUIDE COMPANION, 6th Edition
by Robert M. Overstreet   76911-5/$6.00 US/$8.00 Can

o   o   o

FINE ART
Identification and Price Guide, 2nd Edition
by Susan Theran   76924-7/$20.00 US/$24.00 Can

QUILTS
Identification and Price Guide, 1st Edition
by Liz Greenbacker and Kathleen Barach   76930-1/$14.00 US/$17.00 Can

ORIGINAL COMIC ART
Identification and Price Guide, 1st Edition
by Jerry Weist   76965-4/$15.00 US/$18.00 Can

ART DECO
Identification and Price Guide, 2nd Edition
by Tony Fusco   77012-1/$16.00 US/$19.00 Can

COLLECTIBLE MAGAZINES
Identification and Price Guide, 1st Edition
by David K. Henkel   76926-3/$15.00 US/$17.50 Can